Reading About The World

Volume 2

Third Edition

Paul Brians
Editor-in-Chief

Mary Gallwey
Associate Editor

Douglas Hughes
Associate Editor

Azfar Hussain
Associate Editor

Richard Law
Associate Editor

Michael Myers
Associate Editor

Michael Neville
Associate Editor

Roger Schlesinger
Associate Editor

Alice Spitzer
Associate Editor

Susan Swan
Associate Editor

THOMSON LEARNING
CUSTOM PUBLISHING

Editor: Kathleen Abraham
Production Manager: Staci Powers
Production Coordinator: Lisa Donahue
Marketing Coordinator: Sara L. Hinckley

ISBN 978-0-15-512826-2
(0-15-512826-4)

The Adaptable Courseware Program consists of products and additions to existing Custom Publishing products that are produced from camera-ready copy. Peer review, class testing, and accuracy are primarily the responsibility of the author(s).

Cover design: Courtney Ingebritsen

Contributors and Consultants

at Washington State University:
Roger Chan
Paula Elliot
Shelli Fowler
Bonnie Frederick
Lydia Gerber
Elwood Hartman
Richard Hooker
Azfar Hussain
Noriko Kawamura
John Kicza
Elza Major
Jane Scales
Sumathy Sivamohan
Raymond Sun
Marina Tolmacheva

Nicholas Heer, University of Washington
Mark Olsen, University of Chicago

This publication made possible with a grant from the
International Program Development Office of Washington State University
and support from the Office of General Education
Richard Law, Director.

Introduction

Why read these texts?

As students, you have likely been told that we can learn something about the world by studying literary and philosophical texts. One strong benefit of reading texts from a variety of periods and cultures, such as those found in this book, is that it can contribute to a deeper understanding of the past, of history. When reading about history in conventional textbooks, it is easy to get the assume that what is written down are "the facts" without really thinking about where those ideas came from. Although historians—people whose job it is to write down "what has happened"—have existed in many cultures, much of our information about the past has actually come, not from professional historians, but from such diverse people as lawmakers and dramatists, politicians and poets. These people, through the texts they have written, convey to us from a variety of perspectives fundamental information about their cultures. For example, if a country's ruler issues an edict stating that his subjects should denounce certain religious beliefs to elevate the "true" belief, as in K'ang-Hsi's seventeenth-century "Sacred Edicts," we can conclude that the ruler's society was (and possibly is still) a religious one, as well as one that was suffering from religious conflicts. If a writer states that women should be submissive to her husband, as in the eighteenth-century treatise *Greater Learning for Women*, we can conclude that gender roles were (and possibly are still) of concern in that society. Also, because these accounts of society come from a such a wide range of perspectives (instead of just the perspective of one historian), we can hope to achieve a broader understanding of what a society was really like. This broader understanding of the past, of culture, can in turn give us a greater appreciation of the literature that helped contribute to that culture's creation and history—including one's own culture.

But writings do not only help explain the past; the past can be used to explain writings. Conventional history courses have traditionally asked of the past, "What has happened?" Literature courses, on the other hand, have traditionally asked "What has lasted?" In a literature course the political and social events may be studied in order to explain a work whose main value is that it is still stimulating and enjoyable to read today, regardless of whether it illustrates important historical points. Shakespeare's sonnets are important as poetry, quite apart from anything they tell us about his society. Their very existence is an important item of literary history. This reader is designed to combine both approaches to texts: "sources" used to understand history and texts valuable in themselves.

In order to provide various perspectives about each culture, we have chosen a wide range of materials for you to read Some of the readings have been chosen because they are original sources for the writing of history, such as legal documents, travel books, and speeches. Other readings illustrate the past in a way that brings them vividly to life: comic stories, tragic dramas, or songs of devotion to a loved one or even a god. Some selections are literary works which are generally considered "classics." Finally, many of the readings have profoundly influenced the course of thought—philosophical, religious, social, and so on—of various cultures; Darwin's *The Origin of Species*, Simone de Beauvoir's *The Second Sex*, and Malcolm X's "Declaration of Independence" are some examples. Although the extreme variety of the selections gathered here may seem bewildering, you will find many common themes running through them: religion, social customs, love and sex, death. Many of the readings illustrate contacts or conflicts between cultures or the influences of one culture on another. We have tried especially to illustrate the lives of two groups of people who are often neglected in more traditional histories: those of women and the poor. Finally, as you read the selections in this book, keep in mind that these readings are not merely sources for writing about history; they *are* history—a history that allows a variety of voices to speak, to tell us their stories.

What do these texts "mean"?

One difficulty in learning about the past and about cultures through reading a variety of literature is that it seems a less "straightforward" method than simply reading a history textbook. Furthermore, although you may have studied literature before, your experience with texts may not be as wide-ranging as the selections in this book; perhaps you had to read Robert Frost's popular twentieth-century poem "The Road Not Taken" in an introductory English class, but you have no idea how to approach seventeenth-century Japanese haiku. Although reading strategies vary for different types of literary works, we would like to offer a few suggestions on how to get started when you examine a text. We should also note that because much of what is considered the world's great literature is poetry, this volume contains a great deal of poetry. Many students are convinced that poetry is a deliberately obscure form of writing that one needs special training to read, but we hope that you will find that this is not the case with the poetic selections in this book. We have selected many of these poems on the basis of how readable and enjoyable we hope they are for a typical student reader. Few of these poems are really difficult, and the editors have tried to provide detailed notes to help you through those few, as we understand that there is often not time to do the kind of detailed study of a poem that is common in literature classes. Also for this reason, we have provided some additional reading strategies for poetry at the end of this section.

Finally, most selections in this book (both poetry and prose), besides having the usual introductory note and footnotes, also are prefaced by one or more study questions. These questions may be used as the basis for discussions, quizzes, or exams by your instructor, but even if they are not, you should pay attention to them. Although they may take the form of questions, introductory sections are designed to guide you toward significant points in the reading and to provide valuable information. As you become more comfortable with a variety of literary texts, you may also find that you are able to create study questions for yourself, for example by deciding to compare a text you are reading with another text you have read about a similar theme. Feel free to be creative as you consider new ways to engage with the readings.

Getting Started: Non-Fiction Prose Texts

There are a variety of non-fiction prose texts collected here, including excerpts from philosophical treatises and legal documents. Before you get started with the actual text, be sure to look at the orienting information you are given about the work: identify the culture out of which the piece came and in what period it was written so you get an idea of the "setting" of the piece. Next, skim the introductory notes to get a sense of what's ahead (you can read the notes in more detail later). Now you are ready to read the text itself. One of the first things to do when approaching these sometimes difficult texts is to try to determine what a text means on a literal, sentence-by-sentence level.. Unless you understand what the different thoughts conveyed in a text are, you will not be able to form strong ideas about the work as a whole. For this reason, we recommend that you keep a dictionary handy as you read, and that you look up words you are unfamiliar with. Also, if you see a familiar word but cannot make sense of how it is being used, check to see if there are other definitions or connotations of the word that the writer may be employing. Keep in mind that many of the selections in this book are presented in translation, and wherever possible, the translators have tried to choose the English words that most closely approach the meanings andconnotations of the words in the text's original language. Because of this, it is important to understand these words as clearly as you can.

Once you have an idea of what the sentences literally mean, try to paraphrase the text (put it into your own words). You might jot down your ideas, or perhaps try to explain what you've read to a friend. You may need to read the text and/or specific passages in it several times in order to do this. When you have a general idea of what the text is "about," you can ask yourself a series of questions. What seems to be the purpose of the text? Is it meant to inform? Persuade? Entertain? (You may find that there is a combination of these purposes). What is the writer's tone? (This can help you determine a writer's attitude toward her or his subject; for example, does the writer sound serious? Nostalgic? Angry? Ironic?). Finally, look again at the study questions and try to answer them using specific examples from the text to support your answers.

Getting Started: "Literary" Texts

Along with the prose non-fiction texts discussed above, there are a variety of more specifically "literary" texts in this collection, including fictional prose (such as stories and drama) and different types of poetry (such as epics, hymns, and haiku). The following comments apply especially to the poems. As with the prose non-fiction texts, be sure to identify the culture and period in which the poem was written and skim the introductory notes to get oriented to the poem. Then try skimming the poem to get general sense of it, even if you don't yet have any idea of what the poem might mean. If you sense that it is, for example, a poem about love, how is it different from reading a prose statement about love? One important distinction between poetry and prose literature is the idea that poetry is both (a) somehow more concise than prose; and (b) somehow more rhythmic than prose. This is not to say that prose texts cannot be poetic (parts of the "prose" Hebrew Bible, for example, have been set to music); however, in general, poetry is generally considered to be its own special form of literature. It may also help to remember that much poetry is oral. Early poetry, especially poetry written before the invention of writing (such as Homer's *Odyssey*), was usually performed aloud, often to instrumental accompaniment. In fact, some of the poems in this book are actually songs, such as those poems that are called "hymns." For this reason, you might try reading the poem aloud to see how it sounds. For example, lines in a poem which contain a series of long words might seem to be asking you to slow down as you speak them, perhaps to create a sense of dreaminess or languor, while a series of short, quick words might be asking you to speed up, perhaps to create a sense of cheerfulness or urgency.

After you get a general sense of the poem, go ahead and look at its language. Poets are usually extremely careful in their choice of words, using fewer words to convey an idea than one would in prose. Because each word counts for so much, it especially important to look up those you don't know. Also, when looking at words and phrases in a poem, you will often notice the poet's use of "figurative language," or language that means something beyond its literal definition. You may have learned about "similes," "metaphors," and "personification" in your literature classes; all of these are types of figurative language. For example, in one of her sonnets, Bengali writer Toru Dutt writes that "A sea of foliage girds our garden round." Here, Dutt uses metaphor: she makes an implicit comparison between how foliage in the speaker's garden looks and how the sea looks. When she later writes "palms arise, like pillars gray," Dutt uses simile: she makes an overt comparison between palm trees and gray pillars. When you read poetry, then, look closely at the type of figurative language poets use to convey their ideas, and try to imagine why they chose those particular images. For example, Romeo, in the "Balcony Scene" from Shakespeare's *Romeo and Juliet*, speaks of love and lovers in this way: "How silver-sweet sound lovers' tongues by night,/Like softest music to attending ears!" This description, however, gives a very different sense than the speaker in Louise Labé's sonnet "Ladies, if I have loved," who describes her experience of love as having "felt a thousand torches' burns,/A thousand biting torments and concerns." Poets may also make use of symbols, or words that somehow stand for "more" than what they are. For example, in Faiz Ahmed Faiz's poem "Speak," the second stanza asks us to

See how in the blacksmith's shop
The flame burns wild, the iron glows red;
The locks open their jaws,
And every chain begins to break.

Here, the description of the blacksmith's shop is symbolic, as the poem is not really about blacksmiths; instead, the poet uses the images of locks opening and chains breaking as symbols to show that people who have felt silenced by others may "catch fire" and speak their minds. Learning to understand the use of figurative language is very helpful when approaching poetry, as it allows you to gain a deeper experience of the poem, along with poets' possible feelings or attitudes toward their subjects when they were writing. (At the end of this introduction you will find a glossary that will help explain some of the types of figurative language you may encounter when you read the poetry in this collection, along with some other definitions of literary terms that may be helpful to you).

Once you get a sense of what the poem means on a literal and figurative level (you may even try to paraphrase it, as with prose selections), try to decide what the poet's purpose is. A poem may try to do many things: tell a story, capture a memory, express a certain mood or feeling, convey a particular idea, or even teach a moral lesson; it is your task to consider how and why a poem's "work" is done. Guided by the introductions and study questions, consider how effectively the poets have accomplished their purposes by the choices they have made. Finally, it is important to try to be receptive to all types of experience, even if they are unfamiliar to you, or differ from what you think or believe. You don't have to agree with the ideas in a poem to be able to appreciate it as a piece of literature, and this is true of the other readings in this collection as well. Overall, we hope that *Reading About the World* will help you find ways to grow as a reader of texts and of history, and will guide you toward a deeper appreciation and understanding of the past and of culture.

Glossary

Allusion. A reference to something in previous literary or other works. Example: the use of the phrase "Pan's alphabet" in Rubén Darío's "To Roosevelt" is an allusion to the idea in Greek mythology that the god Pan created the alphabet.

Connotation. The "shade" of a word, or what it suggests beyond its literal meaning. Example: the word "rough" can mean several things, but its use in the description of the "rough beast" in William Butler Yeats' poem "The Second Coming" has the connotation of a beast that is "harsh" or "monstrous" and possibly as yet "unformed."

Denotation. The literal or dictionary definition of a word.

Metaphor. An implied comparison between two things. Example: "O mind, you are a bird encaged" from Lalon Fakir's poem "A Strange Bird."

Paraphrase. Use of one's own words to state what another person has said.

Personification. To give human qualities to something that is not human. Example: in the line "the moon/Looks through their gaps" from a sonnet by Toru Dutt, the moon is treated as if it had eyes as a human would.

Satire. A type of literature that ridicules someone or something. Example: in Mokshodayani Mukhopadhyay's "The Bengali Babu," the speaker, in a biting, negative fashion, describes a clerk working for a colonial employer, presumably to point out that he as not as admirable as he thinks he is. Most traditional satire is conservative, criticizing trends in the author's time in comparison with an idealized past.

Simile. An overt comparison between two things, using such words as "like" or "as." Example: "clouds plod the horizon like caparisoned camels" from Derek Walcott's poem "Hurucan."

Sonnet. A fixed form of poetry with fourteen lines and one of two main types of rhyming patterns. Example: Shakespeare's sonnets 55 and 73.

Symbol. A word or phrase that stands for something more than it is. Example: when the speaker in Raage Ugaas' "Poet's Lament on the Death of his Wife" asks "Have I been borne on a saddle to a distant and desolate place?" this image becomes a symbol of his desolation and grief.

Theme. The central idea (or ideas) in a text. Example: in Abraham Lincoln's "Second Inaugural Address," the themes include the injustice of slavery, the destruction of war, and the righteousness of God.

Tone. A writer's apparent attitude toward her or his subject, audience, or self. Example: the speaker's tone in Kishwar Naheed's Pakistani feminist poem "We Sinful Women" is one of defiance.

Contents

Africa 1500–1750

Leo Africanus: Description of Timbuktu, from *The Description of Africa* (1526)

El Hasan ben Muhammed el-Wazzan-ez-Zayyati was born in the Moorish city of Granada in 1485, but was expelled along with his parents and thousands of other Muslims by Ferdinand and Isabella in 1492. Settling in Morocco, he studied in Fez, and as a teenager accompanied his uncle on diplomatic missions throughout North Africa and to the Sub-Saharan kingdom of Ghana. Still a young man, he was captured by Christian pirates and presented as an exceptionally learned slave to the great Renaissance pope, Leo X. Leo freed him, baptized him under the name "Johannis Leo de Medici," and commissioned him to write in Italian the detailed survey of Africa which provided most of what Europeans knew about the continent for the next several centuries. At the time he visited the Malian city of Timbuktu, it was somewhat past its peak, but still a thriving Islamic city famous for its learning. "Timbuktu" was to become a byword in Europe as the most inaccessible of cities; but at the time Leo visited, it was the center of a busy trade in African products and in books. Leo is said to have died in 1554 in Tunis, having reconverted to Islam.

What evidence does he provide that suggests the importance of learning in Timbuktu? What aspects of the culture do you think he finds attractive or admirable?

The name of this kingdom is a modern one, after a city which was built by a king named Mansa Suleyman in the year 610 of the hegira [1232 CE] around twelve miles from a branch of the Niger River.[1]

The houses of Timbuktu are huts made of clay-covered wattles with thatched roofs. In the center of the city is a temple built of stone and mortar, built by an architect named Granata,[2] and in addition there is a large palace, constructed by the same architect, where the king lives. The shops of the artisans, the merchants, and especially weavers of cotton cloth are very numerous. Fabrics are also imported from Europe to Timbuktu, borne by Berber merchants.[3]

The women of the city maintain the custom of veiling their faces, except for the slaves who sell all the foodstuffs. The inhabitants are very rich, especially the strangers who have settled in the country; so much so that the current king[4] has given two of his daughters in marriage to two brothers, both businessmen, on account of their wealth. There are many wells containing sweet water in Timbuktu; and in addition, when the Niger is in flood canals deliver the water to the city. Grain and animals are abundant, so that the consump-

[1]Mansa Suleyman reigned 1336-1359. The city was in fact probably founded in the 11th century by Tuaregs, but became the chief city of the king of Mali in 1324.

[2]Ishak es Sahili el-Gharnati, brought to Timbuktu by Mansa Suleyman.

[3]By camel caravan across the Sahara Desert from North Africa.

[4]'Omar ben Mohammed Naddi, not in fact the king, but representative of the ruler of the kingdom of Songhai.

tion of milk and butter is considerable. But salt is in very short supply because it is carried here from Tegaza, some 500 miles from Timbuktu. I happened to be in this city at a time when a load of salt sold for eighty ducats. The king has a rich treasure of coins and gold ingots. One of these ingots weighs 970 pounds.[5]

The royal court is magnificent and very well organized. When the king goes from one city to another with the people of his court, he rides a camel and the horses are led by hand by servants. If fighting becomes necessary, the servants mount the camels and all the soldiers mount on horseback. When someone wishes to speak to the king, he must kneel before him and bow down; but this is only required of those who have never before spoken to the king, or of ambassadors. The king has about 3,000 horsemen and infinity of foot-soldiers armed with bows made of wild fennel which they use to shoot poisoned arrows. This king makes war only upon neighboring enemies and upon those who do not want to pay him tribute. When he has gained a victory, he has all of them—even the children—sold in the market at Timbuktu.

Only small, poor horses are born in this country. The merchants use them for their voyages and the courtiers to move about the city. But the good horses come from Barbary. They arrive in a caravan and, ten or twelve days later, they are led to the ruler, who takes as many as he likes and pays appropriately for them.

The king is a declared enemy of the Jews. He will not allow any to live in the city. If he hears it said that a Berber merchant frequents them or does business with them, he confiscates his goods. There are in Timbuktu numerous judges, teachers and priests, all properly appointed by the king. He greatly honors learning. Many hand-written books imported from Barbary are also sold. There is more profit made from this commerce than from all other merchandise.

Instead of coined money, pure gold nuggets are used; and for small purchases, cowrie shells which have been carried from Persia,[6] and of which 400 equal a ducat. Six and two-thirds of their ducats equal one Roman gold ounce.[7]

The people of Timbuktu are of a peaceful nature. They have a custom of almost continuously walking about the city in the evening (except for those that sell gold), between 10 PM and 1 AM, playing musical instruments and dancing. The citizens have at their service many slaves, both men and women.

The city is very much endangered by fire. At the time when I was there on my second voyage,[8] half the city burned in the space of five hours. But the wind was violent and the inhabitants of the other half of the city began to move their belongings for fear that the other half would burn.

There are no gardens or orchards in the area surrounding Timbuktu.

Translated by Paul Brians

[5]Such fabulous nuggets are commonly mentioned by Arab writers about Africa, but their size is probably grossly exaggerated.

[6]Cowrie shells, widely used for money in West Africa, sometimes came in fact from even farther away, from the Maldive Islands southwest of India and Sri Lanka.

[7]A Sudanese gold ducat would weigh .15 oz.

[8]Probably in 1512.

Richard Eden: English merchants at the Royal Court of Benin from *Decades of the New World* (1555)

The Portuguese were the first to begin trading with various West African empires, including the royal court of Benin, whose brilliant sculpture has been famous in Europe ever since. The English, however, were soon looking for profit in the same area. This account of one trading voyage depicts their insatiable desire for gold, or what was almost as good: pepper. (This was not the familiar seed imported at great cost from Southeast Asia, but a different spice used for the same purposes.) Under the guidance of an impoverished Portuguese guide named Captain Pinteado, Captain Windham and several English merchants made their way to Benin. This voyage was to end disastrously, with both captains and many of the crew dying of the tropical diseases which for so long prevented Europeans from penetrating far into Africa.

What evidence is there that the King of Benin was used to dealing with Europeans? Who do you think is more "civilized" in their behavior—the English or the people of Benin? What dangers does Africa pose to the English? What dangers do you think the English might have posed to the Africans?

They were brought with a great company to the presence of the king, who, being a black Moor[1] (although not so black as the rest), sat in a great huge hall, long and wide, the walls made of earth without windows, the roof of thin boards, open in sundry places, like unto louvers to let in the air.

And here to speak of the great reverence they give to their king, it is such that, if we would give as much to Our Savior Christ, we should remove from our heads many plagues which we daily deserve for our contempt and impiety.

So it is, therefore, that, when his noblemen are in his presence, they never look him in the face, but sit cowering, as we upon our knees, so they upon their buttocks with their elbows upon their knees and their hands before their faces, not looking up until the king command them. And when they are coming toward the king, as far as they do see him they do show such reverence, sitting on the ground with their faces covered as before. Likewise, when they depart from him, they turn not their backs toward him, but go creeping backward with like reverence.

And now to speak somewhat of the communication that was between the king and our men, you shall first understand that he himself could speak the Portugal tongue, which he had learned of[2] a child. Therefore, after he had commanded our men to stand up, and demanded of them the cause of their coming into the country, they answered by Pinteado that they were merchants, traveling into those parts for the commodities of his country for exchange of wares, which they had brought from their countries, being such as should be no less commodious for him and his people. The king, then, having of old lying in a certain storehouse 30 or 40 quintals of pepper (every quintal being a hundred weight), willed them to look upon the same, and again to bring him a sight of such merchandise as they had brought with them. And thereupon sent with the captain and the merchants certain of his men to conduct them to the waterside with others to bring the wares from the pinnace to the court. Who, when they were returned and the wares seen, the king grew

[1]That is, a black man, not actually Moorish.
[2]As.

to this end with the merchants to provide in 30 days the lading of all their ships with pepper. And in case their merchandise would not extend to the value of so much pepper, he promised to credit them to their next return, and thereupon sent the country round about to gather pepper, causing the same to be brought to the court. So that within the space of 30 days, they had gathered fourscore tons of pepper.

In the mean season, our men, partly having no rule of themselves, but eating without measure of the fruits of the country and drinking the wine of the palm trees, that drop in the night from the cut of the branches of the same, and in such extreme heat running continuously into the water, not used before to such sudden and vehement alterations (than the which nothing is more dangerous), were thereby brought into swellings and agues:[3] insomuch that the latter time of the year coming on caused them to die sometimes three and sometimes 4 or 5 in a day. Then Windham, perceiving the time of the 30 days to be expired and his men dying so fast, sent to the court in post to Captain Pinteado and the rest to come away and to tarry no longer. But Pinteado with the rest wrote back to him again, certifying him of the great quantity of pepper they had already gathered and looked daily for much more, desiring him furthermore to remember the great praise and name they should win if they came home prosperously, and what shame of the contrary. With which answer Windham, not satisfied, and many of their men dying daily, willed and commanded them again either to come away forthwith or else threatened to leave them behind. When Pinteado heard this answer, thinking to persuade him with reason, he took his way from the court toward the ships, being conducted thither with men by the king's commandment.

In the meantime, Windham, all raging, broke up Pinteado's cabin, broke open his chests, spoiled such provision of cold stilled waters and suckets[4] as he had provided for his health, and left him nothing, neither of his instruments to sail by, nor yet of his apparel; and in the meantime, falling sick, himself died also.

The Adornment of West Africans

The merchants wanted pepper because it could be turned into gold in Europe, of course; and they were fascinated by the quantity of gold and ivory they found circulating along the coast of West Africa.

Among other things . . . touching the manners and nature of the people, this may seem strange, that their princes and noblemen used to pounce[5] and raise their skins with pretty knots in diverse forms, as it were branched damask, thinking that to be a decent ornament. And albeit they go in manner all naked, yet are many of them, and especially their women, in manner laden with collars, bracelets, hoops and chains, either of gold, copper, or ivory. I myself have one of their bracelets of ivory, weighing two pound and six ounces of troy weight, which make eight and thirty ounces. This one of their women did wear upon her arm. It is made of one whole piece of the biggest part of the tooth,[6] turned and somewhat carved, with a hole in the midst, wherein they put their hands to wear it on their arm. Some have on every arm one, and as many on their legs, wherewith some of them are so

---

[3]Aches and fevers.

[4]Candies.

[5]Prick.

[6]Tusk.

galled that, although they are in manner made lame thereby, yet will they by no means leave them off. Some wear also on their legs great shackles of bright copper, which they think to be no less comely. They wear also collars, bracelets, garlands and girdles, of certain blue stones like beads. Likewise, some of their women wear on their bare arms certain foresleeves made of the plates of beaten gold. On their fingers also they wear rings, made of golden wires, with a knot or wreath, like unto that which children make in a ring of a rush. Among other things of gold, that our men bought of them for exchange of their wares, were certain dog-chains and collars.

They are very wary people in their bargaining, and will not lose one spark of gold of any value. They use weights and measures, and are very circumspect in occupying the same.[7] They that shall have to do with them, must use them gently; for they will not traffic[8] or bring in any wares, if they be evil used.

---

[7]Very precise in using their scales.
[8]Trade.

India 1500–1750

Mirabai (1498–1550 CE): Songs for Krishna

Legend says that Mirabai refused to sleep with her husband and wandered the land singing of her exclusive devotion to Lord Krishna, whose most famous lovers were the gopis, *the wives of cowherds, who escaped from their huts at night to dance and make love with the god. Worshippers interpret the frank sexuality of these songs as metaphors for spiritual union: Mirabai uses the language of the flesh to express her passion for spiritual oneness with the divine. The tradition is a long and brilliant one in Hinduism, including the great* Gita Govinda *of Jayadeva. Mirabai remains an extremely popular poet in India even today. Her songs are not only sung in Hindu devotions, but are performed as folksongs and used in musical films. The American composer John Harbison wrote a group of* Mirabai Songs *set to translations by poet Robert Bly. All of the following translations are by A. J. Alston.*

What effects do you think it has on a religion to depict a god as beautiful, and attractive especially to women?

My eyes are spell-bound

My eyes are spell-bound
By the beauty of the angular pose of the Lord.[1]
On beholding the beauty of Madan,[2]
My eyes drink in the nectar
And do not blink.
Attracted by the lotus-petal beauty of His brows,
It is as if they were now entangled
In His curling, odorous locks.
His body is bent at the waist,
His hands curved over the flute,
His turban is aslant and His necklace swinging.
Mira is thrilled by the beauty of the Lord,
Of the courtly Giridhara,[3] dressed as a dancer.

---

[1]Krishna is usually shown dancing, with one leg bent, playing the flute.
[2]Another name for Krishna.
[3]A name which refers to Krishna's feat in holding up an entire mountain on his little finger to protect his village from a jealous god.

Without Krishna I cannot sleep

Devotees of Krishna often speak of longing for him while he dallies with others. They argue that it is necessary to overcome this jealousy and learn to share him with others; yet these poems of longing seem to express the essence of the tormented love that fills his followers.

What are the main effects that Krishna's absence has on the poet? What attitudes might this poem reflect characteristic in a culture where a man might have several wives?

Without Krishna I cannot sleep.
Tortured by longing, I cannot sleep,
And the fire of love
Drives me to wander hither and thither.
Without the light of the Beloved
My house is dark,
And lamps do not please me.
Without the Beloved my bed is uninviting,
And I pass the nights awake.
When will my Beloved return home?
The frogs are croaking, the peacock's cry
And the cuckoo's song are heard.
Low black clouds are gathering,
Lightning flashes, stirring fear in the heart.
My eyes fill with tears.
What shall I do? Where shall I go?
Who can quench my pain?
My body has been bitten
By the snake of "absence,"
And my life is ebbing away
With every beat of the heart.
Fetch the herb quickly.[1]
Which of my companions
Will come bringing the Beloved to meet me?
My Lord when will you come
To meet your Mira?
Manamohan,[2] the Charmer of Hearts,
Fills me with delight. When, my Lord,
Will you come to laugh and talk with me?

---

[1]Medicinal herb, to ease the suffering.
[2]Another title for Krishna.

We do not get a human life

A Hindu may experience rebirth in many forms, often as an animal of some sort. This poem asks Krishna, under his title "Lal Giridhara" to guide the worshipper to a superior future incarnation.

In what ways is "life after death" as depicted here different than or similar to other such beliefs you have encountered in other cultures?

We do not get a human life
Just for the asking.
Birth in a human body
Is the reward for good deeds
In former births.
Life waxes and wanes imperceptibly,
It does not stay long.
The leaf that has once fallen
Does not return to the branch.
Behold the Ocean of Transmigration,
With its swift, irresistible tide.
O Lal Giridhara, O pilot of my soul,
Swiftly conduct my barque[1] to the further shore.
Mira is the slave of Lal Giridhara.
She says: Life lasts but a few days only.

---

[1]Boat.

O Jogi, do not depart

In this song, Mirabi imagines committing sati for Krishna—burning herself alive—so that he may smear his body with the ashes of her corpse. Hindu ascetics often smear themselves with ashes (though not human ones) to symbolize their detachment from worldy life; so this is not as bizarre a symbol as it might seem. Her image is a classic expression of the mystic ideal of complete fusion with the divine. This particular song is movingly performed by Lakshmi Shankar on her compact disc Les heures et les saisons *(Harmonia Mundi 558615/16).*

Is this a suicidal, self-destructive poem, or is something else going on?

O Jogi,[1] do not depart,
I pray you, do not depart.
Behold, I fall at your feet, Your slave.
Strange is the path of love and devotion!
Explain to me its intricacies
Before You depart.
I am laying a pyre of fragrant aloe
And sandalwood.
Light it with Your own hand
Before You depart.
When I am burnt to a heap of ashes,
Smear them on Your body
Before You depart.
Says Mira to her Lord, the courtly Giridhara,
Let my light dissolve in Your light
Before You depart.

---

[1]A name for Krishna.

Kabir: Selected Songs (16th Century?)

Very little is known of Kabir the man. Yet his verses and songs have been recited and sung with love and devotion throughout India and some parts of Bangladesh for about 500 years. Born in or near Kashi (Varanasi) in India and raised in a community of weavers, Kabir is traditionally said to have lived 150 years from 1398 to 1548. Illiterate and always poverty-stricken, Kabir composed most of his songs and verses in medieval Hindi. His work still equally attracts pundits *and the public, trained musicians and street-singers. Always a source of energy and inspiration to the poor and the oppressed, Kabir sings of the glory and strength of human love and union, thus accounting for his influence on numerous poets, singers, mystics, philosophers, and even politicians in India, including Rabindranath Tagore and Mahatma Gandhi. Like a true rebel, Kabir also fearlessly raises his voice against all forms of man-made discrimination based on class, color, creed, gender, and religion. He is particularly noted for his life-long, uncompromising crusade against casteism and communalism that have long plagued Indian societies. Also widely known as a mystic, Kabir comes up with a unique version of mysticism that emphasizes humankind more than God, though now and then Kabir makes fun of "this world" and physical human existence. His songs are at once rugged and smooth, deceptively simple, universal yet deeply rooted in his class and community, and are varied in tone, tune, and tenor. The following songs selected from various works of Kabir represent some of his predominant concerns and themes, though they inadequately reflect Kabir's actual range and scale.*

What are the main messages conveyed in the following songs? What is Kabir's attitude toward scriptures and rituals? How can you tell that Kabir is interested in the small and the insignificant? "Kabir both celebrates and undermines humankind"—explain this statement in the context of the songs represented here. Kabir has a tendency to use a question mark at the end of his song. But to what effect?

This union with the *guru*, O Kabir,
Sets me free; like salt mingled
With flour, I am no more I!

Now I have no caste, no creed,
I am no more what I am!

O dear brother!
By what name would you call me?

I do not quote from the scriptures;
I simply see what I see.

When the bride is one
with her lover,
who cares about
the wedding party?

I am not a Hindu,
Nor a Muslim am I!

I am this body, a play
Of five elements; a drama
Of the spirit dancing
With joy and sorrow.

A drop
Melting into the sea,
Everyone can see.
But the sea
Absorbed
In a drop—
A rare one
can follow!

I am looking at you,
You at him,
Kabir asks, how to solve
This puzzle—
You, he, and I?

Dying, dying, the world
Is dying only.
But lo! None knows how to die
In such a way
That he dies never again.

Man, here is your worth:
Your meat is of no use!
Your bones cannot be sold
For making ornaments,
And your skin cannot be played
On an instrument!

Translated by Azfar Hussain

China 1500–1750

K'ang-Hsi: The Sacred Edicts (1670)

In 1670, when the K'ang-Hsi emperor was sixteen years old he issued a list of sixteen principles that briefly illustrate how he expected his subjects to conduct themselves in order to ensure their goodness, happiness and prosperity. These so-called "Sacred Edicts" were to be read aloud twice a month in every village and town of the empire. The practice of "expounding the Sacred Edicts" was still in use after 1900, yet it was observed that only those that had to attend would be present. It is typical for the Chinese style of rule and the image of the ruler as a benevolent father, that no law or command should be given without a reason. Following the publication of the original edicts, several versions in the Chinese vernacular were published, some with detailed commentaries or illustrations, to make sure that people of all backgrounds were able to fully understand the contents and implications of these imperial commands. The "Sacred Edicts" provide a digest of the practical side of Confucian rule.

What values do these teachings reflect? What is considered valuable? Dangerous?

1. Highly esteem filial piety and the proper relations among brothers in order to give due importance to social relations.[1]
2. Give due weight to kinship in order to promote harmony and peace.
3. Maintain good relations within the neighborhood in order to prevent quarrels and lawsuits.
4. Give due importance to farming and the cultivation of mulberry trees in order to ensure sufficient clothing and food.[2]
5. Be moderate and economical in order to avoid wasting away your livelihood.
6. Make the most of schools and academies in order to honor the ways of scholars.
7. Denounce strange beliefs in order to elevate the true doctrine.[3]
8. Explain laws and regulations in order to warn the ignorant and obstinate.
9. Show propriety and courtesy to improve customs and manners.
10. Work hard in your professions in order to quiet your ambitions.
11. Instruct sons and younger brothers in order to prevent their committing any wrong.
12. Put a stop to false accusations in order to protect the good and honest.
13. Warn against giving shelter to deserters in order to avoid punishment with them.
14. Promptly and fully pay your taxes in order to avoid forced requisition.
15. Get together in groups of ten or a hundred in order to put an end to theft and robbery.
16. Free yourself from resentment and anger to show respect for your body and life.

Translated by Lydia Gerber

---

[1]Since brothers usually remained in the same household, it was not always easy to maintain good relationships. Commentaries mention that often the wives would start sowing dissent.

[2]Mulberry trees were cultivated to provide food for silkworms.

[3]Besides Christianity and witchcraft, Buddhism and Taoism are also listed as "strange beliefs." According to these Edicts, only Confucianism counted as a "true doctrine."

P'u Sung-ling: Painting on the Wall (first made public in 1680)

In general, novelists and story-tellers enjoyed little respect in China. While philosophical or annalistic literature was highly esteemed, fiction was called "small talk" (hsiao shuo)*and neither writing nor reading it was considered worthwhile. P'u Sung-ling (1640-1715) and his collection of about 400 stories published under the title* Liao-chai chih yi (Strange Stories from the Liao-studio*) are an exception. Having passed only one of the three Civil Service examinations, P'u spent most of his life in his native village in Shantung under dire conditions. Just like Jakob and Wilhelm Grimm in 19th-century Germany, he devoted his time to the collection and retelling of folk tales. During P'u's lifetime the* Liao-chai chih yi *collection was circulated in manuscript only since he was too poor to have it printed. In 1740, his grandson had the stories printed for the first time, and P'u's collection subsequently became famous. The stories themselves, though "strange," are not unusual within the context of Chinese fiction. What makes this collection of stories unique is P'u's exquisite style.*

Why does the author suggest that Chu's experience in the temple should have made him a hermit?

When Meng Lung-t'an, a native of Kiang-si, was strolling around in the capital with a Second-Degree-Graduate[1] named Chu, they came upon a Buddhist temple. Its halls were not spacious and only one monk was residing there.

Having caught sight of the visitors, the monk adjusted his robe and stepped forward to greet them and show them around. In the main hall stood a statue of Lord Zhi[2], and on the walls on both sides people and animals were so skillfully painted that they seemed to be alive. On the eastern wall, in a scene depicting the Celestial Maiden scattering flowers there was the image of a girl with her hair in two girlish buns on both sides of her head, holding a flower and smiling. Her cherry lips seemed about to move, her glistening eye seemed about to overflow. Chu fixed his eyes upon her for so long that his mind began to waver. He lost all his determination and, dazed, he sank into deep contemplation. Suddenly, he floated up as if riding on clouds and mist and up he went into the wall.

Now he saw halls and pavilions of all kinds, so beautiful that they resembled heaven. Nothing like it could be seen on earth.

An old priest on a high seat was preaching a Buddhist sermon, surrounded by a crowd of listeners in Buddhist attire, and Chu joined them. Yet suddenly he felt someone tugging at his robe. Turning around he beheld the smiling girl with her hair in buns just as she laughingly slipped away. Without thinking for even a moment Chu followed her as she passed along a balustrade. Yet when she entered a small chamber, Chu hesitated, not daring to enter. But the girl turned around and waving the flower in her hand seemed to beckon him. Swiftly he stepped into the room.

The chamber was empty, and Chu immediately embraced the girl. And since she offered no resistance, they consumated their passion. Later, when she left the room, cautiously closing the door, she told Chu not even to cough and promised to come back at night.

[1]A Second-Degree-Graduate or *Chu-jen* is a Chinese scholar who has passed both the local and provincial examinations and is waiting to take the examination in the Capital.
[2]Lord Chih, a.k.a. Shih Pao-kung, was a Buddhist monk of the Zen (*Chan*) School, who was later on worshipped as a bodhisattva.

After two days had passed in this manner, the girl's sisters began to suspect something and following her discovered the scholar. Jokingly they teased the girl: "How can you still wear your hair in these maiden-buns while there is a baby already growing in your belly?" They brought enameled hairpins and jeweled ornaments and went about binding her hair in a matron's knot. She obediently lowered her head but said nothing. They went on teasing her for a while until one of the girls said with a smile: "Sisters, let us stay no longer, certain people don't want our company!" Giggling, they left.

Chu looked at the girl with her hair piled high like clouds and with phoenix-ornaments dangling, and she seemed even more bewitching than with her hair worn in girlish buns. No one was around, and again they slowly and lovingly embraced each other, inflamed by musk and the orchid's sweet fragrance. Their pleasure had not yet reached its height, when suddenly there arose an uproar: boots tramped, chains clanked, and above all was the noise of angry voices. Terrified, the girl leaped up, and the two stealthily peeped outside. They saw a herald in golden armor, with a face like black laquer, and in his hands were chains and a hammer! As the other girls surrounded him, he asked: "Is everyone here yet?" "Yes, we are all here," they replied.

"It seems as if a man from the lower world is being hidden here," the herald went on. "If so, bring him here or you shall be sorry!" "There is no one here," the girls replied.

The envoy turned around and, scrutinizing everything like an eagle, seemed about to begin a search. The girl grew pale as death with fear. In panic she entreated Chu to hide under the bed. Then she opened a small screen-door in the wall and disappeared. In his hiding-place under the bed Chu did not even dare to breathe. Soon he heard the sound of boots enter the room and leave. Eventually, voices seemed to fade away into the distance, yet he still heard people come and go outside the door. Having been in such a cramped position for so very long, Chu felt increasingly uncomfortable. His ears seemed to buzz as if locusts were nesting inside, and his eyes seemed to be on fire. It was almost too much to bear. Yet he kept quiet, straining his ears for the girl's return and giving no thought to whence he had come and where he was.

Meanwhile, Meng Lung-t'an in the temple noticed that Chu had disappeared and asked the monk where he could be. The monk smiled and said: "He has gone to listen to the preaching of the Doctrine!" "But where is that?" Meng asked. "Not far," the monk answered, and tapping with his finger against the painting on the wall, he called out: "Friend Chu, why does it take you so long to return?" At once there appeared on the wall a portrait of Chu, cocking his ear as if he were eagerly listening. Again the monk called out: "You have kept your companion waiting for quite some time!" And suddenly Chu floated down from the wall. And there he stood: stiff as wood, his heart turned to lead, eyes staring and legs trembling. Meng was startled but quietly asked Chu what had happened. Well, what had happened was that Chu, while hiding under the bed, had heard a noise like thunder and rushed outside to find out what it was.

Now they all looked at the girl in the painting holding a flower: And see, her hair was piled into a matron's knot and no longer fixed in the buns of a maiden!

Chu was dumbfounded and, bowing to the old monk, begged for an explanation. With a chuckle, the monk replied: "Illusions are born in those who see them. How can this old monk possibly offer an explanation?" Upon hearing this, Chu was thoroughly dejected and Meng was greatly alarmed. They stumbled down the stairs and slowly walked away.

The "Teller of Strange Tales" says: "Illusions are born in those who see them" - this seems to be true. If a man turns his mind to lust, then filthy scenes will appear. If a man turns his mind to dirt, terrifying scenes will appear. When a bodhisattva teaches those without knowledge, a thousand illusions will appear. Yet it is the mind itself that creates them. The monk was too keen on seeing results.[3] But it is sad indeed that having heard the monk's words Chu did not become enlightened, loosen his hair and retire to the mountains!

Translated by Lydia Gerber

---

[3]According to the teachings of Zen, being "too keen on seeing results" may lead to failure.

Wu Ch'eng-en: *The Journey to the West* (16th C.)

Perhaps the most popular novel in history is The Journey to the West, *ostensibly an account of the mission of the 7th Century monk Hsüan Tsang to India to bring back Buddhist scriptures; yet its popularity is explained less by its religious themes than by the fantastic and amusing antics of his companion, the magical, impudent, and all-powerful monkey king. In all Chinese-speaking lands and throughout Southeast Asia, the monkey king cavorts in plays, dances, films, cartoons—in every conceivable medium. His adventures are known and loved by children and adults alike. Here is the opening chapter from the translation of the first part of this 100-chapter epic work, published in English as* Monkey.

What fear motivates Monkey to start on his travels?

There was a rock that since the creation of the world had been worked upon by the pure essences of Heaven and the fine savors of Earth, the vigor of sunshine and the grace of moonlight, till at last it became magically pregnant and one day split open, giving birth to a stone egg, about as big as a playing ball. Fructified by the wind it developed into a stone monkey, complete with every organ and limb. At once this monkey learned to climb and run; but its first act was to make a bow towards each of the four quarters. As it did so, a steely light darted from this monkey's eyes and flashed as far as the Palace of the Pole Star. This shaft of light astonished the Jade Emperor as he sat in the Cloud Palace of the Golden Gates, in the Treasure Hall of the Holy Mists, surrounded by his fairy Ministers.[1] Seeing this strange light flashing, he ordered Thousand-league Eye and Down-the-Wind Ears to open the gate of the Southern Heaven and look out. At his bidding these two captains went out to the gate and looked so sharply and listened so well that presently they were able to report, "This steely light comes from the borders of the small country of Ao-lai, that lies to the east of the Holy Continent, from the Mountain of Flowers and Fruit. On this mountain is a magic rock, which gave birth to an egg. This egg changed into a stone monkey, and when he made his bow to the four quarters a steely light flashed from his eyes with a beam that reached the Palace of the Pole Star. But now he is taking a drink, and the light is growing dim."

The Jade Emperor condescended to take an indulgent view. "These creatures in the world below," he said, "were compounded of the essence of heaven and earth, and nothing that goes on there should surprise us." That monkey walked, ran, leapt and bounded over the hills, feeding on grasses and shrubs, drinking from streams and springs, gathering the mountain flowers, looking for fruits. Wolf, panther and tiger were his companions, the deer and civet were his friends, gibbons and baboons his kindred. At night he lodged under cliffs of rock, by day he wandered among the peaks and caves. One very hot morning, after playing in the shade of some pine-trees, he and the other monkeys went to bathe in a mountain stream. See how those waters bounce and tumble like rolling melons!

There is an old saying, "Birds have their bird language, beasts have their beast talk." The monkeys said, "We none of us know where this stream comes from. As we have nothing to do this morning, wouldn't it be fun to follow it up to its source?" With a whoop of joy, dragging their sons and carrying their daughters, calling out to younger brother and to elder brother, the whole troupe rushed along the streamside and scrambled up the steep

---

[1]In Chinese belief, the structure of Heaven is identical to that of the imperial court on earth.

places, till they reached the source of the stream. They found themselves standing before the curtain of a great waterfall.

All the monkeys clapped their hands and cried aloud, "Lovely water, lovely water! To think that it starts far off in some cavern below the base of the mountain, and flows all the way to the Great Sea! If any of us were bold enough to pierce that curtain, get to where the water comes from and return unharmed, we would make him our king!" Three times the call went out, when suddenly one of them leapt from among the throng and answered the challenge in a loud voice. It was the Stone Monkey. "I will go," he cried, "I will go!" Look at him! He screwed up his eyes and crouches; then at one bound he jumped straight through the waterfall. When he opened his eyes and looked about him, he found that where he had landed there was no water. A great bridge stretched in front of him, shining and glinting. When he looked closely at it, he saw that it was made all of burnished iron. The water under it flowed through a hole in the rock, filling in all the space under the arch. Monkey climbed up on to the bridge and, spying as he went, saw something that looked just like a house. There were stone seats and stone couches, and tables with stone bowls and cups. He skipped back to the hump of the bridge and saw that on the cliff there was an inscription in large square writing which said, "This cave of the Water Curtain in the blessed land of the Mountain of Flowers and Fruit leads to Heaven." Monkey was beside himself with delight. He rushed back and again crouched, shut his eyes and jumped through the curtain of water.

"A great stroke of luck," he cried, "A great stroke of luck!"

"What is it like on the other side?" asked the monkeys, crowding round him. "Is the water very deep?" "There is no water," said the Stone Monkey. "There is an iron bridge, and at the side of it a heaven-sent place to live in." "What made you think it would do to live in?" asked the monkeys. "The water," said the Stone Monkey, "flows out of a hole in the rock, filling in the space under the bridge. At the side of the bridge are flowers and trees, and there is a chamber of stone. Inside are stone tables, stone cups, stone dishes, stone couches, stone seats. We could really be very comfortable there. There is plenty of room for hundreds and thousands of us, young and old. Let us all go and live there; we shall be splendidly sheltered in every weather." "You go first and show us how!" cried the monkeys, in great delight. Once more he closed his eyes and was through at one bound. "Come along, all of you !" he cried. The bolder of them jumped at once; the more timid stretched out their heads and then drew them back, scratched their ears, rubbed their cheeks, and then with a great shout the whole mob leapt forward. Soon they were all seizing dishes and snatching cups, scrambling to the hearth or fighting for the beds, dragging things along or shifting them about, behaving indeed as monkeys with their mischievous nature might be expected to do, never quiet for an instant, till at last they were thoroughly worn out. The Stone Monkey took his seat at the head of them and said, "Gentlemen! With one whose word cannot be trusted there is nothing to be done![2] You promised that any of us who managed to get through the waterfall and back again, should be your king. I have not only come and gone and come again, but also found you a comfortable place to sleep, put you in the enviable position of being householders. Why do you not bow down to me as your king?"

Thus reminded, the monkeys all pressed together the palms of their hands and prostrated themselves, drawn up in a line according to age and standing, and bowing humbly they cried, "Great king, a thousand years!" After this the Stone Monkey discarded his old

[2]A quotation from the *Analects* of Confucius, II, 22.

name and became king, with the title "Handsome Monkey King." He appointed various monkeys, gibbons and baboons to be his ministers and officers. By day they wandered about the Mountain of Flowers and Fruit; at night they slept in the Cave of the Water Curtain. They lived in perfect sympathy and accord, not mingling with bird or beast, in perfect independence and entire happiness.

The Monkey King had enjoyed this artless existence for several hundred years when one day, at a feast in which all the monkeys took part, the king suddenly felt very sad and burst into tears. His subjects at once ranged themselves in front of him and bowed down, saying, "Why is your Majesty so sad?" "At present," said the king, "I have no cause for unhappiness. But I have a misgiving about the future, which troubles me sorely." "Your Majesty is very hard to please," said the monkeys, laughing. "Every day we have happy meetings on fairy mountains, in blessed spots, in ancient caves, on holy islands. We are not subject to the Unicorn or Phoenix, nor to the restraints of any human king. Such freedom is an immeasurable blessing. What can it be that causes you this sad misgiving?" "It is true," said the Monkey King, "that to-day I am not answerable to the law of any human king, nor need I fear the menace of any beast or bird. But the time will come when I shall grow old and weak. Yama, King of Death, is secretly waiting to destroy me. Is there no way by which, instead of being born again on earth, I might live forever among the people of the sky?"

When the monkeys heard this they covered their faces with their hands and wept, each thinking of his own mortality. But look! From among the ranks there springs out one monkey commoner, who cries in a loud voice, "If that is what troubles your Majesty, it shows that religion has taken hold upon your heart. There are indeed, among all creatures, three kinds that are not subject to Yama, King of Death." "And do you know which they are?" asked the Monkey King. "Buddhas, Immortals and Sages," he said. "These three are exempt from the Turning of the Wheel, from birth and destruction. They are eternal as Heaven and Earth, as the hills and streams." "Where are they to be found?" asked the Monkey King. "Here on the common earth," said the monkey, "in ancient caves among enchanted hills."

The king was delighted with this news. "To-morrow," he said, "I shall say good-bye to you, go down the mountain, wander like a cloud to the corners of the sea, far away to the end of the world, till I have found these three kinds of Immortal. From them I will learn how to be young forever and escape the doom of death." This determination it was that led him to leap clear of the toils of Re-incarnation and turned him at last into the Great Monkey Sage, equal of Heaven. The monkeys clapped their hands and cried aloud, "Splendid! Splendid! To-morrow we will scour the hills for fruits and berries and hold a great farewell banquet in honor of our king."

Next day they duly went to gather peaches and rare fruits, mountain herbs, yellow-sperm, tubers, orchids, strange plants and flowers of every sort, and set out the stone tables and benches, laid out fairy meats and drinks. They put the Monkey King at the head of the table, and ranged themselves according to their age and rank. The pledge-cup passed from hand to hand; they made their offerings to him of flowers and fruit. All day long they drank, and next day their king rose early and said, "Little ones, cut some pine-wood for me and make me a raft; then find a tall bamboo for pole, and put together a few fruits and such like. I am going to start." He got on to the raft all alone and pushed off with all his might, speeding away and away, straight out to sea, till favored by a following wind he arrived at the borders of the Southern World. Fate indeed had favored him; for days on end, ever since he set foot on the raft, a strong southeast wind blew and carried him at last to the north-western bank, which is indeed the frontier of the Southern World. He tested the water with his pole and found that it was shallow; so he left the raft and climbed ashore. On the beach were people fishing, shooting wild geese, scooping oysters, draining salt. He ran up to them and for fun began to perform queer antics which frightened them so much that they dropped their baskets and nets and ran for their lives. One of them, who stood his ground, Monkey caught hold of, and ripping off his clothes, found out how to wear them himself, and so dressed up went prancing through towns and cities, in market and bazaar, imitating the people's manners and talk. All the while his heart was set only on finding the Immortals and learning from them the secret of eternal youth. But he found the men of the world all engrossed in the quest of profit or fame; there was not one who had any care for the end that was in store for him. So Monkey went looking for the way of Immortality, but found no chance of meeting it. For eight or nine years he went from city to city and town to town till suddenly he came to the Western Ocean. He was sure that beyond this ocean there would certainly be Immortals, and he made for himself a raft like the one he had before. He floated on over the Western Ocean till he came to the Western Continent, where he went ashore, and when he had looked about for some time, he suddenly saw a very high and beautiful mountain, thickly wooded at the base. He had no fear of wolves, tigers or panthers, and made his way up to the very top. He was looking about him when he suddenly heard a man's voice coming from deep amid the woods. He hurried towards the spot and listened intently. It was someone singing, and these were the words that he caught:

I hatch no plot, I scheme no scheme
Fame and shame are one to me
A simple life prolongs my days.
Those I meet upon my way
Are Immortals, one and all,
Who from their quiet seas expound
The Scriptures of the Yellow Court.

When Monkey heard these words he was very pleased. "There must then be Immortals somewhere hereabouts," he said. He sprang deep into the forest and looking carefully saw that the singer was a woodman, who was cutting brushwood. "Reverend Immortal," said Monkey, coming forward, "your disciple raises his hands." The woodman was so astonished that he dropped his ax. "You have made a mistake," he said, turning and answering the salutation, "I am only a shabby, hungry woodcutter. What makes you address me as an 'Immortal?'" "If you are not an Immortal," said Monkey, "why did you talk of yourself as though you were one ?" "What did I say," asked the woodcutter, "that sounded as though I were an Immortal?" "When I came to the edge of the wood," said Monkey, "I heard you singing 'Those I meet upon my way are Immortals, one and all, who from their quiet seats expound the Scriptures of the Yellow Court.' Those scriptures are secret, Taoist texts. What can you be but an Immortal?" "I won't deceive you," said the woodcutter. "That song was indeed taught to me by an Immortal, who lives not very far from my hut. He saw that I have to work hard for my living and have a lot of troubles; so he told me when I was worried by anything to say to myself the words of that song. This, he said, would comfort me and get me out of my difficulties. Just now I was upset about something and so I was singing that song. I had no idea that you were listening."

"If the Immortal lives close by," said Monkey, "how is it that you have not become his disciple? Wouldn't it have been as well to learn from him how never to grow old?" "I have a hard life of it," said the woodcutter. "When I was eight or nine I lost my father. I had no brothers and sisters, and it fell upon me alone to support my widowed mother. There was nothing for it but to work hard early and late. Now my mother is old and I dare not leave her. The garden is neglected, we have not enough either to eat or wear. The most I can do is to cut two bundles of firewood, carry them to market and with the penny or two that I get buy a few handfuls of rice which I cook myself and serve to my aged mother. I have no time to go and learn magic." "From what you tell me," said Monkey, "I can see that you are a good and devoted son, and your piety will certainly be rewarded. All I ask of you is that you will show me where the Immortal lives; for I should very much like to visit him."

"It is quite close," said the woodcutter. "This mountain is called the Holy Terrace Mountain, and on it is a cave called the Cave of the Slanting Moon and Three Stars. In that cave lives an Immortal called the Patriarch Subodhi. In his time he has had innumerable disciples, and at this moment there are some thirty or forty of them studying with him. You have only to follow that small path southwards for eight or nine leagues, and you will come to his home." "Honored brother," said Monkey, drawing the woodcutter toward him, "come with me, and if I profit by the visit I will not forget that you guided me." "It takes a lot to make some people understand," said the woodcutter. "I've just been telling you why I can't go. If I went with you, what would become of my work? Who would give my old mother her food? I must go on cutting my wood, and you must find your way alone."

When Monkey heard this, he saw nothing for it but to say good-bye. He left the wood, found the path, went uphill for some seven or eight leagues and, sure enough, found a cave-dwelling. But the door was locked. All was quiet, and there was no sign of anyone being about. Suddenly he turned his head and saw on top of the cliff a stone slab about thirty feet high and eight feet wide. On it was an inscription in large letters saying, "Cave of the Slanting Moon and Three Stars on the Mountain of the Holy Terrace." "People here," said Monkey, "are certainly very truthful. There really is such a mountain, and such a cave!" He looked about for a while, but did not venture to knock at the door. Instead he jumped up into a pine-tree and began eating the pine-seed and playing among the branches. After a time he heard someone call; the door of the cave opened and a fairy boy of great beauty came out, in appearance utterly unlike the common lads that he had seen till now. The boy shouted, "Who is making a disturbance out there?" Monkey leapt down from his tree, and coming forward said with a bow, "Fairy boy, I am a pupil who has come to study Immortality. I should not dream of making a disturbance." " You a pupil!" said the boy laughing. "To be sure," said Monkey. "My master is lecturing," said the boy. "But before he gave out his theme he told me to go to the door and if anyone came asking for instruction, I was to look after him. I suppose he meant you." "Of course he meant me," said Monkey. "Follow me this way," said the boy. Monkey tidied himself and followed the boy into the cave. Huge chambers opened out before them, they went on from room to room, through lofty halls and innumerable cloisters and retreats, till they came to a platform of green jade, upon which was seated the Patriarch Subodhi, with thirty lesser Immortals assembled before him. Monkey at once prostrated himself and bumped his head three times upon the ground, murmuring, "Master, master! As pupil to teacher I pay you my humble respects." "Where do you come from?" asked the Patriarch. "First tell me your country and name, and then pay your respects again." "I am from the Water Curtain Cave," said Monkey, "on the Mountain of Fruit and Flowers in the country of Ao-lai." "Go away!" shouted the Patriarch. "I know the people there. They're a tricky, humbugging set. It's no good one of them supposing he's going to achieve Enlightenment." Monkey, kowtowing violently, hastened to say, "There's no trickery about this; it's just the plain truth I'm telling you." "If you claim that you're telling the truth," said the Patriarch, "how is it that you say you came from Ao-lai? Between there and here there are two oceans and the whole of the Southern Continent. How did you get here?" "I floated over the oceans and wandered over the lands for ten years and more," said Monkey, "till at last I reached here." "Oh well," said the Patriarch, "I suppose if you came by easy stages, it's not altogether impossible. But tell me, what is your *hsing?*"[3] "I never show *hsing*," said Monkey. "If I am abused, I am not at all annoyed. If I am hit, I am not angry; but on the contrary, twice more polite than before. All my life I have never shown *hsing.*"

"I don't mean that kind of *hsing,*" said the Patriarch. "I mean what was your family, what surname had they?" "I had no family," said Monkey, "neither father nor mother." "Oh indeed!" said the Patriarch. "Perhaps you grew on a tree!" "Not exactly," said Monkey. "I came out of a stone. There was a magic stone on the Mountain of Flowers and Fruit. When its time came, it burst open and I came out."

"We shall have to see about giving you a school-name," said the Patriarch. "We have twelve words that we use in these names, according to the grade of the pupil. You are in the tenth grade." "What are the twelve words?" asked Monkey. "They are Wide, Big, Wise, Clever, True, Conforming, Nature, Ocean, Lively, Aware, Perfect and Illumined. As you belong to the tenth grade, the word Aware must come in your name. How about Aware-of-Vacuity?" "Splendid!" said Monkey, laughing. "From now onwards let me be called Aware-of-Vacuity."[4]

So that was his name in religion. And if you do not know whether in the end, equipped with this name, he managed to obtain enlightenment or not, listen while it is explained to you in the next chapter.

Translated by Arthur Waley

[3]The Patriarch uses the word *hsing* in its meaning of "name," but Monkey uses it in its meaning of "temper."

[4]A very Buddhist name, implying enlightenment.

Japan 1500–1750

Basho (b. 1644): Haiku

It is impossible to convey in translation the complexity and subtlety of Japanese haiku (consisting of seventeen syllables divided into two phrases followed by a third which makes a subtle connection between the first two), with its complex word-play, allusions to other poems both Japanese and Chinese, and the fact that what is left unsaid must often be inferred from a wide background knowledge of other works. However, Basho, the most famous of all writers of haiku, strove radically to simplify the haiku, striving for the utmost in understatement. His love of simplicity has been seen as reflecting the influence of Zen Buddhism. His love of nature is reflected even in his name; born Iga-ueno, he was renamed "Basho" after the banana tree he kept in his yard, and about which he wrote several poems. The influence of haiku on modern Western poetry would be difficult to overstate. Many poets, including especially the early 20th-Century writers known as "Imagists," have been drawn to its esthetic. The African-American novelist Richard Wright devoted the last part of his career to writing thousands of haiku. All haiku are translated by Lucien Stryk.

On a bare branch
A crow is perched—
Autumn evening.

The fragrant orchid:
Into a butterfly's wings
It breathes the incense.

The sea darkens
And a wild duck's call
Is faintly white.

Quietly, quietly,
Yellow mountain roses fall—
Sound of the rapids.

Above a wintry garden
The moon thins to a thread:
Insects singing.

After the chimes fade
Cherry fragrance continues:
Evening dusk.

A monk sipping
His morning tea, and it is quiet—
Chrysanthemum flowers.

Chikamatsu Monzaemon (1653–1725): *The Love Suicides at Sonezaki* The Journey from Dojima to the Sonezaki Shrine

There is a long and popular tradition in Japan of stories about double suicides. In a culture where marriages were usually arranged, fantasizing about the rare couples who dared to rebel was a form of release; but the only way they could stay together permanently was to kill themselves. Thus the social pressures against love matches are both criticized and reinforced. One of the most famous of these stories is told in this work, originally a puppet play (a very serious form of theater in Japan). A shop clerk, Tokubei, in love with a prostitute, Ohatsu, refuses to marry the girl chosen for him by his uncle. He must therefore return to his uncle the dowry money which his mother has already accepted. He obtains it with difficulty, but is at once persuaded by his friend Kuheiji to lend it in turn to him for a few days. Kuheiji tricks Tokubei out of the money. In despair over the consequences Tokubei and Ohatsu decide to commit suicide.

How does their belief in Buddhism affect the two lovers?

NARRATOR
Farewell to this world, and to the night farewell.
We who walk the road to death, to what should we be likened?
To the frost by the road that leads to the graveyard,
Vanishing with each step we take ahead:
How sad is this dream of a dream!
TOKUBEI
Ah, did you count the bell? Of the seven strokes
That mark the dawn, six have sounded.
The remaining one will be the last echo
We shall hear in this life.
OHATSU
It will echo the bliss of nirvana.
NARRATOR
Farewell, and not to the bell alone—
They look a last time on the grass, the trees, the sky.
The clouds, the river go by unmindful of them;
The Dipper's bright reflection shines in the water.
TOKUBEI
Let's pretend that Umeda Bridge
Is the bridge the magpies built[1]
Across the Milky Way, and make a vow
To be husband and wife stars for eternity.
OHATSU
I promise. I'll be your wife forever.

[1]Allusion to the Chinese legend, familiar also in Japan, which tells of two stars (known as the Herd Boy and the Weaver Girl) that meet once a year, crossing over a bridge in the sky built by magpies.

NARRATOR
They cling together—the river waters
Will surely swell with the tears they shed.
Across the river, in a teahouse upstairs,
Some revelers, still not gone to bed,
Are loudly talking under blazing lamps—
No doubt gossiping about the good or bad
Of this year's crop of lovers' suicides;
Their hearts sink to hear these voices.
TOKUBEI
How strange! but yesterday, even today,
We spoke as if such things did not concern us.
Tomorrow we shall figure in their gossip.
If the world will sing about us, let it sing.
NARRATOR
This is the song that now they hear.
        "I'm sure you'll never have me for your wife,
        I know my love means nothing to you . . ."
Yes, for all our love, for all our grieving,
Our lives, our lots, have not been as we wished.
Never, until this very day, have we known
A single night of heart's relaxation—
Instead, the tortures of an ill-starred love.
        "What is this bond between us?
        I cannot forget you.
        But you would shake me off and go.
        I'll never let you!
        Kill me with your hands, then go.
        I'll never release you!"
So she said in tears.[2]
OHATSU
Of all the many songs, that one, tonight!
TOKUBEI
Who is it singing? We who listen
BOTH
Suffer the ordeal of those before us.
NARRATOR
They cling to each other, weeping bitterly.
Any other night would not matter
If tonight were only a little longer,
But the heartless summer night, as is its wont,
Breaks as cockcrows hasten their last hour.
TOKUBEI
It will be worse if we wait for dawn.
Let us die in the wood of Tenjin.

---

[2]The song overheard by Ohatsu and Tokubei is derived from a popular ballad of the time which describes a love suicide.

NARRATOR
He leads her by the hand.
At Umeda Embankment, the night ravens.
TOKUBEI
Tomorrow our bodies may be their meal.
OHATSU
It's strange, this is your unlucky year[3]
Of twenty-five, and mine of nineteen.
It's surely proof how deep are our ties
That we who love each other are cursed alike.
All the prayers I have made for this world
To the gods and to the Buddha, I here and now
Direct to the future:
in the world to come
May we be reborn on the same lotus!
NARRATOR
One hundred eight the beads her fingers tell
On her rosary;[4] tears increase the sum.
No end to her grief, but the road has an end:
Their minds are numbed, the sky is dark, the wind still,
They have reached the thick wood of Sonezaki.

Shall it be here, shall it be there? When they brush the grass, the falling dew vanishes even quicker than their lives, in this uncertain world a lightning flash—or was it something else?

OHATSU
I'm afraid. What was that now?
TOKUBEI
That was a human spirit.[5] I thought we alone would die tonight, but someone else has preceded us. Whoever it may be, we have a companion on the journey to the Mountain of Death. *Namu Amida Butsu. Namu Amida Butsu.*[6]
NARRATOR
She weeps helplessly.
OHATSU
To think that others are dying tonight too! How heartbreaking!
NARRATOR
Man though he is, his tears fall freely.
TOKUBEI
Those two spirits flying together—do you suppose they belong to anyone else? They must be yours and mine!
OHATSU
Those two spirits? Then, are we dead already?

---

[3]According to yin-yang divination, a man's twenty-fifth, forty-second, and sixtieth years were dangerous; for a woman her nineteenth and thirty-third years.
[4]The Buddhist rosary has 108 beads, one for each of the sufferings occasioned by the passions.
[5]*Hitodama,* a kind of will-o'-the-wisp believed to be a human soul.
[6]The invocation to Amida Buddha used in Pure Land Buddhism.

TOKUBEI

Normally, if we saw a spirit, we'd knot our clothes and murmur prayers to keep our souls with us,[7] but now we hurry towards our end, hoping instead our two souls will find the same dwindling. Do not mistake the way, do not lose me!

NARRATOR

They embrace, flesh to flesh, then fall to the ground and weep—how pitiful they are! Their strings of tears unite like entwining branches, or the pine and palm that grow from a single trunk, a symbol of eternal love. Here the dew of their unhappy lives will at last settle.

TOKUBEI

Let this be the spot.

NARRATOR

He unfastens the sash of his cloak. Ohatsu removes her tear-stained outer robe, and throws it on the palm tree; the fronds might now serve as a broom to sweep away the sad world's dust. Ohatsu takes a razor from her sleeve.

OHATSU

I had this razor prepared in case we were overtaken on the way and separated. I was determined not to forfeit our name as lovers. How happy I am that we are to die together as we hoped!

TOKUBEI

How wonderful of you to have thought of that! I am so confident in our love that I have no fears even about death. And yet it would be unfortunate if because of the pain we are to suffer people said that we looked ugly in death. Let us secure our bodies to this twin-trunked tree and die immaculately! We will become an unparalleled example of a lovers' suicide.

OHATSU

Yes, let us do that.

NARRATOR

Alas! She little thought she thus would use her light blue undersash! She draws it taut, and with her razor slashes it through.

OHATSU

The sash is cut, but you and I will never be torn apart.

NARRATOR

She sits, and he binds her twice, thrice to the tree, firmly so that she will not stir.

TOKUBEI

Is it tight?

OHATSU

Very tight.

BOTH

This is the end of our unhappy lives!

TOKUBEI

No I mustn't give way to grief.

NARRATOR

He lifts his head and joins his hands in prayer.

TOKUBEI

My parents died when I was a boy, and I grew up thanks to the efforts of my uncle, who was my master. It disgraces me to die without repaying his kindness. Instead I shall cause him trouble which will last even after my death. Please forgive my sins. Soon I shall see my

---

[7]Exorcism practiced to prevent the soul from leaving the body.

parents in the other world. Father, Mother, welcome me there!

NARRATOR

He weeps. Ohatsu also joins her hands.

OHATSU

I envy you. You say you will meet your parents in the world of the dead. My father and mother are in this world and in good health. I wonder when I shall see them again. I heard from them this spring, but I haven't seen them since the beginning of last autumn. Tomorrow, when word reaches the village of our suicides, how unhappy they will be! Now I must bid farewell for this life to my parents, my brothers and sisters. If at least my thoughts can reach you, please appear before me, if only in dreams. Dear Mother, beloved Father!

NARRATOR

She sobs and wails aloud. Her husband also cries out and sheds incessant tears in all too understandable emotion.

OHATSU

We could talk forever, but it serves no purpose. Kill me, kill me quickly!

NARRATOR

She hastens the moment of death.

TOKUBEI

I am ready.

NARRATOR

He swiftly draws his dagger.

TOKUBEI

The moment has come. *Namu Amida. Namu Amida.*

NARRATOR

But when he tries to bring the blade against the skin of the woman he's loved, and held and slept with so many months and years, his eyes cloud over, his hand shakes. He tries to steady his weakening resolve, but still he trembles, and when he thrusts, the point misses. Twice or thrice the flashing blade deflects this way and that until a cry tells it has struck her throat.

TOKUBEI

Namu Amida. Namu Amida. Namu Amida Butsu.

NARRATOR

He twists the blade deeper and deeper, but the strength has left his arm. When he sees her weaken, he stretches forth his hands. The last agonies of death are indescribable.

TOKUBEI

Must I lag behind you? Let's draw our last breaths together.

NARRATOR

He thrusts and twists the razor in his throat, until it seems the handle or the blade must snap. His eyes grow dim, and his last painful breath is drawn away at its appointed hour. No one is there to tell the tale, but the wind that blows through Sonezaki Wood transmits it, and high and low alike gather to pray for these lovers who beyond a doubt will in the future attain Buddhahood. They have become models of true love.

Translated by Donald Keene

The Middle East 1500–1750

The Lady and Her Five Suitors, from *The Thousand and One Nights*

The sprawling, untidy collection of stories known throughout the Arab-speaking world as the Thousand and One Nights *(and in English long called* The Arabian Nights) *evolved over a long period of time, and it is impossible to say just when a particular story was written. Because the collection reached its more or less definitive form in the 16th century we have chosen to place this example here. Such tales of magic as "Aladdin and the Wonderful Lamp" and "Ali Baba and the Forty Thieves" are actually quite unrepresentative of the bulk of the* Nights. *Most are decidedly adult tales of scandal and treachery, often involving faithless women. It is an irony that cultures which depict women as irrepressibly sexual (including European culture, with its* Decameron *and other story collections), simultaneously tend to portray them as highly intelligent; for in a repressive patriarchal society it takes a good deal of cleverness to break the rules successfully. This story stands out in depicting sympathetically a heroine who manages to cleverly make fools of her would-be lovers by developing her own unique defense against sexual harassment.*

What are the main character traits of the woman in this story, and how are they illustrated?

A woman of the merchant class was married to a man who was a great traveler. Once he set out for a far country and was absent so long that his wife, out of sheer boredom, fell in love with a handsome young man, and they loved each other exceedingly. One day, the youth quarreled with another man, who lodged a complaint against him with the Chief of Police, and he cast him into prison. When the news came to the merchant's wife, she nearly lost her mind. Then she arose and—putting on her richest clothes—went to the house of the Chief of Police. She greeted him and presented him with a petition which read, "The man you have imprisoned is my brother So-and-So, who had a fight with someone; but those who testified against him lied. He has been wrongfully imprisoned, and I have no one else to live with or to support me; therefore I beg you graciously to release him."

When the Chief had read the petition, he looked at her and immediately fell in love with her; so he said to her, "Go into my house, till I bring him out; then I will send for you and you may take him away."

"O, my lord," she replied, "I have no one to protect me except almighty God. I cannot enter any strange man's home."

The Chief said, "I will not let him go unless you come to my home and let me do what I will with you."

She answered, "If it must be, you must come to my home and sleep through the afternoon and evening there."

"And where is your home?" he asked; and she answered, "At such-and-such a place," and arranged a time for him to come.

Then she left him, who had entirely fallen in love with her, and went to the Cadi of the city, to whom she said, "O, our lord the Cadi!"

He said, "Yes?" and she continued, "Examine my case and you will be rewarded by God."

He said, "Who has wronged you?" and she replied, "O my lord, I have a brother, my only brother, and it is on his behalf that I come to you, because the Chief has imprisoned him as a criminal and men have borne false witness against him, claiming that he is an evil man, and I beg you to intercede for him with the Chief of Police."

When the Cadi gazed at her, he immediately fell in love with her and said, "Go into the house and rest awhile with the women in my harem while I send to the Chief to release your brother. If I knew how much his fine was, I would pay it myself out of my own purse so that I could enjoy you, for your sweet speech greatly pleases me."

She said, "If you, O my lord, are to behave in this way, we would not be able to blame others."

Said he, "If you will not come in, go away."

Then she said, "If you insist, O our lord, it will be better and more private at my place than in yours, for here there are slave-girls and eunuchs and people coming and going; and indeed I am not this sort of woman, but I see that I must give in."

The Cadi asked, "And where is your house?" and she answered, "In such-and-such a place," and set for him the same day and time as the Chief of Police.

Then she went from him to the Vizier, to whom she offered her petition for the release from prison of her brother, who was absolutely necessary to her; but he also demanded she give herself to him, saying, "Allow me to do what I will with you and I will set your brother free."

She said, "If you insist, let it be in my house, for there we shall both have more privacy. It is not far away, and you understand that I must wash and dress myself properly for you."

He asked, "Where is your house."

"In such-and-such a place," she answered, and set the same time for as for the two others.

Then she left him to go to the King and told him her story and sought her brother's release. "Who imprisoned him?" he asked; and she replied, "It was the Chief of Police." When the King heard her speech, it pierced his heart with arrows of love, and he asked her to enter this private chamber with him so that he might send to the Cadi to have her brother released.

But she said, "O King, everything is easy for you, whether I agree or not; and if the King indeed wants me, I am fortunate; but if he will come to my house he will do me more honor by entering it, as the poet says: 'O my friends, have you seen or have you heard of his visit whose virtues I hold so high?'"

The King said, "I do not disagree." So she set for him the same time as the three others and told him where her house was.

Then she left him and sought out a carpenter, and told him "I want you to make me a cabinet with four compartments, one above the other, each with a door that can be locked. Let me know how much it will cost and I will pay it."

He replied, "My price is four dinars; but, sweet lady, if you will grant me your favors, I will charge you nothing."

She answered, "If it is absolutely necessary, I will agree; but in that case make five compartments with their padlocks," and she told him to bring it exactly on the day required.

He said, "This is well; sit down, O my lady, and I will make it for you immediately, and then will come with you." So she sat down by him while he began working on the cabinet; and when he had finished it she asked to have it carried home at once and set up in her sitting-room. Then she took four gowns and carried them to the dyer, who dyed each of them a different color; after which she prepared meat and drink, fruits, flowers, and perfumes.

Now when the appointed day came, she put on her costliest dress and adorned herself and scented herself, then spread the sitting-room with various kinds of rich carpets and sat down to await who should come.

The Cadi was the first to appear; and when she saw him, she rose to her feet and kissed the ground before him. Then, taking him by the hand, she made him sit down by her on the couch and lay with him and fell to joking and toying with him. Soon he wanted to fulfill his desires with her, but she said, "O my lord, take off your clothes and turban and put on this yellow robe and bonnet,[1] while I bring you food and drink, and then you shall do what you will." So saying, she took his clothes and turban and dressed him in the robe and bonnet; but hardly had she done this when there was a knocking at the door.

He asked, "Who is that knocking at the door?" and she answered, "My husband!"

"What shall I do? Where shall I go?" the Cadi said.

"Have no fear," she replied; "I will hide you in this cabinet;" and he answered, "Do whatever you think necessary." So she took him by the hand, and pushing him into the lowest compartment, locked the door on him. Then she went to the door of the house, where she found the Chief; so she kissed the ground before him, and taking his hand, brought him into the sitting-room and said to him, "O my lord, make this house your own, this place your place, and I will be your servant. You shall spend all days with me; so take off your clothes and put on this red sleeping gown." So she took away his clothes and made him put on the red gown and set on his head an old patched rag she happened to have; after which she sat by him on the divan and they toyed with each other until he reached to touch her intimately, whereupon she said to him, "O our lord, this is your day, and no one will share it with us; but first, if you will be so kind and generous, write me an order for my brother's release from jail so that my heart can rest easy."

He said, "I hear and obey, by my head and eyes!" and wrote a letter to his treasurer saying, "As soon as this communication reaches you, set So-and-So free, without delay. Do not even wait to give the messenger an answer." Then he sealed it and she took it from him, after which she began to toy with him on the divan again when someone suddenly knocked at the door.

"Who is that?" he asked; and she answered, "My husband." "What shall I do?" he asked, and she replied, "Enter this cabinet, till I send him away and return to you."

So she set him up in the second compartment from the bottom and padlocked the door; and meanwhile the Cadi heard everything they said. Then she went to the house door and opened it, and in entered the Vizier. She kissed the ground before him and received him with all honor, saying "O my lord, you flatter us by coming to our house; may God never deprive us of the light of your countenance!"

Then she seated him on the divan and said to him, "O my lord, take off your heavy clothes and turban and put on these lighter garments." So he took off his clothes and turban and she dressed him in a blue shirt and a tall red bonnet, and said to him, "Those were your official robes; so leave them be for their own time and put on this light gown which is more suitable for carousing and making merry and sleep." Then they began to play with each other, and he was just about to take her when she put him off by saying, "We will get to that."

As they were talking, there came a knock at the door, and the Vizier asked her, "Who is that?" to which she replied, "My husband." "What is to be done?" he said; and she an-

[1]It was customary for party guests to put on special garments supplied by the host.

swered, "Hide in this cabinet until I can get rid of him and come back to you; don't be afraid." So she put him in the third compartment and locked the door on him, after which she went out and opened the house door, and in came the King.

As soon as she saw him she kissed the ground before him, and taking him by the hand, led him into the sitting-room and seated him on the divan at the far end. Then she said to him, "Truly, O King, you honor us highly, and whatever we might give you of all the world contains would not be worth a single one of your steps toward us." And when he had sat down on the divan she said, "Permit me to say one thing."

"Whatever you wish," he answered; and she said, "O my lord, relax and take off your robe and turban." His clothes were worth a thousand dinars; but when he took them off she dressed him in a patched gown worth ten dirhems at the very most, and began talking and joking with him. All this time the men in the cabinet heard everything that went on but did not dare to say a word. Soon the King placed his hand on her breast and sought to fulfill his desire for her; but she said "We will do this soon, but first I promised myself that I would entertain you properly in this room, and I have something to please you."

As they were speaking, someone knocked at the door and he asked her, "Who is that?" "My husband," she answered; and he said, "Make him go away voluntarily, or I will go out and force him to go away."

She replied, "No, O my lord, be patient while I send him away using my cleverness." "And what shall I do?" asked the King; whereupon she took him by the hand and, making him enter the fourth compartment of the cabinet, locked it upon him.

Then she went out and opened the house door to the carpenter, who entered and greeted her. She said, "What kind of a cabinet is this you've made me?" "What's wrong with it, O my lady?" he asked; and she answered, "The top compartment is too narrow." He replied, "No it isn't," and she answered, "Get in yourself and see; you cannot fit in it."

He answered, "it is wide enough for four," and entered the fifth compartment, whereupon she locked the door on him.

Then she took the letter of the Chief of Police and carried it to the treasurer who, having read and understood it, kissed it and delivered her lover to her. She told him all she had done and he said, "But what shall we do now?" She answered, "We will move away to another city, for after all this we cannot remain here." So the two of them packed up what possessions they had and, loading them on camels, set out immediately for another city.

Meanwhile, the five men remained each in his compartment of the cabinet without eating or drinking for three whole days, during which time they held their water, until at last the carpenter couldn't hold back any longer, so he pissed on the King's head, and the King pissed on the Vizier's head, and the Vizier pissed on the Chief, and the Chief pissed on the Cadi, whereupon the Cadi shouted, "What filth is this? Isn't it bad enough that we are trapped like this that you have to piss all over us?"

The Chief of Police recognized the Cadi's voice and answered, "May God reward you, O Cadi!" And when the Cadi heard him, he knew it was the Chief. Then the Chief shouted, "What's the meaning of this filth?" and the Vizier replied, "May God reward you, O Chief!" so that he recognized him as the Vizier. Then the Vizier shouted "What is this nastiness?" But when the King heard his Vizier's voice he recognized it, so he kept silent to conceal his plight.

Then the Vizier said, "May God curse this woman for the way she has dealt with us. She has brought together here all the chief officials of the state, except the King. Said the King, "Silence! For I was the first one to be entrapped by this shameless whore."

At this the carpenter cried out, "And what have I done? I made her a cabinet for four gold pieces, and when I came to get my pay, she tricked me into entering this compartment and locked the door on me." And they began talking with each other, diverting the King and reducing his shame.

Soon, however, the neighbors came by the house and noticed it was deserted. They said to one another, "Only yesterday, our neighbor the wife of So-and-So was home; but now we cannot hear or see anyone. Let's break down the doors and see what is the matter; or news of the case may come to the Chief or the King, and we will be thrown into prison to regret that we had not taken action earlier."

So they broke down the doors and entered the sitting room, where they saw a large wooden cabinet and heard the men in it groaning with hunger and thirst. Then one of them said, "Is there a Genie[2] in this cabinet?" and another said, "Let's pile fuel around it and burn it up."

When the Cadi heard this, he cried out, "Don't!" and they said to each other, "The Genies pretend they are mortals and speak with the voices of men." Thereupon the Cadi recited a passage from the Blessed Qur'an, and said to the neighbors, "Come closer to the cabinet."

So they came closer, and he told him, "I am So-and-so the Cadi, and you are so and so, and here we are all together." The neighbors said, "Who put you in here?" And he told them the whole story from beginning to end. They brought a carpenter to open the five doors and let out the Cadi, the Vizier, the Chief, the King and the carpenter in their bizarre robes; and each one, when he saw how the others were dressed, began laughing at them. She had taken away all their clothes; so all of them sent to their homes for fresh clothing and put it on and went out, shielding themselves from people's eyes.

Translated by Richard Burton, revised by Paul Brians

---

[2]Magic spirit.

Europe 1500–1750

François Rabelais (1494-1593): Letter from Gargantua to his son Pantagruel

So famous is the wildly obscene humor of Gargantua and Pantagruel *that its author's name has given rise to an adjective—"Rabelaisian"—to describe just such humor. Rabelais was a monk and a physician, but in his writings he celebrated his real loves: scholarship and drinking, with the latter often serving as a symbol of the former. As a beneficiary of the age of the printing press, he was intoxicated by the sudden availability of all manner of books. As much as any of the Renaissance Humanists, it is Rabelais who articulates their view that a new age has dawned. If his portrait of the Middle Ages as a time of ignorance and superstition is grossly exaggerated (and it is), it nevertheless helps to convey the excitement of the Humanists during the fifteenth and sixteenth centuries. This passage, a letter from father to son advising him on his education, is written in the elaborate, balanced style of formal prose in the period, quite unlike the tumbling, bawdy narrative that surrounds it. Read aloud, with appropriate pauses at the punctuation marks, it conveys a grand rhythmic majesty.*

Choose one of the inventions of the Renaissance and explain why you think it is important. Of what invention of the Renaissance does Gargantua not *approve?*

But even though my late father Grandgousier, of blessed memory, strove with all his ability that I should profit from and learn political knowledge, and even though my labors and studies matched or even surpassed his desires, nevertheless, as you can well understand, the times were not fit or favorable for learning as is the present; and I did not have the abundance of such instructors as you have had. The times were still dark[1] and reflected the misery and calamity caused by the Goths[2] who had destroyed all good scholarship. But, through divine grace, during my life light and dignity have been restored to learning; and we witness in them so much improvement that now I would have trouble being accepted into a children's beginning class, I who in my maturity was reputed (and not wrongly) the most learned man of the time. I do not say this out of vain boasting—even though I could properly do so in writing to you as you may understand by the authority of Marcus Tullius Cicero in his book *Old Age,* and the teachings of Plutarch in his book titled *How to Praise Oneself Honorably*[3]—but to inspire in you the desire to strive for the highest achieve-

---

[1]The Humanists were fond of referring to the Middle Ages as "dark," but this must not be confused with later definitions of the "Dark Ages" which ended centuries before the Renaissance.

[2]The Goths, headed by Alaric, sacked Rome in 410. This invasion is often considered to have marked the end of the classical world and the beginning of the "Dark Ages" (although many historians reject this latter term). The Humanists used the term broadly to mean "barbaric," and considered the artistic styles which sprang up in their wake barbaric as well, calling the great cathedrals of the High Middle Ages "Gothic" as an insult.

[3]Like the other Humanists, Rabelais delights in making references to ancient Latin works.

ments.

Now all the disciplines have been restored, languages revived: Greek, without which it is shameful for a person to call himself learned: Hebrew, Chaldean,[4] and Latin. Elegant and correct printed editions are available, the result of a divinely-inspired invention of my time, as are in contrast guns, the product of diabolical suggestion. The world is full of learned men, fine teachers, ample libraries; and it is my opinion that neither in the time of Plato,[5] nor of Cicero,[6] nor of Papinian[7] were there such opportunities for study as we see today; and no one should now go out in public who has not been well polished in Minerva's workshop.[8] I see the robbers, hangmen, freebooters and grooms of today more learned than the theologians and preachers of my day. What can I say? Even women and girls aspire to the honor and celestial manna of good learning.[9] Things have changed so much that at my advanced age I have had to learn Greek, which I had not rejected like Cato, but which I had not had the leisure to learn in my youth; and I delight in reading the *Morals* of Plutarch, the beautiful *Dialogues* of Plato, the *Monuments* of Pausanias, and the *Antiquities* of Athenaeus as I await the hour at which it may please God, my Creator, to summon and order me to leave this world.

Translated by Paul Brians

[4]The language of the Biblical Babylonians, famed for their astronomical and astrological studies.
[5]5th Century BCE, Greece.
[6]1st Century BCE, Rome.
[7]3rd Century CE, Rome. Papinian was a great authority on Roman law.
[8]Minerva (Greek Athena) was the goddess of wisdom, so her workshop is scholarship.
[9]Rabelais was a great friend and admirer of the queen and writer, Marguerite de Navarre, to whom he dedicated one of his books.

Desiderius Erasmus: Julius Excluded From Heaven: A Dialogue (1516)

Julius II, Pope 1503-1513, was as responsible as anyone for the bad reputation the leadership of the Catholic Church developed in the Renaissance. He was originally a warrior, and continued waging military campaigns after he was made pope, to increase his own worldly power and that of the Church. In the world of art he is famed as the patron of such great artists as Raphael, Bramante, and Michelangelo. He is said to have told the latter to portray him on his tomb holding a sword rather than a book. He was neither as corrupt nor as debauched as Erasmus' satirical portrait of him suggests; but this dialogue illustrates vividly the indignation with which many Northern Europeans viewed the papacy and which led to the Protestant Reformation. Erasmus was a Dutch priest and humanist who argued strenuously for reform in the Church but opposed the Reformation led by Luther because of its divisiveness. According to Catholic belief, Christ made St. Peter the first pope, and the authority of all succeeding popes descends from his. Erasmus makes much of the irony of Julius audaciously daring to judge the most holy of Christ's apostles as he seeks after his death to enter the gates of heaven.

What Protestant values are apparent in this dialogue? What aspects of the papacy seem most to offend Erasmus?

JULIUS

What the devil is this? The doors won't open? Someone must have changed the lock, or at least tampered with it.

GENIUS[1]

Are you quite sure you haven't brought the wrong key? The key to your treasure-chest won't open this door; and anyway, why didn't you bring both of them with you? The one in your hand is the key of power, not of knowledge.

JULIUS

This is the only one I've ever had and, as I've got it here, I don't see what use the other would be.[2]

GENIUS

Neither do I, except that we're shut out without it.

JULIUS

I'm seething with anger. I'll bang on the doors. Hey! Hey! Someone open this door at once! What's the matter? No one here? What's keeping the doorman? Snoring, I suppose, good and drunk.

GENIUS

He judges everyone by his own standards.

PETER

It's a good thing our gate is as solid as rock or he'd have broken the doors down, whoever he is. This must be some giant or paladin,[3] some wrecker of cities. Immortal God! It smells like a sewer round here! I won't open the door directly, but I'll peep through the bars of this window and find out what kind of monster it is. Who are you? What do you want?

---

[1]In pre-Christian Rome, the guardian spirit of a man or of a place; as used here, the term obviously has satirical pagan associations.

[2]The Pope is represented as holding two keys (from Matthew 16:19) symbolizing the two sorts of power granted the Pope: earthly and spiritual. Julius has no use for the latter.

[3]Knight.

JULIUS

I want you to open the doors, and quickly; if you did your job properly, you'd have come out to meet me with a solemn procession of angels, too.

PETER

He's domineering enough, anyway! But first of all, tell me who you are.

JULIUS

As if you can't see that for yourself.

PETER

See for myself? Well, I can see a strange spectacle, or perhaps I should say monster, unlike anything I've ever seen before.

JULIUS

But I imagine that unless you're quite blind you recognize this key, even if the golden oak[4] isn't familiar; and you can see my triple crown[5] and my robe all glittering with gold and jewels.

PETER

Yes, the silver key is vaguely familiar, but there's only one and it's very different from those which Christ, the true shepherd of the church, entrusted to me long ago. As for that sumptuous crown of yours, why on earth should I recognize it? No barbarian tyrant ever dared wear a thing like that, let alone anyone trying to get in here. I'm certainly not impressed by the robe, because I always scorned gold and jewels and trampled them like so much rubble. But what's this? I see that all your equipment, key, crown, and robe, bears the marks of that villainous huckster and impostor, who had my name but not my nature, Simon, whom I humbled long ago with the aid of Christ.[6]

JULIUS

Stop this nonsense, if you know what's good for you; for your information, I am Julius, the famous Ligurian;[7] and, unless you've completely forgotten your alphabet, I'm sure you recognize these two letters, P.M.

PETER

I suppose they stand for Pestis Maxima.[8]

GENIUS

Ha ha ha! Our soothsayer has hit the nail on the head!

JULIUS

Of course not! Pontifex Maximus.[9]

---

[4]The symbol of the Pope's family.

[5]The traditional headdress of the Pope.

[6]In Acts 8:9-24 the story is told of a magician named Simon who tried to buy from Peter the secret of his miraculous powers, and was strongly condemned for doing so. His name came to be associated with those who sought to use the Church for personal gain, so that the sin of selling Church offices, for instance, was called "simony."

[7]Julius' family came from the town of Liguria.

[8]Supreme Plague.

[9]"Supreme Pontiff," a traditional title for the Pope, derived from ancient Roman terminology.

PETER

Well, you could be thrice Maximus and even greater than Mercurius Trismegistus,[10] but you can't come in here unless you're Optimus,[11] and by that I mean holy.

JULIUS

Oh, if being called "holy" has anything to do with it, it's most impertinent of you to take so long to open the doors; you may have been merely styled "holy" or "saint" for all these years, but everyone has always called me "most holy." There are thousands of bulls. . .[12]

GENIUS

"Cock-and-bulls," you might say!

JULIUS

. . . in which I am many times called "most holy lord;" in fact, I was always referred to as "his Holiness," not just "holy," so that whatever I fancied doing . . .

GENIUS

Even when he was drunk!

JULIUS

. . . people said that "his Holiness, the most holy Lord Julius" had done.

PETER

Then ask your flatterers to let you into heaven, since they made you "most holy," and let those who gave you "Holiness" grant you bliss as well. Do you really think there's no difference between being holy and being called holy?

JULIUS

This is very annoying: if I'd only been allowed to go on living I wouldn't envy you your holiness or your bliss.

PETER

How well your words reveal the holiness of your thoughts! But in any case, I've been watching you closely all this time, and I can see plenty of evidence of impiety, but none of saintliness. What, for instance, is the purpose of that strange escort of yours, so unlike a pope's? You've brought twenty thousand men with you, but not one of the whole mob even looks like a Christian to me. They seem to be the worst dregs of humanity, all stinking of brothels, booze, and gunpowder. I'd say they were a gang of hired thugs, or rather goblins of Tartarus[13] plucked up from hell to wage war on heaven. And the more closely I look at you yourself the less I can see any trace of an apostle. First of all, what monstrous new fashion is this, to wear the dress of a priest on top, while underneath it you're all bristling and clanking with blood-stained armor? Then again, what fierce eyes and stubborn mouth, what a fearsome expression and haughty and arrogant brow you have! I'm ashamed to say, and sorry to see, that your whole body is disfigured by the marks of monstrous and abominable appetites, not to mention that even now you're all belches and that you stink of boozing and hangovers and look as if you've just thrown up. Your whole body is in such a state that I should guess that it's been wasted, withered, and rotted less by old age and illness than by drink.

---

[10]A Greco-Roman form of the name of the "Thrice-Great" Egyptian god Thoth, symbolizing mystical power.

[11]A title for God himself, derived from a title for Jupiter.

[12]Official papal pronouncements. Protestants rejected them.

[13]A Greek name for Hell.

GENIUS

A fine portrait: Julius to the life! . . .

JULIUS

Enough talk, I say! If you don't obey me, and quickly, I'll hurl my thunderbolt of excommunication,[14] even at you; I used to terrify the mightiest kings and even whole kingdoms with it. Do you see this bull, already drawn up for the purpose?

PETER

What on earth is all this about frightful thunderbolts and lightning and bulls and other fine talk? Christ never told us anything about these.

JULIUS

Do as you're told, or you'll find out.

PETER

You may have frightened men once with such fantasies, but they're no use in this place: only truth counts here. This citadel may be taken by good deeds, not foul words. But one question: you threaten me with your thunderbolt of excommunication; by what right?

JULIUS

The best of rights, since you no longer hold office and are no more than a simple priest; no, not even a priest, as you haven't the power to consecrate.[15]

PETER

Because I'm dead, I suppose?

JULIUS

Exactly.

PETER

But by the same token you have no more power over me than a dead man.

JULIUS

Ah, but as long as the cardinals are wrangling over electing a new pope, I'm still in charge.

GENIUS

He's still dreaming the dreams of life.

JULIUS

Now open up, I say.

PETER

And I say that you won't get anywhere unless you give an account of your merits.

JULIUS

What merits?

PETER

I'll explain. Were you eminent in theology?

JULIUS

Certainly not: I hadn't time, I was too busy with my wars. But there are plenty of monks occupied with it, if that's any good to you.

PETER

Well, did you win many souls for Christ by the saintliness of your life?

---

[14]When the Pope excommunicates someone, that person may not receive the holy sacraments, and is considered to be damned unless he or she repents and is reconciled to the Church. Like a wrathful Jupiter hurling his thunderbolts, Julius often excommunicated his enemies for personal rather than religious reasons.

[15]To perform the miracle of consecration of the bread and wine at mass.

GENIUS

He sent a good many to Tartarus.

PETER

Were you famous for your miracles?

JULIUS

This is all old-fashioned stuff.

PETER

Did you pray simply and regularly?

JULIUS

What's he jabbering about? Lot of nonsense!

PETER

Did you mortify the flesh by fasting and vigils?[16]

GENIUS

I'd give up, if I were you; there's no point; you're wasting your time on him.

PETER

I don't know what other qualities make an outstanding pope. If he has some more apostolic ones, let him tell me. . . .

JULIUS

Against all the odds I fought my way up to this position, partly with the help of the French, who took me in as a fugitive, and partly with the aid of an immense amount of money; I raised this both by paying high rates of interest and also by using my wits. . . .

PETER

What does that mean?

JULIUS

It means that I promised benefices in return for cash, and took great care to find guarantors for it, seeing that Crassus[17] himself could hardly have raised so much ready cash all at once. But it's no use telling you all this, when not even all the bankers understand it. Now you know how I reached my position. But since then, as pope, I have managed affairs so well that the church, and Christ himself, owe more to me than any previous pope, even the more recent ones, to say nothing of the early ones who, in my opinion, were popes in name only. . . .

I invented a lot of new offices, as they're called, and considerably enriched the papal treasury. Then I found a way of selling bishoprics[18] without falling into the sin of simony. It had been established by my predecessors that anyone appointed to a bishopric must resign his other offices. I interpreted this as follows: "You are told to resign, but you cannot resign something you don't possess, and so you must buy something to resign."[19] By this device single bishoprics used to bring in six or seven thousand ducats each, apart from the usual extortions for the bulls. Again, I collected no mean profit from the new currency with which I flooded Italy. I've never missed an opportunity to pile up more money, because I understand only too well that nothing, sacred or profane, can be done properly without it. . . .

---

[16] Staying awake praying for long periods of time was considered particularly pious.

[17] An ancient Roman statesman famous for using his office to accumulate a huge personal fortune.

[18] The office of bishop.

[19] That is, Julius only awarded benefices to those who already held an office, which had to be abandoned and could then be sold.

But my finest achievement: even though I maintained so great an army, organized magnificent triumphs, presented many spectacles, and put up buildings all over the place, yet at my death I left five million ducats, and would have gone on to greater things, if the skill of my Jewish doctor, which had already prolonged my life considerably, had been able to extend it still further. Ah, if only some wizard could restore me to life so that I could put the finishing touches to all my splendid plans! Mind you, on my deathbed I took great care to prevent any settlement of the wars I had stirred up throughout the world, and I saw to it that at least the money set aside for this purpose should be untouched: these were my last orders as I expired.[20]

Can you now be reluctant to open the doors of heaven to a pope who has served Christ and the church so well? You'll admire me all the more when you realize that I achieved all this by the strength of my own character alone, having none of the advantages that most other people enjoy: no family connections, as not even I knew who my father was[21] (which indeed adds to the glory of my achievement); no good looks, as everyone shuddered at my ghastly face; no learning, as that was something I never acquired;[22] no physical strength—I've already described the state of my body to you; none of the advantages of youth, as I did all this in old age; no popular support, as everyone hated me; no mercy, since I was so ruthless myself that I even dealt harshly with those to whom other people usually show every indulgence. . . .

PETER

Christ taught me that these doors are to be opened, not to those who bring along bulls heavy with lead, but to those who have clothed the naked, fed the hungry, given drink to the thirsty, visited the prisoner, and taken in the stranger.[23] And if he wished even those who prophesied, cast out devils, and worked miracles in his name to be shut out,[24] do you really think I should let in those who only bring a bull in the name of Julius?

JULIUS

What if I'd found out?

PETER

I see: if some refugees from hell had told you about it, you'd have declared war on me?

JULIUS

More than that: I'd have excommunicated you!

Translated by Michael J. Heath

---

[20]Julius ordered that his treasure should pass only to his successor, not to the conclave as a whole, and that it should be used only for a war against the Turks.

[21]Julius was commonly but incorrectly accused of being illegitimate.

[22]Julius had fine new buildings constructed for the university at Rome, but kept the wages of the teachers low.

[23]Paraphrasing Matthew 25:35–36.

[24]Refers to Matthew 7:22–23.

Galileo Galilei: On Sunspots
From *Dialogue on the Great World Systems* (1632)

Galileo made many discoveries with the telescope, among them sunspots. This was an important discovery in changing the world view of Europeans because the Catholic Church, following Aristotle, had taught that the realm of the Heavens, from the Moon upwards, was perfect and unchanging. Galileo's observations brought the Earth and Sun together into the same flawed realm and made more plausible his defense of Nicolas Copernicus' theory that the Earth was not the center of the universe. This passage from Galileo's dialogue caused him as much trouble as any in his works when the Holy Inquisition charged him with heresy and ordered him to recant (take back) his teachings. The Church temporarily won the argument, but scientific initiative was so damaged in Italy that most European progress in the sciences took place in the Protestant north. In the dialogue which follows, "Simplicius" (simpleton) represents the conservative theologians who opposed Galileo, "Sagredus" is a sophisticated but cautious man, interested in the new science but not ready to commit himself, and "Salvatius" expresses Galileo's own opinions.

How does Salvatius answer the argument that his observations conflict with the theories of Aristotle, whose teaching had been endorsed by the Church? In what way does Sagredus find the earth to be superior to the heavenly bodies which the Church considered perfect?

SALVATIUS

But you, Simplicius, what answer could you give to the opposition of these importunate spots which are started up to disturb the heavens and, more than that, the Peripatetic philosophy? It cannot be but that you, who are so resolute a champion of it, have found some reply or solution for it, of which you ought not to deprive us.

SIMPLICIUS

I have heard sundry opinions about this particular. One says: "They are stars which in their proper circles, like Venus and Mercury, revolve about the Sun, and, in passing under it, look dark themselves to us; as they are many, they often happen to aggregate their parts together, and afterwards separate again." Others believe them to be aerial impressions; others, the illusions of the lenses; and others, other things. But I incline to think that they are an aggregate of several opaque bodies, as it were casually concurrent among themselves. And therefore we often see that in one of these spots one may number ten or more such small bodies, which are of irregular figures, and seem to us like flakes of snow, or flocks of wool, or moths flying: they shift places among themselves, while retaining the over-all shape, and also go beneath the Sun, about which, as about their center, they continually move. But we need not therefore grant that they are generated or dissolved but that at times they are hid behind the body of the Sun, and at other times, though remote from it, are not seen because of the vicinity of the immeasurable light of the Sun. In the eccentric orb of the Sun there is constituted, as it were, an onion, composed of many layers one within another, each of which is studded with certain small spots, and moves; and although their motion at first seems inconstant and irregular, yet, nevertheless, it is said at last to be observed that the very same spots, as before, return again within a determinate time. This seems to me the fittest answer that has been found to maintain the incorruptibility and ingenerability of the heavens; and, if this is not sufficient, there is no lack of

---

[1]Aristotle's philosophy, which dominated late Medieval thought and was endorsed by the Catholic Church.

elevated minds who will give you other more convincing answers.

SALVATIUS

If this of which we dispute were some point of law, or other part of the studies called the humanities, wherein there is neither truth nor falsehood, we might give sufficient credit to the acuteness of wit, readiness of answers, and the greater accomplishments of writers and hope that he who is most proficient in these will make his reason more probable and plausible. But the conclusions of Natural Science are true and necessary, and the judgment of men has nothing to do with them, so that one must be more cautious how he goes about maintaining anything that is false; for a man of an ordinary wit, if by good fortune on the right side, may lay a thousand Demosthenes and a thousand Aristotles[2] at his feet. Therefore reject the hope that there can be any men so much more learned, read, and versed in authors than we, that in spite of Nature they should be able to make that become true which is false. And seeing that, of all the opinions that have been hitherto alleged touching the essence of these solar spots, the one you cite is in your judgment the truest, it follows that all the rest are false; now, to deliver you from this also, which doubtless is a false Chimæra,[3] I shall pass over infinitely many other improbabilities that are therein and propose against it only two experiments. The first is that many of those spots are seen to arise in the midst of the solar ring, and many likewise to dissolve and vanish at a great distance from the rim of the Sun. This implies that they generate and dissolve; for if, without generating or corrupting, they should appear there by local motion, they would all be seen to enter and then pass out over the extreme circumference. The other observation is necessarily conclusive to such as are not totally ignorant in perspective: for the variation of the figures and the apparent changes of the velocity of motion show that the spots are contiguous to the body of the Sun, and that, touching its surface, they move either with it or upon it, and that they in no wise move in circles remote from the same.

[*At this point Salvatius presents a number of other pieces of evidence.*]

SIMPLICIUS

I, for my part, have not made either such long or such exact observations as to enable me to boast myself master of the *quod est*[4] of this matter; but I will more accurately consider it and observe for my own satisfaction whether I can reconcile that which experience shows us with what Aristotle teaches us; for it is a certain maxim that two truths cannot be contrary to one another.

SALVATIUS

If you would reconcile that which sense shows you with the most solid doctrine of Aristotle, you will find no great difficulty in the undertaking; and that it is so, does not Aristotle say, that one cannot confidently treat of the things of heaven by reason of their great remoteness?

SIMPLICIUS

He expressly says so.

SALVATIUS

And does he not likewise affirm that we ought to prefer that which sense demonstrates before all arguments, though in appearance well grounded? And does he not say this without the least doubt or hesitation?

SIMPLICIUS

---

[2]Both revered ancient Greek scholars who speculated about scientific subjects.

[3]Creature of the imagination.

[4]"What is," the facts.

He does so.

SALVATIUS

Well, then, the second of these two doctrines of Aristotle that says that sense is to take the place of Logic is a much more solid and undoubted doctrine than that other which holds the heavens to be unalterable. Therefore, you would argue more Aristotelically by saying, "The heavens are alterable, for so my sense tells me," than if you should say, "The heavens are unalterable, because Logic so persuaded Aristotle." Furthermore, we may discourse of celestial matters much better than Aristotle; because he confesses their knowledge to be difficult to him by reason of their remoteness from the senses; he thereby acknowledges that one to whom the senses can better represent them may philosophize upon them with more certainty. Now we, by help of the Telescope, are brought thirty or forty times nearer to the heavens than Aristotle ever came; so that we may discover in them a hundred things which he could not see, and, among the rest, these spots in the Sun, which were to him absolutely invisible; therefore we may discourse of the heavens and the Sun with more certainty than Aristotle. . . .

SAGREDUS

I cannot without great wonder, nay more, disbelief, hear it being attributed to natural bodies as a great honor and perfection that they are impassable, immutable, inalterable, etc.: as, conversely, I hear it esteemed a great imperfection to be alterable, generable, mutable, etc. It is my opinion that the Earth is very noble and admirable by reason of the many and different alterations, mutations, generations, etc., which incessantly occur in it. And if, without being subject to any alteration, it had been all one vast heap of sand, or a mass of jade, or if, since the time of the deluge, the waters freezing which covered it, it had continued an immense globe of crystal, wherein nothing had ever grown, altered, or changed, I should have esteemed it a wretched lump of no benefit to the Universe, a mass of idleness, and in a word superfluous, exactly as if it had never been in Nature. The difference for me would be the same as between a living and a dead creature. I say the same concerning the Moon, Jupiter, and all the other globes of the Universe. The more I delve into the consideration of the vanity of popular discourses, the more empty and simple I find them. What greater folly can be imagined than to call gems, silver, and gold noble and earth and dirt base? For do not these persons consider that, if there were as great a scarcity of earth as there is of jewels and precious metals, there would be no king who would not gladly give a heap of diamonds and rubies and many ingots of gold to purchase only so much earth as would suffice to plant a jessamine in a little pot or to set a tangerine in it, that he might see it sprout, grow up, and bring forth goodly leaves, fragrant flowers, and delicate fruit? It is scarcity and plenty that make things esteemed and despised by the vulgar, who will say that here is a most beautiful diamond, for it resembles a clear water, and yet would not part with it for ten tons of water. These men who so extol incorruptibility, inalterability, etc., speak thus, I believe, out of the great desire they have to live long and for fear of death, not considering that, if men had been immortal, they would not have had to come into the world. These people deserve to meet with a Medusa's head that would transform them into statues of diamond and jade, that so they might become more perfect than they are.

Translated by Thomas Salusbury & Giorgio de Santillana

William Shakespeare: Sonnets

Not only is Shakespeare the English language's greatest playwright, but one of its greatest lyric poets. Some of the sonnets he wrote contain lines as well known as any in the plays. One of the perennial themes of Western literature—the brevity of life—is given poignantly personal and highly original expression in many of these poems. In the first sonnet he compares the aging process to the onset of winter, to the fading of daylight and to the dying down of a fire so powerfully that one is surprised at the conclusion to realize that this is after all a love poem, expressing in a fresh way the old theme of tempus fugit *("time flies"), to tell his beloved that love can be more intense when one realizes that it is doomed to be brief. The second sonnet takes up another classic theme,* ars longa, vita brevis *("art lasts long, though life is short") in a way that shows Shakespeare was confident of his own greatness. He clearly believed his poetry would last, and used that fact as an argument for love. In the final lines he states, as a Christian, that the lover will live again on Judgment Day, but between this day and the end of the world, will live on through the poem. Shakespeare evidently addressed these poems to a young man, but they have been used to express the longings of lovers of all kinds.*

What do you think the glowing ashes of the poet symbolize? Sonnet 55 maintains that the beloved will be remembered because of this poem, but what does the sonnet actually tell us about the lover?

Sonnet 73

That time of year thou mayst in me behold
When yellow leaves, or none, or few, do hang
Upon those boughs which shake against the cold,
Bare ruined choirs,[1] where late[2] the sweet birds sang.
In me thou see'st the twilight of such day
As after sunset fadeth in the west;
Which by and by black night doth take away,
Death's second self, that seals up all in rest.
In me thou see'st the glowing of such fire,
That on the ashes of his youth doth lie,
As the death-bed whereon it must expire,
Consumed with that which it was nourished by.
This thou perceivest, which makes thy love more strong,
To love that well which thou must leave ere long.

---

[1]The empty tree branches are compared to choir stalls, or benches.
[2]Lately, recently.

Sonnet 55

Not marble, nor the gilded monuments
Of princes, shall outlive this powerful rhyme;[2]
but you shall shine more bright in these contents[3]
Than unswept stone, besmeared with sluttish time.
When wasteful war shall statues overturn,
And broils[4] root out the work of masonry,
Nor[5] Mars his[6] sword nor war's quick fire shall burn
The living record of your memory.
'Gainst death and all-oblivious enmity
Shall you pace forth; your praise shall still find room
Even in the eyes of all posterity
That wear this world out[7] to the ending doom.
  So, till the judgment that yourself arise,
  You live in this, and dwell in lovers' eyes.

---

[2]Poem.
[3]The contents of these poems written about you.
[4]Fights, disturbances.
[5]Neither.
[6]Mars' (the god of war).
[7]Outlast.

Romeo and Juliet (c. 1591), The Balcony Scene (Act 2, Scene 2)

Romeo and Juliet *is one of Shakespeare's most beloved plays, having been turned into paintings, ballets, and several operas. Its hero even became a common noun: "a romeo" used to mean a lover. But it is largely Juliet who makes the play come alive. Although the plot describes her as absurdly young, her passion is expressed with a fine intelligence and wit which makes her irresistible. This most famous of all love scenes shows Romeo at first lusting after the young girl he has just met at the masked ball where he has gone in disguise (because his family is feuding with hers); but she manages eventually to steer his thoughts toward marriage. Romeo has clambered over the wall into the orchard of the Capulet family when he sees the candlelight appear in Juliet's bedroom window, which he immediately compares to the rising sun.*

Which character seems more mature, Romeo or Juliet? Why? How is she affected by the fact that he learns she loves him before he speaks to her in this scene?

[Capulet's orchard.] Enter Romeo. Juliet appears above at a window.
ROMEO
But soft! What light through yonder window breaks?
It is the East, and Juliet is the sun!
Arise, fair sun, and kill the envious moon
Who is already sick and pale with grief,
That[1] thou her maid[2] art far more fair than she:
Be not her maid, since she is envious.
Her vestal livery[3] is but sick and green,[4]
And none but fools do wear it; cast it off.[5]
It is my lady; O, it is my love!
O, that she knew she were!
She speaks, yet she says nothing. What of that?
Her eye discourses; I will answer it.
I am too bold; 'tis not to me she speaks;
Two of the fairest stars in all the heaven,
Having some business, do entreat her eyes
To twinkle in their spheres till they return.[6]
What if her eyes were there, they in her head?
The brightness of her cheek would shame those stars,
As daylight doth a lamp; her eyes in heaven
Would through the airy region stream so bright
That birds would sing and think it were not night.

---

[1]Because.
[2]In classical mythology the moon is ruled by the virgin goddess Diana; hence the innocent Juliet is "her maid," but this maid is more beautiful than her mistress.
[3]Virginal, costume like that worn by the ancient Roman Vestal Virgins.
[4]Young women were said to suffer from "green-sickness" which could only be cured by lovemaking.
[5]That is, stop being a virgin (make love with me).
[6]Her eyes are so bright that it seems two stars have traded places with them.

See, how she leans her cheek upon her hand!
O, that I were a glove upon that hand,
That I might touch that cheek!

JULIET

Ay me!

ROMEO

She speaks.
O, speak again, bright angel! for thou art
As glorious to this night, being o'er my head,
As is a winged messenger of heaven
Unto the white-upturned wondering eyes
Of mortals that fall back to gaze on him,
When he bestrides the lazy puffing clouds
And sails upon the bosom of the air.

JULIET

O Romeo, Romeo! wherefore[7] art thou Romeo?
Deny thy father and refuse thy name;
Or, if thou wilt not, be but sworn my love,
And I'll no longer be a Capulet.

ROMEO *[Aside.]*

Shall I hear more, or shall I speak at this?

JULIET

'Tis but thy name that is my enemy;
Thou art thyself, though not a Montague.
What's Montague? It is nor hand, nor foot,
Nor arm, nor face, nor any other part
Belonging to a man. O, be some other name!
What's in a name? That which we call a rose
By any other word would smell as sweet;
So Romeo would, were he not Romeo call'd,
Retain that dear perfection which he owes[8]
Without that title. Romeo, doff[9] thy name,
And for thy name,[10] which is no part of thee,
Take all myself.

ROMEO

I take thee at thy word.
Call me but love, and I'll be new baptized;
Henceforth I never will be Romeo.

JULIET

What man art thou, that, thus bescreened in night,
So stumblest on my counsel?[11]

---

[7]Why.

[8]Owns, possesses.

[9]Take off, get rid of.

[10]In exchange for your name.

[11]Talk.

ROMEO

By a name
I know not how to tell thee who I am:
My name, dear saint, is hateful to myself
Because it is an enemy to thee;
Had I it written, I would tear the word.

JULIET

My ears have yet not drunk a hundred words
Of thy tongue's uttering, yet I know the sound:
Art thou not Romeo, and a Montague?

ROMEO

Neither, fair maid, if either thee dislike.[12]

JULIET

How camest thou hither, tell me, and wherefore?
The orchard walls are high and hard to climb,
And the place death, considering who thou art,
If any of my kinsmen find thee here.

ROMEO

With love's light wings did I o'erperh[13] these walls,
For stony limits cannot hold love out:
And what love can do, that dares love attempt,
Therefore thy kinsmen are no let[14] to me.

JULIET

If they do see thee, they will murder thee.

ROMEO

Alack, there lies more peril in thine eye
Than twenty of their swords: look thou but sweet,
And I am proof against their enmity.

JULIET

I would not for the world they saw thee here.

ROMEO

I have night's cloak to hide me from their eyes;
And but[15] thou love me, let them find me here.
My life were better ended by their hate
Than death prorogued, wanting[16] of thy love.

JULIET

By whose direction found'st thou out this place?

ROMEO

By Love, that first did prompt me to inquire.
He lent me council, and I lent him eyes.
I am no pilot; yet, wert thou as far

---

[12]If you don't like either of those names.

[13]Climb over.

[14]Hindrance.

[15]Unless

[16]Lacking.

As that vast shore wash'd with the farthest sea,
I should adventure for such merchandise.
JULIET
Thou knowest the mask of night is on my face,
Else[17] would a maiden blush bepaint my cheek
For that which thou hast heard me speak to-night.
Fain[18] would I dwell on form,[19] fain, fain deny
What I have spoke: but farewell compliment!
Dost thou love me? I know thou wilt say "Ay,"
And I will take thy word. Yet, if thou swear'st,
Thou mayst prove false: at lovers' perjuries,
They say, Jove laughs.[20] O gentle Romeo,
If thou dost love, pronounce it faithfully:
Or if thou thinkest I am too quickly won,
I'll frown and be perverse and say thee nay,
So thou wilt woo; but else, not for the world.[21]
In truth, fair Montague, I am too fond;[22]
And therefore thou mayst think my 'haviour[23] light;
But trust me, gentleman, I'll prove more true
Than those that have more cunning to be strange.[24]
I should have been more strange, I must confess,
But[25] that thou overheard'st, ere I was ware,[26]
My true love passion: therefore pardon me,
And not impute this yielding to light love,
Which the dark night hath so discovered.[27]
ROMEO
Lady, by yonder blessed moon I swear,
That tips with silver all these fruit-tree tops—
JULIET
O, swear not by the moon, th' inconstant moon,
That monthly changes in her circle orb,
Lest that thy love prove likewise variable.
ROMEO
What shall I swear by?

---

[17]Otherwise.
[18]Willingly.
[19]Do things correctly, start over following the proper ways of becoming acquainted.
[20]Jove, or Jupiter, an infamously unfaithful husband, was said not to take seriously the failure of lovers to live up to their oaths.
[21]I'll resist you properly if you promise to keep courting me, but not otherwise.
[22]Foolish.
[23]Behavior.
[24]Distant, standoffish.
[25]Except.
[26]Aware.
[27]Revealed.

JULIET
Do not swear at all;
Or if thou wilt, swear by thy gracious self,
Which is the god of my idolatry,
And I'll believe thee.
ROMEO
If my heart's dear love—
JULIET
Well, do not swear. Although I joy in thee,
I have no joy of this contract to-night:
It is too rash, too unadvised, too sudden,
Too like the lightning, which doth cease to be
Ere one can say "it lightens." Sweet, good night!
This bud of love, by summer's ripening breath,
May prove a beauteous flow'r when next we meet.
Good night, good night! As sweet repose and rest
Come to thy heart as that within my breast!
ROMEO
O, wilt thou leave me so unsatisfied?
JULIET
What satisfaction canst thou have to-night?
ROMEO
The exchange of thy love's faithful vow for mine.
JULIET
I gave thee mine before thou didst request it:
and yet I would it were to give again.
ROMEO
Wouldst thou withdraw it? For what purpose, love?
JULIET
But to be frank[28] and give it thee again.
And yet I wish but for the thing I have.
My bounty is as boundless as the sea,
My love as deep; the more I give to thee,
The more I have, for both are infinite.
I hear some noise within; dear love, adieu!
[NURSE calls within.]
Anon,[29] good nurse! Sweet Montague, be true.
Stay but a little, I will come again. *[Exit.]*
ROMEO
O blessed, blessed night! I am afeard,
Being in night, all this is but a dream,
Too flattering-sweet to be substantial.
[Re-enter JULIET, above.]
JULIET
Three words, dear Romeo, and good night indeed.

---

[28]Generous.

[29]Right away.

If that thy bent of love be honorable,
Thy purpose marriage, send me word tomorrow,
By one that I'll procure to come to thee,
Where and what time thou wilt perform the rite;
And all my fortunes at thy foot I'll lay
And follow thee my lord throughout the world.
NURSE *[Within]*
Madam!
JULIET
I come anon.—But if thou meanest not well,
I do beseech thee—
NURSE *[Within]*
Madam!
JULIET
By and by I come.—
To cease thy suit and leave me to my grief
Tomorrow will I send.
ROMEO
So thrive my soul,—
JULIET
A thousand times good night! *[Exit.]*
ROMEO
A thousand times the worse, to want thy light!
Love goes toward love, as schoolboys from their books,
But love from love, toward school with heavy looks.
[Retiring slowly. Re-enter Juliet, above.]
JULIET
Hist! Romeo, hist! O for a falconer's voice,
To lure this tassel-gentle back again![30]
Bondage is hoarse and may not speak aloud;
Else would I tear the cave where Echo lies
And make her airy tongue more hoarse than mine,
With repetition of My Romeo's name.
Romeo!
ROMEO
It is my soul that calls upon my name:
How silver-sweet sound lovers' tongues by night,
Like softest music to attending[31] ears!
JULIET
Romeo!
ROMEO
My dear?

---

[30]Oh for the voice of a falconer who can lure back his tercel-gentle (the male of the goshawk, trained to hunt and return at a master's call).
[31]Listening.

JULIET

At what o'clock tomorrow
Shall I send to thee?
ROMEO

By the hour of nine.
JULIET
I will not fail. 'Tis twenty years till then.
I have forgot why I did call thee back.
ROMEO
Let me stand here till thou remember it.
JULIET
I shall forget, to have thee still stand there,
Remembering how I love thy company.
ROMEO
And I'll still stay, to have thee still forget,
Forgetting any other home but this.
JULIET
'Tis almost morning; I would have thee gone:
And yet no farther than a wanton's bird,
That lets it hop a little from his hand,
Like a poor prisoner in his twisted gyves,[32]
And with a silken thread plucks it back again,
So loving-jealous of his liberty.
ROMEO
I would I were thy bird.
JULIET

Sweet, so would I.
Yet I should kill thee with much cherishing.
Good night, good night! Parting is such sweet sorrow
That I shall say good night till it be morrow. *[Exit.]*
ROMEO
Sleep dwell upon thine eyes, peace in thy breast!
Would I were sleep and peace, so sweet to rest![33]

---

[32] Fetters.

[33] I wish I were sleep and peace so I could rest on your breast.

Louise Labé: Sonnets (1555)

Although the number of her love sonnets is small compared to some of her contemporaries, Louise Labé's contributions to the genre contain some of the most passionate ever written. Attacked as shameless during her lifetime, she defends herself in the first sonnet. She argues that the overwhelming power of love can force even the strongest woman to stray, as Venus did when she fell for Vulcan and Adonis. Both translations below are by Edith R. Farrell.

What warning does she issue to her critics in the final lines?

Ladies, if I have loved

Ladies, if I have loved, don't call it crime;
If I have felt a thousand torches' burns,
A thousand biting torments and concerns;
And if in weeping I have spent my time.

Please do not add your censure to my name,
If I've been weak, I have my pain to bear,
Don't sharpen the cruel barbs already there;
Consider first that Love, if it's his aim,

Without Vulcan, your ardor to excuse,
Without Adonis' beauty to accuse,
Can yet make you love more than I at will;

And more than I you might love out of season
With stranger passion and for far less reason;
Beware lest you be more unhappy still.

Kiss me. Again. More kisses I desire

In this, her most passionate poem, she tells her lover that if her fiery kisses have scorched him she will "kiss the hurt away" with yet more kisses.

What does she mean by living a "double life?" What is her ideal of love?

Kiss me. Again. More kisses I desire.
Give me one your sweetness to express.
Give me the most passionate you possess
Four I'll return, and hotter than the fire.

There, did they burn? I'll change that hurt to pleasure
By giving you ten others—all quite light.
Thus, as we mingle our kisses with delight,
Let us enjoy each other at our leisure.

This to teach one a double life shall give.
Each by himself and in his love shall live.[1]
Allow my love this mad and foolish thought:

I'm always sad when living so discreetly,
And never find my happiness completely,
Unless a sally[2] from my self I've sought.

Translated by Edith R. Farrell

---

[1]That is, everyone should live as part of a couple.
[2]Excursion, going out from.

René Descartes: *Discourse on Method* (1637)

René Descartes, the celebrated mathematician and physicist, is also often considered a founder of modern philosophy, as he sought new ways to move beyond Medieval Aristoteleanism and justify the science of his day. In his Discourse on Method *he expresses his disappointment with traditional philosophy and with the limitations of theology; only logic, geometry and algebra hold his respect, because of the utter certainty which they can offer us. Unfortunately, because they depend on hypotheses, they cannot tell us what is real (i.e., what the world is really like). Therefore Descartes proposes a method of thought incorporating the rigor of mathematics but based on intuitive truths about what is real, basic knowledge which could not be wrong (like the axioms of geometry). He calls into question everything that he thinks he has learned through his senses but rests his whole system on the one truth that he cannot doubt, namely, the reality of his own mind and the radical difference between the mental and the physical aspects of the world.*

Descartes (late in our excerpt) suggests that sensory experience might be like dreaming, i.e., vivid but not matching the way things really are. But what does he realize must be the case even if his senses cannot be trusted?

Part 1:

Good sense is the most evenly distributed thing in the world, for all people suppose themselves so well provided with it that even those who are the most difficult to satisfy in every other respect never seem to desire more than they have. It is not likely that everyone is mistaken; rather this attitude reveals that the ability to judge and distinguish the true from the false, which is properly what one calls good sense or reason, is in fact naturally equally distributed among all people. Thus the diversity of our opinions does not result from some of us being more reasonable than others, but solely from the fact that we conduct our thoughts along different paths, and consider different things. . . .

As far as reason—or good sense—is concerned, since it is the only thing that makes us human and differentiates us from the animals, I should like to believe that it is entirely present in each of us. . . .

I was nourished by study from my earliest childhood; and since I was convinced that this was the means to acquire a clear and certain knowledge of all that is useful in life, I had an extreme desire to learn. But as soon as I had finished a course of studies which usually culminates in one being accepted as one of the learned, I changed my opinion completely; for I found myself troubled by so many doubts and errors that the only profit I had gained in seeking to educate myself was to discover more and more clearly the extent of my ignorance. Nevertheless I had been at one of the most famous schools in Europe, where I thought there must be wise men if such existed anywhere on earth. There I had learned all that the others learned; and besides, not satisfied with the knowledge that we were taught, I had pored over all the unusual and strange books that I could lay my hands on. In addition, I knew how others evaluated me; and I did not want to be considered inferior to my fellow-students, even though some among them were already destined to take the places of my teachers. Finally, our century seemed to me to abound in as many wise spirits as any preceding one, which led me to suppose that I could judge the experience of others by my own, and to think that there was no such knowledge in the world such as I had been led to hope for. . . .

I was especially pleased with mathematics because of the certainty and clarity of its proofs; but I did not as yet realize its true usefulness; and, thinking that it was only useful in the mechanical arts, I was astonished that, since its foundations were so firm and solid, no one had built something higher upon it. To the contrary, I felt that the writings of the ancient pagans[1] who had discussed morality were like superb, magnificent palaces which were built on mere sand and mud: they greatly praised the virtues and made them appear more exalted than anything else in the world; but they did not sufficiently teach how to know them. Often that which they called by the fine name of "virtue" was nothing but apathy, or pride, or despair, or parricide.

I revered our theology, and hoped as much as anyone else to get to heaven; but having learned, as if it were certain, that the road to heaven is as open to the most ignorant as to the most learned, and that the revealed truths which lead one there are beyond our comprehension, I did not dare to submit them to my feeble reasonings, and I thought that to undertake successfully to examine them one would need some extraordinary heavenly aid and be beyond human ability.

Of philosophy I will say nothing except that, seeing that it had been developed by the finest minds that had lived over many centuries and that nevertheless there was no point in it which was not still under dispute, and consequently doubtful, I lacked the presumption to hope that I would succeed any better than the others. When I considered how many different opinions there had been about the same subject put forward by learned men, whereas only one of them could have been correct, I considered that anything which was only probable was as good as false. . . .

It is true that while I considered only the customs of other ordinary men, I found nothing in them to reassure me, and I noticed as much diversity among them as I had earlier done among the opinions of philosophers. The greatest benefit I received from this study was that, having observed many things which, while they seemed quite extravagant and ridiculous, were nevertheless commonly accepted as true and approved by great peoples, I learned not to believe too firmly in anything of which I had been persuaded only by example and custom. Thus I freed myself little by little from many errors which can dim our natural light and even make us less able to listen to reason. But after I had spent several years thus studying the book of the world and trying to get some experience, I one day resolved to study my own self, and to use all the powers of my mind to choose the path I should follow, which was much more successful, it seems to me, than if I had never left my country or my books.

Part 2:

When I was younger I had studied a little among other branches of philosophy, logic, and among types of mathematics, geometrical analysis and algebra: three arts or sciences which seemed as if they ought to contribute something to my goal. But when I examined them, I realized that as far as logic was concerned, its syllogisms and most of its other methods serve only to explain to someone else that which one already knows, or even, like Lully's art,[2] to speak foolishly of things one does not know, rather than to actually learn

---

[1]Descartes means to include here the Greek philosophers; "pagan" covers anyone who was not a part of Christendom.

[2]Alchemy. Although the 14th-century philosopher Ramon Lully was not in fact an alchemist, he had acquired a reputation for dabbling in arcane arts.

anything. Even though logic contains, in fact, many very true and good precepts, they are nevertheless mingled with so many others which are harmful or superfluous that it is almost as hard to separate them out as to carve a Diana or a Minerva from an as yet untouched block of marble. Besides, as far as the analysis of the ancients or modern algebra is concerned, and besides the fact that they can deal only with very abstract matters which seem utterly useless, the former is always so restricted to the study of geometrical figures that it cannot exercise the understanding without greatly tiring the imagination; and the latter is so restricted to certain rules and figures that it has become a confused, obscure art which perplexes the mind instead of being a science which cultivates it. So I thought that I had to look for some other method which, having the advantages of these three, would be free of their defects. Just as a multitude of laws often creates excuses for vices, so that the best regulated state is that which, having very few laws, makes those few strictly observed, instead of the great number or precepts which make up logic, I thought that the four following precepts would suffice, provided that I could make a firm, steadfast resolution not to violate them even once.

The first was to never accept anything as true which I could not accept as obviously true; that is to say, to carefully avoid impulsiveness and prejudice, and to include nothing in my conclusions but whatever was so clearly presented to my mind that I could have no reason to doubt it.

The second was to divide each of the problems I was examining in as many parts as I could, as many as should be necessary to solve them.

The third, to develop my thoughts in order, beginning with the simplest and easiest to understand matters, in order to reach by degrees, little by little, to the most complex knowledge, assuming an orderliness among them which did not at all naturally seem to follow one from the other.

And the last resolution was to make my enumerations so complete and my reviews so general that I could be assured that I had not omitted anything.

These long chains of reasoning, so simple and easy, which geometers customarily use to make their most difficult demonstrations, caused me to imagine that everything which could be known by human beings could be deduced one from the other in the same way, and that, provided only that one refrained from accepting anything as true which was not, and always preserving the order by which one deduced one from another, there could not be any truth so abstruse that one could not finally attain it, nor so hidden that it could not be discovered. And I had little trouble finding which propositions I needed to begin with, for I already knew that they would be the simplest and the easiest to know. . . .

I took the best features of geometrical analysis and of algebra, and corrected all the defects of one by the other.[3]

Part 4:

I had noticed for a long time that it was necessary sometimes to agree with opinions about ethics which I knew to be quite uncertain, even though they were indubitable, as I said earlier; but since I wanted to devote myself solely to the search for truth, I thought that I should act in the opposite manner, and reject as absolutely false anything about

[3]It was Descartes who figured out how to combine algebra and geometry such that, on a pair of intersecting axes, we can geometrically map any algebraic function. Those axes are still called "Cartesian co-ordinates."

which I could imagine the slightest doubt, so that I could see if there would not remain after all that something in my belief which could be called absolutely certain. So, because our senses sometimes trick us, I tried to imagine that there was nothing which is the way that we imagine it; and since there are people who are mistaken about the simplest matters of geometry, making mistakes in logic, and supposing that I was as likely to make mistakes as anyone else, I rejected as false all the reasonings that I had considered as valid demonstrations. Finally, considering that all our thoughts which we have when we are awake can also come to us when we are sleeping without a single one of them being true, I resolved to pretend that everything I had ever thought was no more true that the illusions in my dreams. But I immediately realized that, though I wanted to think that everything was false, it was necessary that the "me" who was doing the thinking was something; and noticing that this truth—I think, therefore I am—was so certain and sure that all the wildest suppositions of skeptics could not shake it, I judged that I could unhesitatingly accept it as the first principle of the philosophy for which I was seeking.

Then, examining closely what I was, and seeing that I could imagine that I had no body and that there was no world or place where I was, I could not imagine that I did not exist at all. On the contrary, precisely because I doubted the existence of other things it followed quite obviously and certainly that I did exist. If, on the other hand, I had only ceased to think while everything else that I had imagined remained true, I would have had no reason to believe that I existed; therefore I realized that I was a substance whose essence, or nature, is nothing but thought, and which, in order to exist, needs no place to exist nor any other material thing. So this self, that is to say the soul, through which I am what I am, is entirely separate from the body, and is even more easily known than the latter, so that even if I did not have a body, my soul would continue to be all that it is.

Translated by Paul Brians

Latin America 1500–1750

Bernal Díaz del Castillo: *The Discovery and Conquest of Mexico* (1560s)

In 1520, when the Spaniards met the Aztecs, their emperor, Montezuma, ruled perhaps fifteen to twenty million people and had an army of over a hundred thousand. Cortés commanded a volunteer force of about 500. But the Europeans had crucial advantages of steel weapons, armor and the horse against the stone-age Aztecs. Further, the Spaniards, like other Europeans of the time, were ruthless in combat, seeking to kill rather than capture and recognizing no settlements or noncombatants as beyond attack. The Spaniards excelled in small-unit combat against the very large but ponderous Aztec forces, which despite their size stressed individual rather than group combat and greatly prized capturing an opponent over slaying him. Their wooden clubs and cotton armor did little to protect them against the Spaniards' swords. Further, the Spaniards learned quickly that to kill or capture the enemy commander forced his entire unit to withdraw. In a flat open area anywhere in the Americas, the Spaniards were invincible against any native army that fought in this manner.

What caused the end of the first battle described? Did the Spaniards have to fight a united Aztec empire? What types of assistance did the Spaniards' Indian allies give them? What strategy did the Spaniards use to successfully invade and hold the Aztecs' island capital city of Tenochtitlan?

That day we reached some farms and huts belonging to a large town named Cuautitlan. Thence we went through some farms and hamlets with the Mexicans always in pursuit of us, and as many of them had got together, they endeavored to kill us and began to surround us, and hurled many stones with their slings and javelins and arrows, and with their broadswords they killed two of our soldiers in a bad pass, and they also killed a horse and wounded many of our men, and we also with cut and thrust killed some of them, and the horsemen did the same. We slept in those houses and we ate the horse they had killed, and the next day very early in the morning we began our march, with the same and even greater precautions than observed before, half of the horsemen always going ahead. On a plain a little more than a league further on (when we began to think that we could march in safety) our scouts, we were on the look out, returned to say that the fields were full of Mexican warriors waiting for us. When we heard this we were indeed alarmed but not so as to be faint-hearted or to fail to meet them and fight to the death. There we halted for a short time and orders were given how the horsemen were to charge and return at a hard gallop, and were not to stop to spear the enemy but to keep their lances aimed at their faces until they broke up their squadrons; and that all the soldiers, in the thrusts they gave, should pass their swords through the bodies of their opponents, and that we should act in such a way as to avenge thoroughly the deaths and wounds of our companions, so that if God willed it we should escape with our lives.

After commending ourselves to God and the Holy Mary, full of courage, and calling on the name of Señor Santiago,[1] as soon as we saw that the enemy began to surround us, and

---

[1]Saint James of Compostella, invoked as the Spanish patron saint of wars against pagans.

that the horsemen, keeping in parties of five, broke through their ranks, we all of us charged at the same time.

Oh! what a sight it was to see this fearful and destructive battle, how we moved all mixed up with them foot to foot, and the cuts and thrusts we gave them, and with what fury the dogs fought, and what wounds and deaths they inflicted on us with their lances and macanas.[2] Then, as the ground was level, to see how the horsemen speared them as they chose, charging and returning, and although both they and their horses were wounded, they never stopped fighting like very brave men. As for all of us who had no horses, it seemed as if we all put on double strength, for although we were wounded and again received other wounds, we did not trouble to bind them up so as not to halt to do so, for there was not time, but with great spirit we closed with the enemy so as to give them sword thrusts. I wish to tell about Cortés and Cristóbal de Olid, Gonzalo de Sandoval, Gonzalo Domínguez and a Juan de Salamanca who although badly wounded rode on one side and the other, breaking through the squadrons; and about the words that Cortés said to those who were in the thick of the enemy, that the cuts and thrusts that we gave should be aimed at distinguished chieftains, for they all of them bore great golden plumes and rich arms and devices. Then to see how the valiant and spirited Sandoval encouraged us and cried: "Now, gentlemen, this is the day when we are bound to be victorious; have trust in God and we shall come out of this alive for some good purpose." They killed and wounded a great number of our soldiers, but it pleased God that Cortés and the Captains whom I have already named who went in his Company reached the place where the Captain General of the Mexicans was marching with his banner displayed, and with rich golden armor and great gold and silver plumes. When Cortés saw him with many other Mexican Chieftains all wearing great plumes, he said to our Captains: "Now, Señores, let us break through them and leave none of them unwounded;" and commending themselves to God, Cortés, Cristóbal de Olid, Sandoval, Alonzo de Ávila, and the other horsemen charged, and Cortés struck his horse against the Mexican Captain, which made him drop his banner, and the rest of our Captains succeeded in breaking through the squadron which consisted of many Indians following the Captain who carried the banner, who nevertheless had not fallen at the shock that Cortés had given him, and it was Juan de Salamanca, who rode with Cortés on a good piebald mare, who gave him a lance thrust and took from him the rich plume that he wore, and afterwards gave it to Cortés, saying that as it was he who first met him and made him lower his banner and deprived his followers of the courage to fight, that the plume belonged to him (Cortés). However, three years afterwards, the King gave it to Salamanca as his coat of arms, and his descendants bear it on their tabards.[3]

Let us go back to the battle. It pleased Our Lord that when that Captain who carried the Mexican banner was dead (and many others were killed there) their attack slackened, and all the horsemen followed them and we felt neither hunger nor thirst, and it seemed as though we had neither suffered nor passed through any evil or hardship, as we followed up our victory killing and wounding. Then our friends the Tlaxcalans were very lions, and with their swords and broadswords which they there captured from the enemy behaved very well and valiantly. When the horsemen returned from following up our victory we all gave many thanks to God for having escaped from such a great multitude of people, for there had never been seen or found throughout the Indies such a great number of warriors

---

[2]*A macana* was the war club that a combatant carried. It was often edged with flint or obsidian chips to make it sharper.

[3]Panels of cloth draped over one's external clothing.

together in any battle that was fought, for there was present there the flower of Mexico and Texcoco and all the towns around the lake, and others in the neighborhood, and the people of Otumba and Tepetexcoco and Saltocan, who came in the belief that this time not a trace of us would be left. Then what rich armor they wore, with so much gold and plumes and devices, and nearly all of them were captains and chieftains. Near the spot where this hard-fought and celebrated battle took place, and where one can say God spared our lives, there stands a town named Otumba.

Our escape from the City of Mexico was on the tenth of the month of July [1520], and this celebrated battle of Otumba was fought on the fourteenth of July. . . .

Let me now say that the towns situated in the lake when they saw how day by day we were victorious both on water and on land, and that the people of Chalco, Tlaxcala, and other pueblos[4] had made friends with us, decided to sue Cortés for peace and with great humility they asked pardon if in any way they had offended us, and said that they had been under orders and could not do otherwise. The towns that came in were Iztapalapa, Churubusco, Culuacan, and Mixquic and all those of the fresh water lake, and Cortés told them that we should not move the camp until the Mexicans sued for peace or he had destroyed them by war. He ordered them to aid us with all the canoes that they possessed to fight against Mexico, and to come and build ranchos[5] for Cortés and to bring him food, and they replied that they would do so, and they built the ranchos but brought very little food. However, our ranchos where we were stationed were never rebuilt so we remained in the rain, for those who have been in this country know that through the months of June, July and August it rains every day in these parts.

We made attacks on the Mexicans every day and succeeded in capturing many idol towers, houses, canals, and other openings and bridges which they had constructed from house to house, and we filled them all up with adobes and the timbers from the houses that we pulled down and destroyed and we kept guard over them, but notwithstanding all this trouble that we took, the enemy came back and deepened them and widened the openings and erected more barricades. And because our three companies considered it a dishonor that some should be fighting and facing the Mexican squadrons and others should be filling up passes and openings and bridges, Pedro de Alvarado, so as to avoid quarrels as to who should be fighting or filling up openings, ordered that one company should have charge of the filling in and look after that work one day, while the other two companies should fight and face the enemy, and another day another company, until each company should have had its turn, and owing to this arrangement there was nothing captured that was not razed to the ground, and our friends the Tlaxcalans helped us. So we went on penetrating into the City, but at the hour for retiring all three companies had to fight in union, for that was the time when we ran the greatest risk. First of all we sent all the Tlaxcalans off the causeway, for it was clear that they were considerable embarrassment when we were fighting.

Guatemoc[6] now ordered us to be attacked at all three camps at the same time by all his troops and with all the energy that was possible both on land and by water, and he ordered them to go by night during the modorra watch,[7] so that the launches should not be able to

---

[4]*Pueblo* is the Spanish word the expeditionaries often used to refer to a Mexican province, typically composed of a headtown and villages scattered through its hinterland.

[5]*Rancho* is a Spanish word with multiple meanings. Here it means an encampment.

[6]The Aztec military leader.

[7]The period of night immediately before daybreak.

assist us on account of the stakes. They came on with so furious an impetus that had it not been for those who were on the watch, who were over one hundred and twenty soldiers well used to fighting, they would have penetrated into our camp, and we ran a great risk as it was, but by fighting in good order we withstood them; however, they wounded fifteen of our men and two of them died of their wounds within eight days.

Also in the camp of Cortés they placed our troops in the greatest straits and difficulties and many were killed and wounded, and in the camp of Sandoval the same thing happened, and in this way they came on two successive nights and many Mexicans also were killed in these encounters and many more wounded. When Guatemoc and his captains and priests saw that the attack that they made on those two nights profited them nothing, they decided to come with all their combined forces at the dawn watch and attack our camp, and they came on so fearlessly that they surrounded us on two sides, and had even half defeated us and cut us off, when it pleased our Lord Jesus Christ to give us strength to turn and close our ranks, and we sheltered ourselves to a certain degree with the launches, and with good cut and thrust, and advancing shoulder to shoulder, we drove them off. In that battle they killed eight and wounded many of our soldiers and they even injured Pedro de Alvarado. If the Tlaxcalans had slept on the causeway that night we should have run great risk from the embarrassment they would have caused us on account of their numbers, but the experience of what had happened before made us get them off the causeway promptly and send them to Tacuba, and we remained free from care. To go back to our battle, we killed many Mexicans and took prisoner four persons of importance. I well understand that interested readers will be surfeited with seeing so many fights every day but one cannot do less, for during the ninety and three days that we besieged this strong and great City we had war and combats every day and every night as well. However, when it seemed to us that we were victorious, great disasters were really coming upon us, and we were in the greatest danger of perishing in all three camps, as will be seen later on.

Translated by A. P. Maudsley

Michel de Montaigne: *On Cannibals* (1580)

The discovery of so many new lands in the Renaissance had less impact on most Europeans than one might suppose. They were largely absorbed in recovering (and competing with) their own classical past and engaging in violent theological and political disputes among themselves. Yet some Europeans were profoundly shaken by the new discoveries into realizing that much of the world thought and lived very differently from what was then known as "Christendom." No writer was more strongly moved to view his own society from a new perspective in the light of reports brought back of the habits of the natives of the "New World" than Michel de Montaigne. He began a long tradition of using non-European peoples as a basis for engaging in a critique of his own culture, undoubtedly in the process romanticizing what Jean-Jacques Rousseau would later call "the noble savage." It is a theme which still appeals to many Westerners.

What reason does Montaigne give for judging cannibalistic Native Americans to be preferable to Europeans? How do you think this essay might have affected Europeans' views of themselves?

When King Pyrrhus invaded Italy, after he had reconnoitered the armed forces that the Romans had sent out against him, he said, "I don't know who these barbarians are"—for the Greeks called all foreign peoples barbarians—"but the organization of the army I see before me is not at all barbaric." The Greeks said the same when Flaminius invaded their country, as did Philip, when he saw from a hill the orderly layout of the Roman camp which had been set up in his kingdom under Publius Sulpicius Galba. These examples illustrate how one must avoid accepting common prejudices: opinions must be judged by means of reason, and not by adopting common opinion.

I had with me for a long time a man who had lived for ten or twelve years in this other world which has been discovered in our time, in the place where Villegaignon landed, which he named Antarctic France.[1] This discovery of an enormous land seems to me to be worth contemplating. I doubt that I could affirm that another such may not be discovered in the future, since so many greater people than I were mistaken about this one. I'm afraid that our eyes are bigger than our stomachs, and that we have more curiosity than comprehension. We try to embrace everything but succeed only in grasping the wind.

I do not find that there is anything barbaric or savage about this nation, according to what I've been told, unless we are to call barbarism whatever differs from our own customs. Indeed, we seem to have no other standard of truth and reason than the opinions and customs of our own country. There at home is always the perfect religion, the perfect legal system—the perfect and most accomplished way of doing everything. These people are wild in the same sense that fruits are, produced by nature, alone, in her ordinary way. Indeed, in that land, it is we who refuse to alter our artificial ways and reject the common order that ought rather to be called wild, or savage.[2] In them the most natural virtues and abilities are alive and vigorous, whereas we have bastardized them and adopted them solely to our corrupt taste. Even so, the flavor and delicacy of some of the wild fruits from those countries is excellent, even to our taste, better than our cultivated ones. After all, it would hardly be reasonable that artificial breeding should be able to outdo our great and powerful

---

[1]Brazil.

[2]*Sauvage* in French means both "wild" and "savage."

mother, Nature. We have so burdened the beauty and richness of her works by our innovations that we have entirely stifled her. Yet whenever she shines forth in her purity she puts our vain and frivolous enterprises amazingly to shame.

> *Et veniunt ederæ sponte sua melius,*
> *surgit et in solis formosior arbutus antris,*
> *et volucres nulla dulcius arte canunt.*[3]

All our efforts cannot create the nest of the tiniest bird: its structure, its beauty, or the usefulness of its form; nor can we create the web of the lowly spider. All things, said Plato are produced by nature, chance, or human skill, the greatest and most beautiful things by one of the first two, the lesser and most imperfect, by the latter.

These nations seem to me, then, barbaric in that they have been little refashioned by the human mind and are still quite close to their original naiveté. They are still ruled by natural laws, only slightly corrupted by ours. They are in such a state of purity that I am sometimes saddened by the thought that we did not discover them earlier, when there were people who would have known how to judge them better than we. It displeases me that Lycurgus or Plato didn't know them, for it seems to me that these peoples surpass not only the portraits which poetry has made of the Golden Age and all the invented, imaginary notions of the ideal state of humanity, but even the conceptions and the very aims of philosophers themselves. They could not imagine such a pure and simple naiveté as we encounter in them; nor would they have been able to believe that our society might be maintained with so little artifice and social structure.

This is a people, I would say to Plato, among whom there is no commerce at all, no knowledge of letters, no knowledge of numbers, nor any judges, or political superiority, no habit of service, riches, or poverty, no contracts, no inheritance, no divisions of property, no occupations but easy ones, no respect for any relationship except ordinary family ones, no clothes, no agriculture, no metal, no use of wine or wheat. The very words which mean "lie," "treason," "deception," "greed," "envy," "slander" and "forgiveness" are unknown. How far his imaginary Republic would be from such perfection:

> *viri a diis recentes*[4]
> *Hos natura modos primum dedit. . . .*[5]

They have their wars against peoples who live beyond their mountains, further inland, to which they go entirely naked, bearing no other arms than bows and sharpened stakes like our hunting spears. The courage with which they fight is amazing: their battles never end except through death of bloodshed, for they do not even understand what fear is. Each one carries back as a trophy the head of the enemy that he has killed, and hangs it up at the entrance to his home. After having treated their prisoners well for a long time, giving them all the provisions that they can, he who is the chief calls a great assembly of his acquaintances. He ties a rope to one of the arms of the prisoner and holds onto the other end, several feet away, out of harm's way, and gives to his best friend the other arm to hold in the same

[3]"The ivy grows best when it grows wild, and the arbutus is most lovely when it grows in solitude; untaught birds sing most sweetly." Propertius, I, ii, 10.

[4]Men freshly molded from the hands of the gods. (Seneca: *Epistles,* 90.)

[5]These are the first laws laid down by Nature. (Virgil: *Georgics,* II, 20.)

way; and the two of them, in the presence of the assembled group, slash him to death with their swords. That done, they roast him and eat him together, sending portions to their absent friends. They do this, not as is supposed, for nourishment as did the ancient Scythians; it represents instead an extreme form of vengeance. The proof of this is that when they saw that the Portuguese, who had allied themselves with their adversaries, executed their captives differently, burying them up to the waist and firing numerous arrows into the remainder of the body, hanging them afterward, they viewed these people from another world, who had spread the knowledge of many vices among their neighbors, and who were much more masterly than they in every sort of evil, and supposed they must have chosen this sort of revenge for a reason. Thinking that it must be more bitter than their own, they abandoned their ancient way to imitate this one.

I am not so concerned that we should remark on the barbaric horror of such a deed, but that, while we quite rightly judge their faults, we are blind to our own. I think it is more barbaric to eat a man alive than to eat him dead, to tear apart through torture and pain a living body which can still feel, or to burn it alive by bits, to let it be gnawed and chewed by dogs or pigs, as we have not only read, but seen, in recent times, not against old enemies but among neighbors and fellow-citizens, and—what is worse—under the pretext of piety and religion.[6] Better to roast and eat him after he is dead.

Translated by Paul Brians

[6]Montaigne is describing the tortures frequently carried out by the Holy Inquisition against heretics.

Two letters from Spanish Settlers in the "New World"

Doña Isabel de Guevara: Letter to Princess doña Juana, regent in Spain (1556)

Doña Isabel was a noblewoman from Seville who joined her husband in an ambitious expedition to conquer Argentina. She and other women in the group proved they could be as hardy pioneers as the men, providing services that the men seldom provided for themselves. In her letter to the ruler of Spain (also a woman), Doña Isabel justifies a request for financial support by enumerating her services to the colonial effort.

What sorts of traditional womanly tasks did the women perform? What more traditionally masculine tasks did they also take on?

Very high and powerful lady:

Several women came to this province of the Río de la Plata along with its first governor don Pedro de Mendoza, and it was my fortune to be one of them. On reaching the port of Buenos Aires, our expedition contained 1,500 men, but food was scarce, and the hunger was such that within three months 1,000 of them died; it was such a famine that the one of Jerusalem cannot equal it, nor any other be compared to it. The men became so weak that all the tasks fell on the poor women, washing the clothes as well as nursing the men, preparing them the little food there was, keeping them clean, standing guard, patrolling the fires, loading the crossbows when the Indians came sometimes to do battle, even firing the cannon, and arousing the soldiers who were capable of fighting, shouting the alarm through the camp, acting as sergeants and putting the soldiers in order, because at that time, as we women can make do with little nourishment, we had not fallen into such weakness as the men. Your highness will readily believe that our contributions were such that if it had not been for us, all would have perished; and were it not for the men's reputation, I could truthfully write you much more and give them as the witnesses. I believe others will write this story to your highness at greater length, so I will cease.

When this so perilous turbulence was over, the few who were still alive decided to ascend the river, weak as they were and with winter coming on, in two brigantines, and the weary women nursed them and looked after them and cooked their meals, carrying firewood on their backs from off the ship, and encouraging them with manly words not to let themselves die, that soon they would reach a fertile land, and carrying them on our shoulders to the brigantines with as much tenderness as if they were our own sons. And when we came upon a kind of Indians called Timbues who are great fishermen, again we served the men in finding different sorts of dishes so that they wouldn't get sick from eating fish without bread when they were so weak.

Afterwards they decided to ascend the Paraná in search of provisions, in which voyage the unfortunate women underwent such hardships that God gave them life miraculously because he saw that the men's lives depended on them, for theyso took all the tasks of the ship to heart that a woman who did less than another felt affronted; they worked the sail, steered the ship, sounded the depth, bailed out the water, took the oar when a soldier was unable to row, and exhorted the soldiers not to be discouraged, that men were meant for hardships. And the truth is, no one forced the women to do those things, nor did they do them out of obligation; only charity obliged them. Thus they arrived at this city of Asunción, which though today it is very rich in provisions, was then greatly in need of them, and the women had to turn to their tasks anew, making clearings with their own hands, clearing and hoeing and sowing and harvesting the crop with no one's aid until such time as the soldiers recovered from their weakness and began to rule the land, acquiring the service of Indian men and women, until the country at last attained its present state.

Andrés García: Letter to his Nephew (1571)

This letter illustrates vividly how even a small trader in Indian-produced goods could prosper in the colonies of the western hemisphere. Andrés García was typical of many immigrant Spaniards who urged their compatriots to join them.

To what degree is García trying to overcome Spanish prejudices? What reasons might he have had for thanking God that he has had no children?

Dear nephew:

In other letters I have written you, telling you where I am and how things are going with me, and I will keep doing the same until I should see a letter from you, as I greatly desire. After leaving you and our kinfolk, I went through many different hardships. As you saw, I came in the ship of Felipe Boquín, and in Veracruz, which is the port of this land of New Spain,[1] he sold off everything I owned to get forty ducats that I owed him. I arrived on the point of dying, and might well have died in fact, if it weren't for a woman called Inés Nuñez, who is of dark skin; she made me very comfortable, and I owe her more than my very mother. If God should bring you here safely, try to go to her house, because I have already told her about you.

Nephew, I live in Mexico City in the tiánguiz[2] of San Juan, among the shops of Tegada. I deal in Campeche wood and cotton blankets and wax, and I also have a certain business in cacao in Soconusco.[3] But now, nephew, I am advanced in years and can no longer take care of all this. I wish, if it please God, that you would come to this land, as I have written you in other letters, so that I could rest and you would remain in the business.

I am married here to a woman very much to my taste. And though there in Spain it might shock you that I have married an Indian woman, here one loses nothing of his honor, because the Indians are a nation held in much esteem. And besides, I can tell you that in the ten years that we have been married we have had no children, praised be our Lord. And she is after me more every day, ever since I told her that I have a nephew whom I raised from infancy and love as if he were my son; she is of the opinion that if God our Lord brings you to this land, we should leave you our property, what we have, as to a legitimate son and heir, because after the end of our days we want to have someone here to do good for our souls. And if you could, bring along your cousin Pedro López, son of Catalina López, our kinswoman, because he could earn as much here from his trade as he wants, and anyway he wouldn't have to, because I have enough for myself and for others, praised be our Lord.

Translated by James Lockhart & Enrique Otte

---

[1]Mexico.

[2] Native market.

[3]In the Mexican uplands. He bought or grew the cacao there for sale in Mexico City.

Sor Juana Ines de la Cruz: A Response to Jealousy (1690)

Juana Ramírez y Asbaje was born between 1648 and 1651 near Mexico City. Although her mother was illiterate, young Juana had access to her grandfather's extensive library and taught herself the forms of classical rhetoric, as well as the language of law, literature, and theology. Because women were not allowed to study at the University in Mexico City, she continued her program of self-education, first as lady-in-waiting at the Spanish Viceroy's court, and then in the convent, which she entered in 1668 to be able to pursue a quiet, intellectual life. In a patriarchal age, however, her confessor and even the Archbishop of Mexico condemned her writing. Nevertheless, Sor Juana's talent earned her the patronage of two Viceroys' wives, and poetry, drama, and prose continued to flow from her pen. Her love poetry, in particular, was viewed as scandalous writing for a nun, as the following selection may illustrate. Probably her most notable work was 1690's The Answer (La Respuesta), *a rebuttal of her clerical critics that justifies her place as a seventeenth century feminist. Unfortunately, when she ventured into theological argument, Sor Juana unleashed such a storm of ecclesiastical condemnation that she ceased writing, selling her library and musical and scientific instruments in 1692. Three years later she was dead, having fallen victim to an epidemic disease contracted while caring for her similarly stricken sisters. Nevertheless, her place as a major figure of Hispanic literature was already assured. Indeed, in her own time, she was known as the "Mexican Phoenix," her work rising as a flame from the ashes of religious disapproval.*

What reasons do you think a nun might have for writing such a poem? Do you think this work is personal, or purely literary?

This afternoon, my dear, when I spoke with you,
In your countenance and in your acts I saw
That with words I could not persuade you,
So I desired that you see into my heart;
And Love, which aided my intent,
Overcame that which seemed impossible,
Since amidst the tears that sadness unleashed,
My heart, undone, dropped within me.
Enough, then, of harshness, my dear, enough:
Neither torment yourself more with these tyrannous doubts
Nor let vile distrust oppose your peace of mind
With foolish shadows or vain evidence,
Since already in flowing humor you saw and held
My helpless heart between your hands.

Translated by Susan Swan

Juan del Valle y Caviedes (1652-1695?): The Privileges of the Poor

Peruvian poet Juan del Valle y Caviedes, a Lima shopkeeper, employed satire, blunt or even vulgar language, and realism, along with a fundamentally religious sense in his poetry. His works were, for the most part, not published until the nineteenth century, but in the intervening two hundred years they circulated widely in manuscript, evidence of their striking a responsive note in many readers. "The Privileges of the Poor" may be considered as an early expression of the sense of injustice toward the poor which underlies the "liberation theology" which has developed within Catholicism. During the seventeenth century and later people's social status was often defined by the privileges to which they were entitled. Here the term is used ironically.

What are some of the main prejudices against poor people? What do you think the poet means to convey by saying that the poor man's nobility is "unseen?"

The poor man is stupid if silent;
and if he speaks, he is an idiot;
if he shows knowledge, he is a chatterer;
and if he is affable, he is a liar;
if he is polite, he is a meddler;
when he doesn't suffer, arrogant;
cowardly when he is humble;
and crazy when he is resolute;
if brave, he is reckless;
conceited, if he is modest;
flattering, if compliant;
and if he begs pardon, coarse;
if he pretends, he is cheeky;
if he is deserving, he gets no appreciation;
his nobility is unseen, and his best clothes, unclean;
if he works, he is greedy, and at the opposite extreme
a lost soul if he rests . . .
Behold! Are these not privileges?

Translated by Mary Gallwey

North America 1500–1750

John Smith: *The Proceedings of the English Colony in Virginia (1612)*

The English who initially settled Jamestown in 1607 struggled to survive and a couple of times came close to abandoning the colony. They could not grow food to sustain themselves and they could not subjugate the local Indian confederacy under the chief Powhatan. They understandably feared that he could wipe them out with a concerted attack, while they remained dependent on supplies that his people could provide from their agricultural surpluses. Captain John Smith, for some months the head of the Jamestown colony, regularly encountered Powhatan or contingents of his people as he himself led small groups into the hinterland. They almost always haggled as each sought to assert his primacy over the other.

Did the Indians already possess some European-made implements when Smith came to visit them? What kinds of ceremonies did the Indians display? What kinds of ceremonies did the English display? Were the Powhatan Indians fearful of the English or vice versa? Did the English need anything of the Indians? Did the English take advantage of Powhatan in the trade that they conducted? What did Powhatan suspect to be the ultimate motive of the English in coming to his territory?

What happened on the second voyage to discover the Bay?

Entering the River of Tockwogh the savages all armed in a fleet of boats round environed us; it chanced one of them could speak the language of Powhatan, who persuaded the rest to a friendly parley. But when they saw us furnished with the Massawomecks' weapons, and we feigning the invention of Kecoughtan to have taken them perforce, they conducted us to their palisaded town, mantled with the barks of trees, with scaffolds like mounts, breasted about with barks very formally. Their men, women, and children, with dances, songs, fruits, fish, furs, and what they had, kindly entertained us, spreading mats for us to sit on, stretching their best abilities to express their loves.

Many hatchets, knives, and pieces of iron, and brass, we saw, which they reported to have from the Sasquesahanocks, a mighty people, and mortal enemies with the Massawomecks. The Sasquesahanocks inhabit upon the chief spring of these 4; two days' journey higher than our barge could pass for[1] rocks. Yet we prevailed with the interpreter to take with him another interpreter to persuade the Sasquesahanocks to come to visit us; for their languages are different: 3 or 4 days we expected their return. Then 60 of these giant-like people came down, with presents of venison, tobacco pipes, baskets, targets, bows and arrows. 5 of their Werowances came boldly aboard us, to cross the bay for Tockwogh; leaving their men and canoes; the wind being so violent that they durst not pass.

Our order was, daily, to have prayer, with a psalm: at which solemnity the poor savages much wonderedf. Our prayers being done, they were long busied with consultation till they had contrived their business. Then they began in most passionate manner to hold up their hands to the sun, with a most fearful song. Then embracing the Captain, they began

[1] Because of.

to adore him in like manner, though he rebuked them, yet they proceeded till their song was finished. Which done, with a most strange furious action, and a hellish voice, began an oration of their loves. That ended, with a great painted bear's skin they covered our Captain. Then one ready with a chain of white beads (weighing at least 6 or 7 pound) hung it about his neck; the others had 18 mantles made of divers sorts of skins sewed together. All these with many other toys, they laid at his feet, stroking their ceremonious hands about his neck for his creation to be their governor, promising their aids, victuals, or what they had to be his, if he would stay with them to defend and revenge them of the Massawomecks; But we left them at Tockwogh, they much sorrowing for our departure, yet we promised the next year again to visit them. Many descriptions and discourses they made us of Atquanahuck, Massawomeck, and other people, signifying they inhabit the river of Cannida, and from the French to have their hatchets, and such like tools by trade. These know no more of the territories of Powhatan than his name, and he as little of them. . . .

Captain Smith's Journey to Pamaunke

This company being victualled but for 3 or 4 days lodged the first night at Weraskoyack, where the President took sufficient provision. This kind savage did his best to divert him from seeing Powhatan; but perceiving he could not prevail, he advised in this manner Captain Smith, "You shall find Powhatan to use you kindly, but trust him not, and be sure he have no opportunity to seize on your arms, for he hath sent for you only to cut your throats:" The Captain thanked him for his good counsel; yet the better to try his love, desired guides to Chowanoke, for he would send a present to that king to bind him his friend. To perform this journey, was sent Michael Sicklemore, a very honest, valiant, and painful[2] soldier; with him two guides, and directions how to search for the lost company of Sir Walter Raleigh, and silk grass. Then we departed thence, the President assuring the king his perpetual love, and left with him Samuell Collier his page to learn the language. . . .

We sent to Powhatan for provision, who sent us plenty of bread, turkeys, and venison. The next day having feasted us after his ordinary manner, he began to ask, when we would be gone, feigning he sent not for us; neither had he any corn, and his people much less; yet for 40 swords he would procure us 40 bushels. The President ,showing him the men there present, that brought him the message and conditions, asked him how it chanced he became so forgetful; thereat the king concluded the matter with a merry laughter, asking for our commodities; but none he liked without guns and swords, valuing a basket of corn more precious than a basket of copper; saying he could eat his corn, but not his copper.

Captain Smith seeing the intent of this subtle savage, began to deal with him after this manner: "Powhatan, though I had many courses to have made my provision, yet believing your promises to supply my wants, I neglected all, to satisfy your desire; and to testify my love, I sent you my men for your building, neglecting my own. What your people had, you have engrossed, forbidding them our trade; and now you think by consuming the time, we shall consume for want, not having [wherewith] to fulfill your strange demands. As for swords, and guns, I told you long ago, I had none to spare. And you shall know, those I have, can keep me from want; yet steal, or wrong you I will not, nor dissolve that friendship we have mutually promised, except you constrain me by your bad usage."

The king having attentively listened to this discourse; promised that both he and his country would spare him what they could; the which within 2 days, they should receive.

---

[2]Painstaking, conscientious.

"Yet Captain Smith," (saith the king) "some doubt I have of your coming hither, that makes me not so kindly seek to relieve you as I would; for many do inform me, your coming is not for trade, but to invade my people and possess my country, who dare not come to bring you corn, seeing you thus armed with your men. To clear us of this fear, leave aboard your weapons; for here they are needless, we being all friends and for ever Powhatan's."

With many such discourses they spent the day, quartering that night in the king's houses. The next day he reviewed his building, which he little intended should proceed. For the Dutchmen finding his plenty, and knowing our want; and perceived his preparation to surprise us, little thinking we could escape, both him and famine. . . .

Many other discourses they had, till at last they began to trade. But the king, seeing his will would not be admitted as a law, our guard [not] dispersed, nor our men disarmed, he, sighing, breathed his mind once more in this manner.

"Captain Smith, I never used any of Werowances so kindly as your self; yet from you I receive the least kindness of any. Captain Newport gave me swords, copper, cloths, a bed, tools, or what I desired, ever taking what I offered him, and would send away his guns when I entreated him. None doth deny to lay at my feet, or do, what I desire, but only you, of whom I can have nothing but what you regard not; and yet you will have whatsoever you demand. Captain Newport you call father, and so you call me; but I see, for all us both, you will do what you list, and we must both seek to content you. But if you intend so friendly as you say, send hence your arms that I may believe you; for you see the love I bear you doth cause me thus nakedly [to] forget my self."

Smith (seeing this savage but trifled the time, to cut his throat), procured the savages to break the ice, that his boat might come to fetch both him and his corn; and gave order for his men to come ashore, to have surprised the king, with whom also he but trifled the time till his men landed, and to keep him from suspicion, entertained the time with this reply:

"Powhatan, you must know as I have but one God, I honor but one king; and I live not here as your subject, but as your friend, to pleasure you with what I can. By the gifts you bestow on me, you gain more than by trade; yet would you visit me as I do you, you should know it is not our custom to sell our courtesy as a vendible commodity. Bring all your country with you for your guard, I will not dislike of it as being over-jealous. But to content you, tomorrow I will leave my arms, and trust to your promise. I call you father indeed, and as a father you shall see I will love you; but the small care you had of such a child, caused my men persuade me to shift for my self."

By this time Powhatan, having knowledge [that] his men were ready, whilst the ice was breaking, his luggage women and children fled. And to avoid suspicion, left 2 or 3 of his women talking with the Captain, whilst he secretly fled, and his men as secretly beset the house, which being at the instant discovered to Captain Smith, with his pistol, sword and target, he made such a passage amongst those naked devils that they fled before him, some one way, some another; so that without hurt he obtained [reached] the corps du guard.[3] When they perceived him so well escaped, and with his 8 men (for he had no more with him), to the uttermost of their skill, they sought by excuses to dissemble the matter. And Powhatan, to excuse his flight and the sudden coming of this multitude, sent our Captain a great bracelet and a chain of pearl, by an ancient orator that bespoke us to this purpose, (perceiving then from our pinnace, a barge and men departing and coming unto us):

---

[3]Reached the bodyguard.

"Captain Smith, our Werowans is fled, fearing your guns, and knowing [that] when the ice was broken, there would come more men, sent those of his to guard his corn from the pilfery that might happen without your knowledge. Now though some be hurt by your misprision,[4] yet he is your friend, and so will continue. And since the ice is open, he would have you send away your corn; and if you would have his company, send also your arms, which so affrighteth this people, that they dare not come to you, as he hath promised they should."

Now having provided baskets for our men to carry the corn, they kindly offered their service to guard our arms, that none should steal them. A great many they were, of goodly well-appointed fellows as grim as devils; yet the very sight of cocking our matches[5] against them, and few words, caused them to leave their bows & arrows to our guard, and bear down our corn on their own backs. We needed not importune them to make quick dispatch. But our own barge being left by the ebb, caused us to stay till the midnight tide carried us safe aboard. Having spent that half night with such mirth as though we never had suspected or intended any thing, we left the Dutchmen to build, Brinton to kill fowl for Powhatan (as by his messengers he importunately desired), and left directions with our men to give Powhatan all the content they could, that we might enjoy his company at our return from Pamaunke.

---

[4]Misunderstanding.
[5]Matchlock guns.

Africa 1750-1900

The Interesting Narrative of the Life of Olaudah Equiano (1789)

Born in Benin in the late 18th century, Equiano was enslaved as a young boy and passed through a variety of experiences, many of them horrible, but managed to acquire enough learning and independence to become a major voice advocating an end to slavery. His Narrative, *written in English in 1789, immediately became a sensation, and has remained a classic source for our knowledge about the European slave trade from the point of view of the slave.*

In what ways does Equiano contrast slavery within Africa with the sort of slavery he encountered in the western hemisphere? What sufferings on the ship does he describe?

Description of his early life

Our tillage is exercised in a large plain or common, some hours' walk from our dwellings, and all the neighbors resort thither in a body. They use no beasts of husbandry, and their only instruments are hoes, axes, shovels, and beaks, or pointed iron to dig with. . . . This common is often the theater of war; and therefore when our people go out to till their land, they not only go in a body, but generally take their arms with them for fear of a surprise; and when they apprehend[1] an invasion they guard the avenues to their dwellings, by driving sticks into the ground, which are so sharp at one end as to pierce the foot, and are generally dipped in poison. From what I can recollect of these battles, they appear to have been irruptions[2] of one little state or district on the other, to obtain prisoners or booty. Perhaps they were incited to this by those traders who brought the European goods I mentioned amongst us. Such a mode of obtaining slaves in Africa is common; and I believe more are procured this way, and by kidnapping than any other. When a trader wants slaves, he applies to a chief for them, and tempts him with his wares. It is not extraordinary, if on this occasion he yields to the temptation with as little firmness, and accepts the price of his fellow creature's liberty with as little reluctance as the enlightened merchant. Accordingly he falls on his neighbors, and a desperate battle ensues. If he prevails and takes prisoners, he gratifies his avarice by selling them; but if his party be vanquished, and he falls into the hands of the enemy, he is put to death; for as he has been known to foment their quarrels, it is thought dangerous to let him survive, and no ransom can save him, though all other prisoners may be redeemed. We have fire-arms, bows and arrows, broad two-edged swords and javelins: we have shields also which cover a man from head to foot. All are taught the use of these weapons; even our women are warriors, and march boldly out to fight along with the men. . . . I was once a witness to a battle in our common. We had been all at work in it one day as usual, when our people were suddenly attacked. I climbed a tree at some distance, from which I beheld the fight. There were many women as well as men on both sides; among others my mother was there, and armed

---

[1]Fear, expect.

[2]Outbreaks.

with a broad sword. After fighting for a considerable time with great fury, and after many had been killed, our people obtained the victory, and took their enemy's Chief prisoner. He was carried off in great triumph, and though he offered a large ransom for his life, he was put to death. A virgin of note among our enemies had been slain in the battle, and her arm was exposed in our market-place where our trophies were always exhibited. The spoils were divided according to the merit of the warriors. Those prisoners which were not sold or redeemed we kept as slaves: but how different was their condition from that of the slaves in the West Indies! With us they do no more work than other members of the community, even their master; their food, clothing and lodging were nearly the same as theirs (except that they were not permitted to eat with those who were freeborn); and there was scarce any other difference between them than a superior degree of importance which the head of a family possesses in our state, and that authority which, as such, he exercises over every part of his household. Some of these slaves have even slaves under them as their own property and for their own use. . . .

Enslavement

My father, besides many slaves, had a numerous family, of which seven lived to grow up, including myself and a sister, who was the only daughter. As I was the youngest of the sons I became, of course, the greatest favorite with my mother, and was always with her; and she used to take particular pains to form my mind. I was trained up from my earliest years in the art of war: my daily exercise was shooting and throwing javelins; and my mother adorned me with emblems, after the manner of our greatest warriors. In this way I grew up till I was turned the age of eleven, when an end was put to my happiness in the following manner:— Generally when the grown people in the neighborhood were gone far in the fields to labor, the children assembled together in some of the neighbors' premises to play, and commonly some of us used to get up a tree to look out for any assailant or kidnapper that might come upon us, for they sometimes took those opportunities of our parents' absence to attack and carry off as many as they could seize. One day, as I was watching at the top of a tree in our yard, I saw one of those people come into the yard of our next neighbor but one, to kidnap, there being many stout young people in it. Immediately on this I gave the alarm of the rogue, and he was surrounded by the stoutest of them, who entangled him with cords, so that he could not escape till some of the grown people came and secured him. But, alas! ere long it was my fate to be thus attacked, and to be carried off, when none of the grown people were nigh. One day, when all our people were gone out to their works as usual and only I and my dear sister were left to mind the house, two men and a woman got over our walls, and in a moment seized us both, and, without giving us time to cry out, or make resistance, they stopped our mouths, and ran off with us into the nearest wood. Here they tied our hands, and continued to carry us as far as they could, till night came on, when we reached a small house, where the robbers halted for refreshment and spent the night. We were then unbound but were unable to take any food; and being quite overpowered by fatigue and grief, our only relief was some sleep, which allayed our misfortune for a short time. The next morning we left the house, and continued traveling all the day. For a long time we had kept to the woods, but at last we came into a road which I believed I knew. I had now some hopes of being delivered;[3] for we had advanced but a little way before I discovered some people at a distance, on which I began to cry out for their assis-

[3]Rescued.

tance; but my cries had no other effect than to make them tie me faster and stop my mouth, and then they put me into a large sack. They also stopped my sister's mouth, and tied her hands and in this manner we proceeded till we were out of the sight of these people. When we went to rest the following night they offered us some victuals; but we refused it; and the only comfort we had was in being in one another's arms all that night, and bathing each other with our tears. But alas! we were soon deprived of even the small comfort of weeping together. The next day proved a day of greater sorrow than I had yet experienced; for my sister and I were then separated, while we lay clasped in each other's arms. It was in vain that we besought them not to part us; she was torn from me, and immediately carried away, while I was left in a state of distraction not to be described. I cried and grieved continually; and for several days I did not eat anything but what they forced into my mouth.

Carried to the coast

Equiano experienced African slavery first hand under several masters, being treated generally less harshly than he had expected; but he found himself at last headed into unfamiliar territory.

All the nations and people I had hitherto passed through, resembled our own in their manners, customs, and language: but I came at length to a country, the inhabitants of which differed from us in all those particulars. I was very much struck with this difference, especially when I came among a people who did not circumcise, and ate without washing their hands. They cooked also in iron pots, and had European cutlasses and cross bows, which were unknown to us, and fought with their fists among themselves. Their women were not so modest as ours, for they ate, and drank, and slept with their men. But above all, I was amazed to see no sacrifices or offerings among them. In some of those places the people ornamented themselves with scars, and likewise filed their teeth very sharp. They wanted sometimes to ornament me in the same manner, but I would not suffer[4] them; hoping that I might some time be among a people who did not thus disfigure themselves, as I thought they did. At last I came to the banks of a large river which was covered with canoes, in which the people appeared to live with their household utensils and provisions of all kinds. I was beyond measure astonished at this, as I had never before seen any water larger than a pond or a rivulet: and my surprise was mingled with no small fear when I was put into one of these canoes, and we began to paddle and move along the river. We continued going on thus till night; and when we came to land, and made fires on the banks, each family by themselves; some dragged their canoes on shore, others stayed and cooked in theirs, and laid in them all night. Those on the land had mats, of which they made tents, some in the shape of little houses; in these we slept: and after the morning meal, we embarked again and proceeded as before. I was often very much astonished to see some of the women, as well as the men, jump into the water, dive to the bottom, come up again, and swim about.

Thus I continued to travel, sometimes by land, sometimes by water, through different countries and various nations, till, at the end of six or seven months after I had been kidnapped, I arrived at the sea coast. . . . The first object which saluted my eyes when I arrived on the coast, was the sea, and a slave ship, which was then riding at anchor, and waiting for its cargo. These filled me with astonishment, which was soon converted into terror, when I was carried on board. I was immediately handled, and tossed up to see if I

[4]Allow.

were sound[5], by some of the crew; and I was now persuaded that I had gotten into a world of bad spirits, and that they were going to kill me. Their complexions, too, differing so much from ours, their long hair, and the language they spoke (which was very different from any I had ever heard), united to confirm me in this belief. Indeed, such were the horrors of my views and fears at the moment, that, if ten thousand worlds had been my own, I would have freely parted with them all to have exchanged my condition with that of the meanest slave in my own country. When I looked round the ship too and saw a large furnace of copper boiling, and a multitude of black people of every description chained together, every one of their countenances expressing dejection and sorrow, I no longer doubted of my fate; and, quite overpowered with horror and anguish, I fell motionless on the deck and fainted. When I recovered a little, I found some black people about me, who I believed were some of those who had brought me on board, and had been receiving their pay; they talked to me in order to cheer me, but all in vain. I asked them if we were not to be eaten by those white men with horrible looks, red faces, and long hair. They told me I was not, and one of the crew brought me a small portion of spirituous[6] liquor in a wine glass; but being afraid of him, I would not take it out of his hand. One of the blacks therefore took it from him and gave it to me, and I took a little down my palate, which, instead of reviving me, as they thought it would, threw me into the greatest consternation at the strange feeling it produced, having never tasted any such liquor before. Soon after this, the blacks who brought me on board went off, and left me abandoned to despair. I now saw myself deprived of all chance of returning to my native country, or even the least glimpse of hope of gaining the shore, which I now considered as friendly; and I even wished for my former slavery in preference to my present situation, which was filled with horrors of every kind, still heightened by my ignorance of what I was to undergo. I was not long suffered to indulge my grief; I was soon put down under the decks, and there I received such a salutation in my nostrils as I had never experienced in my life: so that with the loathsomeness of the stench, and crying together, I became so sick and low that I was not able to eat, nor had I the least desire to taste anything. I now wished for the last friend, death, to relieve me; but soon, to my grief, two of the white men offered me eatables; and on my refusing to eat, one of them held me fast by the hands and laid me across I think the windlass, and tied my feet, while the other flogged me severely. I had never experienced anything of this kind before; and although not being used to the water, I naturally feared that element the first time I saw it, yet nevertheless could I have got over the nettings, I would have jumped over the side, but I could not; and besides, the crew used to watch us very closely who were not chained down to the decks, lest we should leap into the water: and I have seen some of these poor African prisoners most severely cut for attempting to do so, and hourly whipped for not eating. This indeed was often the case with myself. In a little time after, amongst the poor chained men, I found some of my own nation, which in a small degree gave ease to my mind. I inquired of these what was to be done with us; they gave me to understand we were to be carried to these white people's country to work for them. I then was a little revived, and thought, if it were no worse than working, my situation was not so desperate: but still I feared I should be put to death, the white people looked and acted, as I thought, in so savage a manner; for I had never seen among my people such instances of brutal cruelty; and this not only shewn towards us blacks, but also to some of the whites themselves. One white man in particular I saw, when we were per-

[5]Healthy.

[6]Alcoholic.

mitted to be on deck, flogged so unmercifully with a large rope near the foremast, that he died in consequence of it; and they tossed him over the side as they would have done a brute. This made me fear these people the more; and I expected nothing less than to be treated in the same manner. . . .

The stench of the hold while we were on the coast was so intolerably loathsome, that it was dangerous to remain there for any time, and some of us had been permitted to stay on the deck for the fresh air; but now that the whole ship's cargo were confined together it became absolutely pestilential. The closeness of the place, and the heat of the climate, added to the number in the ship, which was so crowded that each had scarcely room to turn himself, almost suffocated us. This produced copious perspirations, so that the air soon became unfit for respiration, from a variety of loathsome smells, and brought on a sickness among the slaves, of which many died, thus falling victims to the improvident avarice, as I may call it, of their purchasers. This wretched situation was again aggravated by the galling of the chains, now become insupportable; and the filth of the necessary tubs, into which the children often fell, and were almost suffocated. The shrieks of the women, and the groans of the dying, rendered the whole a scene of horror almost inconceivable. Happily perhaps for myself I was soon reduced so low here that it was thought necessary to keep me almost always on deck; and from my extreme youth I was not put in fetters. In this situation I expected every hour to share the fate of my companions, some of whom were almost daily brought upon deck at the point of death, which I began to hope would soon put an end to my miseries. Often did I think many of the inhabitants of the deep much more happy than myself. I envied them the freedom they enjoyed, and as often wished I could change my condition for theirs. Every circumstance I met with served only to render my state more painful, and heighten my apprehensions and my opinion of the cruelty of the whites. One day they had taken a number of fishes; and when they had killed and satisfied themselves with as many as they thought fit, to our astonishment who were on the deck, rather than give any of them to us to eat as we expected, they tossed the remaining fish into the sea again, although we begged and prayed for some as well as we could, but in vain; and some of my countrymen, being pressed by hunger, took an opportunity when they thought no one saw them of trying to get a little privately; but they were discovered, and the attempt procured them some very severe floggings. One day, when we had a smooth sea and moderate wind, two of my wearied countrymen who were chained together (I was near them at the time), preferring death to such a life of misery, somehow made through the nettings and jumped into the sea: immediately another quite dejected fellow, who on account of his illness was suffered to be out of irons, also followed their example; and I believe many more would very soon have done the same if they had not been prevented by the ship's crew, who were instantly alarmed. Those of us that were the most active were in a moment put down under the deck, and there was such a noise and confusion amongst the people of the ship as I never heard before, to stop her, and get the boat out to go after the slaves. However two of the wretches were drowned, but they got the other and afterwards flogged him unmercifully for thus attempting to prefer death to slavery. In this manner we continued to undergo more hardships than I can now relate, hardships which are inseparable from this accursed trade.

Life in slavery

Equiano experienced slavery in the Caribbean, in the American colonies, and in England. He writes about slavery at its harshest in the Caribbean.

It was very common in several of the islands, particularly in St Kitt's, for the slaves to be branded with the initial letters of their master's name, and a load of heavy iron hooks hung about their necks. Indeed on the most trifling occasions they were loaded with chains, and often instruments of torture were added. The iron muzzle, thumb-screws, etc., are so well known as not to need a description, and were sometimes applied for the slightest faults. I have seen a negro beaten till some of his bones were broken, for even letting a pot boil over. It is surprising that usage like this should drive the poor creatures to despair, and make them seek refuge in death from those evils which render their lives intolerable—while,

"With shudd'ring horror pale, and eyes aghast,
They view their lamentable lot, and find
No rest !"[7]

This they frequently do. A negro-man on board a vessel of my master, while I belonged to her, having been put in irons for some trifling misdemeanor, and kept in that state for some days, being weary of life, took an opportunity of jumping overboard into the sea; however, he was picked up without being drowned. Another whose life was also a burden to him resolved to starve himself to death, and refused to eat any victuals: this procured him a severe flogging; and he also, on the first occasion which offered, jumped overboard at Charleston, but was saved.

Nor is there any greater regard shown to the little property, than there is to the persons and lives of the negroes. I have already related an instance or two of particular oppression out of many which I have witnessed; but the following is frequent in all the islands. The wretched field-slaves, after toiling all the day for an unfeeling owner, who gives them but little victuals, steal sometimes a few moments from rest or refreshment to gather some small portion of grass, according as their time will admit. This they commonly tie up in a parcel; (either a bit, worth six pence, or half a bit's-worth); and bring it to town, or to the market, to sell. Nothing is more common than for the white people on this occasion to take the grass from them without paying for it; and not only so, but too often also to my knowledge, our clerks, and many others, at the same time have committed acts of violence on the poor, wretched, and helpless females, whom I have seen for hours stand crying to no purpose, and get no redress or pay of any kind. Is not this one common and crying sin enough to bring down God's judgment on the islands? He tells us the oppressor and the oppressed are both in his hands; and if these are not the poor, the broken-hearted, the blind, the captive, the bruised, which our Savior speaks of, who are they? . . .

The small account in which the life of a negro is held in the West Indies is so universally known that it might seem impertinent to quote the following extract, if some people had not been hardy enough of late to assert that negroes are on the same footing in that respect as Europeans. By the 329th Act, page 125, of the assembly of Barbadoes it is enacted "That if any negro, or other slave, under punishment by his master, or his order, for running away, or any other crime or misdemeanour towards his said master, unfortunately shall suffer in life or member, no person whatsoever shall be liable to a fine, but if any man shall out of *wantonness, or only of bloody-mindedness, or cruel intention, willfully kill a negro, or other slave, of his own, he shall pay into the public treasury fifteen pounds sterling.*" And it is the same in most, if not all, of the West India islands.

[7]These lines describe the plight of the damned in Milton's *Paradise Lost.*

African Proverbs (19th Century)

The languages of Africa are rich in proverbs. These examples were collected in the 19th century and reflect traditional values. They were collected and translated by various Europeans and edited by the famous explorer Richard F. Burton in 1865 in Wit and Wisdom from West Africa.

Try rewording some of these proverbs to explain their meaning.

Wolof::
The house-roof fights with the rain, but he who is sheltered ignores it.
To love the king is not bad, but a king who loves you is better.
Allah does not destroy the men whom one hates.

Oji (Ashanti):
If nothing touches the palm-leaves they do not rustle.[1]
He is a fool whose sheep runs away twice.

Yoruba:
The man who has bread to eat does not appreciate the severity of a famine.
Because friendship is pleasant, we partake of our friend's entertainment; not because we have not enough to eat in our own house.
When your neighbor's horse falls into a pit, you should not rejoice at it, for your own child may fall into it too.
The pot-lid is always badly off: the pot gets all the sweet, the lid nothing but steam.[2]

Efik:
His opinions are like water in the bottom of a canoe, going from side to side.
You lament not the dead, but lament the trouble of making a grave; the way of the ghost is longer than the grave.

---

[1]Compare English "Where there's smoke there's fire."
[2]Said of slaves who work without pay.

India 1750-1900

Raja Rammohan Roy: A Second Conference Between an Advocate for, and An Opponent of, the Practice of Burning Widows Alive (1820)

This is an imaginary dialogue arguing for and against sati, *the practice of encouraging—and often forcing—widows to burn themselves alive on their husbands' funeral pyres, here referred to as "Concremation." This practice was outlawed by the British not long after the great Indian reformer Rammohan Roy made this argument, and is now extremely rare, as are the polygamous arrangements which he describes; but many of his comments on the burdens borne by women are applicable even today.*

What are the main disadvantages towomen that Roy sees in traditional marriage?

ADVOCATE

I alluded . . . to the real reason for our anxiety to persuade widows to follow their husbands, and for our endeavors to burn them pressed down with ropes: viz., that women are by nature of inferior understanding, without resolution, unworthy of trust, subject to passions, and void of virtuous knowledge; they, according to the precepts of the Sastra, are not allowed to marry again after the demise of their husbands, and consequently despair at once of all worldly pleasure; hence it is evident, that death to these unfortunate widows is preferable to existence; for the great difficulty which a widow may experience by living a purely ascetic life, as prescribed by the Shastras, is obvious; therefore, if she do not perform Concremation, it is probable that she may be guilty of such acts as may bring disgrace upon her paternal and maternal relations, and those that may be connected with her husband. Under these circumstances, we instruct them from their early life in the idea of Concremation, holding out to them heavenly enjoyments in company with their husbands, as well as the beatitude of their relations, both by birth and marriage, and their reputation in this world. From this many of them, on the death of their husbands, become desirous of accompanying them; but to remove every chance of their trying to escape from the blazing fire, in burning them we first tie them down to the pile.

OPPONENT

The reason you have now assigned for burning widows alive is indeed your true motive, as we are well aware; but the faults which you have imputed to women are not planted in their constitution by nature; it would be, therefore, grossly criminal to condemn that sex to death merely from precaution. By ascribing to them all sorts of improper conduct, you have indeed successfully persuaded the Hindu community to look down upon them as contemptible and mischievous creatures, whence they have been subjected to constant miseries. I have, therefore, to offer a few remarks on this head.

Women are in general inferior to men in bodily strength and energy; consequently the male part of the community, taking advantage of their corporeal weakness, have denied to them those excellent merits that they are entitled to by nature, and afterwards they are apt to say that women are naturally incapable of acquiring those merits. But if we give the subjects consideration, we may easily ascertain whether or not your accusation against them is consistent with justice. As to their inferiority in point of understanding, when did you ever afford them a fair opportunity of exhibiting their natural capacity? How then can you accuse them of want of understanding? If, after instruction in knowledge and wisdom, a person cannot comprehend or retain what has been taught him, we may consider him as deficient; but as you keep women generally void of education and acquirements, you cannot, therefore, in justice pronounce on their inferiority. On the contrary, Lilavati, Bhanumati, the wife of the prince of Karnat, and that of Kalidasa, are celebrated for their thorough knowledge of all the Shastras: moreover in the *Vrihadaranyaka Upanishhad* of the *Yajur Veda* it is clearly stated that Yajnavalkya imparted divine knowledge of the most difficult nature to his wife Maitreyi, who was able to follow and completely attain it!

Secondly. You charge them with want of resolution, at which I feel exceedingly surprised: for we constantly perceive, in a country where the name of death makes the male shudder, that the female, from her firmness of mind, offers to burn with the corpse of her deceased husband; and yet you accuse those women of deficiency in point of resolution.

Thirdly. With regard to their trustworthiness, let us look minutely into the conduct of both sexes, and we may be enabled to ascertain which of them is the most frequently guilty of betraying friends. If we enumerate such women in each village or town as have been deceived by men, and such men as have been betrayed by women, I presume that the number of the deceived women would be found ten times greater than that of the betrayed men. Men are, in general, able to read and write, and manage public affairs, by which means they easily promulgate such faults as women occasionally commit, but never consider as criminal the misconduct of men towards women. One fault they have, it must be acknowledged; which is, by considering others equally void of duplicity as themselves, to give their confidence too readily, from which they suffer much misery, even so far that some of them are misled to suffer themselves to be burnt to death.

In the fourth place, with respect to their subjection to the passions, this may be judged of by the custom of marriage as to the respective sexes; for one man may marry two or three, sometimes even ten wives and upwards; while a woman, who marries but one husband, desires at his death to follow him, forsaking all worldly enjoyments, or to remain leading the austere life of an ascetic.

Fifthly. The accusation of their want[1] of virtuous knowledge is an injustice. Observe what pain, what slighting, what contempt, and what afflictions their virtue enables them to support![2] How many Kulin Brahmans are there who marry ten or fifteen wives for the sake of money, that never see the greater number of them after the day of marriage, and visit others only three or four times in the course of their life. Still amongst those women, most, even without seeing or receiving any support from their husbands, living dependent on their fathers or brothers, and suffering much distress, continue to preserve their virtue; and when Brahmans, or those of other tribes, bring their wives to live with them, what misery do the women not suffer? At marriage the wife is recognized as half of her husband, but in after-conduct they are treated worse than inferior animals. For the woman is employed to do the work of a slave in the house, such as, in her turn, to clean the place very early in the morning, whether cold or wet, to scour the dishes, to wash the floor, to cook night and day, to prepare and serve food for her husband, father, mother-in-law, sisters-in-

[1]Lack.

[2]Bear.

law, brothers-in-law, and friends and connections! (for amongst Hindus more than in other tribes relations long reside together, and on this account quarrels are more common amongst brothers respecting their worldly affairs). If in the preparation or serving up of the victuals they commit the smallest fault, what insult do they not receive from their husband, their mother-in-law, and the younger brothers of their husband? After all the male part of the family have satisfied themselves, the women content themselves with what may be left, whether sufficient in quantity or not. Where Brahmans or Kayasthas are not wealthy, their women are obliged to attend to their cows, and to prepare the cow-dung for firing. In the afternoon they fetch water from the river or tank, and at night perform the office of menial servants in making the beds. In case of any fault or omission in the performance of those labors they receive injurious treatment. Should the husband acquire wealth, he indulges in criminal amours to her perfect knowledge and almost under her eyes, and does not see her perhaps once a month. As long as the husband is poor, she suffers every kind of trouble, and when he becomes rich, she is altogether heart-broken. All this pain and affliction their virtue alone enables them to support. Where a husband takes two or three wives to live with him, they are subjected to mental miseries and constant quarrels. Even this distressed situation they virtuously endure. Sometimes it happens that the husband, from a preference for one of his wives, behaves cruelly to another. Amongst the lower classes, and those even of the better class who have not associated with good company, the wife, on the slightest fault, or even on bare suspicion of her misconduct, is chastised as a thief. Respect to virtue and their reputation generally makes them forgive even this treatment. If unable to bear such cruel usage, a wife leaves her husband's house to live separately from him, then the influence of the husband with the magisterial authority is generally sufficient to place her again in his hands; when, in revenge for her quitting him, he seizes every pretext to torment her in various ways, and sometimes even puts her privately to death. These are facts occurring every day, and not to be denied. What I lament is, that, seeing the women thus dependent and exposed to every misery, you feel for them no compassion, that might exempt them from being tied down and burnt to death.

Lalon Fakir: Songs (19th Century)

Lalon Fakir was born in 1774 in an obscure village in the district of Kushtia, now in Bangladesh. One of the greatest mystic-singers the Indian subcontinent has ever produced, Lalon was perhaps the most radical voice in India during British colonial rule. Like Kabir, he had no formal education and lived in extreme poverty. Writing in nineteenth-century lyrical Bengali. Lalon composed numerous songs which still provide spiritual and political inspiration to the Bengali rural peasant—a class from which Lalon himself came, and also to freedom-fighters all over the world. He celebrates the freedom of body, soul, and even language from all repressive and divisive forces. Always opposed to casteism, sectarianism, and colonialism, Lalon represents and exemplifies the true revolutionary and secular nature of his community known as "Baul"—a community of low-class, illiterate, wandering singers whose wisdom and wit do not come from academic training, but from an active contact with a life intensely lived.

What images are used here to symbolize mental freedom? How are women used to argue against distinctions based on caste in the second poem?

A Strange Bird

Look, how a strange bird flits in and out of the cage!
O brother, I wish I could bind it with my mind's fetters.
Have you seen a house of eight rooms with nine doors
Closed and open, with windows in between, mirrored?
O mind, you are a bird encaged! And of green sticks
Is your cage made, but it will be broken one day.
Lalon says: Open the cage, look how the bird wings away!

Casteism

People ask, what is Lalon's caste?
Lalon says, my eyes fail to detect
The signs of caste. Don't you see that
Some wear garlands, some rosaries
Around the neck? But does it make any
Difference brother? O, tell me,
What mark does one carry when
One is born, or when one dies?
A Muslim is marked by the sign
Of circumcision; but how should
You mark a woman? If a Brahmin male
Is known by the thread he wears,
How is a woman known? People of the world,
O brother, talk of marks and signs,
But Lalon says: I have only dissolved
The raft of signs, the marks of caste
In the deluge of the One!

Translated by Azfar Hussain

Muddupalani: Appeasing Radhika (18th Century)

Muddupalani (c. 1730-1790) was a courtesan in the court of the Nayaka king Pratapasinha of Tanjavur, in South India. The Nayaka kings were great patrons of art. There is evidence to show that distinguished women poets were attached to their courts in various periods. Courtesans were highly educated and were economically independent, unlike many other women of the time. The selection here is taken from Muddupalani's erotic epic of four parts called Radhika Santawanam (Appeasing Radhika). *In this selection Radhika (also known as Radha) the lover of Krishna instructs him on how to make love to his bride-to-be. "Honey" is a more literal term in the original than the rather worn epithet it has become in English; one thinks of the sweetness and sensuousness of liquid honey.*

How do you think Radhika feels about Krishna as she is speaking to him? What does she seem to be most concerned about in her instructions? Does this poem strike you as reflecting female attitudes? Explain.

Move on her lips
the tip of your tongue;
   do not scare her
   by biting hard.
Place on her cheeks
a gentle kiss;
   do not scratch her
   with your sharp nails.
Hold her nipple
with your fingertips;
   do not scare her
by squeezing it tight.
Make love
gradually;
   do not scare her
   by being aggressive.
        I am a fool
        to tell you all these.
        When you meet her
        and wage your war of love
        would you care to recall
        my "do's and dont's," Honey?

Translated by B. V. L. Narayanarow

Toru Dutt: Sonnet (1876)

Toru Dutt was born in Bengal, but her father wanted his daughters to have a Western education, so the family moved to France, where she learned both French and English. She traveled to England (where for a brief while she attended special lectures for women at Cambridge) and Italy. On her return home she published, at the age of twenty, her only volume of verse and died the next year. Virtually unknown during her brief lifetime, her work gave her some posthumous celebrity in Europe. Fond of Hindu myth but raised a Christian, loving both France and India, she illustrates the influence that colonialism had on many writers seeking an audience as she expresses her love for her home in English, which was not even her second language.

What aspects of this work reflect European influence?

A sea of foliage girds[1] our garden round,
   But not a sea of dull unvaried green,
   Sharp contrasts of all colors here are seen;
The light-green graceful tamarinds abound
Amid the mango clumps of green profound,
   And palms arise, like pillars gray, between;
   And o'er the quiet pools the seemuls lean,
Red—red, and startling like a trumpet's sound.
But nothing can be lovelier than the ranges
   Of bamboos to the eastward, when the moon
Looks through their gaps, and the white lotus changes
   Into a cup of silver. One might swoon
         Drunken with beauty then, or gaze and gaze
         On a primeval Eden, in amaze.[2]

---

[1]Encircles.
[2]Amazement.

China 1750–1900

Hung Hsiu-Ch'uan: A Visit to Heaven (1862)

From 1852 to 1864 the uprising of the T'ai-p'ings devastated a huge part of China, in particular the fertile plains of the Yangtse Valley and most of Chekiang and Kiangsu. At least 20 million people died in the uprising, more than in World War I. Hung Hsiu-ch'uan, the leader of the rebellion was born into a poor Hakka family in Canton. Since he appeared to be the brightest son, the whole family made many sacrifices to let him study for the Civil Service examinations. The greater was Hong's humiliation when he repeatedly failed. While he stayed in Canton taking part in the provincial examination, he received a pamphlet written by a Chinese Christian. (Both Catholic and Protestant missionaries regularly distributed Christian tracts during Civil Service examinations, hoping to attract the future leaders of China to Christianity, but Christianity had little attraction for upper class Chinese.) Back home Hung suffered a nervous breakdown. He used the Christian tract he had received to interpret his feverish visions and claimed to be the younger brother of Jesus called upon to save mankind from evil and in particular China from the evils of Manchu rule. He attracted a large number of followers who formed the "Army of Universal Peace"(T'ai-p'ing chun). *In 1850 rebellion broke out and by 1853 the T'ai-p'ings had conquered the city of Nanking. Hung declared himself emperor of the T'ai-p'ing Heavenly Kingdom with Nanking as its capital. Equal rights for men and women, the equal distribution of land, and mandatory church attendance were some of the goals of Hung's reign. Western observers, however, who had initially been attracted to this allegedly Christian kingdom grew increasingly weary of the corruption of the T'ai-p'ing court and the megalomania of its ruler. For more than a decade, the armies of the reigning Ch'ing dynasty were incapable of reconquering the territory occupied by the T'ai-'ping. Fundamental reforms of the imperial army had to be enacted, a new military leadership had to be established and the assistance of Western troops secured until the Ch'ing were finally able to defeat the T'ai-p'ing in 1864. In spite of its partly Christian ideology the T'ai-p'ing rebellion has been praised by Chinese Communists as a predecessor to the Communist movement. The following text is a description by Hung Hsiu-ch'uan of his vision of a visit to Heaven.*

Which of Hung's images strike you as coming from Christian sources; which do you consider Chinese in origin?

When the True Lord[1] [Hung Hsiu-ch'uan] was twenty-five years old, on the first day of the third month of the year Ting-yu (April 5, 1837) at noon, he saw a multitude of angels floating down who said they would escort him to heaven. He also saw little children in yellow robes. Fluttering towards him they looked like roosters of several ch'ih[2] in size.

When, seated in a sedan chair, the True Lord had reached the gate of Heaven, there were countless beautiful girls lined up on both sides welcoming him. Yet without even looking

[1]The Chinese text says "Lord." Here "True" is added to distinguish between Hung and Jesus or God.

[2]1 ch'ih = about 13 inches.

at them, the True Lord entered heaven. He was dazzled by the brightness and colors so different from the world below. He saw that a multitude of men dressed in dragon robes and three-cornered hats[3] had assembled to receive him.

As for the True Lord's belly, old parts were taken out and exchanged for new parts. In addition, an order was given that books should be lined up for him, so that the True Lord might read them one after the other.

Later the Heavenly Mother came to welcome him. She said: "My son, dwelling on earth has soiled you. Let your mother clean you in the river, and then you may go and see your Father."

Having cleaned him, the Heavenly mother led him to see the Heavenly Father Supreme Lord and August God.[4] He wore a hat with a high brim and was dressed in a dragon robe of black color. His mouth was covered by a thick golden beard that hung down to his belly. He was truly imposing in appearance, extremely tall, his seated posture very severe, his attire most proper, his hands resting on his knees. Having prostrated himself, the True Lord stood by his side.

The Heavenly Father dejectedly said: "So you have come up here? You know this: Truly, most people on earth are heartless. Who on earth was not made and raised by Me? Who does not eat My food or wear My clothes? Who does not enjoy My blessings? The ten thousand beings in heaven and on earth have all been created by Me. I gave them all food and clothing. How then do the people on earth while enjoying My blessings betray and obscure their innermost feelings? Really, there is not even half a dot of a heart worshipping Me! They are in fact deluded by devils, and they use the goods bestowed upon them by Me as offerings in worship of those devils! It is just as if these devils had created and raised them! They have no clue that these devils will harm and kill them. The devils snare and seize them, yet they still don't understand! I truly despise and pity them for such ignorance."

Upon hearing this, the True Lord became greatly distressed and wished to go and exhort and raise the people and make everyone understand the dangerous plans of the devils and have them turn their hearts around to the worship of the Heavenly Father.

Yet the Heavenly Father replied: "Difficult, difficult!"

The Heavenly Father then taught the True Lord how to sit and dress, that his robe should be straightened right, his head should be held high, his body should be upright, his hands should rest on his knees, and his legs should be planted apart.[5]

The Heavenly Father also took the True Lord around High Heaven and showed him how the devils secretly harm the people on earth. . . . The True Lord became very angry and asked the Heavenly Father: "My Father! Since they are doing so much harm, why don't you eliminate them?"

The Heavenly Father replied: "Not only are there devils on earth, they even intrude in the 33rd heaven!"[6]

Thereupon the True Lord said: "My Father, you are so powerful that whomever you command to be born is born and whomever you command to die shall die, why do you

---

[3]This attire is exactly what Chinese officials traditionally wore.

[4]This form of address includes all possible honorific titles both for "god" and "emperor." In the original Chinese the full title is repeated whenever the "Heavenly Father" is mentioned.

[5]This is the posture expected of Chinese emperors and high officials.

[6]According to Buddhist tradition, the 33rd heaven is that of Indra.

permit them to intrude?"

The Heavenly Father replied: "Let them do harm for a while and then I shall deal with them. It is impossible that they should get the better of me!"

The True Lord answered: "Yet if you let them roam for a while, it would be quite understandable for my brothers and sisters to get angry."

The Heavenly Father thereupon said: "If you really see it like this, I shall not allow them to roam but send everyone forth to pursue them. . . ."

Among the reasons for the harm done by the devils, he [the Heavenly Father] also mentioned that the books by Confucius were full of mistakes. The Heavenly Father had books piled in three categories and pointing them out to the True Lord said: "In this category are the books I Myself left behind while performing miracles down on earth, and they are truly faultless. In this second category are books your Elder Brother Jesus left behind having dwelt on earth, performed miracles and in obedience to my command sacrificed his own life to redeem the sins of mankind. These are also truly faultless. In this next category are books Confucius left behind. These are the books you have read during your stay on earth. They are so full of mistakes and errors, that even you have adopted wrong ideas through reading them."

The Heavenly Father thereupon summoned and reproached Confucius and said: "Why do you teach people this way and distort facts in a way that the people on earth don't recognize Me and that your name is considered greater than Mine?"

At first Confucius tried to argue, but soon he had neither thought nor speech.

The Heavenly Elder Brother Jesus also reproached Confucius saying: "Since you created such books to teach the people, even my younger brother got muddled studying them."

Even the assembled angels blamed him: "You made such books to educate the people? How could you make such books!"

When Confucius became aware that all people in Heaven were accusing him, he secretly left heaven planning to join the head of the devils and go with him.

But the Heavenly Father immediately told the True Lord and the angels to pursue Confucius. He was tied up and brought before the Heavenly Father.

The Heavenly Father was furious and ordered the angels to whip him. Confucius fell on his knees before the Heavenly Elder Brother Jesus and three times asked for forgiveness. While receiving a severe flogging, Confucius wailed and begged without end.[7]

The Heavenly Father, thinking that merits might now sufficiently counterbalance his shortcomings, announced that Confucius might henceforth enjoy felicity in Heaven, yet forbade him to ever again go down to earth.

Then the Heavenly Father ordered the True Lord to fight and pursue the devils. He bestowed a golden seal on the True Lord and a knife and ordered him to pursue the devils together with the angels. They should gradually drive the devils out from the 33rd heaven, pursue the head of the devils and his brothers and sisters, bind them together and bring them back to High Heaven. . . .

---

[7]To a contemporary Chinese audience this description of Confucius being flogged in heaven must have appeared rather unusual. According to Chinese tradition, whoever had passed one of the Civil Service examinations and thus professed some knowledge of Confucian literature was exempt from suffering corporeal punishment during a court hearing. All others could be beaten and tortured during an interrogation. If not even a young student could be flogged, how much less would any Chinese even think about having Confucius beaten up!

While the True Lord was fighting against the head devil, the Heavenly Father was behind the True Lord, and the Heavenly Elder Brother Jesus was also behind the True Lord and blinded the devil, so that he could not harm the True Lord. . . . When the True Lord became furious during the fight and attempted to kill him, the Heavenly Father cried out: "No, you can't do that, just immobilize him."

Since the True Lord could not understand why, the Heavenly Father explained: "This evil spirit is an old snake and can bewitch people and eat their souls. If he is killed, all the souls he has eaten can't be saved and this holy place will be polluted. Therefore, for the time being, we have to spare his life. . . ." Whenever the True Lord got tired fighting, angels would crowd around him so that the devil could do him no harm. Having rested he would continue fighting. . . .

Whenever the True Lord got hungry fighting, his Heavenly Mother and Younger Sisters would pluck for him the sweet fruit of heaven, which were of a deep yellow color and had a wonderful aroma. During his fights, the Heavenly Mother and Younger Sisters also helped him so that he was always victorious. Having defeated the devils, he went back to high heaven. The Heavenly Father was immensely pleased and bestowed on the True Lord the title "Ch'uan, the Heavenly King of Universal Peace and Sovereign of the Supreme Truth. . . ."

The Heavenly Father would often teach the True Lord to sing psalms. . . . The Heavenly Father also sometimes ordered the Heavenly Elder Brother Jesus to teach the True Lord by reading characters to him without pause, yet the Heavenly Elder Brother Jesus got very angry and the Heavenly Sister-in-Law had to urge him to restrain himself. The Heavenly Sister-in-Law was truly considerate of the True Lord and could be called an "older sister-in-law acting like a mother." Whenever the Heavenly Elder Brother Jesus was in a bad mood, the Heavenly Mother would exhort him to restrain himself.

The Heavenly Mother deeply loved the True Lord, and she could truly be called graceful and highborn. The True Lord also had a wife in high heaven. In all matters the True Lord was respectful and attentive, and at the appropriate time a son was born. . . .

The Heavenly Father said to the True Lord: "Your Father told you that you should read more books and psalms to be prepared for your future, but you have to descend to earth again. If you don't go back to earth, how can the people on the earth be awakened and ascend to heaven?" The True Lord agreed to this, but in his heart he did not want to go back to earth. Whenever the Heavenly Father insisted too strongly, the True Lord would travel down a few heavens and come back again. Finally, the Heavenly Father became very angry, so that the True Lord said to his wife: "Look after our son and stay here with my father, mother, elder brother, sister-in-law and all my little sisters and wait here while I go down to earth and do what my father told me to do. Afterwards I will ascend to heaven and enjoy peace and happiness with you."

Thereupon the Heavenly Father, the Heavenly Elder Brother Jesus and all the angels bade him farewell.

Translated by Lydia Gerber

Li Ju-chen: The Land of the Great (1828)

Like several other distinguished Chinese novelists, Li Ju-chen (1763-1830) failed to pass the Chinese Civil Service examination. During most of his life he was supported by his understanding elder brother and could thus pursue a wide range of interests: astrology, calligraphy, chess, mathematics, painting, medicine, gardening and particularly phonetics. Li started writing Flowers in the Mirror *when he was fifty years old "to amuse himself" and eventually spent more than a decade on it.* Flowers in the Mirror *is a very complex novel combining historical facts with metaphysical concepts. It takes place during the T'ang Dynasty. Frustrated with the cruel reign of Empress Wu who had usurped the throne in 684 A.D., T'ang Ao decides to leave China and embark on a voyage with his brother-in-law Lin, a merchant, and an old sailor named Tuo. Like Johnathan Swift's Gulliver, they visit several strange lands. Comparing their customs and institutions with those of China they do at times find much to improve in their own country. While on the surface the critique is directed against the situation in T'ang China, it is quite possible to understand it as directed against the China during Li Ju-chen's lifetime. Even in contemporary China, historical topics are at times used in order to point to current problems.*

What attitude toward the rich is reflected in this selection?

They sailed for several days until they came to the Land of the Great. As this country lay next to the Land of Gentlemen, its customs, language and products were much the same. . . .

"I have always wanted to come here," said T'ang, "ever since I heard that the people here ride around on clouds instead of walking. Heaven has granted my wish today."

Having walked for a few hours they approached a mountain and for the first time saw people. They seemed two or three feet taller than men elsewhere and moved around on clouds about half a foot above the ground. Whenever they wanted to stop, the clouds would come to a halt.

When they had climbed the mountain and passed two cliffs a labyrinth of small trails spread before them. . . .

"We have apparently lost our way," said Tuo, "but over there is a temple with a thatched roof. Let's go and ask the monk for directions!"

They walked up to the temple and were just going to knock when an old man in ordinary clothes arrived on his cloud carrying a vessel of wine in one hand and a piece of pork in the other. He opened the gate and was about to enter, when T'ang addressed him: "Excuse me, sir," he said, "could you give us the name of the temple and tell us whether a monk is residing here?" Apologizing, the old man hastened in to put down the wine and meat and upon his return bowed in formal greeting. "This temple is devoted to the Goddess of Mercy, and this insignificant person is the monk here," the old man replied.

"If you are a monk, why is your head not shaved?" Lin asked in astonishment. "And since you appear to drink wine and eat meat, you are probably also keeping nuns?"[1]

"There is only one nun here, my wife," the monk replied. "There are just the two of us living here, and we have been looking after this temple ever since we were young."

"Originally, we had never heard of monks in this country. But when we discovered that ever since the Han Dynasty, people in the Celestial Empire[2] have shaved their heads and

[1]In China, Buddhist monks and nuns were expected to shave their heads, abstain from meat and wine and to remain celibate.

[2]This is another name for China.

called themselves monks and nuns, we decided to follow their example. But we don't shave our heads or fast, and I, as a monk, have a wife who is a nun. May I ask where you three gentlemen come from?"

Once Tuo had told him, the old man made a deep bow, excused himself for not having recognized them as citizens of the Celestial Empire, and invited them in to take some refreshment. T'ang however explained that they still had to cross the mountains and had no time to rest.

"What is the correct name for the offspring of monks and nuns?" Lin asked. "They could hardly be called the same as other children!"

Smiling, the old man replied: "I and my wife are looking after this temple. Since we, like other good citizens don't break the law, steal or engage in illicit sexual relations, why should our children bear a special name? If you can tell me how the children of caretakers of your Confucian halls are called, we are quite willing to use the same word for our children!"

"We observed that all your esteemed fellow-citizens have clouds under their feet," T'ang said. "Is one born with them in this country?"

"They naturally grow from our feet. It is beyond our control," said the old man. "The most honorable are the rainbow-colored clouds, followed by those that are yellow. The others are of equal value, except for the black clouds: they are the lowest."

At Tuo's request, the monk gave them directions, and having passed several hills they arrived at a large city. Everything appeared to be very much the same as in the Land of Gentlemen, only that here the people moved on clouds of various shapes and colors. When a beggar passed them on rainbow-colored clouds, T'ang turned around to Tuo and asked: "Uncle, if rainbow-colored clouds are honored and black clouds are looked down upon, how can this filthy beggar be riding on a rainbow-colored cloud?"

"That monk we met eats pork, drinks wine and took a wife," Lin pointed out, "but he also had a rainbow-colored cloud. Certainly neither of them could be called men of distinguished virtue!"

"When I was here before," Tuo explained, "the same thing intrigued me. I heard that although the colors of the clouds are ranked and some are better than others, this has nothing to do with a person's wealth or position but is entirely dependent on his disposition and character. If a man is true and honest, rainbow-colored clouds will spread under his feet. If he is wicked and malicious, the clouds will be black. The color of the clouds spreading under his feet is determined by his heart. He cannot control it. Because of this, the rich and the influential often have black clouds, while those of the poor are rainbow-colored. Yet in general the morality is high, and in a hundred people you won't discover more than one or two whose clouds are black. And since there is nothing petty-minded about them, this country is being called the Land of the Great by its neighbors. . . ."

At this moment, people started scurrying to the sides of the road to make way for an official. He was truly an imposing sight with his high-brimmed hat of black silk, a wide collar and a purple canopy carried above him to screen him from the sun. Runners and attendants were following him. But at his feet, a red silk veil made it impossible to discern the color of his clouds.

"It is certainly much more convenient for officials here to move around on their clouds. They don't have to use carriages [like our Chinese officials]," remarked T'ang. "But why do they have veils around their feet?"

Tuo explained: "Quite often their clouds turn an ugly grayish-blackish color, and that is considered unlucky. People with clouds of this kind have secretly committed evil deeds. Yet while they are able to fool their countrymen, these clouds have no pity on them: They change into this awful color, and their owners no longer dare to face the world. This is why they have veils around their feet to screen them from the public. This is very much like a robber, who, planning to steal a bell, plugs his own ears. Unless they change their hearts, these unfortunates are incapable of changing the color of their clouds. If, however, their repentance is sincere and they attempt to do good, the color of their clouds will gradually change. But if someone has appeared with unsightly clouds for a very long time, the king will start an investigation and punish him accordingly. His fellow-citizens will avoid him, since he is obviously unwilling to repent and even seems to take pleasure in his evil doing."

"Heaven is not fair," was Lin's reaction to this. "How can you say that?" T'ang asked. "Wouldn't you call it unfair that only here in the Land of the Great these clouds are provided? If there was a signal like this everywhere in the world, and black clouds would spread from every scoundrel's feet and shame him publicly, everyone who saw them could be on their guard. Wouldn't that be wonderful?"

"Well, it is true that not every bad man in the world has black clouds under his feet. But there is black vapor over their heads that reaches Heaven, which is even worse," Tuo replied. "If there is such vapor, why can't I see it?" Lin asked.

"You may not see it," Tuo replied "but Heaven does and distinguishes between good and evil. And all will be judged according to fixed principles, and the good will receive a good end and the evil will receive a bad end."

"If this is true, I will no longer accuse Heaven of being unfair," Lin conceded. They walked around a bit longer and then started back to their ship lest they be late.

Translated by Lydia Gerber

Lin tse-hsü's letter to Queen Victoria, protesting the opium trade (1839)

Lin tse-hsü was the Chinese Commissioner who blockaded British opium ships in the harbor of Canton. He then tried to appeal to Queen Victoria's sense of morality, but failed. The result was the infamous Opium War.

What passages in the letter show that Lin felt the Chinese were superior to the English?

We have read your successive tributary memorials saying, "In general our countrymen who go to trade in China have always received His Majesty the Emperor's gracious treatment and equal justice," and so on. Privately we are delighted with the way in which the honorable rulers of your country deeply understand the grand principles and are grateful for the Celestial grace. For this reason the Celestial Court in soothing those from afar has redoubled its polite and kind treatment. The profit from trade has been enjoyed by them continuously for two hundred years. This is the source from which your country has become known for its wealth.

But after a long period of commercial intercourse, there appear among the crowd of barbarians both good persons and bad, unevenly. Consequently there are those who smuggle opium to seduce the Chinese people and so cause the spread of the poison to all provinces. Such persons who only care to profit themselves, and disregard their harm to others, are not tolerated by the laws of heaven and are unanimously hated by human beings. His Majesty the Emperor, upon hearing of this, is in a towering rage. He has especially sent me, his commissioner, to come to Kwantung, and together with the governor-general and governor jointly to investigate and settle this matter.

All those people in China who sell opium or smoke opium should receive the death penalty. If we trace the crime of those barbarians who through the years have been selling opium, then the deep harm they have wrought and the great profit they have usurped should fundamentally justify their execution according to law. We take into consideration, however, the fact that the various barbarians have still known how to repent their crimes and return to their allegiance to us by taking the 20,183 chests of opium from their storeships and petitioning us, through their consular officer,[1] Elliot, to receive it. It has been entirely destroyed and this has been faithfully reported to the Throne in several memorials by this commissioner and his colleagues. . . .

We find that your country is sixty or seventy thousand *li*[2] from China. Yet there are barbarian ships that strive to come here for trade for the purpose of making a great profit. The wealth of China is used to profit the barbarians. That is to say, the great profit made by barbarians is all taken from the rightful share of China. By what right do they then in return use the poisonous drug to injure the Chinese people? Even though the barbarians may not necessarily intend to do us harm, yet in coveting profit to an extreme, they have no regard for injuring others. Let us ask, where is your conscience? I have heard that the smoking of opium is very strictly forbidden by your country; that is because the harm caused by opium is very clearly understood. Since it is not permitted to do harm to your own country, then even less should you let it be passed on to the harm of other countries—how much less to China! Of all that China exports to foreign countries, there is not a single

[1]Superintendent of trade.

[2]Three *li* equal one mile.

thing which is not beneficial to people: they are of benefit when eaten, or of benefit when used, or of benefit when resold: all are beneficial. Is there a single article from China which has done any harm to foreign countries? Take tea and rhubarb, for example; the foreign countries cannot get along for a single day without them.[3] If China cuts off these benefits with no sympathy for those who are to suffer, then what can the barbarians rely upon to keep themselves alive? Moreover the woolens, camlets, and longells[4] of foreign countries cannot be woven unless they obtain Chinese silk. If China, again, cuts off this beneficial export, what profit can the barbarians expect to make? As for other foodstuffs, beginning with candy, ginger, cinnamon, and so forth, and articles for use, beginning with silk, satin, chinaware, and so on, all the things that must be had by foreign countries are innumerable. On the other hand, articles coming from the outside to China can only be used as toys. We can take them or get along without them. Since they are not needed by China, what difficulty would there be if we closed the frontier and stopped the trade? Nevertheless our Celestial Court lets tea, silk, and other goods be shipped without limit and circulated everywhere without begrudging it in the slightest. This is for no other reason but to share the benefit with the people of the whole world. . . .

Suppose there were people from another country who carried opium for sale to England and seduced your people into buying and smoking it; certainly your honorable ruler would deeply hate it and be bitterly aroused. We have heard heretofore that your honorable ruler is kind and benevolent. Naturally you would not wish to give unto others what you yourself do not want. . . .

May you, O [Queen], check your wicked and sift your vicious people before they come to China, in order to guarantee the peace of your nation, to show further the sincerity of your politeness and submissiveness, and to let the two countries enjoy together the blessings of peace. How fortunate, how fortunate indeed! After receiving this dispatch will you immediately give us a prompt reply regarding the details and circumstances of your cutting off the opium traffic. Be sure not to put this off."

Translated by Ssu-Yu Teng and John K. Fairbank

[3]Although the English might have been hard pressed to do without tea, the Chinese were mistaken in thinking that rhubarb (used as a medicine) was of any great importance to them or could not be grown in their own country.

[4]I.e., textiles.

Japan 1750-1900

Kaibara Ekken or Kaibara Token: *Greater Learning for Women* (1762)

This treatise on proper roles for women was widely influential in the later Edo Period (1600–1868), and denounced as retrograde during the progressive period that followed the Meiji Restoration of 1868. It is commonly attributed to the Confucian scholar Kaibara Ekken (1630–1714), based on its similarities to one of his works; but it has also been suggested that it may be an adaptation of his ideas by his wife, Kaibara Token (1652–1713), also a scholar.

What qualities are considered undesirable in women in this passage?

Seeing that it is a girl's destiny, on reaching womanhood, to go to a new home, and live in submission to her father-in-law and mother-in-law, it is even more incumbent upon her than it is on a boy to receive with all reverence her parents' instructions. Should her parents, through excess of tenderness, allow her to grow up self-willed, she will infallibly show herself capricious in her husband's house, and thus alienate his affection, while, if her father-in-law be a man of correct principles, the girl will find the yoke of these principles intolerable. . . .

More precious in a woman is a virtuous heart than a face of beauty. The vicious woman's heart is ever excited; she glares wildly around her, she vents her anger on others, her words are harsh and her accent vulgar. When she speaks it is to set herself above others, to upbraid others, to envy others, to be puffed up with individual pride, to jeer at others, to outdo others,—all things at variance with the "way" in which a woman should walk. The only qualities that befit a woman are gentle obedience, chastity, mercy, and quietness.

From her earliest youth, a girl should observe the line of demarcation separating women from men; and never, even for an instant, should she be allowed to see or hear the slightest impropriety. The customs of antiquity did not allow men and women to sit in the same apartment, to keep their wearing-apparel in the same place, to bathe in the same place or to transmit to each other anything directly from hand to hand. . . .

Let her never even dream of jealousy. If her husband be dissolute, she must expostulate with him, but never either nurse or vent her anger. If her jealousy be extreme, it will render her countenance frightful and her accents repulsive, and can only result in completely alienating her husband from her, and making her intolerable in his eyes. Should her husband act ill[1] and unreasonably, she must compose her countenance and soften her voice to remonstrate with him; and if he be angry and listen not to the remonstrance, she must wait over a season, and then expostulate with him again when his heart is softened. Never set thyself up against thy husband with harsh features and a boisterous voice! . . .

The five worst maladies that afflict the female mind are: indocility,[2] discontent, slander, jealousy, and silliness. Without any doubt, these five maladies infest seven or eight out of every ten women, and it is from these that arises the inferiority of women to men. A woman should cure them by self-inspection and self-reproach. The worst of them all, and the parent of the other four, is silliness.

[1]Badly.

[2]Lacking submissiveness.

Woman's nature is passive. This passiveness, being of the nature of the night, is dark. Hence, as viewed from the standard of man's nature, the foolishness of woman fails to understand the duties that lie before her very eyes, perceives not the actions that will bring down blame upon her own head, and comprehends not even the things that will bring down calamities on the heads of her husband and children. Neither when she blames and accuses and curses innocent persons, nor when, in her jealousy of others, she thinks to set up herself alone, does she see that she is her own enemy. . . . Again, in the education of her children, her blind affection induces an erroneous system. Such is the stupidity of her character that it is incumbent on her, in every particular, to distrust herself and to obey her husband.

Translated by Basil Hall Chamberlain

Katsu Kokichi: *Musui's Story* *The Autobiography of a Tokugawa Samurai* (1844)

Katsu Kokichi was born into the Samurai class, but began life in extreme poverty and experienced many ups and downs in fortune during a tumultuous career marked by his short temper and sometimes unscrupulous schemes for making money. His autobiography unabashedly and entertainingly recounts the catastrophes he encountered as well as the triumphs. The first part of the following passage is a good example of his candor in revealing his own shortcomings. Suicide was often used as a threat of last resort, since it was a great disgrace to have caused someone else to commit suicide. Katsu prided himself on his swordsmanship, even conducting a school for samurai at one point. The wild and violent impoverished samurai plays much the same role in the lore of Japan as the lawless western gunfighter does in U.S. culture; and Katsu embodies that figure well.

How is Katsu convinced that he should devote himself to his wife rather than to the woman he has become infatuated with?

It was when I was still living on Yamaguchi's property. I became hopelessly smitten with a certain woman. In desperation I told my wife about it.

"Leave everything to me," she said. "I'll get her for you."

"Oh, would you—"

"But first you must give me some time off."

"What ever for?"

"I intend to go to the woman's house and persuade her family one way or another to give her to you. You say they're samurai, too, so they could very well try to put me off. Don't worry, I'll get her for you even if I have to kill myself."

I handed my wife a dagger.

She said, "I'll go tonight and bring her back without fail."

I took off for the day looking for something to do and ran into Tonomura Nanpei. As we stood chatting, he said to me, "Katsu-san, I'll bet you're prone to woman trouble—I can tell by the features on your face. Can you think of any particular problem of that nature?"

I told him about the conversation I'd had with my wife earlier on.

"How very commendable of her," he said and went on his way.

I decided to drop by to see my friend Sekikawa Sanuki, a fortune teller. He took one look at me and said, "Something dreadful's about to happen. Come in and we'll talk about it." Inside, Sanuki went on to say that he could see right away that I was having woman trouble. "And this very night I foresee trouble over a sword. A lot of people may be hurt. Tell me, can you think of anything along these lines?" I told him about my infatuation with a woman and my wife's determination to get her for me. He was speechless at first but then started to give me counsel, saying how fortunate I was to have such a devoted wife and how I should take better care of her in the future. I thought about it for a moment. He was right. I was clearly in the wrong. I flew home.

My wife was just about to leave—she had sent her grandmother with our baby daughter to Hikoshiro's in Kamezawa-cho and had finished writing me a note. It took a lot of talking to convince her to give up the idea, but the incident ended without mishap. It wasn't the first time she got me out of trouble.

After that I tried to be more gentle and considerate to my wife. Until then not a day had passed without my hitting her for one reason or another.

Maybe it's because of these past beatings, but she's suddenly become sickly over the last four or five years. I know what—from now on I'll treat her like the retired lady of the house!

A year before my retirement a great fire had ravaged the Yoshiwara, and many of the pleasure houses had been forced to move to temporary quarters. One day at the Sanotsuchiya—it had been relocated to Yamanoyado—I got into a big fight with Kuma, the son of an employee at the copper mint in Hashiba. We were on the second floor, so I picked up Kuma and threw him down the stairs. He had to be carried home by some men who came running from the mint.

In a while about thirty men appeared with hooked spears. They began surrounding the house. I flung off my outer garments, hitched up the hem of my kimono, and rushed outside swinging my sword. I forced the men to retreat two or three hundred yards, but just then a band of men arrived from the local patrol office to break up the fight.

After this even the crones and shrews who were hired to escort customers to the brothels drew away as soon as they saw me. The brothels in Yamanoyado closed shop for three days, and the incident ended quietly. I was also in a great many other fights, but I've forgotten most of them.

The sword I used that time in Yamanoyado was two feet four inches. In another fight—I'd gone with Tarao Shichirosaburo, Otani Chujiro, and several others to the Asakusa fair—I had with me the sword made by Seki no Kane . . . It was two feet seven inches long and had a leather loop at the tip of the scabbard.

Tarao had asked me at the last minute, and I'd had no time to put on my hakama. In the crush of people going through the Kaminarimon gate, my sword got caught in the folds of my kimono. Unable to move my legs, I was carried forward willy-nilly by the crowd.

Out of the blue a man hit Tarao on the head with a big wooden pestle. A samurai, no less. Even while jostled by the crowd, I tried to hold the fellow back by his haori, but he hit me on the shoulder with the pestle. Then when I tried to draw my sword, the tip of the scabbard got caught. "Just wait—I'll cut you to pieces!" I roared. The people around me shied away, so I whipped out my sword and struck at the samurai.

The blade grazed his back in a straight line, slashing his obi and making his pouch and pair of swords fall out. He ran off without stopping to pick up his belongings.

A man from the guard station at Denboin came with a long stick. I waved my sword in his face a couple of times and sent the passersby flying. I scooped up the swords and pouch and threw them into the guard station. My friends and I headed immediately for Okuyama.

I had to admit that in a crowd a long sword had its drawbacks—the blade must have barely skimmed the samurai. Tarao got a nasty cut right on his bald head, too. We picked fights along the way and went as far as Ryogoku Bridge. That evening, with nothing special to do, I went home.

There were scores of other adventures, but they took place so long ago I have all but forgotten them.

Translated by Teruko Craig

Fukuzumi Masae: The "Pill" of the Three Religions

Fukuzumi's life spanned two major episodes in modern Japanese history, the fall of the Tokugawa Shogunate (1600–1868) and the modernization efforts of the Meiji Restoration (1868–1912). As the disciple of Ninomiya Sonotoku (1787–1856), a champion of the peasantry, Fukuzumi perpetuated his master's teachings of exhorting the peasantry to return to the rural foundation of Japanese tradition. In the early 20th century, he organized the "Society for Returning Virtue" with the twin goals of helping the Japanese people to return to their rural roots and uniting the poor peasants so they could help each other. The passage below is an explanation of both the complexity and basis of Japanese culture.

Discuss the different roles Shinto, Confucianism, and Buddhism played in traditional Japanese society.

Old Ninomiya once said, "I have long pondered about Shinto—what it calls the Way, what are its virtues and what its deficiencies; and about Confucianism—what its teaching consists in, what are its virtues and deficiencies; and also about Buddhism—what do its various sects stand for, and what are their virtues and deficiencies. And so I wrote a poem:

Yo no naka wa	The things of this world
Sute ajirogi no	Are like lengths
Take-kurabe	Of bamboo rod
Sore kore tomo ni	For use in fish nets—
Nagashi mijikashi	This one's too long,
	That one too short.

"Such was my dissatisfaction with them. Now let me state the strong and weak points of each. Shinto is the Way which provides the foundation of the country; Confucianism is the Way which provides for governing the country; and Buddhism is the Way which provides for governing one's mind. Caring no more for lofty speculation than for humble truth, I have tried simply to extract the essence of each of these teachings. By essence I mean their importance to mankind. Selecting what is important and discarding what is unimportant, I have arrived at the best teaching for mankind, which I call the teaching of Repaying Virtue. I also call it the 'pill containing the essence of Shinto, Confucianism and Buddhism. . . .'"

Kimigasa Hyodayu asked the proportions of the prescription in this "pill," and the old man replied, "One spoon of Shinto, and a half-spoon each of Confucianism and Buddhism."

Then someone drew a circle, one half of which was marked Shinto and two quarter-segments labeled Confucianism and Buddhism respectively. "Is it like this?" he asked. The old man smiled. "You won't find medicine like that anywhere. In a real pill all the ingredients are thoroughly blended so as to be indistinguishable. Otherwise it would taste bad in the mouth and feel bad in the stomach. . . ."

The old man said: "The Buddhists say that this life is temporary and only the life hereafter is important. Nevertheless, we have obligations to our masters, our parents, our wives, and our children. Even if we could renounce this world, leaving behind our masters and parents and wives and children, still our bodily life goes on. And as long as our bodily life goes on, we cannot do without food and clothing. In this world you cannot get across the river or sea without paying the boat fare. So Saigyo says in his poem:

Sute hatete	Having renounced all,
Mi wa naki mono to	I feel myself utterly nonexistent,
Omoedomo	And yet when it snows,
Yuki no furu hi wa	I know
Samuku koso are	How cold I am!"

Translated b y Ryusaku Tsunoda

Fukuzawa Yukichi: Chinese vs. Western Learning (1899)

Born in 1834 into a lower samurai family in the province of Buzen in Northern Kyushu, Fukuzawa Yukichi would emerge as perhaps the most influential intellectual of his generation. A fervent advocate of modernization, his ideas transformed an entire generation of youths and intellectuals of the Meiji Era (1868-1912). His three-volume work, Conditions of the West, *published 1866–1870, provided the Japanese people with their initial glimpse of the everyday social practices and institutions of America and Europe. Fukuzawa's later works, in particular* An Encouragement of Learning *(1872–1876) and* An Outline of Civilization *(1875) severely criticized the paternalistic, hierarchic, and repressive values of traditional Japanese society while highly praising the individualistic, egalitarian, and progressive ideals of modern Western society. Reflecting the fact that Japan had borrowed heavily from China in the past, Fukuzawa critiques the ineffectiveness of the Chinese tradition in modern society.*

Why did Fukuzawa believe that Japan must abandon classical Chinese learning and adopt Western learning? What are some of his most severe criticisms of classical Chinese learning?

To show that my belief in the underlying anti-foreign spirit of the regime was not groundless, I can cite an instance of a proceeding of the time.

Soon after the Restoration—either in the first or second year of the Meiji era—an English prince arrived to pay a formal visit at the Tokyo castle. It seems there was much discussion as to the ethics of conducting a foreign visitor into the imperial presence. It was decided that some ritual of purification of the English prince would be proper before he crossed the bridge (Nijubashi) over the moat to the castle. All this became the basis of a ridiculous incident. At that time the acting minister from the United States was Mr. Portman. It seemed that the President of the United States was not in the habit of personally reading the reports of the ministers in foreign lands unless they contained unusual or very pertinent matters. Now, when Mr. Portman heard of this purification of the English prince, he realized it would be a good episode to base his message on and thus have it reach the President. So he headed his report with the remarkable title, "The Purification of the Duke of Edinburgh." It continued something like this:

"Japan is a small secluded country, very self-respecting and very self-important. It is customary, therefore, for its inhabitants to regard foreigners as belonging to the lower order of animals, below human beings. Actually, when the English prince arrived to be received by the Emperor, they held a ceremony of purification over the person of the prince at the entrance to the castle. This ritual of purification traces its history to ancient times when water was used in cleansing the bodies of persons entering sacred precincts. In the middle ages when paper was invented, they simplified the ceremony by substituting paper for water. In this reformed rite, they use a streamer of paper at the end of a staff which is called gohei. The body of the subject is swept by this staff and so is cleansed of all impurities and pollution. Such being the ancient rite in the land, they employed this method on the person of the Duke of Edinburgh, because in the eyes of the Japanese, all foreigners, whether of noble lineage or common, are alike impure as animals."

So ran the clever report of the American then serving as interpreter at the American embassy. Seki told me minutely of this incident, repeating as closely as he remembered the words of the original message. He laughed over it, thinking it a good joke on our government. But I did not laugh; I felt like crying over this revelation of our national superstition.

About that time the former American Secretary of State, Mr. Seward, arrived with his daughter on a tour through Japan. He was a noted statesman in America, having been Secretary under Abraham Lincoln, and at the time of the assassination he had also been attacked. Mr. Seward had never been congenial with the English, but had always shown friendship for Japan. But now on his tour in the country itself, he declared that after seeing the condition of things, he could not say much more in commendation of Japan. He was sorry, he said, but Japan with her stubborn inflexible nature would hardly be expected to keep her independence.

In truth I could see that the officials of the government knew nothing better than the dregs of the Chinese philosophy with which to guide their actions. So they were simply lording it over the people with arrogance and pretense, and there was little that pointed to the establishment of the new culture. Now that I had the corroboration of the foreign statesman, Mr. Seward, I was truly discouraged.

Yet I was Japanese and I could not sit still. If I could do nothing toward improving the condition of politics, I could at least try something by teaching what I had learned of Western culture to the young men of my land, and by translating Western books and writing my own. Then perhaps through good fortune I might be able to lead my countrymen out of their present obscurity. So, helpless but resolute, I took my stand alone.

I have never told anyone of the dire, helpless state of my mind at that time. But I will confess it now. Watching the unfortunate condition of the country, I feared in reality that we might not be able to hold our own against foreign aggressiveness. Yet no one in all the land was there with whom I could talk over my anxiety—no one anywhere, east, west, north or south, as I searched whom I could depend upon. I seemed alone in my anxiety and I knew I did not have the power to save my country.

If in the future there should come signs of foreign aggression, and we were to be subjected to insult from foreigners, I would probably find some way to extricate myself. But when I thought of my children in the more distant future, again I was afraid. They should never fall into the power of the foreigners; I would save them with my own life first. At one time I thought even of having my sons enter the Christian priesthood. If in that calling they could be independent of others in their living, and if they could, be accepted as Christian priests, I thought, my sons would be spared any insult or injury. So, in my anxiety, though I was not a believer in that religion, I once planned to make priests of my boys.

As I look back today—over thirty years since—it all seems a dream. How advanced and secure the country is now! I can do nothing but bless with a full heart this glorious enlightenment of Japan today. . . .

[O]urs was the only center in the country where Western learning was being taught. Indeed, I think it was until after the completion of *haihan-chiken* (the abolition of the clan system and the organization of the prefectural government) that Keio-gijuku remained the only school specializing in European studies. After that, the department of education was established and the government began to give more attention to the general education. Our own school went on in the same way, the number of students being always between two and three hundred.

The chief subject of instruction in my school was English, and the Chinese, which was the basis of all previous education in Japan, was left in the second place. So it happened that there were many students who could not read Chinese at all though they were reading

English with ease. Things were reversed in my school. While elsewhere the boys had to know Chinese before taking up English, we were teaching English first and Chinese later.

There was Hatano Shogoro, for instance, who at first had difficulty in reading even his letters from home. But he was especially gifted and had a spirit keen for literature. He went on and quickly mastered the Chinese classics, and became, as everyone knows today, an accomplished scholar.

The final purpose of all my work was to create in Japan a civilized nation, as well equipped in both the arts of war and peace as those of the Western world. I acted as if I had become the sole functioning agent for the introduction of Western culture. It was natural then that I should be disliked by the older type of Japanese, and suspected of working for the benefit of foreigners. In my interpretation of education, I try to be guided by the laws of nature in man and the universe, and I try to coordinate all the physical actions of human beings by the very simple laws of "number and reason." In spiritual or moral training, I regard the human being as the most sacred and responsible of all orders, unable therefore, in reason, to do anything base. So in self-respect, a man cannot change his sense of humanity, his justice, his loyalty or anything belonging to his manhood even when driven by circumstances to do so. In short, my creed is that a man should find his faith in independence and self-respect.

From my own observations in both the Occidental and Oriental civilizations, I find that each has certain strong points and weak points bound up in its moral teaching and scientific theory. But when I examine which excels the other as to wealth, armament, and general well-being, I have to put the Orient below the Occident. Granting that a nation's destiny depends upon the education of its people, there must be some fundamental difference in the education of the Western and Eastern peoples.

In the education of the East, so often saturated with Confucian teaching, I find two points lacking; that is to say, the lack of studies in "number and reason" in material culture, and the lack of the idea of independence in the spiritual culture. But in the West I think I see why their statesmen are successful in managing their national affairs, and the businessmen in theirs, and the people generally ardent in their patriotism and keen in their family circles.

I regret that in our country I have to acknowledge that people are not formed in these two principles though I believe no one can escape the laws of "number and reason" nor can anyone depend on anything but the doctrine of independence as long as nations are to exist and mankind is to thrive. Japan could not assert herself among the great nations of the world without full recognition and practice of these two principles. And so I reasoned that Chinese philosophy as the root of education was responsible for our obvious shortcomings.

With this as the fundamental theory of education, I began instructing young men in the fields of "number and reason." And though lacking both funds and equipment, I did what I could in teaching the rudiments of sciences. On the other hand I always took the opportunity in public speech, in my writing, and in casual conversations, to advocate my doctrine of independence. Also I tried in many ways to demonstrate the theory in my actual life. During my endeavor, I came to believe less than ever in the old Chinese teachings.

So today, when many of the former students of Keio-gijuku have gone out into the world of men, if I hear that they are practicing the sciences of "number and reason" whatever business they may follow, if I hear that they are upright in character, sharing in the principle of independence—that is the chief pleasure I find in enlivening my old age.

It is not only that I hold little regard for the Chinese teachings, but I have even been endeavoring to drive its degenerate influences from my country. It is not unusual for scholars in Western learning and for interpreters of languages to make this denouncement. But too often they lack the knowledge of Chinese which would make their attacks truly effective. But I know a good deal of Chinese, for I have given real effort to study it under a strict teacher. And I am familiar with most of the references made from histories, ethics and poetry. Even the peculiarly subtle philosophy of Lao Tzu and Chuang Tzu, I have studied after hearing any teacher lecture on them. All of this experience I owe to the great scholar of Nakatsu, Shiraishi. So, while I frequently pretend that I do not know much, I often take advantage of the more delicate points for attack both in my writings and speeches. I realize I am a pretty disagreeable opponent of the Chinese scholars—"a worm in the lion's body."

The true reason of my opposing the Chinese culture with such vigor is my belief that as long as the old retrogressive doctrine of the Chinese school remains at all in our young men's minds, our country can never enter the rank of civilized nations of the world. In my determination to save our coming generation from this detrimental influence, I was prepared even to face, single-handed, the Chinese scholars of the country as a whole.

Gradually the new education was showing its results among the younger generation; yet men of middle age or past, who held responsible positions, were for the most part uninformed as to the true spirit of the Western culture, and so whenever they had to make decisions, they turned invariably to their Chinese sources for guidance. And so again and again I had to rise up and denounce the all-important Chinese influence before this weighty opposition. It was not altogether a very safe road for my reckless spirit to follow.

Translated by Eiichi Kiyooka

Europe 1750–1900

Voltaire: *A Treatise on Toleration* (1763)

Voltaire was the most eloquent and tireless advocate of the anti-dogmatic movement known as "The Enlightenment." He argued in favor of "deism," a vague substitute for traditional religion which acknowledged a creator and some sort of divine justice, but rejected most of the other fundamental beliefs of Christianity. Instead he preached that all are obliged to tolerate each other. When he defends even false religion as superior to none, it is obvious that his objections to atheism are superficial and that he looks on religious beliefs as useful, but not necessarily true. It should be remembered that atheism was strictly illegal in Voltaire's time, and he had been imprisoned repeatedly and finally exiled for his challenges to traditional religion. Deism provided a convenient (and legal) screen for his attacks on Christianity; but many scholars believe that despite his statements to the contrary, he was in fact an atheist. His arguments for religious freedom have become commonplaces in the modern Western world, even among religious believers.

What reasons does Voltaire give that we should all tolerate each other?

Whether it is Useful to Maintain People in their Superstition

Such is the feebleness of humanity, such is its perversity, that doubtless it is better for it to be subject to all possible superstitions, as long as they are not murderous, than to live without religion. Man always needs a rein, and even if it might be ridiculous to sacrifice to fauns, or sylvans, or naiads,[1] it is much more reasonable and more useful to venerate these fantastic images of the Divine than to sink into atheism. An atheist who is rational, violent, and powerful, would be as great a pestilence as a blood-mad, superstitious man.

When men do not have healthy notions of the Divinity, false ideas supplant them, just as in bad times one uses counterfeit money when there is no good money. The pagan feared to commit any crime, out of fear of punishment by his false gods; the Malabarian[2] fears to be punished by his pagoda.[3] Wherever there is a settled society, religion is necessary; the laws cover manifest crimes, and religion covers secret crimes.

But whenever human faith comes to embrace a pure and holy religion, superstition not only becomes useless, but very dangerous. We should not seek to nourish ourselves on acorns when God gives us bread.

Superstition is to religion what astrology is to astronomy: the foolish daughter of a very wise mother. These two daughters, superstition and astrology, have subjugated the world for a long time.

When, in our ages of barbarity, scarcely two feudal lords owned between them a single New Testament, it might be pardonable to offer fables to the vulgar, that is, to these feudal lords, to their imbecile wives, and to their brutish vassals; they were led to believe that

[1]Ancient Greek demigods.

[2]Inhabitant of the Malabar Coast in India.

[3]Voltaire mistakenly supposes a pagoda to be a god rather than a building.

Saint Christopher carried the infant Jesus from one side of a river to the other; they were fed stories about sorcerers and their spiritual possessions; they easily imagined that Saint Genou[4] would cure the gout, and that Saint Claire[5] would cure eye problems. The children believed in the werewolf, and the fathers in the rope girdle of Saint Francis. The number of relics[6] was innumerable.

The sediment of these superstitions still survived among the people, even at that time that religion was purified. We know that when Monsieur de Noailles, the Bishop of Châlons, removed and threw into the fire the false relic of the holy navel of Jesus Christ, then the entire village of Châlons began proceedings against him; however, he had as much courage as he had piety, and he succeeded in making the Champenois believe that they could adore Jesus Christ in spirit and truth, without having his navel in the church.

Those we call Jansenists[7] contributed greatly to rooting out gradually from the spirit of the nation the greater part of the false ideas which dishonored the Christian religion. People ceased to believe that it was sufficient to recite a prayer to the Virgin Mary for thirty days so that they could do what they wish and sin with impunity the rest of the year.

Finally the bourgeoisie began to realize that it was not Saint Geneviève who gave or withheld rain, but that it was God Himself who disposed of the elements. The monks were astonished that their saints did not bring about miracles any longer; and if the writers of *The Life of Saint Francis Xavier* returned to the world, they would not dare to write that the saint revived nine corpses, that he was in two places, on the sea and on land, at the same time, and that his crucifix fell into the sea and was restored to him by a crab.

It is the same with excommunications. Our historians tells us that when King Robert was excommunicated by Pope Gregory V, for marrying his godmother, the princess Bertha, his domestic servants threw the meats to be served to the king right out the window, and Queen Bertha gave birth to a goose in punishment for the incestuous marriage. One could seriously doubt that in this day and age the servants of the king of France, if he were excommunicated, would throw his dinner out the window, or that the queen would give birth to a goose.

There are still a few convulsive fanatics[8] in remote corners of the suburbs; but this disease only attacks the most vile population. Each day reason penetrates further into France, into the shops of merchants as well as the mansions of lords. We must cultivate the fruits of this reason, especially since it is impossible to check its advance. One cannot govern France, after it has been enlightened by Pascal, Nicole, Arnauld, Bossuiet, Descartes, Gassendi, Bayle, Fontenelle, and the others, as it as been governed in the times of Garasse and Menot.

If the masters of errors, and I'm speaking here of the grand masters, so long paid and honored for abusing the human species, ordered us today to believe that the seed must die in order to germinate; that the world is immovable on its foundations, that it does not orbit around the sun; that the tides are not a natural effect of gravitation; that the rainbow is not formed by the refraction and the reflection of rays of light, and so on, and they based

[4]His name means "knee" in French.

[5]Her name suggests light.

[6] Physical remains of saints, either their body parts, clothing, or any other physical object associated with them; these relics were supposed to display remarkable curative and other magical properties.

[7]Reformers who agreed in many ways with Protestant ideas.

[8]Ecstatics who fell into religious fits.

their ordinances on passages poorly understood from the Holy Bible, how would educated men regard these men? Would the term "beasts" seem too strong? And if these wise masters used force and persecution to enforce their insolent stupidity, would the term "wild beasts" seem too extreme?

The more the superstitions of monks are despised, the more the bishops are respected and the priests listened to; while they do no good, these monkish superstitions from over the mountains[9] do a great deal of harm. But of all these superstitions, is not the most dangerous that of hating your neighbor for his opinions? And is it not evident that it would be much more reasonable to worship the Holy Navel, the Holy Foreskin, or the milk or the robe of the Virgin Mary,[10] than to detest and persecute your brother?

Virtue is Better than Science

The fewer dogmas, the fewer disputes; the fewer disputes, the fewer miseries: if this is not true, then I'm wrong.

Religion was instituted to make us happy in this life and in the other. What must we do to be happy in the life to come? Be just.

What must we do in order to be happy in this life, as far as the misery of our nature permits? Be indulgent.

It would be the height of folly to pretend to improve all men to the point that they think in a uniform manner about metaphysics. It would be easier to subjugate the entire universe through force of arms than to subjugate the minds of a single village. . . .

On Universal Tolerance

It does not require great art, or magnificently trained eloquence, to prove that Christians should tolerate each other. I, however, am going further: I say that we should regard all men as our brothers. What? The Turk my brother? The Chinaman my brother? The Jew? The Siam? Yes, without doubt; are we not all children of the same father and creatures of the same God?

But these people despise us; they treat us as idolaters! Very well! I will tell them that they are grievously wrong. It seems to me that I would at least astonish the proud, dogmatic Islam imam or Buddhist priest, if I spoke to them as follows:

"This little globe, which is but a point, rolls through space, as do many other globes; we are lost in the immensity of the universe. Man, only five feet high, is assuredly only a small thing in creation. One of these imperceptible beings says to another one of his neighbors, in Arabia or South Africa: 'Listen to me, because God of all these worlds has enlightened me: there are nine hundred million little ants like us on the earth, but my ant-hole is the only one dear to God; all the other are cast off by Him for eternity; mine alone will be happy, and all the others will be eternally damned.'"

They would then interrupt me, and ask which fool blabbed all this nonsense. I would be obliged to answer,"You, yourselves." I would then endeavor to calm them, which would be very difficult.

---

[9] Rome.

[10] These are all relics actually venerated in his time.

I would then speak with the Christians, and I would dare to say, for example, to a Dominican Inquisitor of the Faith:[11] "My brother, you know that each province of Italy has its own dialect, and that people do not speak at Venice or Bergamo the same way they speak at Florence. The Academy of Crusca near Florence has fixed the language; its dictionary is a rule which one dare not depart from, and the *Grammar* of Buonmattei is an infallible guide that one must follow. But do you believe that the consul of the Academy, or Buonmattei in his absence, could in conscience cut the tongues out of all the Venetians and all the Bergamese who persist in speaking their dialect?"

The inquisitor responds, "There is a difference between your example and our practice. For us, it is a matter of the health of your soul. It is for your good that the director of the Inquisition ordains that you be siezed on the testimony of a single person, however infamous or criminal that person might be; that you will have no advocate to defend you; that the name of your accuser will not even be known by you; that the inquisitor can promise you mercy, and immediately condemn you; that five different tortures will be applied to you, and then you will be flogged, or sent to the galleys, or ceremoniously burned. Father Ivonet, Doctor Cuchalon, Zanchinus, Campegius, Roias, Felynus, Gomarus, Diabarus, Gemelinus, are explicit on this point, and this pious practice cannot suffer any contradiction."

I would take the liberty to respond, "My brother, perhaps you are reasonable; I am convinced that you wish to do me good; but could I not be saved without all that?"

It is true that these absurd horrors do not stain the face of the earth every day; but they are frequent, and they could easily fill a volume much greater than the gospels which condemn them.[12] Not only is it extremely cruel to persecute in this brief life those who do not think the way we do, but I do not know if it might be too presumptuous to declare their eternal damnation. It seems to me that it does not pertain to the atoms of the moment, such as we are, to anticipate the decrees of the Creator.

Translated by Richard Hooker

[11]The Dominicans ran the notorious Inquisition which tortured and condemned to death people who departed from orthodox Catholicism.

[12]Note how he slips in this comment, arguing that the Inquisition itself is contrary to the teachings of Christ.

Jean-Jacques Rousseau: *The Social Contract* (1762)

Jean-Jacques Rousseau, in The Social Contract, *propounds a doctrine which already had a long history in the struggle against the older view of the divine right of kings, namely, that government gets its authority over us by a willing consent on our part, not by the authorization of God. While Rousseau's famous opening line condemns the society of his day for its limiting of our natural spontaneity (indeed, its corruption of our natural goodness), he thinks that a good government can be justified in terms of the compromise to which each of us submits so as to gain "civil liberty and the proprietorship of all he possesses." Rousseau even thinks that we mature as human beings in such a social setting, where we are not simply driven by our appetites and desires, but become self-governing, self-disciplined beings.*

How, as Rousseau himself asks, can one enter into an agreement which limits one's power without thereby "harming his own interests and neglecting the care he owes to himself?" What is the difference between "natural liberty" and "civil liberty"?

Subject of the First Book

Man is born free; and everywhere he is in chains. One thinks himself the master of others, and still remains a greater slave than they. How did this change come about? I do not know. What can make it legitimate? That question I think I can answer.

If I took into account only force, and the effects derived from it, I should say: "As long as a people is compelled to obey, and obeys, it does well; as soon as it can shake off the yoke, and shakes it off, it does still better; for, regaining its liberty by the same right as took it away, either it is justified in resuming it, or there was no justification for those who took it away." But the social order is a sacred right which is the basis of all rights. Nevertheless, this right does not come from nature, and must therefore be founded on conventions. . . .[1]

Slavery

Since no man has a natural authority over his fellow, and force creates no right, we must conclude that conventions form the basis of all legitimate authority among men.

The Social Compact

I suppose men to have reached the point at which the obstacles in the way of their preservation in the state of nature show their power of resistance to be greater than the resources at the disposal of each individual for his maintenance in that state. That primitive condition can then subsist no longer; and the human race would perish unless it changed its manner of existence.

But, as men cannot engender new forces, but only unite and direct existing ones, they have no other means of preserving themselves than the formation, by aggregation, of a sum of forces great enough to overcome the resistance. These they have to bring into play by means of a single motive power, and cause to act in concert.[2]

This sum of forces can arise only where several persons come together: but, as the force and liberty of each man are the chief instruments of his self-preservation, how can he

[1]That is, agreements which are not inevitable but are entered into voluntarily.
[2]Jointly.

pledge them without harming his own interests, and neglecting the care he owes to himself? This difficulty, in its bearing on my present subject, may be stated in the following terms:

"The problem is to find a form of association which will defend and protect with the whole common force the person and goods of each associate, and in which each, while uniting himself with all, may still obey himself alone, and remain as free as before." This is the fundamental problem of which the *Social Contract* provides the solution. . . .

The Civil State

The passage[3] from the state of nature to the civil state produces a very remarkable change in man, by substituting justice for instinct in his conduct, and giving his actions the morality they had formerly lacked. Then only, when the voice of duty takes the place of physical impulses and right of appetite, does man, who so far had considered only himself, find that he is forced to act on different principles, and to consult his reason before listening to his inclinations. Although, in this state, he deprives himself of some advantages which he got from nature, he gains in return others so great, his faculties are so stimulated and developed, his ideas so extended, his feelings so ennobled, and his whole soul so uplifted that, did not the abuses of this new condition often degrade him below that which he left, he would be bound to bless continually the happy moment which took him from it for ever, and, instead of a stupid and unimaginative animal, made him an intelligent being and a man.

Let us draw up the whole account in terms easily commensurable. What man loses by the social contract is his natural liberty and an unlimited right to everything he tries to get and succeeds in getting; what he gains is civil liberty and the proprietorship of all he possesses. If we are to avoid mistakes in weighing one against the other, we must clearly distinguish natural liberty, which is bounded only by the strength of the individual, from civil liberty, which is limited by the general will; and possession, which is merely the effect of force or the right of the first occupier, from property, which can be founded only on a positive title.

We might, over and above all this, add, to what man acquires in the civil state, moral liberty, which alone makes him truly master of himself; for the mere impulse of appetite is slavery, while obedience to a law which we prescribe to ourselves is liberty. . . .

Translated by G. D. H. Cole

[3]Transition.

The Declaration of the Rights of Man (August 27, 1789)

Drawing on the ideas of Rousseau and other Enlightenment thinkers, the French National Assembly exalted the idea of laws democratically passed as supreme; no longer would the sovereign will of a monarch be able to override all legal restrictions. The rulers of the rest of Europe confidently predicted that mob rule would result in severe restrictions on liberty, and that is in fact what occurred. Yet after a delay of a half a century, these ideas were to be accepted by those very nations.

Which provisions seem particularly aimed at taking away the privileges of the aristocracy?Explain which of these rights you think are the most important? Which one seem less important? Why?

The representative of the French people, organized as a National Assembly, believing that the ignorance, neglect or contempt of the rights of man are the sole cause of public calamities and of the corruption of governments, have determined to set forth in a solemn declaration the natural, inalienable and sacred rights of man, in order that this declaration, being constantly before all the members of the social body, shall remind them continually of their rights and duties; in order that the acts of the legislative power, as well as those of the executive power, may be compared at any moment with the ends[1] of all political institutions and may thus be more respected; and, lastly, in order that the grievances of the citizens, based hereafter upon simple and incontestable principles, shall tend to the maintenance of the constitution and redound to the happiness of all. Therefore the National Assembly recognizes and proclaims, in the presence and under the auspices of the Supreme Being, the following rights of man and of the citizen:—

ARTICLE 1. Men are born and remain free and equal in rights. Social distinctions may only be founded upon the general good.

2. The aim of all political association is the preservation of the natural and imprescriptible[2] rights of man. These rights are liberty, property, security and resistance to oppression.

3. The principle of all sovereignty resides essentially in the nation. No body nor individual may exercise any authority which does not proceed directly from the nation.

4. Liberty consists in the freedom to do everything which injures no one else; hence the exercise of the natural rights of each man has no limits except those which assure to the other members of the society the enjoyment of the same rights. These limits can only be determined by law.

5. Law can only prohibit such actions as are hurtful to society. Nothing may be prevented which is not forbidden by law, and no one may be forced to do anything not provided for by law.

6. Law is the expression of the general will. Every citizen has a right to participate personally or through his representative in its formation. It must be the same for all, whether it protects or punishes. All citizens, being equal in the eyes of the law, are equally eligible to all dignities and to all public positions and occupations, according to their abilities, and without distinction except that of their virtues and talents.

---

[1] Purposes.

[2] Not able to be confined by law because they are natural.

7. No person shall be accused, arrested or imprisoned except in the cases and according to the forms prescribed by law. Any one soliciting, transmitting, executing or causing to be executed any arbitrary order shall be punished. But any citizen summoned or arrested in virtue of the law shall submit without delay, as resistance constitutes an offense.

8. The law shall provide for such punishments only as are strictly and obviously necessary, and no one shall suffer punishment except it be legally inflicted in virtue of a law passed and promulgated before the commission of the offense.

9. As all persons are held innocent until they shall have been declared guilty, if arrest shall be deemed indispensable, all harshness not essential to the securing of the prisoner's person shall be severely repressed by law.

10. No one shall be disquieted on account of his opinions, including his religious views, provided their manifestation does not disturb the public order established by law.

11. The free communication of ideas and opinions is one of the most precious of the rights of man. Every citizen may, accordingly, speak, write and print with freedom, but shall be responsible for such abuses of this freedom as shall be defined by law.

12. The security of the rights of man and of the citizen requires public military force. These forces are, therefore, established for the good of all and not for the personal advantage of those to whom they shall be entrusted.

13. A common contribution is essential for the maintenance of the public forces and for the cost of administration. This should be equitably distributed among all the citizens in proportion to their means.[3]

14. All the citizens have a right to decide, either personally or by their representatives, as to the necessity of the public contribution; to grant this freely; to know to what uses it is put; and to fix the proportion, the mode of assessment, and of collection, and the duration of the taxes.

15. Society has the right to require of every public agent an account of his administration.

16. A society in which the observance of the law is not assured, nor the separation of powers defined, has no constitution at all.

17. Since property is an inviolable and sacred right, no one shall be deprived thereof except where public necessity, legally determined, shall clearly demand it, and then only on condition that the owner shall have been previously and equitably indemnified.

Translated by James Harvey Robinson

[3]In pre-revolutionary France the wealthy nobles had been exempt from taxation.

Adam Smith: *An Inquiry into the Nature and Causes of the Wealth of Nations* (1776)

This Scottish economist is the most influential thinker in the history of capitalist economics, a fact that is all the more remarkable in that he was writing during the earliest phases of the industrial revolution. He is still cited in support of arguments for an unregulated economy: the less government interferes with business the more prosperous the nation will be, runs this theory. Although not an absolutist (he did believe that some tariffs were necessary), he generally opposed restrictions on international trade. These arguments have been repeated in recent years in the U.S. in regard to such Japanese imports as automobiles and in the context of debates over the North American Free Trade Agreement (NAFTA) and the General Agreement on Tariffs and Trade (GATT).

Which group does Smith seem to be trying most to protect: workers, manufacturers, or consumers? Explain.

The Case for Free Trade and Lower Taxes

By restraining, either by high duties, or by absolute prohibitions, the importation of such goods from foreign countries as can be produced at home, the monopoly of the home-market is more or less secured to the domestic industry employed in producing them. Thus the . . . high duties upon the importation of corn,[1] which in times of moderate plenty amount to a prohibition, give a like advantage to the growers of that commodity. The prohibition of the importation of foreign woolens is equally favorable to the woolen manufacturers. The silk manufacture, though altogether employed upon foreign materials, has lately obtained the same advantage. The linen manufacture has not yet obtained it, but is making great strides towards it. Many other sorts of manufacturers have, in the same manner, obtained in Great Britain, either altogether, or very nearly a monopoly against their countrymen. . . .

That this monopoly of the home-market frequently gives great encouragement to that particular species of industry which enjoys it . . . cannot be doubted. But whether it tends either to increase the general industry of the society, or to give it the most advantageous direction, is not, perhaps, altogether so evident. . . .

The natural advantages which one country has over another in producing particular commodities are sometimes so great, that it is acknowledged by all the world to be in vain to struggle with them. By means of glasses, hotbeds, and hotwalls, very good grapes can be raised in Scotland, and very good wine too can be made of them at about thirty times the expense for which at least equally good can be brought from foreign countries. Would it be a reasonable law to prohibit the importation of all foreign wines, merely to encourage the making of claret and burgundy in Scotland? But if there would be a manifest absurdity in turning towards any employment, thirty times more of the capital and industry of the country, than would be necessary to purchase from foreign countries an equal quantity of the commodities wanted, there must be an absurdity, though not altogether so glaring, yet exactly of the same kind, in turning towards any such employment a thirtieth, or even a three hundredth part more of either. . . . As long as the one country has those advantages,

[1]Grains such as wheat.

and the other wants[2] them, it will always be more advantageous for the latter, rather to buy of the former than to make. It is an acquired advantage only, which one artificer has over his neighbor, who exercises another trade; and yet they both find it more advantageous to buy of one another, than to make what does not belong to their particular trades.

Merchants and manufacturers are the people who derive the greatest advantage from this monopoly of the home market. The prohibition of the importation of foreign cattle, and of salt provisions, together with the high duties upon foreign corn, which in times of moderate plenty amount to a prohibition, are not near so advantageous to the graziers and farmers of Great Britain, as other regulations of the same kind are to its merchants and manufacturers. Manufactures, those of the finer kind especially, are more easily transported from one country to another than corn or cattle. It is in the fetching and carrying manufactures, accordingly, that foreign trade is chiefly employed. In manufactures, a very small advantage will enable foreigners to undersell our own workmen, even in the home market. It will require a very great one to enable them to do so in the rude produce of the soil. If the free importation of foreign manufacturers were permitted, several of the home manufactures would probably suffer, and some of them, perhaps, go to ruin altogether, and a considerable part of the stock and industry at present employed in them, would be forced to find out some other employment. But the freest importation of the rude produce of the soil could have no such effect upon the agriculture of the country.

---

[2]Lacks.

G.W.F. Hegel: Introduction to the *Lectures on the Philosophy of History* (1840 edition)

G.W.F. Hegel has summarized much of his all-encompassing system of philosophy in the introduction to a series of lectures on world history. He sees an inevitable progress taking place through history: the coming-into-its-own of consciousness, which he also calls "spirit." That word covers both the mind of the individual person and what we might call the "mind of an age," which is the whole of what people think and value, as passed on and developed through culture (i.e., shared language, morality, science, art, religion and philosophy). The self-understanding of such spirit is liberating, in that our realization that we are free (or can be free) actually makes us free! Just as a single human being progresses from childhood through youth to maturity, so, Hegel thinks, human cultures have progressed from what he calls the "Oriental world" through the Greek and Roman experiences and into the "Christian world," by which he means medieval and modern Europe.

Hegel's vision of the whole world developing toward freedom, rationality, and understanding was typical of one strain of nineteenth-century European thought. Today we might ask ourselves whether, in spite of a current appreciation of diversity, the world isn't inevitably moving toward homogeneity, and if so, whether that homogeneity will embody the ideals which Hegel posited or some other conditions.

What socio-economic condition among the Greeks and Romans does Hegel cite as seeming to belie his thesis about progress toward freedom? How does he explain that such a practice lingered on even into the Christian world?

Universal history is the exhibition of Spirit in the process of working out the knowledge of what it [Spirit] potentially is. Just as the seed bears in itself the whole nature of the tree, including the taste and form of its fruit, so do the first traces of Spirit virtually contain the whole of its own history. The Orientals did not attain the knowledge that Spirit, in the form of mankind, is free. They only knew that "one is free." But in those terms, the freedom of that one person was only caprice, whether exhibited as ferocity, a brutal recklessness of passion, or as mildness and tameness of the desires, either of which is merely an accident of nature. That "one" was thus only a despot, not a really free man. The consciousness of freedom first arose among the Greeks, and therefore they were free, though they, just as the Romans, knew only that "some are free," not man as such. Even Plato and Aristotle did not know that. Thus the Greeks had slaves, and the whole of their life and the maintenance of their splendid liberty was implicated with the institution of slavery. That fact, on the one hand, made their liberty only an accidental, transient and limited growth and, on the other hand, constituted it a rigorous thralldom of our common nature, i.e., of the human. The Germanic nations, under the influence of Christianity, were the first to attain the consciousness that man, as man, is free, that it is the freedom of Spirit which constitutes Spirit's essence. This consciousness arose first in religion, the most inward region of Spirit. But the introduction of the principle [of consciousness] into the various relations of the actual world has involved a more extensive problem than did its simple implantation [into the soul], a problem whose solution and application have required a severe and lengthened process of culture. In proof of this, we may note that slavery did not cease immediately on the reception of Christianity. Still less did liberty predominate in states or did governments and constitutions adopt a rational organization or recognize freedom as their own basis. The application of the principle to political relations and its thorough molding and interpenetration of the constitution of society is a process identical with history itself. . . . The history of the world is none other than the progress of the consciousness of freedom. . . .

Translated by J. Sibree, adapted by Michael Neville

August Comte: *The Positive Philosophy* (1830)

August Comte, in response to philosophers such as Kant and Hegel, sought to base all philosophy on the sciences. He claimed that the human race had passed through two earlier phases: the theological (from ancient times up through the Medieval), in which all phenomena were explained in terms of the gods and divine forces; and the metaphysical (beginning with the Greeks and culminating in Renaissance and early modern thought), in which reason was supposed to explain all phenomena in terms of underlying non-physical forces. Now, he posits, we are entering the scientific (or positivist) age, in which all phenomena will be explained simply in terms of patterns of events which have been observed, not in terms of unexperienced forces. The one subject matter which he finds that science has not yet explained is the human being himself; in calling for the scientific study of human individuals and communities, Comte is considered the founder of modern sociology, which he calls "social physics." Indeed, he goes so far with this notion that he claims to derive ethical principles themselves from a scientific study of the human, and he eventually founded a sort of humanistic religion.

What problem does Comte find in trying to define so basic a notion as that of attraction? How does he think that people are still trying to explain "Social subjects?"

[T]he first characteristic of the Positive Philosophy is that it regards all phenomena as subjected to invariable natural *Laws.* Our business is . . . to pursue an accurate discovery of these Laws, with a view to reducing them to the smallest possible number. By speculating upon causes, we could solve no difficulty about origin and purpose. Our real business is to analyze accurately the circumstances of phenomena, and to connect them by the natural relations of succession and resemblance. The best illustration of this is in the case of the doctrine of Gravitation. We say that the general phenomena of the universe are *explained* by it, because it connects under one head the whole immense variety of astronomical facts; exhibiting the constant tendency of atoms toward each other in direct proportion to their masses, and in inverse proportion to the squares of their distance; while the general fact itself is a mere extension of one which is perfectly familiar to us, and which we therefore say that we know—the weight of bodies on the surface of the earth. As to what weight and attraction are, we have nothing to do with that, for it is not a matter of knowledge at all. Theologians and metaphysicians may imagine and refine about such questions; but positive philosophy rejects them. When any attempt has been made to explain them, it has ended only in saying that attraction is universal weight, and that weight is terrestrial attraction: that is, that the two orders of phenomena are identical; which is the point from which the question set out. . . .

In mentioning just now the four principal categories of phenomena,—astronomical, physical, chemical, and physiological,[1]—there was an omission which will have been noticed. Nothing was said of Social phenomena. Though involved with the physiological, Social phenomena demand a distinct classification, both on account of their importance and of their difficulty. They are the most individual, the most complicated, the most dependent on all others; and therefore they must be the latest,—even if they had no special obstacle to encounter. This branch of science has not hitherto entered into the domain of

[1]That is, biological.

Positive philosophy. Theological and metaphysical methods, exploded in other departments,[2] are as yet exclusively applied, both in the way of inquiry and discussion, in all treatment of Social subjects, though the best minds are heartily weary of eternal disputes about divine right and the sovereignty of the people. This is the great, while it is evidently the only, gap which has to be filled, to constitute, solid and entire, the Positive Philosophy. Now that the human mind has grasped celestial and terrestrial physics,—mechanical and chemical; organic physics, both vegetable and animal,—there remains one science, to fill up the series of sciences of observation,—Social physics. This is what men have now most need of: and this it is the principal aim of the present work to establish.

Translated by Abraham S. Blumberg

[2] Discredited in other fields.

John Stuart Mill: *On Liberty* (1859)

John Stuart Mill, one of the foremost nineteenth-century spokesmen for liberalism, advocated Utilitarianism in ethics, i.e., the view that we should each act so as to promote the greatest happiness for the greatest number of people. Yet he was a champion of individual rights, calling, among other things, for more power and freedom for women. In his treatise On Liberty *he argues that in the past the danger had been that monarchs held power at the expense of the common people and the struggle was one of gaining liberty by limiting such governmental power. But now that power has largely passed into the hands of the people at large through democratic forms of government, the danger is that the majority will deny liberty to individuals, whether explicitly through laws, which he calls "acts of public authority," or more subtly through morals and social pressure, which he calls "collective opinion."*

Why doesn't the establishment of democratic forms of government automatically lead to true self-government? What does Mill mean by "the tyranny of the majority"? Can you think of examples of this sort of tyranny in our own time?

The aim, therefore, of patriots was to set limits to the power which the ruler should be suffered[1] to exercise over the community; and this limitation was what they meant by liberty. It was attempted in two ways. First, by obtaining a recognition of certain immunities, called political liberties or rights, which it was to be regarded as a breach of duty in the ruler to infringe; and which if he did infringe, specific resistance, or general rebellion, was held to be justifiable. A second, and generally a later expedient, was the establishment of constitutional checks, by which the consent of the community, or of a body of some sort, supposed to represent its interests, was made a necessary condition to some of the more important acts of the governing power. To the first of these modes of limitation, the ruling power, in most European countries, was compelled, more or less, to submit. It was not so with the second; and, to attain this, or when already in some degree possessed, to attain it more completely, became everywhere the principal object of the lovers of liberty. And so long as mankind were content to combat one enemy by another, and to be ruled by a master, on condition of being guaranteed more or less efficaciously against his tyranny, they did not carry their aspirations beyond this point.

A time, however, came, in the progress of human affairs, when men ceased to think it a necessity of nature that their governors should be an independent power, opposed in interest to themselves. It appeared to them much better that the various magistrates of the State should be their tenants or delegates, revocable at their pleasure. In that way alone, it seemed, could they have complete security that the powers of government would never be abused to their disadvantage. By degrees this new demand for elective and temporary rulers became the prominent object of the exertions of the popular party, wherever any such party existed; and superseded, to a considerable extent, the previous efforts to limit the power of rulers. As the struggle proceeded for making the ruling power emanate from the periodical choice of the ruled, some persons began to think that too much importance had been attached to the limitation of the power itself. *That* (it might seem) was a resource against rulers whose interests were habitually opposed to those of the people. What was now wanted was, that the rulers should be identified with the people; that their interest and will should be the interest and will of the nation. The nation did not need to be protected against its

[1]Allowed.

own will. There was no fear of its tyrannizing over itself. Let the rulers be effectually responsible to it, promptly removable by it, and it could afford to trust them with power of which it could itself dictate the use to be made. Their power was but the nation's own power, concentrated, and in a form convenient for exercise. This mode of thought, or rather perhaps of feeling, was common among the last generation of European liberalism, in the Continental section of which it still apparently predominates. . . .[2]

In time, however, a democratic republic came to occupy a large portion of the earth's surface, and made itself felt as one of the most powerful members of the community of nations; and elective and responsible government became subject to the observations and criticisms which wait upon a great existing fact. It was now perceived that such phrases as "self-government," and "the power of the people over themselves," do not express the true state of the case. The "people" who exercise the power are not always the same people with those over whom it is exercised; and the "self-government" spoken of is not the government of each by himself, but of each by all the rest. The will of the people, moreover, practically means the will of the most numerous or the most active *part* of the people; the majority, or those who succeed in making themselves accepted as the majority; the people, consequently *may* desire to oppress a part of their number; and precautions are as much needed against this as against any other abuse of power. The limitation, therefore, of the power of government over individuals loses none of its importance when the holders of power are regularly accountable to the community, that is, to the strongest party therein. This view of things, recommending itself equally to the intelligence of thinkers and to the inclination of those important classes in European society to whose real or supposed interests democracy is adverse, has had no difficulty in establishing itself; and in political speculations "the tyranny of the majority" is now generally included among the evils against which society requires to be on its guard.

Like other tyrannies, the tyranny of the majority was at first, and is still vulgarly, held in dread, chiefly as operating through the acts of the public authorities. But reflecting[3] persons perceived that when society is itself the tyrant—society collectively over the separate individuals who compose it—its means of tyrannizing are not restricted to the acts which it may do by the hands of its political functionaries. Society can and does execute its own mandates: and if it issues wrong mandates instead of right, or any mandates at all in things with which it ought not to meddle, it practices a social tyranny more formidable than many kinds of political oppression, since, though not usually upheld by such extreme penalties, it leaves fewer means of escape, penetrating much more deeply into the details of life, and enslaving the soul itself. Protection, therefore, against the tyranny of the magistrate is not enough; there needs protection also against the tyranny of the prevailing opinion and feeling; against the tendency of society to impose, by other means than civil penalties, its own ideas and practices as rules of conduct on those who dissent from them; to fetter the development, and, if possible, prevent the formation, of any individuality not in harmony with its ways, and compel all characters to fashion themselves upon the model of its own. There is a limit to the legitimate interference of collective opinion with individual independence: and to find that limit, and maintain it against encroachment, is as indispensable to a good condition of human affairs, as protection against political despotism.

---

[2]Mill was writing in 1859.

[3]Thoughtful.

Johann Wolfgang von Goethe: *Faust* (1808) "Prologue in Heaven"

Goethe's Faust *is the quintessential Romantic masterpiece. Set in the Renaissance, the play nevertheless reflects the themes and concerns of the late 18th and early 19th centuries. It contains all the major Romantic themes: nostalgia for earlier ages, a preference for emotional and lived experience over learning and reason, magic, drugs and eroticism. As children of the Enlightenment, Goethe's generation rebelled against the traditional fascination with classical mythology but felt free to treat Christianity itself as myth. In the opening scene of the play he uses Biblical imagery to announce the work's major theme: that life at its truest is a matter of endless striving and transformation. The man that interests this god is not an obedient saint, but a rebellious skeptic, never satisfied with life as he finds it. The stage is set by the song of the three angels (the only three given names in the Bible), describing the universe as a place of constant conflict and motion. Mephistopheles (the Devil himself or one of his companions—Goethe is deliberately ambiguous on this point) enters to mock their raptures and describe the pitiful state of tortured humanity. In a parody of the opening of Job, the Lord proposes a wager: whichever of them shall win Faust as his own will be proven right. It is never explained why God chooses Faust as his example, since he is not only selfish and destructive, but an atheist and a dabbler in black magic. It is paradoxical that he will be willing to sign a contract with the Devil to sell his soul in return for magical powers, for he does not believe in the Hell from which Mephistopheles comes. The drama is not a Christian morality play, but a wild, gleefully self-contradictory journey through a Romantic view of life.*

What aspects of Mephistopheles' character make him an attrractive or sympathetic figure?

RAPHAEL
The sun intones,[1] in ancient tourney[2]
With brother spheres, a rival air;[3]
And his predestinated journey,
He closes with a thundrous blare.[4]
His sight, as none can comprehend it,
Gives strength to angels; the array
Of works, unfathomably splendid,
Is glorious as on the first day.

---

[1]Sings. According to Medieval belief, each object in the sky is borne in its orbit by a huge crystal sphere which emits a single pure tone. Altogether these tones make up the "harmony of the spheres," which can be heard only by Heavenly beings.
[2]Contest, combat.
[3]An "air" is a melody. Goethe turns the traditional harmony of the spheres into a contest, a struggle, in keeping with his Romantic theme.
[4]The sunset is imagined as emitting a grand concluding sound as it sets. Part Two of *Faust* will begin with the clattering chariot wheels of the sun rising at dawn. Both are meant to gently mock primitive geocentric notions of the universe.

GABRIEL
Unfathomably swiftly speeded,
Earth's pomp revolves in whirling flight,[5]
As Eden's brightness is succeeded
By deep and dread-inspiring night;
In mighty torrents foams the ocean
Against the rocks with roaring song—
In ever-speeding spheric motion,
Both rock and sea are swept along.
MICHAEL
And rival tempests roar and ravage
From sea to land, from land to sea,
And, raging, form a chain of savage,
Deeply destructive energy.
There flames a flashing devastation
To clear the thunder's crashing way;
Yet, Lord, thy herald's admiration
Is for the mildness of thy day.[6]
THE THREE
The sight, as none can comprehend it,
Gives strength to angels; thy array
Of works, unfathomably splendid,
Is glorious as on the first day.
MEPHISTOPHELES
Since you, oh Lord, have once again drawn near,
And ask how we have been, and are so genial,
And since you used to like to see me here,
You see me, too, as if I were a menial.[7]
I cannot speak as nobly as your staff,
Though by this circle here I shall be spurned:
My pathos would be sure to make you laugh,
Were laughing not a habit you've unlearned.

---

[5]Although the angels do not appear aware of it, Raphael has described a geocentric (Ptolemaic) universe while Gabriel now proceeds to describe a heliocentric (Copernican) one. In Goethe's mythological cosmology both are combined so that everything is in motion: sun, earth, and everything on earth. Note how he chooses in the following lines precisely the least stable, most constantly moving portions of the earth to describe: the sea and storm-filled air.

[6]Michael underlines the theme that runs throughout the angels' opening song: the universe is an amazing but chaotic and incomprehensible place; not the stable set of neatly nested spheres or the orderly chain of being imagined by the Renaissance.

[7]Servant. Mephistopheles is God's servant in two ways: he tempts sinners and punishes the damned in Hell, both tasks which God wants done. Goethe explores throughout the play the paradox that God's greatest enemy who wants the opposite of what God wants, nevertheless ends by doing God's will.

Of suns and worlds I know nothing to say;
I only see how men live in dismay.[8]
The small god of the world[9] will never change his ways
And is as whimsical—as on the first of days.
His life might be a bit more fun,
Had you not given him that spark of heaven's sun;
He calls it reason and employs it, resolute
To be more brutish than is any brute.[10]
He seems to me, if you don't mind, Your Grace,
Like a cicada of the long-legged race,
That always flies and, flying, springs,
And in the grass the same old ditty sings;
If only it were grass he could repose in!
There is no trash he will not poke his nose in.
THE LORD
Can you not speak but to abuse?
Do you come only to accuse?
Does nothing on the earth seem to you right?[11]
MEPHISTOPHELES
No, Lord. I find it still a rather sorry sight.
Man moves me to compassion, so wretched is his plight.
I have no wish to cause him further woe.[12]
THE LORD
Do you know Faust?
MEPHISTOPHELES
The doctor?
THE LORD
Aye, my servant.
MEPHISTOPHELES
Lo!
He serves you most peculiarly, I think.
Not earthly are the poor fool's meat and drink.
His spirit's ferment drives him far,
And he half knows how foolish is his quest:
From heaven he demands the fairest star,
And from the earth all joys that he thinks best:
And all that's near and all that's far
Cannot soothe the upheaval in his breast.

---

[8]The entire universe is God's concern, but Mephistopheles is a specialist, concerned only with humanity.

[9]Humanity.

[10] An ironic reply to the Enlightenment view that reason could solve most human problems.

[11]The Lord gives notably weak and ambiguous replies in this dialogue. He seems put on the defensive.

[12] Note that Mephistopheles seems more compassionate toward humanity than the Lord.

THE LORD
Though now he serves me but confusedly,
I shall soon lead him where the vapor clears.
The gardener knows, however small the tree,
That bloom and fruit adorn its later years.
MEPHISTOPHELES
What will you bet? You'll lose him yet to me,
If you will graciously connive
That I may lead him carefully.
THE LORD
As long as he may be alive,
So long you shall not be prevented.
Man errs as long as he will strive.[13]
MEPHISTOPHELES
Be thanked for that; I've never been contented
To waste my time upon the dead.
I far prefer full cheeks, a youthful curly-head.
When corpses come, I have just left the house—
I feel as does the cat about the mouse.
THE LORD
Enough—I grant that you may try to clasp him,
Withdraw this spirit from his primal source
And lead him down, if you can grasp him,
Upon your own abysmal course—
And stand abashed when you have to attest:
A good man in his darkling aspiration
Remembers the right road throughout his quest.
MEPHISTOPHELES
Enough—he will soon reach his station;
About my bet I have no hesitation,
And when I win, concede your stake
And let me triumph with a swelling breast:
Dust he shall eat, and that with zest.
As my relation does, the famous snake.[14]
THE LORD
Appear quite free on that day, too;
I never hated those who were like you:
Of all the spirits that negate.

---

[13] Goes wrong as long as he is continuing to strive for greater things. Yet the Lord himself notes later that rest is not what he desires. Goethe is creating a substitute for conventional morality by drawing a distinction not between good and evil, but between rest and activity. Activity leads to trouble, but life is trouble. A life of perfect peace and contentment would be no life at all from this perspective.

[14] The snake which tempted Adam and Eve in the Garden of Eden is often interpreted as being the Devil himself, but nothing in the text of Genesis requires that this be so.

The knavish jester gives me least to do.
For man's activity can easily abate,
He soon prefers uninterrupted rest;
To give him this companion hence seems best
Who roils[15] and must as Devil help create.[16]
But you, God's rightful sons, give voice
To all the beauty in which you rejoice;
And that which ever works and lives and grows
Enfold you with fair bonds that love has wrought
And what in wavering apparition flows
That fortify with everlasting thought.
(The heavens close, the Archangels disperse.)
MEPHISTOPHELES *(alone)*
I like to see the Old Man now and then
And try to be not too uncivil.
It's charming in a noble squire when
He speaks humanely with the very Devil.[17]

Translated by Walter Kaufmann

[15] Agitates, stirs up.
[16] So restless activity, while it inevitably leads to error, is creative; and creativity, not virtue, is here the highest good.
[17] Throughout the play Mephistopheles' casual, cynical attitude is contrasted with Faust's frenetic romanticism and Heaven's pious solemnity. Goethe doesn't allow one to efface the other; he simply mixes them together and delights in the ensuing struggle.

William Wordsworth: The World Is Too Much with Us (1807)

Wordsworth was born and lived most of his life in the rural northwest of England known as the Lake District. Like many other Romantic writers, he saw in Nature an emblem of god or the divine and his poetry often celebrates the beauty and spiritual values of the natural world. He revolutionized English poetry with the publication of Literary Ballads *(1798), co-authored with his friend Samuel Taylor Coleridge who contributed "The Rime of the Ancient Mariner" for the volume. In this book Wordsworth sought to break the pattern of artificial situations of eighteenth-century poetry, which had been written for the upper classes, and to write in simple, straightforward language for the common man. Other English Romantic poets would follow Wordsworth's lead in taking apparently insignificant moments and, by observation and contemplation, raising them to illuminations of experience. Wordsworth defined poetry as the "spontaneous overflow of powerful feelings," intense "emotion recollected in tranquillity." In the sonnet "The World Is Too Much with Us" the poet contrasts Nature with the world of materialism and "making it." Because we are insensitive to the richness of Nature, we may be forfeiting our souls. To us there is nothing wonderful or mysterious about the natural world, but ancients who were pagans created a colorful mythology out of their awe of Nature.*

What does Wordsworth think is wrong with the modern world?

The world is too much with us; late and soon,
Getting and spending, we lay waste our powers;
Little we see in Nature that is ours;
We have given our hearts away, a sordid boon!
This Sea that bares her bosom to the moon,
The winds that will be howling at all hours,
And are up-gathered now like sleeping flowers,
For this, for everything, we are out of tune;
It moves us not.—Great God! I'd rather be
A Pagan suckled in a creed outworn;[1]
So might I, standing on this pleasant lea,[2]
Have glimpses that would make me less forlorn;
Have sight of Proteus[3] rising from the sea;
Or hear old Triton[4] blow his wreathed horn.

---

[1]Brought up in an outdated religion.
[2]Meadow.
[3]Greek sea god capable of taking many shapes.
[4]Another sea god, often depicted as trumpeting on a shell.

Emile Zola: *Germinal* (1885)

Zola's technique of "naturalism" attempted through scrupulous research to depict the lives of ordinary people. For Germinal, *he descended into a mineshaft very much like the one he describes below, taking detailed notes. Zola's works portray groups of humans in the grip of circumstances beyond their control, often destined to be destroyed in monumental catastrophes. Each mining disaster hinted at in the following passage will actually occur, leaving almost every one of the characters mentioned dead by the end of the novel.* Germinal *was an eloquent protest against the inhuman working conditions common in late Nineteenth-Century European factories and mines. Etienne Lantier is an out-of-work railway worker who by sheer luck has secured a job in the coal mine called "Le Voreux" (a name suggesting a voracious beast which consumes workers wholesale). This passage depicts the journey into the hell of the mine of the team headed by an experienced miner named Maheu, which includes his teenage daughter, Catherine.*

What are some striking instances of Zola's use of sounds *to convey a vivid impression of the mine? What are the main dangers threatening the miners?*

"Damn! It's not warm here," muttered Catherine, shivering.

Étienne simply nodded. He found himself before the shaft, in the center of a huge hall swept by drafts. Of course he thought of himself as brave, yet an unpleasant emotion caused his throat to contract among the thundering of the carts, the clanking of the signals, the muffled bellowing of the megaphone, facing the continuously flying cables, unrolling and rolling up again at top speed on the spools of the machine. The cages rose and fell, slithering like some nocturnal animal, continually swallowing men that the hole seemed to drink down. It was his turn now. He was very cold. He kept silent out of nervousness which made Zacharie and Levaque snicker, for both disapproved of the hiring of this stranger—Levaque especially, hurt because he had not been consulted. So Catherine was happy to hear her father explaining things to the young man.

"Look, up on top of the cage; there's a parachute and iron hooks that catch in the guides in case the cable breaks. It works . . . most of the time. . . . Yes, the shaft is divided into three vertical compartments, sealed off by planks from top to bottom. In the center are the cages; on the left the ladder-well. . . ."[1]

But he broke off to complain, without daring to speak very loudly, "What the hell are we doing waiting here, for God's sake? How can they let us freeze here like this?"

Richomme, the foreman, who was also going down, his open miner's lamp hanging from a nail in his leather cap, heard him complaining.

"Be careful; the walls have ears!" he muttered paternalistically, as a former miner who still sided with the workers.

"They've got to make the adjustments . . . See? Here we are, get in with your team."

And in fact, the cage, banded with sheet iron and covered by a fine-meshed screen, was waiting for them, resting on its catches. Maheu, Zacherie, Levaque, and Catherine slid into a cart at the back; and since it was supposed to hold five people, Étienne got in as well; but all the good places were taken and he had to squeeze in beside the young girl, whose elbow poked into his belly. His lamp got in his way; he was advised to hang it from a buttonhole of his jacket. He didn't hear this advice and kept it awkwardly in his hand. The loading continued, above and below, a jumbled load of cattle. Couldn't they get going?

[1]An emergency escape shaft.

What was happening? It seemed as if he'd been waiting for a long time. Finally a jolt shook him and everything fell away, the objects around him seemed to fly past while he felt a nervous dizziness that churned his guts. This lasted as long as he was in the daylight, passing the two landing levels, surrounded by the wheeling flight of the timbers. Then, falling into the blackness of the pit, he remained stunned, no longer able to interpret his feelings.

"We're off," said Maheu tranquilly.

They seemed relaxed. He, however, wondered at moments whether he was going down or up. There were moments at which they seemed immobile, when the cage was dropping straight down without touching the guides; then brusquely there were shudders, a sort of dancing between the planks, which made him fear a catastrophe was going to happen. In addition, he couldn't make out the walls of the shaft behind the grill to which his face was pressed. The lamps only dimly lit the heap of bodies at his feet. Alone, the open lamp of the foreman shone from the next cart like a beacon.

"This one is fifteen feet wide," continued Maheu, instructing him. "The casing needs to be redone; water's leaking everywhere. . . . Listen, we're down at the water level. Can you hear it?"

Etienne had just been asking himself what this sound of a downpour could be. A few big drops had splashed first on the roof of the cage, like at the beginning of a storm; and now the rain grew, streamed, was transformed into a real deluge. The roof must have had a hole in it, for a trickle of water, flowing onto his shoulder, was soaking him to the skin. The cold became glacial; they entered a damp blackness, then there was a blinding flash and a glimpse of a cave where men were moving about. But already they were plunging back into nothingness.

Maheu said:

"That's the first landing. We're a hundred feet down now . . . Look how fast we're going."

Lifting his lamp, he lit up a guide timber flying past like the rail beneath a train running full steam ahead; beyond that, nothing else was could be seen. Three other platforms flew out of the shadows.

"How deep it is!" murmured Étienne.

The fall seemed to have lasted for hours. He was suffering because of the awkward position he was in, not daring to move, above all tortured by Catherine's elbow. She didn't say a word; he only felt her pressed against him, warming him. When the cage finally halted at the bottom, at 1,828 feet, he was astonished to learn that the descent had lasted just one minute. But the sound of the catches taking hold and the feeling of something solid underneath him suddenly cheered him up. . . .

The cage was emptying; the workers crossed the landing dock, a room carved out of the rock vaulted over with bricks lit by three huge lamps with open flames. The loaders were violently shoving full carts across the cast-iron floor. A cellar-like odor seeped from the walls, a chilly smell of saltpeter traversed by warm gusts from the stable nearby. Four galleries gaped into the opening.

"This way," said Maheu to Étienne. "You're not there yet. We have another good mile and a quarter to go. . . ."

The miners were separating, disappearing by groups into these black holes. Some fifteen of them had just entered the one on the left; and Étienne walked behind them following Maheu, who led Catherine, Zacharie and Levaque. It was a good tunnel for hauling the carts, cutting through a layer of rock so solid that only partial timbering had been necessary. They walked single file, walking always onward, without a word, led by the tiny flames in their lamps. The young man stumbled at every step, catching his feet in the rails. suddenly a muffled sound worried him, the distant noise of a storm whose violence seemed to being growing, coming from the bowels of the earth. Was it the thunder of a cave-in which would crush down onto their heads the enormous mass cutting them off from the light of day. . . ?

The further they went, the more narrow the gallery became, lower, with an uneven ceiling forcing them constantly to bend over.

Étienne bumped his head painfully. If he hadn't been wearing a leather cap, his skull would have been cracked. Yet he had been following closely the smallest movements of Maheu ahead of him, his somber silhouette created by the flow of the lamps. None of the workers bumped into anything; they must have known every hump in the ground, every knot in the timbers, every protrusion in the rock. The young man was also bothered by the slippery ground, which was getting more and more damp. Sometimes he passed through virtual seas which he discovered only as his feet plunged into the muddy mess. But what surprised him the most were the abrupt changes in temperature. At the bottom of the shaft it was very cold, and in the haulage tunnel, through which all the air in the mine flowed, a freezing wind was blowing, like a violent storm trapped between narrow walls. Further on, as they gradually traveled down other passageways which got less ventilation, the wind dropped and the warmth increased, creating a suffocating, leaden heat.

Maheu had not said another word. He turned right into a new gallery saying only to Étienne, without turning around, "The Guillaume vein."

This was the vein whose coal face they were to work. After a few steps Étienne bruised his head and elbows. The sloping roof descended so far that they had to walk doubled over for fifty or a hundred feet at a time. The water reached his ankles. They went on in this way for more than 600 feet when suddenly, Levaque, Zacharie and Catherine disappeared, seemingly swallowed by a tiny crack that opened in front of him.

"You have to climb up," said Maheu. "Hang your lamp from a buttonhole and hang on to the timbers."

He too disappeared. Étienne had to follow him. This chimney was left for the miners to allow them to reach all the secondary passageways, just the width of the coal vein, barely two feet. Fortunately the young man was thin: still clumsy, he drew himself up with a wasteful expense of strength, pulling in his shoulders and buttocks, hand over hand, clinging to the timbers. Fifty feet higher up they came to the first secondary passageway, but they had to go on; the work area of Maheu and his team was at the sixth level, "in Hell" as they said, and every fifty feet there was another passageway to be crossed. The climb seemed to go on forever, through this crack which scraped against his back and chest. Étienne gasped as if the weight of the rocks were crushing his limbs; his hands were skinned, his legs bruised. Worst of all, he was suffocating, feeling as if the blood was going to burst out through his skin. He could vaguely see down one of the passageways two animals crouched down, one small and one large, shoving carts ahead of them: Lydie and La Mouquette, already at work. And he still had to clamber up two more levels! Sweat blinded him, he despaired of catching up to the others whose agile legs he could hear constantly brushing against the rock.

"Come on; here we are!" said Catherine's voice. . . .

Little by little the veins had filled, the faces were being worked at each level, at the end of each passageway. The all-devouring mine had swallowed its daily ration of men, more than 700 workers laboring now in this giant ant heap, burrowing through the earth in every direction, riddling it like an old piece of wood infested by worms. And in the midst of this heavy silence, under the crushing weight of these deep layers of earth, could be heard—if you put your ear to the rock—the movement of these human insects at work, from the flight of the cable raising and lowering the extraction cage to the bite of the tools digging into the coal at the bottom of the mine. . . .

The four cutters had stretched out one above the other across the sloping coal face. . . . Maheu was the one who suffered most. High up where he was the temperature was as high as 95°, the air did not circulate, and eventually you would suffocate. In order to see clearly he had had to hang his lamp on a nail near his head; but this lamp broiled his skull, making his blood seethe. His torture was worsened above all by the damp. Water kept flowing over the rock above him a few inches from his face; and huge drops kept rapidly, continuously, in a maddening rhythm, falling, always on the same spot. It was no use twisting his neck or bending his head, the drops fell on his face, beating at him, splattering endlessly. After a quarter of an hour he was soaked, covered with his own sweat, steaming like a laundry tub. He didn't want to stop cutting and gave huge blows which jolted him violently between the two rocks, like a flea caught between the pages of a book, threatened by being completely crushed.

Not a word was spoken. They all hammered away, and nothing could be heard but these irregular blows, muffled, seemingly far-off. The sounds took on a harsh quality in the dead, echoless air, and it seemed as if the shadows created a mysterious blackness, thickened by the flying coal dust and made heavier by the gas which weighed down their eyes. The wicks of their lamps displayed only glowing red tips through their metal screens. You couldn't make out anything clearly. The work space opened out into a large chimney, flat and sloping, on which the soot of ten winters had created a profound night. Ghostly forms moved about, random light beams allowing a glimpse of the curve of a thigh, a brawny arm, a savage face, blackened as if in preparation for a crime. Sometimes blocks of coal stood out, suddenly lit up, their facets glinting like crystals. Then everything was plunged back into darkness, the picks beating out their heavy, dull blows; and there was nothing but the sound of heavy breathing, groans of pain and fatigue beneath the weight of the air and the showers from the underground streams.

Translated by Paul Brians

Karl Marx and Friedrich Engels: *The Communist Manifesto* (1848)

Although it at first had little or no impact on the widespread and varied revolutionary movements of the mid-19th century Europe, the Communist Manifesto *was to become one of the most widely read and discussed documents of the 20th century. Marx sought to differentiate his brand of socialism from others by insisting that it was scientifically based in the objective study of history, which he saw as being a continuous process of change and transformation. Just as feudalism had naturally evolved into mercantilism and then capitalism, so capitalism would inevitably give way to its logical successor, socialism (a term which in Marx's usage includes its most advanced form, communism) as the necessary result of class struggle. Marx's insistence that tough-minded realism should replace the utopian idealism of earlier socialists had profound consequences: it enabled revolutionaries like Lenin to put it into action, but it also tended to encourage its followers to accept ruthless means to justify what they believed were historically necessary ends. Radical politics were being much more widely discussed than the small number of radicals justified; but Marx uses this fact to his advantage by proclaiming that any ideology so feared must be important and worth explaining clearly. In the notes, "Marx" is used as shorthand for both Marx (the theoretician) and Engels (the more eloquent writer of the two). The* Manifesto *was originally issued in several languages, including this English version.*

What kinds of changes does Marx say have been characteristic of the bourgeois era? Choose some of Marx's arguments that you either agree or disagree with and explain what you think is most and least effective in them. Discuss anything that you find surprising or unexpected in this selection, based on your prior knowledge of Marxism.

Prologue

A specter is haunting Europe—the specter of communism. All the powers of old Europe have entered into a holy alliance to exorcise this specter: Pope and Czar, Metternich and Guizot,[1] French Radicals and German police spies.

Where is the party in opposition that has not been decried as communistic by its opponents in power? Where the Opposition that has not hurled back the branding reproach of communism, against the more advanced opposition parties, as well as against its reactionary adversaries?

Two things result from this fact:

I. Communism is already acknowledged by all European powers to be itself a power.

II. It is high time that Communists should openly, in the face of the whole world, publish their views, their aims, their tendencies, and meet this nursery tale of the specter of communism with a manifesto of the party itself.[2]

[1]German and French conservatives.

[2]Marx opposed secret conspiratorial communist organizations because he felt that the only successful revolution would need the support of the overwhelming mass of society; and people could not be expected to support what they did not understand or even know about.

Part I: Bourgeois And Proletarians

The history of all hitherto existing society is the history of class struggles.

Freeman and slave,[3] patrician and plebeian,[4] lord and serf,[5] guildmaster and journeyman,[6] in a word, oppressor and oppressed, stood in constant opposition to one another, carried on an uninterrupted, now hidden, now open fight, a fight that each time ended, either in a revolutionary reconstitution of society at large, or in the common ruin of the contending classes.

In the earlier epochs of history, we find almost everywhere a complicated arrangement of society into various orders, a manifold gradation of social rank. In ancient Rome we have patricians, knights, plebeians, slaves; in the Middle Ages, feudal lords, vassals, guild-masters, journeymen, apprentices, serfs; in almost all of these classes, again, subordinate gradations.

The modern bourgeois society that has sprouted from the ruins of feudal society, has not done away with class antagonisms. It has but established new classes, new conditions of oppression, new forms of struggle in place of the old ones.

Our epoch, the epoch of the bourgeoisie,[7] possesses, however, this distinctive feature: It has simplified the class antagonisms. Society as a whole is more and more splitting up into two great hostile camps, into two great classes directly facing each other—bourgeoisie and proletariat. . . .[8]

Modern industry has established the world market, for which the discovery of America paved the way.[9] This market has given an immense development to commerce, to navigation, to communication by land. This development has, in its turn, reacted on the extension of industry; and in proportion as industry, commerce, navigation, railways extended, in the same proportion the bourgeoisie developed, increased its capital, and pushed into the background every class handed down from the Middle Ages.

We see, therefore, how the modern bourgeoisie is itself the product of a long course of development, of a series of revolutions in the modes of production and of exchange.

Each step in the development of the bourgeoisie was accompanied by a corresponding political advance of that class.[10] An oppressed class under the sway of the feudal nobility, it became an armed and self-governing association in the medieval commune; here indepen-

---

[3]Typical of ancient civilizations like that of the Greeks.

[4]Roman social classes.

[5]From the European Middle Ages.

[6]Representing the later Middle Ages and Renaissance.

[7]The term originally meant simply the class of people who lived in cities, but here it means those whose income comes from doing business rather than—like the aristocracy—from inherited estates or—like the proletariat—from wages.

[8]The working class, people who make their living by working for others rather than owning or investing in businesses.

[9]Marx's comments on the importance of the world market, developed further in passages here omitted, sound very modern. He argued that the differences between countries would diminish as they adopted capitalism and increased their international trade, paving the way for a stateless world united in communism.

[10]Marx particularly has in mind the European revolutions of 1789–1848, in which the bourgeoisie, which had long before become the dominant economic force in society, asserted its claims to political power as well.

dent urban republic (as in Italy and Germany), there taxable "third estate" of the monarchy (as in France); afterwards, in the period of manufacture proper, serving either the semi-feudal or the absolute monarchy as a counterpoise against the nobility, and, in fact, corner-stone of the great monarchies in general—the bourgeoisie has at last, since the establishment of modern industry and of the world market conquered for itself, in the modern representative state, exclusive political sway. The executive of the modern state is but a committee for managing the common affairs of the whole bourgeoisie.[11]

The bourgeoisie has played a most revolutionary role in history.[12]

The bourgeoisie, wherever it has got the upper hand, has put an end to all feudal, patriarchal, idyllic relations. It has pitilessly torn asunder the motley feudal ties that bound man to his "natural superiors," and has left no other bond between man and man than naked self-interest, than callous "cash payment." It has drowned the most heavenly ecstasies of religious fervor, of chivalrous enthusiasm, of philistine sentimentalism, in the icy water of egotistical calculation. It has resolved personal worth into exchange value, and in place of the numberless indefeasible chartered freedoms, has set up that single, unconscionable freedom—Free Trade. In one word, for exploitation, veiled by religious and political illusions, it has substituted naked, shameless, direct, brutal exploitation.[13]

Part II: Proletarians and Communists

What else does the history of ideas prove, than that intellectual production changes its character in proportion as material production is changed? The ruling ideas of each age have ever[14] been the ideas of its ruling class.[15]

When people speak of ideas that revolutionize society, they do but express the fact that within the old society the elements of a new one have been created, and that the dissolution of the old ideas keeps even pace with the dissolution of the old conditions of existence.

When the ancient world was in its last throes, the ancient religions were overcome by Christianity. When Christian ideas succumbed in the eighteenth century to rationalist ideas, feudal society fought its death-battle with the then revolutionary bourgeoisie. The

---

[11]In this famous comment, the modern democratic states are dismissed as mere tools of the bourgeoisie, since it is the wealthy who run them and set their agendas, despite their claims to popular representation.

[12]Although the following paragraph outlines this role in negative terms, Marx believed that the transformation of the world wrought by capitalism was absolutely necessary to provide the foundations for communism; so the bourgeoisie are revolutionary in fact, though unwittingly so.

[13]Although this is harshly put, Marx believes that the idealism which justified earlier class structures was indeed an illusion, a repressive deception that needed to be destroyed.

[14]Always.

[15]One of Marx's most influential concepts. In a capitalist society people think competition natural because capitalism requires competition; but in the Middle Ages submission to one's social "superiors" was seen as equally natural. Communism is not "against human nature" because there is no such thing—only the social values produced by certain kinds of economic organization. Contemporary Marxist analysis attempts to trace society's values back to the economic and political interests of the most powerful people in society.

ideas of religious liberty and freedom of conscience, merely gave expression to the sway of free competition within the domain of knowledge.

"Undoubtedly," it will be said, "religious, moral, philosophical and juridical ideas have been modified in the course of historical development. But religion, morality, philosophy, political science, and law constantly survived this change."

"There are, besides, eternal truths, such as Freedom, Justice, etc., that are common to all states of society. But communism abolishes eternal truths, it abolishes all religion, and all morality, instead of constituting them on a new basis; it therefore acts in contradiction to all past historical experience."

What does this accusation reduce itself to? The history of all past society has consisted in the development of class antagonisms, antagonisms that assumed different forms at different epochs.

But whatever form they may have taken, one fact is common to all past ages, viz., the exploitation of one part of society by the other. No wonder, then, that the social consciousness of past ages, despite all the multiplicity and variety it displays, moves within certain common forms, or general ideas, which cannot completely vanish except with the total disappearance of class antagonisms.

The Communist revolution is the most radical rupture with traditional property relations; no wonder that its development involves the most radical rupture with traditional ideas.[16]

Part IV: Position of the Communists in Relation to the Various Existing Opposition Parties

In short, the Communists everywhere support every revolutionary movement against the existing social and political order of things.[17]

In all these movements they bring to the front, as the leading question in each case, the property question, no matter what its degree of development at the time.

Finally, they labor everywhere for the union and agreement of the democratic parties of all countries.

The Communists disdain to conceal their views and aims.[18] They openly declare that their ends can be attained only by the forcible overthrow of all existing social conditions. Let the ruling classes tremble at a Communist revolution. The proletarians have nothing to lose but their chains. They have a world to win.

Workingmen of all countries, unite![19]

---

[16]Marx spent relatively little time outlining the nature of communist society, but the goals were widely understood to be 1) complete equality of all citizens, 2) abolition of private ownership of the means of production (factories, mines, railways, etc.), 3) the replacement of a market economy with one in which everyone got whatever they needed in return for such labor as they were able to give. In addition, Marx envisions the abolition of all states and governments, and as a consequence, an end to war.

[17]Marx argues that communists should work with all "progressive" movements in what were later to be called "united fronts."

[18]Note the repeated emphasis on openness. When communists were viewed as conspirators, they risked being seen as enemies of the people they were trying to help.

[19]This stirring conclusion is almost always misquoted as "Working men of all countries, unite! You have nothing to lose but your chains!"

Friedrich Nietzsche: The Death of God (1882)

This passage from The Gay Science *contains the most famous—and most misunderstood—words Nietzsche ever wrote. The German philosopher combined elements of romanticism and rationalism to create a philosophy of heroic, skeptical individualism. For Nietzsche God is an illusion that conceals from humanity its true creative powers. For him it is people who are the true creators of ethics and all other values, and they should take responsibility for the ethical systems they create rather than attributing them to a god. By asserting that God is dead, Nietzsche is not suggesting that he has ever been alive. What he means is that the idea of God which played a vital role in earlier periods of civilization has lost its vitality and should be discarded as outworn. This parable builds on a famous story about the Greek philosopher Diogenes who, when asked why he was carrying a lantern about in the daylight, replied that he was looking for an honest man, implying that such a creature was rare indeed. Nietzsche's "madman" similarly carries out his quest in a mocking manner only to demonstrate how impossible it is.*

What does it mean to say that we should become gods to become worthy of the murder of God?

The Madman. Have you not heard of that madman who lit a lantern in the bright morning hours, ran to the market place, and cried incessantly, "I seek God! I seek God!" As many of those who do not believe in God were standing around just then, he provoked much laughter. Why, did he get lost? said one. Did he lose his way like a child? said another. Or is he hiding? Is he afraid of us? Has he gone on a voyage? or emigrated? Thus they yelled and laughed. The madman jumped into their midst and pierced them with his glances.

"Whither is God?" he cried. "I shall tell you. We have killed him—you and I. All of us are his murderers. But how have we done this? How were we able to drink up the sea? Who gave us the sponge to wipe away the entire horizon? What did we do when we unchained this earth from its sun? Whither is it moving now? Whither are we moving now? Away from all suns? Are we not plunging continually? Backward, sideward, forward, in all directions? Is there any up or down left? Are we not straying as through an infinite nothing? Do we not feel the breath of empty space? Has it not become colder? Is not night and more night coming on all the while? Must not lanterns be lit in the morning? Do we not hear anything yet of the noise of the gravediggers who are burying God? Do we not hear anything yet of God's decomposition? Gods too decompose. God is dead. God remains dead. And we have killed him. How shall we, the murderers of all murderers, comfort ourselves? What was holiest and most powerful of all that the world has yet owned has bled to death under our knives. Who will wipe this blood off us? What water is there for us to clean ourselves? What festivals of atonement, what sacred games shall we have to invent? Is not the greatness of this deed too great for us? Must not we ourselves become gods simply to seem worthy of it? There has never been a greater deed; and whoever will be born after us—for the sake of this deed he will be part of a higher history than all history hitherto."

Here the madman fell silent and looked again at his listeners; and they too were silent and stared at him in astonishment. At last he threw his lantern on the ground, and it broke and went out. "I come too early," he said then; "my time has not come yet. This tremendous event is still on its way, still wandering—it has not yet reached the ears of man. Lightning and thunder require time, the light of the stars requires time, deeds require time even after they are done, before they can be seen and heard. This deed is still more distant from them than the most distant stars— *and yet they have done it themselves."*

It has been related further that on that same day the madman entered divers churches and there sang his *requiem aeternam deo.*[1] Led out and called to account, he is said to have replied each time, "What are these churches now if they are not the tombs and sepulchers of God?"

Translated by Walter Kaufmann

[1]May God rest in peace: funeral mass for God.

Charles Darwin: *The Origin of Species* (1859)

Opposition to evolutionary theory has always been most vigorous among those who feel that their religious beliefs requires them to reject it. Darwin was acutely aware of this fact and tried whenever he could to accommodate religious sensibilities. In the following overview of his theory of natural selection he emphasizes not only how much more rational the theory is than the claim that each species was separately created, but argues that it is marvelous and worthy of a majestic creator as well. In the final paragraph he lays down the basic elements of his theory: that individuals in every species tend naturally to vary from the norm, and that when there are so many members of a species sharing an ecological niche that they are competing for survival, only those whose variations give them decisive advantages will survive. They will pass these characteristics on to their descendants. Despite many disagreements among scientists about the details of evolution, some of which are mentioned in the footnotes below, most of them agree that a century and a half of accumulated evidence supports the broad outlines of this elegant theory which explains nature's oddities, failures and even occasional ugliness as the products of chance operations rather than of an omnipotent god.

What examples does Darwin give of features of nature that seem like errors ("less than perfect")?

As natural selection acts solely by accumulating slight, successive, favorable variations, it can produce no great or sudden modifications; it can act only by short and slow steps.[1] Hence, the canon of "Natura non facit saltum,"[2] which every fresh addition to our knowledge tends to confirm, is on this theory intelligible. We can see why throughout nature the same general end is gained by an almost infinite diversity of means, for every peculiarity when once acquired is long inherited, and structures already modified in many different ways have to be adapted for the same general purpose. We can, in short, see why nature is prodigal in variety, though niggard[3] in innovation. But why this should be a law of nature if each species has been independently created no man can explain.

Many other facts are, as it seems to me, explicable on this theory. How strange it is that a bird, under the form of a woodpecker, should prey on insects on the ground; that upland geese which rarely or never swim, should possess webbed feet; that a thrush-like bird should dive and feed on sub-aquatic insects; and that a petrel should have the habits and structure fitting it for the life of an auk! and so in endless other cases. But on the view of each species constantly trying to increase in members, with natural selection always ready to adapt the slowly varying descendants of each to any unoccupied or ill-occupied place in nature, these facts cease to be strange, or might even have been anticipated.

We can to a certain extent understand how it is that there is so much beauty throughout nature; for this may be largely attributed to the agency of selection. That beauty, according to our sense of it, is not universal, must be admitted by every one who will look at some venomous snakes, at some fishes, and at certain hideous bats with a distorted resemblance to the human face. Sexual selection has given the most brilliant colors, elegant patterns,

---

[1]One modern school of evolutionary thought rejects Darwin's gradualism, arguing that sudden and widespread change after long periods of stability has been more characteristic of evolutionary history.

[2]Nature makes no leaps.

[3]Miserly.

and other ornaments to the males, and sometimes to both sexes of many birds, butterflies, and other animals. With birds it has often rendered the voice of the male musical to the female, as well as to our ears. Flowers and fruit have been rendered conspicuous by brilliant colors in contrast with the green foliage, in order that the flowers may be easily seen, visited, and fertilized by insects, and the seeds disseminated by birds. How it comes that certain colors, sounds, and forms should give pleasure to man and the lower animals,—that is, how the sense of beauty in its simplest form was first acquired,—we do not know any more than how certain odors and flavors were first rendered agreeable.

As natural selection acts by competition, it adapts and improves the inhabitants of each country only in relation to their co-inhabitants; so that we need feel no surprise at the species of any one country, although on the ordinary view supposed to have been created and specially adapted for that country, being beaten and supplanted by the naturalized productions from another land. Nor ought we to marvel if all the contrivances in nature be not, as far as we can judge, absolutely perfect, as in the case even of the human eye; or if some of them be abhorrent to our ideas of fitness. We need not marvel at the sting of the bee, when used against an enemy, causing the bee's own death; at drones being produced in such great numbers for one single act, and being then slaughtered by their sterile sisters; at the astonishing waste of pollen by our fir-trees; at the instinctive hatred of the queen-bee for her own fertile daughters; at ichneumonidæ[4] feeding within the living bodies of caterpillars; or at other such cases. The wonder indeed is, on the theory of natural selection, that more cases of the want [5] of absolute perfection have not been detected. . . .

Authors of the highest eminence seem to be fully satisfied with the view that each species has been independently created. To my mind it accords better with what we know of the laws impressed on matter by the Creator, that the production and extinction of the past and present inhabitants of the world should have been due to secondary causes, like those determining the birth and death of the individual. When I view all beings not as special creations, but as the lineal descendants of some few beings which lived long before the first bed of the Cambrian[6] system was deposited, they seem to me to become ennobled. Judging from the past, we may safely infer that not one living species will transmit its unaltered likeness to a distant futurity. And of the species now living very few will transmit progeny of any kind to a far distant futurity; for the manner in which all organic beings are grouped, shows that the greater number of species in each genus, and all the species in many genera, have left no descendants, but have become utterly extinct. We can so far take a prophetic glance into futurity as to foretell that it will be the common and widely-spread species, belonging to the larger and dominant groups within each class, which will ultimately prevail and procreate new and dominant species. As all the living forms of life are the lineal descendants of those which lived long before the Cambrian epoch, we may feel certain that the ordinary succession by generation has never once been broken, and that no cataclysm has desolated the whole world.[7] Hence we may look with some confidence to a secure future of great length. And as natural selection works solely by

---

[4]A kind of wasp.

[5]Lack.

[6]About 700,000,000 years ago.

[7]Darwin has in mind not only the Biblical flood, but theories of nature which attributed all traces of large-scale change to various catastrophes. Ironically, most modern Darwinians have integrated the belief in at least one great cataclysm—the cometary impact which evidently ended the age of the dinosaurs—into evolutionary theory.

and for the good of each being, all corporeal and mental endowments will tend to progress towards perfection.[8]

It is interesting to contemplate a tangled bank, clothed with many plants of many kinds, with birds singing on the bushes, with various insects flitting about, and with worms crawling through the damp earth, and to reflect that these elaborately constructed forms, so different from each other, and dependent upon each other in so complex a manner, have all been produced by laws acting around us. These laws, taken in the largest sense, being Growth with Reproduction; Inheritance which is almost implied by reproduction; Variability from the indirect and direct action of the conditions of life, and from use and disuse: a Ratio of Increase so high as to lead to a Struggle for Life, and as a consequence to Natural Selection, entailing Divergence of Character and the Extinction of less-improved forms. Thus, from the war of nature, from famine and death, the most exalted object which we are capable of conceiving, namely, the production of the higher animals, directly follows. There is grandeur in this view of life, with its several powers, having been originally breathed by the Creator into a few forms or into one; and that, whilst this planet has gone cycling on according to the fixed law of gravity, from so simple a beginning endless forms most beautiful and most wonderful have been, and are being evolved.

---

[8]This view has been disputed by some scientists who argue that later forms are not necessarily "better" than earlier ones.

Rudyard Kipling, The White Man's Burden (1899)

Born in British India in 1865, Rudyard Kipling was educated in England before returning to India in 1882, where his father was a museum director and authority on Indian arts and crafts. Thus Kipling was thoroughly immersed in Indian culture: by 1890 he had published in English about 80 stories and ballads previously unknown outside India. As a result of financial misfortune, from 1892-96 he and his wife, the daughter of an American publisher, lived in Vermont, where he wrote the two Jungle Books. *After returning to England, he published "The White Man's Burden" in 1899, an appeal to the United States to assume the task of developing the Philippines, recently won in the Spanish-American War. As a writer, Kipling perhaps lived too long: by the time of his death in 1936, he had come to be reviled as the poet of British imperialism, though being regarded as a beloved children's book author. Today he might yet gain appreciation as a transmitter of Indian culture to the West.*

What is it today's reader finds so repugnant about Kipling's poem? If you were a citizen of a colonized territory, how would you respond to Kipling?

Take up the White Man's burden—
Send forth the best ye breed—
Go bind your sons to exile
To serve your captives' need;
To wait in heavy harness,
On fluttered folk and wild—
Your new-caught, sullen peoples,
Half-devil and half-child.

Take up the White Man's burden—
In patience to abide,
To veil the threat of terror
And check the show of pride;
By open speech and simple,
An hundred times made plain
To seek another's profit,
And work another's gain.

Take up the White Man's burden—
The savage wars of peace—
Fill full the mouth of Famine
And bid the sickness cease;
And when your goal is nearest
The end for others sought,
Watch sloth and heathen Folly
Bring all your hopes to nought.

Take up the White Man's burden—
No tawdry rule of kings,
But toil of serf and sweeper—
The tale of common things.

The ports ye shall not enter,
The roads ye shall not tread,
Go mark them with your living,
And mark them with your dead.

Take up the White Man's burden—
And reap his old reward:
The blame of those ye better,
The hate of those ye guard—
The cry of hosts ye humour
(Ah, slowly!) toward the light:—
"Why brought he us from bondage,
Our loved Egyptian night?"

Take up the White Man's burden—
Ye dare not stoop to less—
Nor call too loud on Freedom
To cloke[1] your weariness;
By all ye cry or whisper,
By all ye leave or do,
The silent, sullen peoples
Shall weigh your gods and you.

Take up the White Man's burden—
Have done with childish days—
The lightly proferred laurel,[2]
The easy, ungrudged praise.
Comes now, to search your manhood
Through all the thankless years
Cold, edged with dear-bought wisdom,
The judgment of your peers!

---

[1]Cloak, cover.
[2]Since the days of Classical Greece, a laurel wreath has been a symbolic victory prize.

Latin America 1750–1900

María Eugenia Echenique Letter to Elena (From a Ravine, 1875)

María Eugenia Echenique (Argentina; 1851-1878) had more formal education than most women of her day, having studied law, as her intelligent, insightful essays reflect. Two series of articles in particular brought her both respect and controversy: the first was "Letters to Elena" (1874), a series of letters written from various places in nature. She found in the contemplation of nature the inspiration for meditations about science, education, the future of women, and even space travel. Although many writers wrote about the emancipation of women, Echenique's essays stand out for their intellectual depth and for her understanding of the economics of the issue; for example, she pointed out the irony of the government's support of immigrant workers while native-born Argentine women were unable to work. When Echenique died at the age of just 26 (probably of cancer), she was mourned both in her hometown of Cordoba and in Buenos Aires.

At the time this essay was written, women were still struggling for the right to vote, and their social roles were greatly restricted. Why does Echenique feel that the 19th century is nevertheless a time of great advances for women?

I am in one of those nebulous and melancholic afternoons in the month of June.

If through a lens or by means of one of those dreams that sometimes force themselves upon our mind, you were to observe me for a moment in the middle of this wild nature, in these moments in which a profound stillness reigns everywhere, you would say: "She is alone, completely alone."

But it isn't so; though far from society, a world is with me, Elena.

Bossuet,[1] Balmes,[2] Lacordaire,[3] Almeida, Byron,[4] and Lamartine[5] accompany me in their immortal works.

With one of these philosophers on the right and one of these poets on the left, I believe that no one could be alone in this world. No one except someone who has never been delighted by the waters of life in the fountains of civilization.

---

[1]Jacques-Bégnigne Bossuet (1627-1704), French Bishop famous for his funeral orations on famous people.

[2]Jaime Luciano Balmes (1810-1848), Spanish clergyman best known for defending Catholicism against the accusation of its being opposed to progress. His works would have obviously appealed to the liberal leanings of Echenique.

[3]Henri Lacordaire (1802-1861), liberal French priest who advocated the separation of church and state.

[4]George Gordon Byron ("Lord Byron," 1788-1824), enormously popular English Romantic poet, famous for his rebellious attitudes.

[5]Alphonse de Lamartine (1790-1869), leading French Romantic poet who, like Byron, was associated with liberal movements in politics.

The savage and the ignorant who have no past, present, nor future, who are like atoms lost in the world's atmosphere, live alone: but someone who wants to, can live at least on memories and dreams and knows how to turn inward and meditate.

In these moments I live on the ideas of these great men, Elena, and I live on the past, present, and future, that is, on memories and dreams of all that forms the charm of civilized life and constitutes the man of society. And why not? I have had the good fortune to be born into the nineteenth century, the splendid theater in which the events narrated by those men have taken place; century of enlightenment, of liberty, of the emancipation of women, and of great marvels. I do not feel alone when I contemplate it from afar.

For how can I live alone if I live in history? If in my thoughts I explore the four corners of the earth and read one by one the great acts that the century embraces in its midst?"

While I read these sublime geniuses, I am where they are. I navigate the muddy waters of the Mediterranean, and of course I see the carob trees turn into Lebanese pines, into Chinese palms, into Lidian rushes, or else leaving Lamartine, I enter a populous city and with Bossuet study the passions of men, the great conquests of humankind and its religious expansion. I visit with them all the seas, all the continents, all the islands, I converse with all men and study every race.

And isn't that being accompanied, Elena?

Isn't it being in communication no longer with one society but with many societies?

Since the center of ideas has established itself definitely in the world,[6] granting to humankind freedom of thought and the freedom to express thoughts by means of the word and the pen, every civilized person lives accompanied within himself, there are no more hermits in politics, in philosophy, nor in social ideas.

Everyone who thinks, speaks and expresses their thinking, and even if far from society, is always in communication with it through ideas and the press.

Because everyone who professes ideas, beliefs, and opinions is a social being, and the recognition of that in practice or adopted as a principle, is one of the great miracles accomplished by the nineteenth century.

Because you and I, Elena, have been born in the century of miracles: I speak of the miracles accomplished by the sciences, by the arts, and by ideas.

To the ideas of the nineteenth century, we owe the miracle of the emancipation of women. If I were not free, I would not say what I am saying, I would not write what I am writing now. Two centuries ago, a book of philosophy or geometry on my lap would have been ridiculous, a useless thing; all my ideas would have been buried in chaos; a pen in my hand would have been like a crime. Any man would have thought he had the right to strangle the voice in my throat, any man, even if he himself were nothing.

Thanks to the century in which we live, not only can I freely read and study those books, but also no one raises his voice at the door of my room while I write! no one: because I am free; because I am free and I can speak and write what I like, no one opposes me, no one interrupts me.

Because I am free I have a heart full of hopes and dreams, and like most young women of this century, through the black storms that constantly agitate our existence, I see fortune smiling, I see happiness. I am in the spring of my life, all flowers must bloom.

Because women are free in the nineteenth century, one day they will not depend on anyone for their living; they can better themselves as they are doing now, one day in one

[6]As opposed to the Heavens.

aspect and another day in another, in spite of attitudes still rooted in some societies, to obtain a position which is deserving of their mission, of their talent, and of their virtue.

The miracles of the nineteenth century are all those great doings that have been happening for the last seventy years, and that astonish the world with their effects. Pope Pius IX[7] is a miracle, a repentant France is a miracle,[8] the abolition of slavery in the New and Old World is yet another miracle. A century of miracles, there is not a single person born in it who has not lived through one of them; who does not profess an idea, who does not have an ambition, who does not live from a hope, from a memory.

From the depth of this ravine, I study the century, I am already living on its ideas, I am already living on its convictions; from here I listen to the laments of humanity, the sad sighs of society's people; because just as this century is the century of miracles, it is also a cursed century in which the passions of men have overflowed, and men no longer listen to the weeping of others. Europe is crying, and its tears are lost in the Atlantic before we hear them; America is crying and its sobs are soon buried in its own solitude. Who worries about tears these days? Is there someone who would wipe the ones from my eyes?

But I do laugh at my tears, and I laugh because laughter is the salvation of the nineteenth century. To laugh, to cry and then to ponder that same laughter and crying, that is the life of a philosopher, the life of a poet, the life of all people who like me live in the presence of an idea and an emotion.

Translated by Bonnie Frederick

---

[7]Echenique is probably seeking to pacify her conservative readers by praising Pius IX, pope from 1846 to 1878, who was in fact opposed to many of the ideas of her favorite writers. It was under him that the very conservative doctrines of papal infallibility and the immaculate conception of Mary were promulgated; and he launched in his "Syllabus of Errors" an attack on all sorts of modern liberal movements, including women's rights. He certainly made a huge impression on the Catholic Church of the 19th century, so in that sense could be considered "miraculous."

[8]She is probably thinking of the collapse of the anti-clerical Paris Commune in 1871. Echenique was a liberal, but still considered herself a good Catholic.

Silvia Fernández: He and She (1876)

The elevated, idealized language that characterized romantic discourse in the nineteenth century attracted many followers but also many critics. Women writers in Latin America often portray exalted language as dangerous, misleading young women into false expectations. The following poem, published in 1876 by Silvia Fernández (Argentina, 1857–1945) pokes fun at the difference between the couple's words and their real feelings.

What does each not understand about the other?

"Goodbye, light of my life, my beauty,
Woman with skin of roses and lilies,
   My lovely angel.
Tomorrow I will return, and while I am
Away from you, pure and innocent angel,
   Remember me."

"Goodbye, absolute lord of my life,
My most beautiful and blessed hope,
   Remember me.
Don't forget that I adore you madly,
Don't forget that your love and your tenderness
   Sustain my existence."

"This woman's endearments bore me,
Her beauty isn't worth two cents,
   What skin! what a color!
I must tell her, with no hesitation,
That even if she is dying for love of me,
   It's all over."

"Finally, thank God, I'm alone!
Oh! how the gallantries of that boring man
   Tire me out!
He loves me to distraction, I am his greatest desire;
But I must get rid of him, even if, I fear,
   He should die of sorrow."

Translated by the Palouse Translation Project

Joaquim Maria Machado de Assis: *A Canary's Ideas*

Brazilian author Machado de Assis (1839-1908), the grandson of slaves and son of a mulatto father and Portuguese immigrant mother, became fluent in several languages, including French, Spanish and English. However, because he wrote in his native Portuguese, his work remained largely unknown outside his own country until the 1950s, when his Posthumous Memoirs of Bras Cubas (Epitaph of a Small Winner) *was published in English. Curiously, although he actually wrote in the last half of the 19th Century, his work has a decidedly modern appeal, as the following selection reveals in its rather surreal narrative.*

How "realistic" is this story? What does it say about the nature of "reality," e.g., How is it perceived? And who decides what it is?

A man by the name of Macedo, who had a fancy for ornithology, related to some friends an incident so extraordinary that no one took him seriously. Some came to believe he had lost his mind. Here is a summary of his narration.

At the beginning of last month, as I was walking down the street, a carriage darted past me and nearly knocked me to the ground. I escaped by quickly side-stepping into a secondhand shop. Neither the racket of the horse and carriage nor my entrance stirred the proprietor, dozing in a folding chair at the back of the shop. He was a man of shabby appearance: his beard was the color of dirty straw, and his head was covered by a tattered cap which probably had not found a buyer. One could not guess that there was any story behind him, as there could have been behind some of the objects he sold, nor could one sense in him that austere, disillusioned sadness inherent in the objects which were remnants of past lives.

The shop was dark and crowded with the sort of old, bent, broken, tarnished, rusted articles ordinarily found in secondhand shops, and everything was in that state of semidisorder befitting such an establishment. This assortment of articles, though banal, was interesting. Pots without lids, lids without pots, buttons, shoes, locks, a black skirt, straw hats, fur hats, picture frames, binoculars, dress coats, a fencing foil, a stuffed dog, a pair of slippers, gloves, nondescript vases, epaulets, a velvet satchel, two hatracks, a slingshot, a thermometer, chairs, a lithographed portrait by the late Sisson, a backgammon board, two wire masks for some future Carnival—all this and more, which I either did not see or do not remember, filled the shop in the area around the door, propped up, hung, or displayed in glass cases as old as the objects inside them. Further inside the shop were many objects of similar appearance. Predominant were the large objects—chests of drawers, chairs, and beds—some of which were stacked on top of others which were lost in the darkness.

I was about to leave, when I saw a cage hanging in the doorway. It was as old as everything else in the shop, and I expected it to be empty so it would fit in with the general appearance of desolation. However, it wasn't empty. Inside, a canary was hopping about. The bird's color, liveliness, and charm added a note of life and youth to that heap of wreckage. It was the last passenger of some wrecked ship, who had arrived in the shop as complete and happy as it had originally been. As soon as I looked at the bird, it began to hop up and down, from perch to perch, as if it meant to tell me that a ray of sunshine was frolicking in the midst of that cemetery. I'm using this image to describe the canary only because I'm speaking to rhetorical people, but the truth is that the canary thought about neither cemetery nor sun, according to what it told me later. Along with the pleasure the sight of the bird brought me, I felt indignation regarding its destiny and softly murmured these bitter words:

"What detestable owner had the nerve to rid himself of this bird for a few cents? Or what indifferent soul, not wishing to keep his late master's pet, gave it away to some child, who sold it so he could make a bet on a soccer game?"

The canary, sitting on top of its perch, trilled this reply:

"Whoever you may be, you're certainly not in your right mind. I had no detestable owner, nor was I given to any child to sell. Those are the delusions of a sick person. Go and get yourself cured, my friend . . ."

"What?" I interrupted, not having had time to become astonished. "So your master didn't sell you to this shop? It wasn't misery or laziness that brought you, like a ray of sunshine, to this cemetery?"

"I don't know what you mean by 'sunshine' or 'cemetery.' If the canaries you've seen use the first of those names, so much the better, because it sounds pretty, but really, I'm sure you're confused."

"Excuse me, but you couldn't have come here by chance, all alone. Has your master always been that man sitting over there?"

"What master? That man over there is my servant. He gives me food and water every day, so regularly that if I were to pay him for his services, it would be no small sum, but canaries don't pay their servants. In fact, since the world belongs to canaries, it would be extravagant for them to pay for what is already in the world."

Astonished by these answers, I didn't know what to marvel at more—the language or the ideas. The language, even though it entered my ears as human speech, was uttered by the bird in the form of charming trills. I looked all around me so I could determine if I were awake and saw that the street was the same, and the shop was the same dark, sad, musty place. The canary, moving from side to side, was waiting for me to speak. I then asked if it were lonely for the infinite blue space . . .

"But, my dear man," trilled the canary, "what does 'infinite blue space' mean?"

"But, pardon me, what do you think of this world? What is the world to you?"

"The world," retorted the canary, with a certain professorial air, "is a secondhand shop with a small rectangular bamboo cage hanging from a nail. The canary is lord of the cage it lives in and the shop that surrounds it. Beyond that, everything is illusion and deception."

With this, the old man woke up and approached me, dragging his feet. He asked me if I wanted to buy the canary. I asked if he had acquired it in the same way he had acquired the rest of the objects he sold and learned that he had bought it from a barber, along with a set of razors.

"The razors are in very good condition," he said.

"I only want the canary."

I paid for it, ordered a huge, circular cage of wood and wire, and had it placed on the veranda of my house so the bird could see the garden, the fountain, and a bit of blue sky.

It was my intention to do a lengthy study of this phenomenon, without saying anything to anyone until I could astound the world with my extraordinary discovery. I began by alphabetizing the canary's language in order to study its structure, its relation to music, the bird's appreciation of aesthetics, its ideas and recollections. When this philological and psychological analysis was done, I entered specifically into the study of canaries: their origin, their early history, the geology and flora of the Canary Islands, the bird's knowledge of navigation, and so forth. We conversed for hours while I took notes, and it waited, hopped about, and trilled.

As I have no family other than two servants, I ordered them not to interrupt me, even to deliver a letter or an urgent telegram or to inform me of an important visitor. Since they both knew about my scientific pursuits, they found my orders perfectly natural and did not suspect that the canary and I understood each other.

Needless to say, I slept little, woke up two or three times each night, wandered about aimlessly, and felt feverish. Finally, I returned to my work in order to reread, add, and emend. I corrected more than one observation, either because I had misunderstood something or because the bird had not expressed it clearly. The definition of the world was one of these. Three weeks after the canary's entrance into my home, I asked it to repeat to me its definition of the world.

"The world," it answered, "is a sufficiently broad garden with a fountain in the middle, flowers, shrubbery, some grass, clear air, and a bit of blue up above. The canary, lord of the world, lives in a spacious cage, white and circular, from which it looks out on the rest of the world. Everything else is illusion and deception."

The language of my treatise also suffered some modifications, and I saw that certain conclusions which had seemed simple were actually presumptuous. I still could not write the paper I was to send to the National Museum, the Historical Institute, and the German universities, not due to a lack of material but because I first had to put together all my observations and test their validity. During the last few days, I neither left the house, answered letters, nor wanted to hear from friends or relatives. The canary was everything to me. One of the servants had the job of cleaning the bird's cage and giving it food and water every morning. The bird said nothing to him, as if it knew the man was completely lacking in scientific background. Besides, the service was no more than cursory, as the servant was not a bird lover.

One Saturday I awoke ill, my head and back aching. The doctor ordered complete rest. I was suffering from an excess of studying and was not to read or even think, nor was I even to know what was going on in the city or the rest of the outside world. I remained in this condition for five days. On the sixth day I got up, and only then did I find out that the canary, while under the servant's care, had flown out of its cage. My first impulse was to strangle the servant—I was choking with indignation and collapsed into my chair, speechless and bewildered. The guilty man defended himself, swearing he had been careful, but the wily bird had nevertheless managed to escape.

"But didn't you search for it?"

"Yes, I did, sir. First it flew up to the roof, and I followed it. It flew to a tree, and then who knows where it hid itself? I've been asking around since yesterday. I asked the neighbors and the local farmers, but no one has seen the bird."

I suffered immensely. Fortunately, the fatigue left me within a few hours, and I was soon able to go out to the veranda and the garden. There was no sign of the canary. I ran everywhere, making inquiries and posting announcements, all to no avail. I had already gathered my notes together to write my paper, even though it would be disjointed and incomplete, when I happened to visit a friend who had one of the largest and most beautiful estates on the outskirts of town. We were taking a stroll before dinner when this question was trilled to me:

"Greetings, Senhor Macedo, where have you been since you disappeared?"

It was the canary, perched on the branch of a tree. You can imagine how I reacted and what I said to the bird. My friend presumed I was mad, but the opinions of friends are of no importance to me. I spoke tenderly to the canary and asked it to come home and continue our conversations in that world of ours, composed of a garden, a fountain, a veranda, and a white circular cage.

"What garden? What fountain?"

"The world, my dear bird."

"What world? I see you haven't lost any of your annoying professorial habits. The world," it solemnly concluded, "is an infinite blue space, with the sun up above."

Indignant, I replied that if I were to believe what it said, the world could be anything—it had even been a secondhand shop . . .

"A secondhand shop?" it trilled to its heart's content. "But is there really such a thing as a secondhand shop?"

Translated by Jack Schmitt and Lorie Ishimatsu

North America 1750–1900

Thomas Paine: Profession of Faith, from *The Age of Reason* (1794)

Thomas Paine came to America from his native England in 1774 with a passion for liberty and hatred of tyranny, and within two years he had become the most well-known, persuasive journalistic voice of the American Revolution. Before enlisting in the Continental Army, Paine had earned a reputation as an effective political satirist and his inflammatory pamphlet Common Sense *(1776), urging rebellion against British oppression, sold 100,000 copies in three months. Less an original thinker than an articulate conduit for the ideas of others, Paine initially participated in and wrote on the French Revolution until the excesses of the revolution became insupportable. The essay below is taken from his* The Age of Reason *(1795), written in reaction to the atheism spread by the revolutionaries. In it Paine expresses an acceptance of Deism, that widely-held belief of the eighteenth century in a rational god who has ordained the laws of nature but who is far removed from the prayers and dogmas of Christians, Jews, and Muslims.*

Having acknowledged with tolerance that there are religious beliefs other than his own, what does Paine focus on as intellectually dishonest with respect to faith? Why does he object to a close connection between church and state?

It has been my intention for several years past to publish my thoughts upon Religion. I am well aware of the difficulties that attend the subject; and from that consideration had reserved it to a more advanced period of life. I intended it to be the last offering I should make to my fellow-citizens of all nations, and that at a time when the purity of the motive that induced me to it could not admit of a question, even by those who might disapprove the work.

The circumstance that has now taken place in France, of the total abolition of the whole national order of priesthood and of everything appertaining to compulsive systems of religion and compulsive articles of faith, has not only precipitated my intention, but rendered a work of this kind exceedingly necessary; lest, in the general wreck of superstition, of false systems of government, and false theology, we lose sight of morality, of humanity, and of the theology that is true.

As several of my colleagues, and others of my fellow-citizens of France, have given me the example of making their voluntary and individual profession of faith, I also will make mine; and I do this with all that sincerity and frankness with which the mind of man communicates with itself.

I believe in one God, and no more; and I hope for happiness beyond this life.

I believe in the equality of man, and I believe that religious duties consist in doing justice, loving mercy, and endeavoring to make our fellow creatures happy.

But lest it should be supposed that I believe many other things in addition to these, I shall, in the progress of this work, declare the things I do not believe and my reasons for not believing them.

I do not believe in the creed professed by the Jewish church, by the Roman church, by the Greek church, by the Turkish church, by the Protestant church, nor by any church that

I know of. My own mind is my own church.

All national institutions of churches—whether Jewish, Christian, or Turkish—appear to me no other than human inventions set up to terrify and enslave mankind and monopolize power and profit.

I do not mean by this declaration to condemn those who believe otherwise. They have the same right to their belief as I have to mine. But it is necessary to the happiness of man that he be mentally faithful to himself. Infidelity does not consist in believing or in disbelieving; it consists in professing to believe what he does not believe.

It is impossible to calculate the moral mischief, if I may so express it, that mental lying has produced in society. When a man has so far corrupted and prostituted the chastity of his mind as to subscribe his professional belief to things he does not believe, he has prepared himself for the commission of every other crime. He takes up the trade of a priest for the sake of gain, and, in order to qualify himself for that trade, he begins with a perjury. Can we conceive anything more destructive to morality than this?

Soon after I had published the pamphlet, COMMON SENSE, in America, I saw the exceeding probability that a revolution in the system of government would be followed by a revolution in the system of religion. The adulterous connection of church and state, wherever it had taken place, whether Jewish, Christian, or Turkish, had so effectually prohibited, by pains and penalties, every discussion upon established creeds and upon first principles of religion, that until the system of government should be changed those subjects could not be brought fairly and openly before the world; but that whenever this should be done, a revolution in the system of religion would follow. Human inventions and priestcraft would be detected, and man would return to the pure, unmixed, and unadulterated belief of one God, and no more.

Abraham Lincoln: Second Inaugural Address (March 4, 1865)

Abraham Lincoln, sixteenth President of the United States, is regarded by his countrymen and women as possibly the nation's greatest political leader, principally for his successful effort to preserve the Union at a time when the Confederate states sought to secede. Although reared in the then frontier of Illinois and regarded by many Eastern politicians as uncouth and socially awkward, Lincoln was in fact a skilled politician and superb writer and speaker. The speech below, which marked his re-election to a second term, was delivered a month before the Civil War would end and six weeks before his assassination on April 14, 1865. The speech displays a simple eloquence, and like most of Lincoln's speeches contains a number of biblical quotations or allusions. Lincoln's references to the causes of the bloody war and the injustices of slavery are muted here, and end of the speech is justly celebrated for its conciliatory and magnanimous tone.

How does Lincoln contrast the attitude toward slavery common in the Union at the beginning of the war with that which he proclaims here?

Fellow Countrymen:

At this second appearing to take the oath of the presidential office, there is less occasion for an extended address than there was at the first. Then a statement, somewhat in detail, of a course to be pursued, seemed fitting and proper. Now, at the expiration of four years, during which public declarations have been constantly called forth on every point and phase of the great contest which still absorbs the attention, and engrosses the energies of the nation, little that is new could be presented. The progress of our arms, upon which all else chiefly depends, is as well known to the public as to myself; and it is, I trust, reasonably satisfactory and encouraging to all. With high hope for the future, no prediction in regard to it so ventured.

On the occasion corresponding to this four years ago, all thoughts were anxiously directed to an impending civil-war. All dreaded it—all sought to avert it. While the inaugural address was being delivered from this place, devoted altogether to *saving* the Union without war, insurgent agents were in the city seeking to *destroy* it without war—seeking to dissolve the Union, and divide effects, by negotiation. Both parties deprecated war; but one of them would *make* war rather than let the nation survive; and others would *accept* war rather than let it perish. And the war came.

One eighth of the whole population were colored slaves, not distributed generally over the Union, but localized in the Southern part of it. These slaves constituted a peculiar and powerful interest. All knew that this interest was somehow, the cause of the war. To strengthen, perpetuate, and extend this interest was the object for which the insurgents would rend the Union, even by war; while the government claimed no right to do more than to restrict the territorial enlargement of it. Neither party expected for the war, the magnitude, or the duration, which it has already attained. Neither anticipated that the cause of the conflict might cease with, or even before, the conflict itself should cease. Each looked for an easier triumph, and a result less fundamental and astounding. Both read the same Bible, and pray to the same God; and each invokes His aid against the other. It may seem strange that any men should dare ask a just God's assistance in wringing their bread from the sweat of other men's faces; but let us judge not that we will be not judged.[1] The prayers of both could not be answered; that of neither has been answered fully. The Al-

[1]See Matthew 7:1.

mighty has His own purposes. "Woe unto the world because of offenses! for it must needs be that offenses come; but woe to that man by whom the offense cometh!"[2] If we shall suppose that American Slavery is one of those offenses which, in the providence of God, must needs come, but which, having continued through His appointed time, He now wills to remove, and that He gives to both North and South, this terrible war, as the woe due to those by whom the offense came, shall we discern therein any departure from those divine attributes which the believers in a Living God always ascribe to Him? Fondly do we hope—fervently do we pray—that this mighty scourge of war may speedily pass away. Yet, if God wills that it continue, until all the wealth piled by the bond-man's two hundred and fifty years of unrequited toil shall be sunk, and until every drop of blood drawn with the lash, shall be paid by another drawn with the sword, as was said three thousand years ago, so still it must be said "the judgments of the Lord, are true and righteous altogether."[3]

With malice toward none; with charity for all; with firmness in the right, as God gives us to see the right, let us strive on to finish the work we are in, to bind up the nation's wounds; to care for him who shall have borne the battle, and for his widow, and his orphan—to do all which may achieve and cherish a just, and a lasting peace, among ourselves, and with all nations.

---

[2]Matthew 18:7.
[3]Psalms 19:9.

Mark Twain: An American's View of Europe from *Innocents Abroad* (1869)

Throughout its early history Americans suffered from ambivalent feelings about Europe. As settlers in the "New World," they claimed to have begun civilization afresh on a fairer footing than the corrupt culture of old Europe, and often took some pleasure in boasting about the superior attractions of their native land. However, they also had to acknowledge that the United States lacked the long historical traditions and great artistic achievements of a country like France. Having founded their nation on a rejection of monarchy, they were often fascinated by the actual monarchs they encountered. As many writers such as Henry James and Edith Wharton were to be later, Mark Twain was fascinated by the splendors and wretchedness he encountered on this first trip to Europe, where he had been sent by a newspaper to report on a grand tour mostly populated with pious travelers whose main interest was in the culminating exploration of sacred sites in Palestine. Twain was self-consciously a rowdy Westerner and a scoffer, but he was also a Victorian in his attitudes toward sex, as is revealed in his account of the popular French can-can. He appreciated little of the art he saw, and many of the pictures in the Louvre offended his democratic instincts. Although there are many lavish portraits of nobles in that museum, he may have been reacting even more to the numerous pictures which depict titled lords and ladies familiarly posing with Mary and the infant Jesus.

What is his reaction when he encounters a real-life monarch in the Bois de Boulogne? What contrast in attitudes toward history does he suggest between the U.S. and Europe in the final paragraph?

The dance had begun, and we adjourned to the temple.[1] Within it was a drinking-saloon; and all around it was a broad circular platform for the dancers. I backed up against the wall of the temple, and waited. Twenty sets formed, the music struck up, and then—I placed my hands before my face for very shame. But I looked through my fingers. They were dancing the renowned "Can-can." A handsome girl in the set before me tripped forward lightly to meet the opposite gentleman—tripped back again, grasped her dresses vigorously on both sides with her hands, raised them pretty high, danced an extraordinary jig that had more activity and exposure about it than any jig I ever saw before, and then, drawing her clothes still higher, she advanced gaily to the center and launched a vicious kick full at her vis-a-vis[2] that must infallibly have removed his nose if he had been seven feet high. It was a mercy he was only six.

That is the Can-can. The idea of it is to dance as wildly, as noisily, as furiously as you can; expose yourself as much as possible if you are a woman; and kick as high as you can, no matter which sex you belong to. There is no word of exaggeration in this. Any of the staid, respectable, aged people who were there that night can testify to the truth of that statement. There were a good many such people present. I suppose French morality is not of that strait-laced description which is shocked at trifles.

I moved aside and took a general view of the Can-can. Shouts, laughter, furious music, a bewildering chaos of darting and intermingling forms, stormy jerking and snatching of gay dresses, bobbing heads, flying arms, lightning flashes of white-stockinged calves and dainty slippers in the air, and then a grand final rush, riot, a terrific hubbub, and a wild

[1]Ironic term for a dance-hall.

[2]Partner facing her.

stampede! Heavens! Nothing like it has been seen on earth since trembling Tam O'Shanter saw the devil and the witches at their orgies that stormy night in "Alloway's auld haunted kirk."[3]

We visited the Louvre . . . and looked at its miles of paintings by the old masters. Some of them were beautiful, but at the same time they carried such evidences about them of the cringing spirit of those great men that we found small pleasure in examining them. Their nauseous adulation of princely patrons was more prominent to me and chained my attention more surely than the charms of color and expression which are claimed to be in the pictures. Gratitude for kindnesses is well, but it seems to me that some of those artists carried it so far that it ceased to be gratitude, and became worship. If there is a plausible excuse for the worship of men, then by all means let us forgive Rubens and his brethren.

But I will drop the subject, lest I say something about the old masters that might as well be left unsaid.

Of course we drove in the Bois de Boulogne, that limitless park, with its forests, its lakes, its cascades, and its broad avenues. There were thousands upon thousands of vehicles abroad, and the scene was full of life and gaiety. There were very common hacks,[4] with father and mother and all the children in them; conspicuous little open carriages with celebrated ladies of questionable reputation in them; there were Dukes and Duchesses abroad, with gorgeous footmen perched behind, and equally gorgeous outriders perched on each of the six horses; there were blue and silver, and green and gold, and pink and black, and all sorts and descriptions of stunning and startling liveries out, and I almost yearned to be a flunkey myself, for the sake of the fine clothes.

But presently the Emperor[5] came along and he outshone them all. He was preceded by a body-guard of gentlemen on horseback in showy uniforms, his carriage-horses (there appeared to be somewhere in the remote neighborhood of a thousand of them) were bestridden by gallant-looking fellows, also in stylish uniforms, and after the carriage followed another detachment of body-guards. Everybody got out of the way; everybody bowed to the Emperor and his friend the Sultan, and they went by on a swinging trot and disappeared.

I will not describe the Bois de Boulogne. I cannot do it. It is simply a beautiful, cultivated, endless, wonderful wilderness. It is an enchanting place. It is in Paris, now, one may say, but a crumbling old cross in one portion of it reminds one that it was not always so. The cross marks the spot where a celebrated troubadour was waylaid and murdered in the fourteenth century.[6] It was in this park that that fellow with an unpronounceable name made the attempt upon the Russian Czar's life last spring with a pistol.[7] The bullet struck a tree. Ferguson[8] showed us the place. Now in America that interesting tree would be chopped down or forgotten within the next five years, but it will be treasured here. The guides will point it out to visitors for the next eight hundred years, and when it decays and falls down they will put up another there and go on with the same old story just the same.

---

[3]A church ("kirk") in the Scottish town of Alloway, from "Tam O'Shanter," a poem by Robert Burns, written 1790.

[4]Horse-drawn cabs.

[5]Napoleon III, overthrown the year after this was published.

[6]The Pré Catelan in the Bois is named after Catelan, a now obscure troubadour.

[7]The would-be asssasin of Czar Alexander II was named Berezovsky. Several assassins tried to kill him before one succeeded in 1881.

[8]The name Twain jokingly gave to all his tour guides.

Henry David Thoreau: *Civil Disobedience* (1846)

When the U.S. annexed Texas in 1845 it precipitated a war of which many in the U.S. disapproved, including the philosopher and social critic Henry David Thoreau, who went to jail for refusing to pay his taxes in protest. Like Sophocles' Antigone, Thoreau argues in this essay that individual rights must sometimes take precedence over state authority. It has inspired many protesters since, people as varied as civil rights advocates and libertarian militarists.

What does Thoreau mean by "casting your whole vote?"

I heartily accept the motto—"That government is best which governs least;" and I should like to see it acted up to more rapidly and systematically. Carried out, it finally amounts to this, which also I believe,—"That government is best which governs not at all;" and when men are prepared for it, that will be the kind of government which they will have. Government is at best but an expedient; but most governments are usually, and all governments are sometimes, inexpedient. The objections which have been brought against a standing army, and they are many and weighty, and deserve to prevail, may also at last be brought against a standing government. The standing army is only an arm of the standing government. The government itself, which is only the mode which the people have chosen to execute their will, is equally liable to be abused and perverted before the people can act through it. Witness the present Mexican war, the work of comparatively a few individuals using the standing government as their tool; for in the outset, the people would not have consented to this measure. . . .

Under a government which imprisons any unjustly, the true place for a just man is also in prison. The proper place to-day, the only place which Massachusetts has provided for her freer and less desponding spirits, is in her prisons, to be put out and locked out of the State by her own act, as they have already put themselves out by their principles. It is there that the fugitive slave, and the Mexican prisoner on parole, and the Indian come to plead the wrongs of his race, should find them; on that separate, but more free and honorable ground, where the State places those who are not *with* her, but *against* her,—the only house in a slave-state in which a free man can abide with honor. If any think that their influence would be lost there, and their voices no longer afflict the ear of the State, that they would not be as an enemy within its walls, they do not know by how much truth is stronger than error, nor how much more eloquently and effectively he can combat injustice who has experienced a little in his own person. Cast your whole vote, not a strip of paper merely, but your whole influence. A minority is powerless while it conforms to the majority; it is not even a minority then; but it is irresistible when it clogs by its whole weight. If the alternative is to keep all just men in prison, or give up war and slavery, the State will not hesitate which to choose. If a thousand men were not to pay their tax-bills this year, that would not be a violent and bloody measure, as it would be to pay them, and enable the State to commit violence and shed innocent blood. This is, in fact, the definition of a peaceable revolution, if any such is possible. If the tax-gatherer, or any other public officer, asks me, as one has done, "But what shall I do?" my answer is, "If you really wish to do anything, resign your office." When the subject has refused allegiance, and the officer has resigned his office, then the revolution is accomplished. But even suppose blood should flow. Is there not a sort of blood shed when the conscience is wounded? Through this wound a man's real manhood and immortality flow out, and he bleeds to an everlasting death. I see this blood flowing now.

Walt Whitman: *Song of Myself* (1855)

Before he published his first volume of poetry, Leaves of Grass, *in 1855 at the age of thirty-six, Walt Whitman had dirtied his hands as a typesetter and carpenter, had lived in New York City and traveled to the American South, had been a newspaper reporter and editor, and had become an astute political observer of his country on the verge of civil war. His poetry reflects the depth and breadth of his intellectual and existential experience and it displays a particularly American tone. Like much of his work, "Song of Myself" is an experimental form of poetry that would help revolutionize American poetry by the turn of the century. It broke with the conventional blank verse (unrhymed iambic pentameter) and presented autobiography unashamedly almost as a stream of consciousness. But the poem, which runs to fifty-two sections, gradually moves beyond drama of a single self as the "I" of the poem becomes associated mystically with all of humanity. Whitman's poetry skillfully balances the vaguely spiritual with an insistent, concrete reality, often achieved by piling up catalogues of ordinary things.*

What makes these long, unrhymed lines poetic? What is the effect of the I or Self of the poem alternating between assertions of specialness and identification with others? What kind of attitude toward living is he trying to encourage in this poem? What do you think his attitude toward nature is?

1

I celebrate myself, and sing myself,
And what I assume you shall assume,
For every atom belonging to me as good belongs to you.

I loafe and invite my soul,
I lean and loafe at my ease observing a spear of summer grass.

My tongue, every atom of my blood, form'd from this soil, this air,
Born here of parents born here from parents the same, and their parents the same,
I, now thirty-seven years old in perfect health begin,
Hoping to cease not till death.

Creeds and schools in abeyance,
Retiring back a while sufficed at what they are, but never forgotten,
I harbor for good or bad, I permit to speak at every hazard,
Nature without check with original energy.

2

Houses and rooms are full of perfumes, the shelves are crowded with perfumes,
I breathe the fragrance myself and know it and like it,
The distillation would intoxicate me also, but I shall not let it.
The atmosphere is not a perfume, it has no taste of the distillation, it is odorless,
It is for my mouth forever, I am in love with it,
I will go to the bank by the wood and become undisguised and naked:
I am mad for it to be in contact with me.

The smoke of my own breath,
Echoes, ripples, buzz'd whispers, love-root, silk-thread, crotch and vine
My respiration and inspiration, the beating of my heart, the passing of blood and air through my lungs,
The sniff of green leaves and dry leaves, and of the shore and dark color'd sea-rocks, and of hay in the barn,
The sound of the belch'd words of my voice loos'd to the eddies of the wind,
A few light kisses, a few embraces, a reaching around of arms,
The play of shine and shade on the trees as the supple boughs wag,
The delight alone or in the rush of the streets, or along the fields and hill-sides.
The feeling of health, the full-noon trill, the song of me rising from bed and meeting the sun.

Have you reckon'd a thousand acres much? have you reckon'd the earth much?
Have you practis'd so long to learn to read?
Have you felt so proud to get at the meaning of poems?
Stop this day and night with me and you shall possess the origin of all poems,
You shall possess the good of the earth and sun, (there are millions of suns left),
You shall no longer take things at second or third hand, nor look through the eyes of the dead, nor feed on the spectres in books,
You shall not look through my eyes either, nor take things from me,
You shall listen to all sides and filter them from your self.

3

I have heard what the talkers were talking, the talk of the beginning and the end
But I do not talk of the beginning or the end.
There was never any more inception than there is now,
Nor any more youth or age than there is now,
And will never be any more perfection than there is now,
Nor any more heaven or hell than there is now.

Urge and urge and urge,
Always the procreant urge of the world.
Out of the dimness opposite equals advance, always substance and increase, always sex,
Always a knit of identity, always distinction, always a breed of life.
To elaborate is no avail, learn'd and unlearn'd feel that it is so.

Sure as the most certain sure, plumb in the uprights, well entretied,[1] braced in the beams,
Stout as a horse, affectionate, haughty, electrical,
I and this mystery here we stand.

Clear and sweet is my soul, and clear and sweet is all that is not my soul.

Lack one lacks both, and the unseen is proved by the seen,
Till that becomes unseen and receives proof in its turn.

---

[1]Supported. A term from carpentry.

Showing the best and dividing it from the worst age vexes age,
Knowing the perfect fitness and equanimity of things, while they discuss I am silent, and go bathe and admire myself.

Welcome is every organ and attribute of me, and of any man hearty and clean,
Not an inch nor a particle of an inch is vile, and none shall be less familiar than the rest.

I am satisfied—I see, dance, laugh, sing;
As the hugging and loving bed-fellow[2] sleeps at my side through the night, and withdraws at the peep of the day with stealthy tread.
Leaving me baskets cover'd with white towels swelling the house with their plenty,
Shall I postpone my acceptation and realization and scream at my eyes,
That they turn from gazing after and down the road,
And forthwith cipher[3] and show me to a cent,
Exactly the value of one and exactly the value of two, and which is ahead?

4

Trippers and askers[4] surround me,
People I meet, the effect upon me of my early life or the ward and city I live in, or the nation,
The latest dates, discoveries, inventions, societies, authors old and new,
My dinner, dress, associates, looks, compliments, dues,
The real or fancied indifference of some man or woman I love,
The sickness of one of my folks or of myself, or ill-doing or loss or lack of money, or depressions or exaltations,
Battles, the horrors of fratricidal[5] war, the fever of doubtful news, the fitful events;
These come to me days and nights and go from me again,
But they are not the Me myself.

Apart from the pulling and hauling stands what I am,
Stands amused, complacent, compassionating, idle, unitary,
Looks down, is erect, or bends an arm on an impalpable certain rest,
Looking with side-curved head curious what will come next,
Both in and out of the game and watching and wondering at it.

Backward I see in my own days where I sweated through fog with linguists and contenders,
I have no mockings or arguments, I witness and wait.

5

I believe in you my soul, the other I am must not abase itself to you,
And you must not be abased to the other.

---

[2]God.
[3]Calculate.
[4]Travelers and panhandlers.
[5]Brother killing brother, as in the American Civil War.

Loafe with me on the grass, loose the stop from your throat,
Not words, not music or rhyme I want, not custom or lecture, not even the best,
Only the lull I like, the hum of your valved voice.

I mind how once we lay such a transparent summer morning,
How you settled your head athwart my hips and gently turn'd over upon me,
And parted the shirt from my bosom-bone, and plunged your tongue to my bare-stript heart,
And reach'd till you felt my beard, and reach'd till you held my feet.

Swiftly arose and spread around me the peace and knowledge that pass all the argument of the earth,
And I know that the hand of God is the promise of my own,
And I know that the spirit of God is the brother of my own,
And that all the men ever born are also my brothers, and the women my sisters and lovers,
And that a kelson[6] of the creation is love,
And limitless are leaves stiff or drooping in the fields,
And brown ants in the little wells beneath them,
And mossy scabs of the worm fenced heap'd stones, elder, mullein and poke-weed.

6

A child said *What is the grass?* fetching it to me with full hands;
How could I answer the child? I do not know what it is any more than he.

I guess it must be the flag of my disposition, out of hopeful green stuff woven.

Or I guess it is the handkerchief of the Lord,
A scented gift and remembrancer designedly dropt,
Bearing the owner's name someway in the corners, that we may see and remark, and say *Whose?*
Or I guess the grass is itself a child, the produced babe of the vegetation.

Or I guess it is a uniform hieroglyphic,
And it means, Sprouting alike in broad zones and narrow zones,
Growing among black folks as among white,
Kanuck, Tuckahoe, Congressman, Cuff,[7] I give them the same, I receive them the same.

And now it seems to me the beautiful uncut hair of graves.

Tenderly will I use you curling grass,
It may be you transpire from the breasts of young men,
It may be if I had known them I would have loved them.
It may be you are from old people, or from offspring taken soon out of their mothers' laps,

---

[6]Keel, basis.

[7]French Canadian, Tuckahoe Indian, Virginian, African-American.

And here you are the mothers' laps.

This grass is very dark to be from the white heads of old mothers.
Darker than the colorless beards of old men,
Dark to come from under the faint red roofs of mouths.

O I perceive after all so many uttering tongues,
And I perceive they do not come from the roofs of mouths for nothing.

I wish I could translate the hints about the dead young men and women,
And the hints about old men and mothers, and the offspring taken soon out of their laps.

What do you think has become of the young and old men?
And what do you think has become of the women and children?

They are alive and well somewhere,
The smallest sprout shows there is really no death,
And if ever there was it led forward life, and does not wait at the end to arrest it,
And ceas'd the moment life appear'd.

All goes onward and outward, nothing collapses,
And to die is different from what any one supposed, and luckier.

Emily Dickinson (1830-86)

Emily Dickinson wrote a highly idiosyncratic poetry on the joy and pain of existence. Her poetry is compressed, sharp, but sometimes ambiguous. She is exciting because she combines passion with intellectual wit. In "After Great Pain" she refers to nerves sitting like tombs and uses "hour of lead" and "quartz contentment" as metaphors of special awareness of emotional hurt. In "Because I Could not Stop for Death," she personifies death as a kindly gentleman taking a lady for a ride and on their journey they pass the vitality of life en route to eternity. In "Wild Nights" she displays a desire for love which combines the security of a harbor with the passion of a storm. Moored safely in her love's arms she would have no need for the tools of travel: compass, sailing chart, or winds for the sails.

What metaphors for emotional numbness can you find in this poem?

After great pain

After great pain, a formal feeling comes—
The Nerves sit ceremonious, like Tombs—
The stiff Heart questions was it He, that bore,
And Yesterday, or Centuries before?

The Feet, mechanical, go round—
Of Ground, or Air, or Ought—[1]
A Wooden way
Regardless grown,
A Quartz contentment, like a stone—

This is the Hour of Lead—
Remembered, if outlived,
As Freezing persons, recollect the Snow—
First—Chill—then Stupor—then the letting go—

---

[1]Emptiness, nothingness.

Because I could not stop for Death

Judging by the end of the poem, from what perspective is the voice in the poem describing these events?

Because I could not stop for Death—
He kindly stopped for me—
The Carriage held but just Ourselves—
and Immortality.

We slowly drove—He knew no haste
And I had put away

My labor and my leisure too,
For His Civility—
We passed the School, where Children strove
At Recess—in the Ring—
We passed the Fields of Gazing Grain—
We passed the Setting Sun—

Or rather—He passed Us—
The Dews drew quivering and chill—
For only Gossamer, my Gown—
My Tippet[2]—only Tulle[3]—

We paused before a House that seemed
A Swelling of the Ground—
The Roof was scarcely visible—
The Cornice—in the Ground—

Since then—'Tis Centuries—and yet
Feels shorter than the Day
I first surmised the Horses Heads
Were toward Eternity—

---

[2]Scarf
[3]Both gossamer and tulle are fine sheer fabrics, providing little or no warmth.

Wild nights—wild nights!

What sort of "wildness" is this poem about? What is unusual about longing to experience wildness in port rather than out at sea?

Wild nights—wild nights!
Were I with thee,
Wild nights should be
Our luxury.

Futile the winds
To a heart in port
Done with the compass,
Done with the chart.

Rowing in Eden—
Ah, the sea!
Might I but moor tonight
In thee.

Africa 1900-Present

Joseph Conrad: *Heart of Darkness* (1902)

Heart of Darkness *has been considered for most of this century not only as a literary classic, but as a powerful indictment of the evils of imperialism. It reflects the savage repressions carried out in the Congo by the Belgians in one of the largest acts of genocide committed up to that time. Conrad's narrator encounters at the end of the story a man named Kurtz, dying, insane, and guilty of unspeakable atrocities. More recently, African critics like Chinua Achebe have pointed out that the story can be read as a racist or colonialist parable in which Africans are depicted as innately irrational and violent, and in which Africa itself is reduced to a metaphor for that which white Europeans fear within themselves. The people of Africa and the land they live in remain inscrutably alien, other. The title, they argue, implies that Africa* is *the "heart of darkness," where whites who "go native" risk releasing the "savage" within themselves. Defenders of Conrad sometimes argue that the narrator does not speak in Conrad's own voice, and that a layer of irony conceals his true views.*

What is your impression of these opening pages from Heart of Darkness? *Do the Africans seem stereotyped to you? What signs are there that the narrator is sympathetic to them?*

"I left in a French steamer, and she called in every blamed port they have out there, for, as far as I could see, the sole purpose of landing soldiers and custom-house officers. I watched the coast. Watching a coast as it slips by the ship is like thinking about an enigma. There it is before you— smiling, frowning, inviting, grand, mean, insipid, or savage, and always mute with an air of whispering, Come and find out. This one was almost featureless, as if still in the making, with an aspect of monotonous grimness. The edge of a colossal jungle, so dark-green as to be almost black, fringed with white surf, ran straight, like a ruled line, far, far away along a blue sea whose glitter was blurred by a creeping mist. The sun was fierce, the land seemed to glisten and drip with steam. Here and there grayish-whitish specks showed up clustered inside the white surf, with a flag flying above them perhaps. Settlements some centuries old, and still no bigger than pinheads on the untouched expanse of their background. We pounded along, stopped, landed soldiers; went on, landed custom-house clerks to levy toll in what looked like a God-forsaken wilderness, with a tin shed and a flagpole lost in it; landed more soldiers—to take care of the custom-house clerks, presumably. Some, I heard, got drowned in the surf; but whether they did or not, nobody seemed particularly to care. They were just flung out there, and on we went. Every day the coast looked the same, as though we had not moved; but we passed various places—trading places—with names like Gran' Bassam, Little Popo; names that seemed to belong to some sordid farce acted in front of a sinister back-cloth. The idleness of a passenger, my isolation amongst all these men with whom I had no point of contact, the oily and languid sea, the uniform somberness of the coast, seemed to keep me away from the truth of things, within the toil of a mournful and senseless delusion. The voice of the surf heard now and then was a positive pleasure, like the speech of a brother. It was something natural, that had its reason, that had a meaning. Now and then a boat from the shore gave one a momentary contact with reality. It was paddled by black fellows. You could see from afar the white of their eyeballs glistening. They shouted, sang; their bodies streamed with perspiration; they had faces like grotesque masks—these chaps; but they had bone, muscle, a wild vitality, an intense energy of movement, that was as natural and true as the surf along their coast. They wanted no excuse for being there. They were a great comfort to look at. For a time I would feel I belonged still to a world of straightforward facts; but the feeling would not last long. Something would turn up to scare it away. Once, I remember, we came upon a man-of-war anchored off the coast. There wasn't even a shed there, and she was shelling the bush. It appears the French had one of their wars going on thereabouts. Her ensign[1] dropped limp like a rag; the muzzles of the long six-inch guns stuck out all over the low hull; the greasy, slimy swell swung her up lazily and let her down, swaying her thin masts. In the empty immensity of earth, sky, and water, there she was, incomprehensible, firing into a continent. Pop, would go one of the six-inch guns; a small flame would dart and vanish, a little white smoke would disappear, a tiny projectile would give a feeble screech—and nothing happened. Nothing could happen. There was a touch of insanity in the proceeding, a sense of lugubrious drollery in the sight; and it was not dissipated by somebody on board assuring me earnestly there was a camp of natives—he called them enemies!—hidden out of sight somewhere.

"We gave her her letters (I heard the men in that lonely ship were dying of fever at the rate of three a day) and went on. We called at some more places with farcical names, where the merry dance of death and trade goes on in a still and earthy atmosphere as of an overheated catacomb; all along the formless coast bordered by dangerous surf, as if Nature herself had tried to ward off intruders; in and out of rivers, streams of death in life, whose banks were rotting into mud, whose waters, thickened into slime, invaded the contorted mangroves that seemed to writhe at us in the extremity of an impotent despair. Nowhere did we stop long enough to get a particularized impression, but the general sense of vague and oppressive wonder grew upon me. It was like a weary pilgrimage amongst hints for nightmares.

"It was upward of thirty days before I saw the mouth of the big river. We anchored off the seat of the government. But my work would not begin till some two hundred miles farther on. So as soon as I could I made a start for a place thirty miles higher up.

"I had my passage on a little sea-going steamer. Her captain was a Swede, and knowing me for a seaman, invited me on the bridge. He was a young man, lean, fair, and morose, with lanky hair and a shuffling gait. As we left the miserable little wharf, he tossed his head contemptuously at the shore. 'Been living there?' he asked. I said, 'Yes.' 'Fine lot these government chaps—are they not?' he went on, speaking English with great precision and considerable bitterness. 'It is funny what some people will do for a few francs a month. I wonder what becomes of that kind when it goes up country?' I said to him I expected to see that soon. 'So-o-o!' he exclaimed. He shuffled athwart, keeping one eye ahead vigilantly. 'Don't be too sure,' he continued. 'The other day I took up a man who hanged himself on the road. He was a Swede, too.' 'Hanged himself! Why, in God's name?' I cried. He kept on looking out watchfully. 'Who knows? The sun too much for him, or the country perhaps.'

"At last we opened a reach.[2] A rocky cliff appeared, mounds of turned-up earth by the

---

[1]A small flag

[2]Reached a straight stretch of river.

shore, houses on a hill, others with iron roofs, amongst a waste of excavations, or hanging to the declivity. A continuous noise of the rapids above hovered over this scene of inhabited devastation. A lot of people, mostly black and naked, moved about like ants. A jetty projected into the river. A blinding sunlight drowned all this at times in a sudden recrudescence of glare. 'There's your Company's station,' said the Swede, pointing to three wooden barrack-like structures on the rocky slope. 'I will send your things up. Four boxes did you say? So. Farewell.'

"I came upon a boiler wallowing in the grass, then found a path leading up the hill. It turned aside for the boulders, and also for an undersized railway-truck lying there on its back with its wheels in the air. One was off. The thing looked as dead as the carcass of some animal. I came upon more pieces of decaying machinery, a stack of rusty rails. To the left a clump of trees made a shady spot, where dark things seemed to stir feebly. I blinked, the path was steep. A horn tooted to the right, and I saw the black people run. A heavy and dull detonation shook the ground, a puff of smoke came out of the cliff, and that was all. No change appeared on the face of the rock. They were building a railway. The cliff was not in the way or anything; but this objectless blasting was all the work going on.

"A slight clinking behind me made me turn my head. Six black men advanced in a file, toiling up the path. They walked erect and slow, balancing small baskets full of earth on their heads, and the clink kept time with their footsteps. Black rags were wound round their loins, and the short ends behind waggled to and fro like tails. I could see every rib, the joints of their limbs were like knots in a rope; each had an iron collar on his neck, and all were connected together with a chain whose bights swung between them, rhythmically clinking. Another report from the cliff made me think suddenly of that ship of war I had seen firing into a continent. It was the same kind of ominous voice; but these men could by no stretch of imagination be called enemies. They were called criminals, and the outraged law, like the bursting shells had come to them, an insoluble mystery from the sea. All their meager breasts panted together, the violently dilated nostrils quivered, the eyes stared stonily up-hill. They passed me within six inches, without a glance, with that complete, deathlike indifference of unhappy savages. Behind this raw matter one of the reclaimed, the product of the new forces at work, strolled despondently, carrying a rifle by its middle. He had a uniform jacket with one button off, and seeing a white man on the path, hoisted his weapon to his shoulder with alacrity. This was simple prudence, white men being so much alike at a distance that he could not tell who I might be. He was speedily reassured, and with a large, white, rascally grin, and a glance at his charge, seemed to take me into partnership in his exalted trust. After all, I was also a part of the great cause of these high and just proceedings.

"Instead of going up, I turned and descended to the left. My idea was to let that chain-gang get out of sight before I climbed the hill. You know I am not particularly tender; I've had to strike and to fend off. I've had to resist and to attack sometimes—that's the only way of resisting—without counting the exact cost, according to the demands of such sort of life as I had blundered into. I've seen the devil of violence, and the devil of greed, and the devil of hot desire; but, by all the stars! these were strong, lusty, red-eyed devils, that swayed and drove men—men, I tell you. But as I stood on this hillside, I foresaw that in the blinding sunshine of that land I would become acquainted with a flabby, pretending, weak-eyed devil of a rapacious and pitiless folly. How insidious he could be, too, I was only to find out several months later and a thousand miles farther. For a moment I stood appalled, as though by a warning. Finally I descended the hill, obliquely, towards the trees I had seen.

Chinua Achebe: *Things Fall Apart* (1958)

Things Fall Apart *is a moving and detailed account of life in a typical Ibo village (the name "Umuofia" means "people of the forest") in what is now Nigeria, on the eve of its first encounter with Europeans. Although the novel depicts some traditional patterns negatively, it generally depicts a vital, thriving society in which complex social sanctions regulate the behavior of its members. The protagonist, Okonkwo, is a misfit whose shame at having had an indolent father has caused him to exaggerate his aggressive qualities. Fiercely proud and quick to anger, his refusal to compromise repeatedly causes trouble for himself and ultimately brings disaster to the entire village. The title of this novel slyly inverts the meaning of the phrase in William Butler Yeats' apocalyptic poem, "The Second Coming." Whereas Yeats anticipated the destruction of European civilization through the collapse of its values; it is precisely the arrival of the "civilized" Europeans in Africa that causes the culture of the Ibo to collapse. At the beginning of the following passage, Ikemefuna, a boy taken hostage from another tribe with which the Umuofians have been at war, has come to live with Okonkwo's family. Note that his polygamous household is arranged in traditional fashion, in a large compound, with separate dwellings for each wife and her children and a private residence for the husband.*

In this society, women are clearly subordinated to men, but they do have some rights and privileges. What social patterns can you discern in the following passage which serve to protect women? What limits can you see to those protections? How does Achebe challenge the stereotype that traditional societies are static and unchanging?

Ikemefuna came to Umuofia at the end of the carefree season between harvest and planting.[1] In fact he recovered from his illness only a few days before the Week of Peace began. And that was also the year Okonkwo broke the peace, and was punished, as was the custom, by Ezeani, the priest of the earth goddess.

Okonkwo was provoked to justifiable anger by his youngest wife, who went to plait her hair at her friend's house and did not return early enough to cook the afternoon meal. Okonkwo did not know at first that she was not at home. After waiting in vain for her dish he went to her hut to see what she was doing. There was nobody in the hut and the fireplace was cold.

"Where is Ojiugo?" he asked his second wife, who came out of her hut to draw water from a gigantic pot in the shade of a small tree in the middle of the compound.

"She has gone to plait her hair."

Okonkwo bit his lips as anger welled up within him.

"Where are her children? Did she take them?" he asked with unusual coolness and restraint.

"They are here," answered his first wife, Nwoye's mother. Okonkwo bent down and looked into her hut. Ojiugo's children were eating with the children of his first wife.

"Did she ask you to feed them before she went?"

"Yes," lied Nwoye's mother, trying to minimize Ojiugo's thoughtlessness.

Okonkwo knew she was not speaking the truth. He walked back to his obi[2] to await

---

[1]This child has been temporarily adopted into Okonkwo's family as a hostage from a just-concluded war with another village.

[2]The large living quarters of the head of the household.

Ojiugo's return. And when she returned he beat her very heavily. In his anger he had forgotten that it was the Week of Peace. His first two wives ran out in great alarm pleading with him that it was the sacred week. But Okonkwo was not the man to stop beating somebody half-way through, not even for fear of a goddess.

Okonkwo's neighbors heard his wife crying and sent their voices over the compound walls to ask what was the matter. Some of them came over to see for themselves. It was unheard of to beat somebody during the sacred week.

Before it was dusk Ezeani, who was the priest of the earth goddess, Ani, called on Okonkwo in his obi. Okonkwo brought out kola nut[3] and placed it before the priest.

"Take away your kola nut. I shall not eat in the house of a man who has no respect for our gods and ancestors."

Okonkwo tried to explain to him what his wife had done, but Ezeani seemed to pay no attention. He held a short staff in his hand which he brought down on the floor to emphasize his points.

"Listen to me," he said when Okonkwo had spoken. "You are not a stranger in Umuofia. You know as well as I do that our forefathers ordained that before we plant any crops in the earth we should observe a week in which a man does not say a harsh word to his neighbor. We live in peace with our fellows to honor our great goddess of the earth without whose blessing our crops will not grow. You have committed a great evil." He brought down his staff heavily on the floor. "Your wife was at fault, but even if you came into your obi and found her lover on top of her, you would still have committed a great evil to beat her." His staff came down again "The evil you have done can ruin the whole clan. The earth goddess whom you have insulted may refuse to give us her increase, and we shall all perish." His tone now changed from anger to command. "You will bring to the shrine of Ani tomorrow one she-goat, one hen, a length of cloth and a hundred cowries." He rose and left the hut.

Okonkwo did as the priest said. He also took with him a pot of palm-wine.[4] Inwardly, he was repentant. But he was not the man to go about telling his neighbors that he was in error. And so people said he had no respect for the gods of the clan. His enemies said his good fortune had gone to his head. They called him the little bird nza who so far forgot himself after a heavy meal that he challenged his *chi*.[5]

No work was done during the Week of Peace. People called on their neighbors and drank palm-wine. This year they talked of nothing else but the *nso-ani*[6] which Okonkwo had committed. It was the first time for many years that a man had broken the sacred peace. Even the oldest men could only remember one or two other occasions somewhere in the dim past.

Ogbuefi Ezeudu, who was the oldest man in the village, was telling two other men who came to visit him that the punishment for breaking the Peace of Ani had become very mild in their clan.

"It has not always been so," he said. "My father told me that he had been told that in the past a man who broke the peace was dragged on the ground through the village until he died. But after a while this custom was stopped because it spoiled the peace which it was meant to preserve."

---

[3]A stimulant, served on almost all social occasions, like coffee. It is the ingredient which gives the soft drinks called "colas" their name.

[4]The fermented sap of the palm-wine tree, commonly used as a mild alcoholic beverage.

[5]Personal god.

[6]"Earth's taboo," ritual offence.

"Somebody told me yesterday," said one one the younger men, "that in some clans it is an abomination for a man to die during the Week of Peace."

"It is indeed true," said Ogbuefi Ezeudu. "They have that custom in Obodoani. If a man dies at this time he is not buried but cast into the Evil Forest.[7] It is a bad custom which these people observe because they lack understanding. They throw away large numbers of men and women without burial. And what is the result? Their clan is full of the evil spirits of these unburied dead, hungry to do harm to the living."

After the Week of Peace every man and his family began to clear the bush to make new farms. The cut bush was left to dry and fire was then set to it. As the smoke rose into the sky kites appeared from different directions and hovered over the burning field in silent valediction. The rainy season was approaching when they would go away until the dry season returned.

Okonkwo spent the next few days preparing his seed-yams. He looked at each yam carefully to see whether it was good for sowing. Sometimes he decided that a yam was too big to be sown as one seed and he split it deftly along its length with his sharp knife. His eldest son, Nwoye, and Ikemefuna helped him by fetching the yams in long baskets from the barn and in counting the prepared seeds in groups of four hundred. Sometimes Okonkwo gave them a few yams each to prepare. But he always found fault with their effort, and he said so with much threatening.

"Do you think you are cutting up yams for cooking?" he asked Nwoye. "If you split another yam of this size, I shall break your jaw. You think you are still a child. I began to own a farm at your age. And you," he said to Ikemefuna, "do you not grow yams where you come from?"

Inwardly Okonkwo knew that the boys were still too young to understand fully the difficult art of preparing seed-yams. But he thought that one could not begin too early. Yam stood for manliness, and he who could feed his family on yams from one harvest to another was a very great man indeed. Okonkwo wanted his son to be a great farmer and a great man. He would stamp out the disquieting signs of laziness which he thought he already saw in him.

"I will not have a son who cannot hold up his head in the gathering of the clan. I would sooner strangle him with my own hands. And if you stand staring at me like that," he swore, "Amadiora will break your head for you!"

Some days later, when the land had been moistened by two or three heavy rains, Okonkwo and his family went to the farm with baskets of seed-yams, their hoes and machetes, and the planting began. They made single mounds of earth in straight lines all over the field and sowed the yams in them.

Yam, the king of crops, was a very exacting king. For three or four moons it demanded hard work and constant attention from cock-crow till the chickens went back to roost. The young tendrils were protected from earth-heat with rings of sisal leaves. As the rains became heavier the women planted maize, melons and beans between the yam mounds. The yams were then staked, first with little sticks and later with tall and big tree branches.[8] The women weeded the farm three times at definite periods in the life of the yams, neither early nor late.

---

[7] A taboo area outside the village.

[8] Note that both men and women are involved in agriculture, though their roles are carefully defined.

And now the rains had really come, so heavy and persistent that even the village rain-maker no longer claimed to be able to intervene. He could not stop the rain now, just as he would not attempt to start it in the heart of the dry season, without serious danger to his own health. The personal dynamism required to counter the forces of these extremes of weather would be far too great for the human frame.

And so nature was not interfered with in the middle of the rainy season. Sometimes it poured down in such thick sheets of water that earth and sky seemed merged in one gray wetness. It was then uncertain whether the low rumbling of Amadiora's thunder came from above or below. At such times, in each of the countless thatched huts of Umuofia, children sat around their mother's cooking fire telling stories, or with their father in his obi warming themselves from a log fire, roasting and eating maize. It was a brief resting period between the exacting and arduous planting season and the equally exacting but light-hearted month of harvests.

Ngugi Wa Thiong'o: The Return (1961)

Ngugi is the most famous of the East African writers who have written in English. His works have portrayed fearlessly and vividly both the crimes of colonialism and the corruption of postcolonial Kenyan society. In recent years he has advocated writing in traditional African languages, and produced works in Gikuyu. This story is set during the violent uprising led by the Mau Mau in Kenya against the English colonialists and their black supporters (1950-1963). The British retaliated fiercely, imposing a state of emergency and arresting thousands of Africans, many innocent of any participation in the Mau Mau movement. Over 11,000 were killed. This story depicts the effects of that violence on one man; but the story of his homecoming is all too familiar from the experience of other wars.

On the surface this story is about the betrayal of one African by another. What passages can you find in the story which are aimed at criticizing the British government?

The road was long. Whenever he took a step forward, little clouds of dust rose, whirled angrily behind him, and then slowly settled again. But a thin train of dust was left in the air, moving like smoke. He walked on, however, unmindful of the dust and ground under his feet. Yet with every step he seemed more and more conscious of the hardness and apparent animosity of the road. Not that he looked down; on the contrary, he looked straight ahead as if he would, any time now, see a familiar object that would hail him as a friend and tell him that he was near home. But the road stretched on.

He made quick, springing steps, his left hand dangling freely by the side of his once white coat, now torn and worn out. His right hand, bent at the elbow, held onto a string tied to a small bundle on his slightly drooping back. The bundle, well wrapped with a cotton cloth that had once been printed with red flowers now faded out, swung from side to side in harmony with the rhythm of his steps. The bundle held the bitterness and hardships of the years spent in detention camps. Now and then he looked at the sun on its homeward journey. Sometimes he darted quick side-glances at the small hedged strips of land which, with their sickly-looking crops, maize, beans, and peas, appeared much as everything else did—unfriendly. The whole country was dull and seemed weary. To Kamau, this was nothing new. He remembered that, even before the Mau Mau emergency, the overtilled Gikuyu holdings wore haggard looks in contrast to the sprawling green fields in the settled area.[1]

A path branched to the left. He hesitated for a moment and then made up his mind. For the first time, his eyes brightened a little as he went along the path that would take him down the valley and then to the village. At last home was near and, with that realization, the faraway look of a weary traveler seemed to desert him for a while. The valley and the vegetation along it were in deep contrast to the surrounding country. For here green bush and trees thrived. This could only mean one thing: Honia river still flowed. He quickened his steps as if he could scarcely believe this to be true till he had actually set his eyes on the river. It was there; it still flowed. Honia, where so often he had taken a bathe, plunging stark naked into its cool living water, warmed his heart as he watched its serpentine movement round the rocks and heard its slight murmurs. A painful exhilaration passed all over him, and for a moment he longed for those days. He sighed. Perhaps the river would not recognize in his hardened features that same boy to whom the riverside world had meant

[1]Area settled by white colonists.

everything. Yet as he approached Honia, he felt more akin to it than he had felt to anything else since his release.

A group of women were drawing water. He was excited, for he could recognize one or two from his ridge. There was the middle-aged Wanjiku, whose deaf son had been killed by the Security Forces just before he himself was arrested. She had always been a darling of the village, having a smile for everyone and food for all. Would they receive him? Would they give him a "hero's welcome?" He thought so. Had he not always been a favorite all along the Ridge? And had he not fought for the land? He wanted to run and shout: "Here I am. I have come back to you." But he desisted. He was a man.

"Is it well with you?" A few voices responded. The other women, with tired and worn features, looked at him mutely as if his greeting was of no consequence. Why! Had he been so long in the camp? His spirits were damped as he feebly asked: "Do you not remember me?" Again they looked at him. They stared at him with cold, hard looks; like everything else, they seemed to be deliberately refusing to know or own him. It was Wanjiku who at last recognized him. But there was neither warmth nor enthusiasm in her voice as she said, "Oh, is it you, Kamau? We thought you—" She did not continue. Only now he noticed something else—surprise? fear? He could not tell. He saw their quick glances dart at him and he knew for certain that a secret from which he was excluded bound them together.

"Perhaps I am no longer one of them!" he bitterly reflected. But they told him of the new village. The old village of scattered huts spread thinly over the Ridge was no more.

He left them, feeling embittered and cheated. The old village had not even waited for him. And suddenly he felt a strong nostalgia for his old home, friends and surroundings. He thought of his father, mother and— and— he dared not think about her. But for all that, Muthoni, just as she had been in the old days, came back to his mind. His heart beat faster. He felt desire and a warmth thrilled through him. He quickened his step. He forgot the village women as he remembered his wife. He had stayed with her for a mere two weeks; then he had been swept away by the Colonial Forces. Like many others, he had been hurriedly screened and then taken to detention without trial. And all that time he had thought of nothing but the village and his beautiful woman.

The others had been like him. They had talked of nothing but their homes. One day he was working next to another detainee from Muranga. Suddenly the detainee, Njoroge, stopped breaking stones. He sighed heavily. His worn-out eyes had a faraway look.

"What's wrong, man? What's the matter with you?" Kamau asked.

"It is my wife. I left her expecting a baby. I have no idea what has happened to her."

Another detainee put in: "For me, I left my woman with a baby. She had just been delivered. We were all happy. But on the same day, I was arrested . . ."

And so they went on. All of them longed for one day—the day of their return home. Then life would begin anew.

Kamau himself had left his wife without a child. He had not even finished paying the bride-price. but now he would go, seek work in Nairobi, and pay off the remainder to Muthoni's parents. Life would indeed begin anew. They would have a son and bring him up in their own home. With these prospects before his eyes, he quickened his steps. He wanted to run— no, fly to hasten his return. He was now nearing the top of the hill. He wished he could suddenly meet his brothers and sisters. Would they ask him questions? he would, at any rate, not tell them all: the beating, the screening and the work on roads and in quarries with an askari always nearby ready to kick him if he relaxed. Yes. He had suffered many humiliations, and he had not resisted. Was there any need? but his soul and all the vigor of his manhood had rebelled and bled with rage and bitterness.

One day these wazungu would go!

One day his people would be free! Then, then—he did not know what he would do. However, he bitterly assured himself no one would ever flout his manhood again.

He mounted the hill and then stopped. The whole plain lay below. The new village was before him— rows and rows of compact mud huts, crouching on the plain under the fast-vanishing sun. Dark blue smoke curled upwards from various huts, to form a dark mist that hovered over the village. Beyond, the deep, blood-red sinking sun sent out finger-like streaks of light that thinned outwards and mingled with the gray mist shrouding the distant hills.

In the village, he moved from street to street, meeting new faces. He inquired. He found his home. He stopped at the entrance to the yard and breathed hard and full. This was the moment of his return home. His father sat huddled up on a three-legged stool. He was now very aged and Kamau pitied the old man. But he had been spared—yes, spared to see his son's return—

"Father!"

The old man did not answer. He just looked at Kamau with strange vacant eyes. Kamau was impatient. He felt annoyed and irritated. Did he not see him? Would he behave like the women Kamau had met at the river?

In the street, naked and half-naked children were playing, throwing dust at one another. The sun had already set and it looked as if there would be moonlight.

"Father, don't you remember me?" Hope was sinking in him. He felt tired. Then he saw his father suddenly start and tremble like a leaf. He saw him stare with unbelieving eyes. Fear was discernible in those eyes. His mother came, and his brothers too. They crowded around him. His aged mother clung to him and sobbed hard.

"I knew my son would come. I knew he was not dead."

"Why, who told you I was dead?"

"That Karanja, son of Njogu."

And then Kamau understood. He understood his trembling father. He understood the women at the river. But one thing puzzled him: he had never been in the same detention camp with Karanja. Anyway he had come back. He wanted now to see Muthoni. Why had she not come out? He wanted to shout, "I have come Muthoni; I am here." He looked around. his mother understood him. She quickly darted a glance at her man and then simply said:

"Muthoni went away."

Kamau felt something cold settle in his stomach. He looked at the village huts and the dullness of the land. He wanted to ask many questions but he dared not. He could not yet believe that Muthoni had gone. But he knew by the look of the women at the river, by the look of his parents, that she was gone.

"She was a good daughter to us," his mother was explaining. "She waited for you and patiently bore all the ills of the land. Then Karanja came and said that you were dead. Your father believed him. She believed him too and keened for a month. Karanja constantly paid us visits. He was of your Rika, you know. Then she got a child. We could have kept her. But where is the land? Where is the food? Ever since land consolidation, our last security was taken away. We let Karanja go with her. Other women have done worse—gone to town.[2] Only the infirm and the old have been left here."

---

[2]To become prostitutes.

He was not listening; the coldness in his stomach slowly changed to bitterness. He felt bitter against all, all the people including his father and mother. They had betrayed him. They had leagued against him, and Karanja had always been his rival. Five years was admittedly not a short time. But why did she go? Why did they allow her to go? He wanted to speak. Yes, speak and denounce everything—the women at the river, the village and the people who dwelt there. But he could not. This bitter thing was choking him.

"You—you gave my own away?" he whispered.

"Listen, child, child—"

The big yellow moon dominated the horizon. He hurried away bitter and blind, and only stopped when he came to the Honia river.

And standing at the bank, he saw not the river, but his hopes dashed on the ground instead. The river moved swiftly, making ceaseless monotonous murmurs. In the forest the crickets and other insects kept up an incessant buzz. And above, the moon shone bright. He tried to remove his coat, and the small bundle he had held on to so firmly fell. It rolled down the bank and before Kamau knew what was happening, it was floating swiftly down the river. For a time he was shocked and wanted to retrieve it. What would he show his—Oh, had he forgotten so soon? His wife had gone. And the little things that had so strangely reminded him of her and that he had guarded all those years, had gone! He did not know why, but somehow he felt relieved. Thoughts of drowning himself dispersed. He began to put on his coat, murmuring to himself, "Why should she have waited for me? Why should all the changes have waited for my return?"

Raage Ugaas: Poet's Lament on the Death of his Wife

Poetry has always been very popular in Somalia, and a largely oral tradition still flourishes there, now often circulated on cassette. An official system of writing Somali was established only as recently as 1972. Somali politics and history play a large role in poetry, and need extensive knowledge to be comprehensible to outsiders; but there are also many love poems which can be readily understood by anyone.

Which images in the poem are about the pain of separation? What other kinds of emotions does the poet express through this series of metaphors?

Like the *vu'ubl* wood bell tied to gelded camels that are running away,
Or like camels which are being separated from their young,
Or like people journeying while moving camp,
Or like a well which has broken its sides or a river which has overflowed its banks,
Or like an old woman whose only son was killed,
Or like the poor, dividing the scraps for their frugal meal,
Or like the bees entering their hive, or food crackling in the frying,
Yesterday my lamentations drove sleep from all the camps.
Have I been left bereft in my house and shelter?
Has the envy of others been miraculously fulfilled?
Have I been deprived of the fried meat and reserves for lean times which were so
plentiful for me?
Have I today been taken from the chessboard of life?
Have I been borne on a saddle to a distant and desolate place?
Have I broken my shin, a bone which cannot be mended?

Translated by B. W. Andrezejewski & I. M. Lewis

Léopold Sédar Senghor: *Long, long you have held* (1949)

Senghor was one of a number of Caribbean and African students in Paris who together founded the négritude movement, celebrating the beauty of blackness and of the African landscape. It has often been noted that their insistence on the qualities which set Africans apart from Europeans sometimes reinforced European stereotypes, and their poetry has been much criticized by other African writers in consequence. But their intention was to generate a militant pan-African anticolonial movement, rooted in pride, rejecting foreign domination. In this they were successful. Senghor became the first President of Sénégal in 1960, and governed that country with distinction until his retirement twenty years later. Some of Senghor's verse is among the most beautiful of twentieth-century French poetry. The following poem, like much of his verse, connects the beauty of an African woman to the beauty of the African landscape.

How does the departing poet seek to console his beloved as he leaves for Europe? Why might life abroad reinforce his awareness of things African?

For khalam[1]

Long, long you have held between your hands the black face of the warrior
Held as if already there fell on it a twilight of death.
From the hill I have seen the sun set in the bays of your eyes.
When shall I see again, my country, the pure horizon of your face?
When shall I sit down once more at the dark table of your breast?

Hidden in the half-darkness, the nest of gentle words.

I shall see other skies and other eyes
I shall drink at the spring of other mouths cooler than lemons
I shall sleep under the roof of other heads of hair in shelter from storms.
But every year, when the rum of springtime sets my memory ablaze
I shall be full of regret for my homeland and the rain from your eyes on the thirsty
savannahs.

Translated by John Reed and Clive Wake

---

[1]A traditional stringed instrument. In other words, this poem is a song to be performed to the accompaniment of a *khalam*.

Frantz Fanon (1925-1961): *Black Skin, White Masks* (1952)

Fanon was born in Forte-de-France, the capital of the French colony of Martinique in the Caribbean. He studied medicine and psychiatry at the University of Lyon in France, returned to Martinique to work as a doctor, thebn moved on to Algeria which became his adopted country. Apart from treating patients in Algeria, Fanon was involved as an intellectual-activist in the Algerian independence war of 1954 waged against French colonialism. Fanon's last and most well-known work, The Wretched of the Earth *(published in 1961), analyzes the socio-economic, historical and psychological causes and consequences of colonialism, while also suggesting revolutionary strategies for anti-colonial movements. Written with fiery eloquence, this work was immediately hailed as a kind of manifesto for many national independence struggles and decolonization movements and later by the Black Power Movement in the United States. Almost equally well known is Fanon's other important work,* Black Skins, White Masks *(1952). Fanon in this work diagnoses signs and symptoms of the alienated black consciousness and analyzes the problems of racism besetting people of color under white domination. The work is also striking for its revolutionary humanism. Fanon was influenced by theorists like Marx and Freud, among others. The following is from the conclusion of* this second work. *Note that, typical of the style of the time in which it was written, this selection uses "man" and "him" to refer to humanity generally—both men and women.*

Some anti-racists argue that an "Afro-centric" approach to history which emphasizes the great achievements of blacks in the past can help to increase the self-esteem of oppressed blacks whose ancestors were cut off from their heritage by the experience of slavery. What arguments does he make against this position? Do you agree or disagree with these arguments? What does he mean by saying that the white man has "killed man"? In the last line of the passage, what kind of ideas do you think Fanon wants to question (challenge)?

I am not the slave of the Slavery that dehumanized my ancestors.

To many colored intellectuals European culture has a quality of exteriority.[1] What is more, in human relationships, the Negro may feel himself a stranger to the Western world. Not wanting to live the part of a poor relative, of an adopted son, of a bastard child, shall he feverishly seek to discover a Negro civilization?

Let us be clearly understood. I am convinced that it would be of the greatest interest to be able to have contact. with a Negro literature or architecture of the third century before Christ. I should be very happy to know that a correspondence had flourished between some Negro philosopher and Plato. But I can absolutely not see how this fact would change anything in the lives of the eight- year-old children who labor in the cane fields of Martinique or Guadeloupe.

No attempt must be made to encase man, for it is his destiny to be set free.

The body of history does not determine a single one of my actions.

I am my own foundation.

And it is by going beyond the historical, instrumental hypothesis that I will initiate the cycle of my freedom.

The disaster of the man of color lies in the fact that he was enslaved.

The disaster and the inhumanity of the white man lie in the fact that somewhere he has killed man.

---

[1]That is, it seems alien, foreign .

And even today they subsist, to organize this dehumanization rationally. But I as a man of color, to the extent that it becomes possible for me to exist absolutely, do not have the right to lock myself into a world of retroactive reparations.

I, the man of color, want only this:

That the tool never possess the man. That the enslavement of man by man cease forever. That is, of one by another. That it be possible for me to discover and to love man, wherever he may be.

The Negro is not. Any more than the white man.[2]

Both must turn their backs on the inhuman voices which were those of their respective ancestors in order that authentic communication be possible. Before it can adopt a positive voice, freedom requires an effort at disalienation. At the beginning of his life a man is always clotted, he is drowned in contingency. The tragedy of the man is that he was once a child.[3]

It is through the effort to recapture the self and to scrutinize the self, it is through the lasting tension of their freedom that men will be able to create the ideal conditions of existence for a human world.

Superiority? Inferiority?

Why not the quite simple attempt to touch the other,, to feel the other, to explain the other to myself?

Was my freedom not given to me then in order to build the world of the You? [4]

At the conclusion of this study, I want the world to recognize, with me, the open door of every consciousness.

My final prayer:

O my body, make of me always a man who questions!

Translated by Constance Farrington

[2]Neither one of these abstractions is ultimately real. All people must be seen as essentially human, whatever their color.

[3]People are influenced—often negatively—by their origins.

[4]"The You" consists of other persons treated as real human beings, and not as abstractions.

Umkhonto we Sizwe: We Are at War! (1967)

Umkhonto we Sizwe ("Spear of the Nation") was founded as the military arm of the African National Congress (ANC) in 1961, partly in response to the 1960 Sharpeville Massacre in which at least 72 people died when South African police fired upon non-violent demonstrators. They were protesting the policy of racial apartheid *(segregation) which divided South Africa's population into Blacks, Whites, Asians (largely Indians), and Coloreds (people of mixed ancestry). Nelson Mandela, Commander-in-Chief of Umkhonto we Sizwe, was in prison under a life sentence when this manifesto was published.*

What are the main complaints of Umkhonto we Sizwe about the government of South Africa?

On 16th December, 1961, Umkhonto we Sizwe, military wing of the ANC, made it known that we, the oppressed people of South Africa, would fight for our rights. We made this known not only with words. Dynamite blasts announced it.

From 13th August, 1967, our men of Umkhonto we Sizwe, together with our brothers of ZAPU (Zimbabwe African People's Union[1]) have been fighting the oppressors in Matabeleland, Wankie and further south.

The Vorster[2] government, through the radio and newspapers, continues to lie about this fighting.

The truth is very different from what these newspapers have reported. Our men are armed and trained freedom-fighters, not "terrorists." They are fighting with courage, discipline and skill. The forces of the Rhodesian racialists[3] suffered heavy losses. So also did the white soldiers sent to Rhodesia by Vorster to save the Smith regime from collapse.

The freedom-fighters have inflicted heavy losses on the enemy. Apart from those who have been ambushed and killed, hospitals at Bulawayo and Wankie are crowded with wounded Smith and Vorster forces. Several South African helicopters and military transport planes have been brought down over the past three months.

The fighting will go on in Rhodesia and South Africa. We will fight until we have won, however long it takes and however much it will cost.

Why we fight

To you, the sons and daughters of the soil, our case is clear.

The white oppressors have stolen our land. They have destroyed our families. They have taken for themselves the best that there is in our rich country and have left us the worst. They have the fruits and the riches. We have the backbreaking toil and the poverty.

---

[1]Zimbabwe is the former British colony of Rhodesia. Its white leader, Ian Smith, was a militant advocate of white minority domination and segregation, and was a strong ally of the apartheid government of the Union of South Africa.

[2]John Vorster was an outspoken opponent of racial equality in South Africa, imprisoned during World War II for his support of fascism. He was an important leader in the construction of apartheid during the fifties, organizing the segregated system of education which was to become the focus of much of the ANC's future protests. In 1961 he was made Minister of Justice, and was Prime Minister from 1966 to 1978.

[3]Racists.

We burrow into the belly of the earth to dig out gold, diamonds, coal, uranium. The white oppressors and foreign investors grab all this wealth. It is used for their enrichment and to buy arms to suppress and kill us.

In the factories, on the farms, on the railways, wherever you go, the hard, dirty, dangerous, badly paid jobs are ours. The best jobs are for whites only.

In our own land we have to carry passes; we are restricted and banished while the white oppressors move about freely.

Our homes are hovels; those of the whites are luxury mansions, flats and farmsteads.

There are not enough schools for our children; the standard of education is low, and we have to pay for it. But the government uses our taxes and the wealth we create to provide free education for white children.

We have suffered long enough.

Over 300 years ago the white invaders began a ceaseless war of aggression against us, murdered our forefathers, stole our land and enslaved our people.

Today they still rule by force. They murder our people. They still enslave us.

Only by meeting force with force can we win back our motherland.

We have tried every way to reason with the white supremacists. For many years our leaders and organizations sent petitions and deputations to Cape Town and Pretoria, even overseas, to London and the United Nations in New York. We organized mass demonstrations, pass-burnings, peaceful stay-at-homes.

What answer was given by the government?

Strikers and demonstrators were shot in cold blood. New acts of oppression and injustice were heaped upon us. Our leaders and spokesmen were banned, gagged, jailed, banished—even murdered. Our organization, the African National Congress, was outlawed. Our meetings, journals and leaflets were prohibited.

The Nazi Vorster, who was interned for helping Hitler, is now the Prime Minister of South Africa. This man is the murderer of Mini, Mkaba, Khayingo, Bongco, Saloojee and other brave sons of Africa. He has condemned Mandela, Sisulu, Mbeki, Mhlaba, Motsoaledi, Mlangeni, Kathrada, Fischer and many others to rot away in jails for life.

They have declared war on us. We have to fight back!

Our *Indian* brothers know full well the hardships and bitterness of white baaskaap[4] rule. Since the time of Mahatma Gandhi[5] and before, they have had to face persecution—attempts to deport them to India, Ghetto Acts, Group Areas and other forms of oppression.

The South African Indian Congress fought back. Led by men like Yusuf Dadoo, Monty Naicker and Nana Sita, the Indian community marched hand in hand with the ANC for liberty, for the rights of all South Africans.

Our *Colored* brothers know how even the few privileges they were allowed—crumbs from the master's table—have been taken away from them. Votes, skilled jobs, trade union rights—one by one they are being taken away. Now apartheid madness is conscripting the Colored youth into labor camps and jails for pass offenders. The ghetto walls grow higher.

[4]Afrikaans for "domination," in this context ,white supremacy.

[5]Gandhi led a somewhat successful campaign of rights for the Indian minority in South Africa in the years just before World War I.

That is why the Colored People's Congress (CPC) pledged its support to the Freedom Charter and why its leaders are driven into jail or exile.

And what of the *white* minority? For years they have been misled by racialist politicians, dominees and fascists who told them they were the superior race. They have followed the Vorsters and the de Villiers Graffs, and now they are being called upon to fight and die in defense of apartheid. Let them ask themselves: is it worth it? Has it brought anything but uncertainty and fear, isolation and contempt at home and abroad? Is this a future to fight and die for—a life in an armed camp, surrounded by the hate and anger of the oppressed non-white people?

The African National Congress, remembering also the Bram Fischers and the Dennis Goldbergs,[6] calls on white South Africans to take their place on the side of liberty and democracy, the side of our freedom fighters—now *before it is too late.*

What we fight for

We are fighting for democracy—majority rule—the right of the Africans to rule Africa. We are fighting for a South Africa in which there will be peace and harmony and equal rights for all people.

We are not racialists, as the white oppressors are. The African National Congress has a message of freedom for all who live in our country.

What you should do

The battle has begun.

In Rhodesia, we have met the oppressors with guns in our hands! That was the start. Soon there will be battles in South Africa.

We will speak to them with guns, again and again, now here, now there, until their day is done and apartheid destroyed for ever.

We call on you to be prepared.

Stand up and speak out against Vorster and his Nazis. Don't collaborate with them! Take courage from our immortal freedom-fighters who died in the name of freedom for all.

Our country will be free. We fight for all South Africans, for you and your children and your children's children.

Prepare to support our fighting men!

Pass this message to your friends and relatives, throughout Southern Africa—in Botswana, Lesotho, South-West Africa, or Swaziland; in Rhodesia, Mozambique or Angola, and in every corner of South Africa itself.

HELP THE FREEDOM FIGHTERS!

MAKE THEIR PATH EASY! MAKE THE ENEMY'S PATH HARD!

WE ARE ANSWERING THE WHITE OPPRESSORS IN THE LANGUAGE THEY HAVE CHOSEN!

THIS IS A WAR TO DESTROY APARTHEID, TO WIN BACK OUR COUNTRY FOR ALL OUR PEOPLE!

WE SHALL WIN! FORWARD TO VICTORY OR DEATH!

AFRIKA! MAYIBUYE! AMANDLA NGAWETHU!

MATLA KE ARONA! POWER TO THE PEOPLE!

---

[6]Prominent white opponents of apartheid.

Nelson Mandela: Inaugural Address, May 10, 1994

Nelson Mandela was trained as a lawyer, and joined the African National Congress in 1944 to aid in its struggle against apartheid. During over 25 years in prison he became the world's most famous political prisoner. After a long campaign of resistance within South Africa and political and economic pressure from without, President F. W. de Klerk ended the government ban on the ANC and freed Mandela in 1990, whereupon he assumed leadership of the organization. He worked tirelessly over the next few years to negotiate an end to apartheid and minority rule, gaining widespread respect and support in the process. National elections were held in April 1994, and on May 10th of that year Nelson Mandela was inaugurated as the first Black president of South Africa.

What are the most important ideals for the South African future stated in this speech?

Your Majesties, Your Highnesses, Distinguished Guests, Comrades and Friends:

Today, all of us do, by our presence here, and by our celebrations in other parts of our country and the world, confer glory and hope to newborn liberty.

Out of the experience of an extraordinary human disaster that lasted too long, must be born a society of which all humanity will be proud.

Our daily deeds as ordinary South Africans must produce an actual South African reality that will reinforce humanity's belief in justice, strengthen its confidence in the nobility of the human soul and sustain all our hopes for a glorious life for all.

All this we owe both to ourselves and to the peoples of the world who are so well represented here today.

To my compatriots, I have no hesitation in saying that each one of us is as intimately attached to the soil of this beautiful country as are the famous jacaranda trees of Pretoria and the mimosa trees of the bushveld.

Each time one of us touches the soil of this land, we feel a sense of personal renewal. The national mood changes as the seasons change.

We are moved by a sense of joy and exhilaration when the grass turns green and the flowers bloom.

That spiritual and physical oneness we all share with this common homeland explains the depth of the pain we all carried in our hearts as we saw our country tear itself apart in a terrible conflict, and as we saw it spurned, outlawed and isolated by the peoples of the world, precisely because it has become the universal base of the pernicious ideology and practice of racism and racial oppression.

We, the people of South Africa, feel fulfilled that humanity has taken us back into its. bosom, that we, who were outlaws not so long ago, have today been given the rare privilege to be host to the nations of the world on our own soil.

We thank all our distinguished international guests for having come to take possession with the people of our country of what is, after all, a common victory for justice, for peace, for human dignity.

We trust that you will continue to stand by us as we tackle the challenges of building peace, prosperity, non-sexism, non-racialism and democracy.

We deeply appreciate the role that the masses of our people and their political mass democratic, religious, women, youth, business, traditional and other leaders have played to bring about this conclusion. Not least among them is my Second Deputy President, the Honorable F.W. de Klerk.

We would also like to pay tribute to our security forces, in all their ranks, for the distinguished role they have played in securing our first democratic elections and the transition to democracy, from blood-thirsty forces which still refuse to see the light.

The time for the healing of the wounds has come.

The moment to bridge the chasms that divide us has come.

The time to build is upon us.

We have, at last, achieved our political emancipation. We pledge ourselves to liberate all our people from the continuing bondage of poverty, deprivation, suffering, gender and other discrimination.

We succeeded to take our last steps to freedom in conditions of relative peace. We commit ourselves to the construction of a complete, just and lasting peace.

We have triumphed in the effort to implant hope in the breasts of the millions of our people. We enter into a covenant that we shall build the society in which all South Africans, both black and white, will be able to walk tall, without any fear in their hearts, assured of their inalienable right to human dignity—a rainbow nation at peace with itself and the world.

As a token of its commitment to the renewal of our country, the new Interim Government of National Unity will, as a matter of urgency, address the issue of amnesty for various categories of our people who are currently serving terms of imprisonment.

We dedicate this day to all the heroes and heroines in this country and the rest of the world who sacrificed in many ways and surrendered their lives so that we could be free.

Their dreams have become reality. Freedom is their reward.

We are both humbled and elevated by the honor and privilege that you, the people of South Africa, have bestowed on us, as the first President of a united, democratic, non-racial and non-sexist South Africa, to lead our country out of the valley of darkness.

We understand it still that there is no easy road to freedom.

We know it well that none of us acting alone can achieve success.

We must therefore act together as a united people, for national reconciliation, for nation building, for the birth of a new world.

Let there be justice for all.

Let there be peace for all.

Let there be work, bread, water and salt for all.

Let each know that for each the body, the mind and the soul have been freed to fulfill themselves.

Never, never and never again shall it be that this beautiful land will again experience the oppression of one by another and suffer the indignity of being the skunk of the world.

Let freedom reign.

The sun shall never set on so glorious a human achievement!

God bless Africa!

Thank you.

Middle East & North Africa 1900–Present

Naguib Mahfouz: Half a Day (1989)

This 1988 Egyptian Nobel Prize-winning author depicts modern life in his homeland, sometimes in a rather surreal fashion, as in this story. It is a poetic reflection on the shortness of life written by a 78-year-old man who might have looked back on his childhood as "only yesterday."

What aspects of modern life in Cairo might an old man find unpleasant?

I proceeded alongside my father, clutching his right hand, running to keep up with the long strides he was taking. All my clothes were new: the black shoes, the green school uniform, and the red tarboosh.[1] My delight in my new clothes, however, was not altogether unmarred, for this was no feast day but the day on which I was to be cast into school for the first time.

My mother stood at the window watching our progress, and I would turn toward her from time to time, as though appealing for help. We walked along a street lined with gardens; on both sides were extensive fields planted with crops, prickly pears, henna trees, and a few date palms.

"Why school?" I challenged my father openly. "I shall never do anything to annoy you."

"I'm not punishing you," he said, laughing. "School's not a punishment. It's the factory that makes useful men out of boys. Don't you want to be like your father and brothers?"

I was not convinced. I did not believe there was really any good to be had in tearing me away from the intimacy of my home and throwing me into this building that stood at the end of the road like some huge, high-walled fortress, exceedingly stern and grim.

When we arrived at the gate we could see the courtyard, vast and crammed full of boys and girls. "Go in by yourself," said my father, "and join them. Put a smile on your face and be a good example to others."

I hesitated and clung to his hand, but he gently pushed me from him. "Be a man," he said. "Today you truly begin life. You will find me waiting for you when it's time to leave."

I took a few steps, then stopped and looked but saw nothing. Then the faces of boys and girls came into view. I did not know a single one of them, and none of them knew me. I felt I was a stranger who had lost his way. But glances of curiosity were directed toward me, and one boy approached and asked, "Who brought you?"

"My father," I whispered.

"My father's dead," he said quite simply.

I did not know what to say. The gate was closed, letting out a pitiable screech. Some of the children burst into tears. The bell rang. A lady came along, followed by a group of men. The men began sorting us into ranks. We were formed into an intricate pattern in the great courtyard surrounded on three sides by high buildings of several floors; from each floor we were overlooked by a long balcony roofed in wood.

---

[1]Traditional red felt cap.

"This is your new home," said the woman. "Here too there are mothers and fathers. Here there is everything that is enjoyable and beneficial to knowledge and religion. Dry your tears and face life joyfully."

We submitted to the facts, and this submission brought a sort of contentment. Living beings were drawn to other living beings, and from the first moments my heart made friends with such boys as were to be my friends and fell in love with such girls as I was to be in love with, so that it seemed my misgivings had had no basis. I had never imagined school would have this rich variety. We played all sorts of different games: swings, the vaulting horse, ball games. In the music room we chanted our first songs. We also had our first introduction to language. We saw a globe of the Earth, which revolved and showed the various continents and countries. We started learning the numbers. The story of the Creator of the universe was read to us, we were told of His present world and of His Hereafter, and we heard examples of what He said.[2] We ate delicious food, took a little nap, and woke up to go on with friendship and love, play and learning.

As our path revealed itself to us, however, we did not find it as totally sweet and unclouded as we had presumed. Dust-laden winds and unexpected accidents came about suddenly, so we had to be watchful, at the ready, and very patient. It was not all a matter of playing and fooling around. Rivalries could bring about pain and hatred or give rise to fighting. And while the lady would sometimes smile, she would often scowl and scold. Even more frequently she would resort to physical punishment.

In addition, the time for changing one's mind was over and gone and there was no question of ever returning to the paradise of home. Nothing lay ahead of us but exertion, struggle, and perseverance. Those who were able took advantage of the opportunities for success and happiness that presented themselves amid the worries.

The bell rang announcing the passing of the day and the end of work. The throngs of children rushed toward the gate, which was opened again. I bade farewell to friends and sweethearts and passed through the gate. I peered around but found no trace of my father, who had promised to be there. I stepped aside to wait. When I had waited for a long time without avail, I decided to return home on my own. After I had taken a few steps, a middle-aged man passed by, and I realized at once that I knew him. He came toward me, smiling, and shook me by the hand, saying, "It's a long time since we last met—how are you?"

With a nod of my head, I agreed with him and in turn asked, "And you, how are you?"

"As you can see, not all that good, the Almighty be praised!"

Again he shook me by the hand and went off. I proceeded a few steps, then came to a startled halt. Good Lord! Where was the street lined with gardens? Where had it disappeared to? When did all these vehicles invade it? And when did all these hordes of humanity come to rest upon its surface? How did these hills of refuse come to cover its sides? And where were the fields that bordered it? High buildings had taken over, the street surged with children, and disturbing noises shook the air. At various points stood conjurers showing off their tricks and making snakes appear from baskets. Then there was a band announcing the opening of a circus, with clowns and weight lifters walking in front. A line of trucks carrying central security troops crawled majestically by. The siren of a fire engine shrieked, and it was not clear how the vehicle would cleave its way to reach the blazing fire. A battle raged between a taxi driver and his passenger, while the passenger's wife called out for help and no one answered. Good God! I was in a daze. My head spun. I almost went

[2] From the Qur'an.

crazy. How could all this have happened in half a day, between early morning and sunset? I would find the answer at home with my father. But where was my home? I could see only tall buildings and hordes of people. I hastened on to the crossroads between the gardens and Abu Khoda. I had to cross Abu Khoda to reach my house, but the stream of cars would not let up. The fire engine's siren was shrieking at full pitch as it moved at a snail's pace, and I said to myself, "Let the fire take its pleasure in what it consumes." Extremely irritated, I wondered when I would be able to cross. I stood there a long time, until the young lad employed at the ironing shop on the corner came up to me. He stretched out his arm and said gallantly, "Grandpa, let me take you across."

Translated by Denys Johnson-Davies

Mahmoud Darwish (1942–): Identity Card

When Mahmoud Darwish was six, he saw his native village called Al-Birwa destroyed by the Israeli army. Repeatedly imprisoned and exiled, he has devoted himself to eloquently supporting the cause of the Palestinians and speaking out for human rights and equality. He has earned numerous awards, some of which include the Lotus Prize (1969), the Mediterranean Award (1980), and the Lenin Prize (1982). In the following poem, Darwish protests the strict supervision under which his people lived in the modern state of Israel.

Why does the poet continuously ask, "Does this bother you?" Who is the "usurper?"

Write down
I am an Arab
& my I.D. card number is 50,000
& my children are eight in number
& the ninth
   arrives next summer.
Does this bother you?

Write down
I am an Arab
& I work with comrades in a stone quarry
& my children are eight in number.
For them I hack out
   a loaf of bread
   clothing
   a school exercise-book
from the rocks
rather than begging for alms
   at your door
rather than making myself small
   at your doorsteps.
Does this bother you ?

Write down
I am an Arab.
I am a name without a family-name.
I am patient in a country where everything
lives by the eruption of anger.
My roots
   gripped down before time began
   before the blossoming of ages
   before cypress trees & olive trees
   . . . before grass sprouted.
My father
   is from the family of the plough
   not from a noble line

& my grandfather
   was a peasant
   without nobility without genealogy!
& my house
   is a crop-warden's shack
   built of sticks & reeds.
Does my social status satisfy you?
I am a name without a family name.

Write down
I am an Arab
& colour of hair: jet black
& colour of eyes: brown
distinguishing features:
   on my head a camel-hair headband
   over a keffyeh[1]
   & my palm is solid as rock
   scratching whoever touches it
   & to me the most delicious food
   is olive oil & thyme.
Address:
   I come from a remote forgotten village.
   Its streets are nameless
   & all its men in the fields & the quarry
   love communism!
Does this bother you ?

Write down
I am an Arab.
You usurped my grandfather's vineyards
& the plot of land I used to plough
I & all my children
& you left us
   & all my grandchildren
nothing but these rocks . . . so
your government
will it take them too as rumour has it?
So be it.
   Write down at the top of the first page:
   I do not hate people.
   I steal from no-one.
However
   if I am hungry
   I will eat the flesh of my usurper.
Beware beware of my hunger
& of my anger.

Translated by Ian Wedde & Fawwaz Tuqan

[1]Traditional head scarf.

The Ayatollah Khomeini: America, the Great Satan (1980)

By 1960, the Ayatollah ("theologian") Ruhollah Khomeini had become the leader of Iran's Shiite Muslims. Khomeini and his followers believed in a strict interpretation of the Qur'an *whereby government should serve the religious establishment. The head of the government, Shah Reza Pahlavi—supported by the United States—used his power to persecute Iran's Shiite community. In 1964, Khomeini fled to Paris, where at least one attempt was made on his life (his elder son was assassinated in Iraq). When Khomeini returned to Iran in February, 1979, he imposed strict Islamic standards for public and private life. He gave this speech, calling for Muslim unity and condemning the United States, in Teheran on September 13, 1980.*

Why is the United States the "Great Satan?" In Khomeini 's opinion, what has the United States done wrong? According to Khomeini , how can Muslims defeat their enemies? What does this speech reveal about Khomeini's personality? About his skill as an orator?

Muslims the world over who believe in the truth of Islam, arise and gather, beneath the banner of tauhid [divine unity] and the teachings of Islam! Repel the treacherous superpowers from your countries and your abundant resources. Restore the glory of Islam, and abandon your selfish disputes and differences, for you possess everything! Rely on the culture of Islam, resist Western imitation, and stand on your own feet. Attack those intellectuals who are infatuated with the West and the East, and recover your true identity. Realize that intellectuals in the pay of foreigners have inflicted disaster upon their people and countries. As long as you remain disunited and fail to place your reliance in true Islam, you will continue to suffer what you have suffered already. We are now in an age when the masses act as the guides to the intellectuals and are rescuing them from abasement and humiliation by the East and the West. For today is the day that the masses of the people are on the move; they are the guides to those who previously sought to be the guides themselves.

Know that your moral power will overcome all other powers. With a population of almost one billion and with infinite sources of wealth, you can defeat all the powers. Aid God's cause so that He may aid you. Great ocean of Muslims, arise and defeat the enemies of humanity. If you turn to God and follow the heavenly teachings, God Almighty and His vast hosts will be with you.

The most important and painful problem confronting the subjugated nations of the world, both Muslim and non-Muslim, is the problem of America. In order to swallow up the material resources of the countries it has succeeded in dominating, America, the most powerful country in the world, will spare no effort.

America is the number-one enemy of the deprived and oppressed people of the world. There is no crime America will not commit in order to maintain its political, economic, cultural, and military domination of those parts of the world where it predominates. It exploits the oppressed people of the world by means of the large-scale propaganda campaigns that are coordinated for it by international Zionism. By means of its hidden and treacherous agents, it sucks the blood of the defenseless people as if it alone, together with its satellites, had the right to live in this world.

Iran has tried to sever all its relations with this Great Satan and it is for this reason that it now finds wars imposed upon it. America has urged Iraq to spill the blood of our young men, and it has compelled the countries that are subject to its influence to boycott us

Assia Djebar: A Little Arab Girl's First Day at School (1985)

This is the first chapter of Djebar's novel, Fantasia: An Algerian Cávalcade. *In it she details the long history of the sufferings inflicted on the Algerian people—and most especially on the women—by the French colonizers, and explores the experiences of the women who fought so hard for independence only to find themselves newly oppressed in liberated Algeria. She views French with ambivalence, both as the language of the oppressor, in which she was early trained and which tended to alienate her from her own culture, and as a vehicle of expression which has allowed her to speak about her own plight and that of other North African women.*

What objections does Djebar say traditional Algerians had to education for girls? How does her childhood experience described here affect her behavior toward her own daughter years later?

A little Arab girl going to school for the first time, one autumn morning, walking hand in hand with her father. A tall erect figure in a fez and a European suit, carrying a bag of school books. He is a teacher at the French primary school. A little Arab girl in a village in the Algerian Sahel.

Towns or villages of narrow white alleyways and windowless houses. From the very first day that a little girl leaves her home to learn the ABC, the neighbors adopt that knowing look of those who in ten or fifteen years' time will be able to say "I told you so!" while commiserating with the foolhardy father, the irresponsible brother. For misfortune will inevitably befall them. Any girl who has had some schooling will have learned to write and will without a doubt write that fatal letter. For her the time will come when there will be more danger in love that is committed to paper than love that languishes behind enclosing walls.

So wrap the nubile girl in veils. Make her invisible. Make her more unseeing than the sightless, destroy in her every memory of the world without. And what if she has learned to write? The jailer who guards a body that has no words—and written words can travel—may sleep in peace: it will suffice to brick up the windows, padlock the sole entrance door, and erect a blank wall rising up to heaven.

And what if the maiden does write? Her voice, albeit silenced, will circulate. A scrap of paper. A crumpled cloth. A servant-girl's hand in the dark. A child, let into the secret. The jailer must keep watch day and night. The written word will take flight from the patio, will be tossed from a terrace. The blue of heaven is suddenly limitless. The precautions have all been in vain.

At seventeen I am introduced to my first experience of love through a letter written by a boy, a stranger. Whether acting thoughtlessly or out of bravado, he writes quite openly. My father, in a fit of silent fury, tears up the letter before my eyes and throws it into the waste-paper basket without letting me read it.

As soon as term ends at my boarding school, I now spend the summer holidays back in the village, shut up in the flat overlooking the school playground. During the siesta hour, I piece together the letter which has aroused my father's fury. The mysterious correspondent says he remembers seeing me go up on to the platform during the prize-giving ceremony which took place two or three days previously, in the neighboring town. I recall staring at him rather defiantly as I passed him in the corridors of the boys' high school. He writes very formally suggesting that we exchange friendly letters. In my father's eyes, such a request is not merely completely indecent but this invitation is tantamount to setting the stage for rape.

Simply because my father wanted to destroy the letter, I interpreted the conventional French wording used by this student on holiday as the cryptic expression of some sudden, desperate passion.

During the months and years that followed, I became absorbed by this business of love, or rather by the prohibition laid on love; my father's condemnation only served to encourage the intrigue. In these early stages of my sentimental education,[1] our secret correspondence is carried on in French: thus the language that my father had been at pains for me to learn, serves as a go-between, and from now a double, contradictory sign reigns over my initiation. . . .

As with the heroine of a Western romance, youthful defiance helped me break out of the circle that whispering elders traced around me and within me. . . . Then love came to be transformed in the tunnel of pleasure, soft clay to be molded by matrimony.

Memory purges and purifies the sounds of childhood; we are cocooned by childhood until the discovery of sensuality, which washes over us and gradually bedazzles us. . . . Voiceless, cut off from my mother's words by some trick of memory, I managed to pass through the dark waters of the corridor, miraculously inviolate, not even guessing at the enclosing walls. The shock of the first words blurted out: the truth emerging from a break in my stammering voice. From what nocturnal reef of pleasure did I manage to wrest this truth?

I blew the space within me to pieces, a space filled with desperate voiceless cries, frozen long ago in a prehistory of love. Once I had discovered the meaning of the words—those same words that are revealed to the unveiled body—I cut myself adrift.

I set off at dawn, with my little girl's hand in mine.

Translated by Dorothy S. Blair

[1] The expression alludes to the title of a novel by Gustave Flaubert, *L'éducation sentimentale* and refers to the development of one's feelings.

Nawal El Saadawi: The Veil (1987)

Nawal El Saadawi was trained as a medical doctor and been Director of Public Health of Egypt. She has been writing often controversial fiction for over forty years. In 1972 she published her first study of Arab women's problems, Women and Sex. *She was imprisoned, along with other leading Egyptian intellectuals, during the regime of Anwar Sadat. Her fiction includes* Woman at Point Zero *and* The Hidden Face of Eve.

What evidence is there that most of this story is taking place within the mind of the narrator? What are the different ways in which she uses veils as symbols? What do you think her thoughts tell us about the society in which she lives? What are her attitudes toward sexuality?

All of a sudden I awake to find myself sitting, a bottle of wine in front of me of which only a little remains, and an ashtray full of cigarette ends of a strange kind I think I have not seen before, until I remember that they are the new brand I began smoking three or four years ago.

I look up from the ashtray to see a man I've never seen before. He is naked, apart from a silken robe which is open to reveal hairy chest and thighs. Between the chest and thighs are a pair of close-fitting striped underpants. I raise my surprised eyes to his face. Only now do I realize that I've seen him before. My eyes rest on his for a moment and I smile a strange, automatic smile, as fleeting as a flash of light or an electric current, leaving behind no trace other than a curious kind of perplexity like the eternal confusion of a person in search of God or happiness. Why is there such confusion in the world and in my body at this particular moment, even though each day my eyes meet hundreds or thousands of eyes and the world and my body remain as they are? But it is soon over. The world and my body return to normal and life continues as usual. It is three or four years since I saw him for the first time and I'd almost forgotten him in the tumult of work and home and people.

My eyes fall on to his naked body and hairy thighs once more. The expression on my face, as I look at his body, is not the same as when I look into his eyes, for my problem is that what I feel inside shows instantly on my face. His eyes are the only part of his body with which I have real contact. They dispel strangeness and ugliness and make my relationship with him real in the midst of numerous unreal ones. Three years, maybe four, and every time I run into him in a street or office or corridor, I stop for a moment in surprise and confusion. Then I continue on my way, knowing that whilst this relationship is very strange, it is at the same time familiar and accepted, among numerous unfamiliar and unaccepted relationships.

When we began meeting regularly or semi-regularly, my relationship with him did not extend to parts of his body other than his eyes. For long hours we would sit and talk, my eyes never leaving his. It was a sort of meeting of minds, and gratifying, but the gratification was somehow lacking. What did it lack?

I asked myself whether it was the body's desire for contact with another body? And why not? In the final analysis, isn't he a man and I a woman? The idea strikes me as new, even strange, and a frightening curiosity takes hold of me. I wonder what the meeting of my body with his could be like. A violent desire to find out can sometimes be more violent than the desire for love and can, at times, draw me into loveless contacts simply in order to satisfy that curiosity. And every time that happens, I experience a repulsion, certain in my mind that my body repulses the body of a man except in one situation: that of love.

I understand the cause of this repulsion. It's an explicable repulsion linked not to the body but to history. To the extent that man worships his masculinity, so woman repulses him. A woman's repulsion is the other face of the worship of the male deity. No power on earth can rid woman of her repulsion other than the victory of love over the male deity. Then history will go back six thousand years to when the deity was female. Will love be victorious? Is the relationship between us love? I do not know. I have no proof. Can love be proved? Is it the desire which rises to the surface of my crowded life, to look into his eyes? Like a person who, from time to time, goes to a holy water spring to kneel down and pray and then goes home? I do not kneel down and neither do I pray. I recognize no deity other than my mind inside my head. What is it that draws me to his eyes?

Is love simply a fairy tale, like the stories of Adam and Eve or Cinderella or Hassan the Wise? All the fairy tales came to an end and the veil fell from each of them. Many veils fell from my mind as I grew up. Each time a veil fell, I would cry at night in sadness for the beautiful illusion which was lost. But in the morning, I'd see my eyes shining, washed by tears as the dew washes the blossom, the jasmine and the rose. I would leave the mirror, trample the fallen veil underfoot and stamp on it with new-found strength, with more strength than I'd had the previous day.

He has filled the tenth or twentieth glass. My hand trembles a little as I hold it, but the deity inside my head is as steady and immobile as the Sphinx. My eyes are still on his and do not leave them, even though I realize, somehow, that he is no longer wearing the silken robe nor even the tight striped underpants.

I notice that his body is white, blushed with red, revealing strength, youthfulness, cleanliness and good eating. My eyes must still have been staring into his, for in another moment, I realize that he has taken my head in his hand and moved it so that my eyes fall on to his body.

I look at him steadily and once again see the strength and youthfulness and cleanliness and good eating. I almost tell him what it is I see.

But I look up and my eyes meet his. I do not know whether it is he who looks surprised or whether the surprise is in my own eyes. I tell myself that the situation calls for surprise, for it is nearly three in the morning. The glass is empty. There is no one in the house and the world outside is silent, dark, dead, fallen into oblivion. What is happening between my body and his?

When I next turn towards him, he is sitting, dressed in the robe with the belt carefully tied around his waist, hiding his chest and thighs. I no longer see anything of him other than his head and eyes and feet inside a pair of light houseshoes. From the side, his face looks tired, as though he's suddenly grown old and weary. His features hang loose, like a child needing to sleep after staying up late. I put out my hand like a mother does to stroke the face of a child, and place a tender motherly kiss on his forehead.

In the street I lift my burning face to the cold and humid dawn breeze. Mysterious feelings of joy mingle with strange feelings of sadness. I put my head on my pillow; my eyes open, filled with tears. My mind had got the better of the wine until I put my head on the pillow; but then the wine took over and sadness replaced joy.

When I open my eyes the following day, the effect of the wine has gone and the veil has lifted from my eyes. I look in the mirror at my shining eyes washed with tears. I am about to walk away from the mirror, like every other time, to trample on the fallen veil at my feet and stamp on it with new-found strength. But this time I do not leave my place. I bend down, pick up the veil from the ground and replace it once again on my face.

Translated by Shirley Eber

South Asia 1900–Present

Rabindranath Tagore: Once There Was a King (1916)

Tagore won the Nobel Prize for literature in 1913—the first to be awarded a non-European—on the belief that he represented the romantic, mysterious East judged by the sentimental translations he had made from the poems in his book Gitanjli. *But poetic fashions were changing in the West, and his work soon lost its popularity abroad, though it continued to be loved at home in India. In fact he had a sophisticated Western-oriented education and was not particularly religious. He wrote plays, novels, essays and stories, including this charming one whose mixture of humorous fantasy and thoughtfulness foreshadows the work of a much later Indian-born writer, Salman Rushdie.*

What does this story have to say about death?

"Once upon a time there was a king."

When we were children there was no need to know who the king in the fairy story was. It didn't matter whether he was called Shiladitya or Shaliban, whether he lived at Kashi or Kanauj. The thing that made a seven-year-old boy's heart go thump, thump with delight was this one sovereign truth, this reality of all realities: "Once there was a king."

But the readers of this modern age are far more exact and exacting. When they hear such an opening to a story, they are at once critical and suspicious. They apply the searchlight of science to its legendary haze and ask: "Which king?"

The story-tellers have become more precise in their turn. They are no longer content with the old indefinite, "There was a king," but assume instead a look of profound learning, and begin: "Once there was a king named Ajatasatru."

The modern reader's curiosity, however, is not so easily satisfied. He blinks at the author through his scientific spectacles, and asks again: "Which Ajatasatru?"

"Every schoolboy knows," the author proceeds, "that there were three Ajatasatrus. The first was born in the twentieth century B.C., and died at the tender age of two years and eight months. I deeply regret that it is impossible to find, from any trustworthy source, a detailed account of his reign. The second Ajatasatru is better known to historians. If you refer to the new Encyclopedia of History . . ."

By this time the modern reader's suspicions are dissolved. He feels he may safely trust his author. He says to himself: "Now we shall have a story that is both improving and instructive."

Ah! how we all love to be deluded! We have a secret dread of being thought ignorant. And we end by being ignorant after all, only we have done it in a long and roundabout way.

There is an English proverb: "Ask me no questions, and I will tell you no lies." The boy of seven who is listening to a fairy story understands that perfectly well; he withholds his questions, while the story is being told. So the pure and beautiful falsehood of it all remains naked and innocent as a babe; transparent as truth itself; limpid as a fresh bubbling spring. But the ponderous and learned lie of our moderns has to keep its true character draped and veiled. And if there is discovered anywhere the least little peephole of deception, the reader turns away with a prudish disgust, and the author is discredited.

When we were young, we understood all sweet things; and we could detect the sweets of a fairy story by an unerring science of our own. We never cared for such useless things as knowledge. We only cared for truth. And our unsophisticated little hearts knew well where the Crystal Palace of Truth lay and how to reach it. But today we are expected to write pages of facts, while the truth is simply this:

"There was a king."

I remember vividly that evening in Calcutta when the fairy story began. The rain and the storm had been incessant. The whole of the city was flooded. The water was knee-deep in our lane. I had a straining hope, which was almost a certainty, that my tutor would be prevented from coming that evening. I sat on the stool in the far corner of the veranda looking down the lane, with a heart beating faster and faster. Every minute I kept my eye on the rain, and when it began to grow less I prayed with all my might: "Please, God, send some more rain till half-past seven is over." For I was quite ready to believe that there was no other need for rain except to protect one helpless boy one evening in one corner of Calcutta from the deadly clutches of his tutor.

If not in answer to my prayer, at any rate according to some grosser law of physical nature, the rain did not give up.

But, alas! nor did my teacher.

Exactly to the minute, in the bend of the lane, I saw his approaching umbrella. The great bubble of hope burst in my breast, and my heart collapsed. Truly, if there is a punishment to fit the crime after death, then my tutor will be born again as me, and I shall be born as my tutor.

As soon as I saw his umbrella I ran as hard as I could to my mother's room. My mother and my grandmother were sitting opposite one another playing cards by the light of a lamp. I ran into the room, and flung myself on the bed beside my mother, and said:

"Mother dear, the tutor has come, and I have such a bad headache; couldn't I have no lessons to-day?"

I hope no child of immature age will be allowed to read this story, and I sincerely trust it will not be used in text-books or primers for schools. For what I did was dreadfully bad, and I received no punishment whatever. On the contrary, my wickedness was crowned with success.

My mother said to me: "All right," and turning to the servant added: "Tell the tutor that he can go back home."

It was perfectly plain that she didn't think my illness very serious, as she went on with her game as before, and took no further notice. And I also, burying my head in the pillow, laughed to my heart's content. We perfectly understood one another, my mother and I.

But every one must know how hard it is for a boy of seven years old to keep up the illusion of illness for long time. After about a minute I got hold of Grandmother, and said: "Grannie, do tell me a story."

I had to ask this many times. Grannie and Mother went on playing cards, and took no notice. At last Mother said to me: "Child, don't bother. Wait till we've finished our game." But I persisted: "Grannie, do tell me a story." I told Mother she could finish her game to-morrow, but she must let Grannie tell me a story there and then.

At last Mother threw down the cards and said: "You had better do what he wants. I can't manage him." Perhaps she had it in her mind that she would have no tiresome tutor on the morrow, while I should be obliged to be back to those stupid lessons.

As soon as ever Mother had given way, I rushed at Grannie. I got hold of her hand, and, dancing with delight, dragged her inside my mosquito curtain on to the bed. I clutched hold of the bolster with both hands in my excitement, and jumped up and down with joy, and when I had got a little quieter, said: "Now, Grannie, let's have the story!"

Grannie went on: "And the king had a queen." That was good to begin with. He had only one.

It is usual for kings in fairy stories to be extravagant in queens. And whenever we hear that there are two queens, our hearts begin to sink. One is sure to be unhappy. But in Grannie's story that danger was past. He had only one queen.

We next hear that the king had not got any son. At the age of seven I didn't think there was any need to bother if a man had had no son. He might only have been in the way.

Nor are we greatly excited when we hear that the king has gone away into the forest to practice austerities in order to get a son.[1] There was only one thing that would have made me go into the forest, and that was to get away from my tutor!

But the king left behind with his queen a small girl, who grew up into a beautiful princess.

Twelve years pass away, and the king goes on practicing austerities, and never thinks all this while of his beautiful daughter. The princess has reached the full bloom of her youth. The age of marriage has passed, but the king does not return. And the queen pines away with grief and cries: "Is my golden daughter destined to die unmarried? Ah me! what a fate is mine."

Then the queen sent men to the king to entreat him earnestly to come back for a single night and take one meal in the palace. And the king consented.

The queen cooked with her own hand, and with the greatest care, sixty-four dishes, and made a seat for him of sandal-wood, and arranged the food in plates of gold and cups of silver. The princess stood behind with the peacock-tail fan in her hand. The king, after twelve years' absence, came into the house, and the princess waved the fan, lighting up all the room with her beauty. The king looked in his daughter's face, and forgot to take his food.

At last he asked his queen: "Pray, who is this girl whose beauty shines as the gold image of the goddess? Whose daughter is she?"

The queen beat her forehead, and cried: "Ah, how evil is my fate! Do you not know your own daughter?"

The king was struck with amazement. He said at last: "My tiny daughter has grown to be a woman."

"What else?" the queen said with a sigh. "Do you not know that twelve years have passed by?"

"But why did you not give her in marriage?" asked the king.

"You were away," the queen said. "And how could I find her a suitable husband?"

The king became vehement with excitement. "The first man I see to-morrow," he said, "when I come out of the palace shall marry her."

The princess went on waving her fan of peacock feathers, and the king finished his meal.

The next morning, as the king came out of his palace, he saw the son of a Brahman

---

[1]Strict asceticism practiced for a while might lead the gods to grant fertility.

gathering sticks in the forest outside the palace gates. His age was about seven or eight.[2]

The king said: "I will marry my daughter to him."

Who can interfere with a king's command? At once the boy was called, and the marriage garlands were exchanged between him and the princess.

At this point I came up close to my wise Grannie and asked her eagerly: "What then?"

In the bottom of my heart there was a devout wish to substitute myself for that fortunate wood-gatherer of seven years old. The night was resonant with the patter of rain. The earthen lamp by my bedside was burning low. My grandmother's voice droned on as she told the story. And all these things served to create in a corner of my credulous heart the belief that I had been gathering sticks in the dawn of some indefinite time in the kingdom of some unknown king, and in a moment garlands had been exchanged between me and the princess, beautiful as the Goddess of Grace. She had a gold band on her hair and gold earrings in her ears. She had a necklace and bracelets of gold, and a golden waist-chain round her waist, and a pair of golden anklets tinkled above her feet.

If my grandmother were an author how many explanations she would have to offer for this little story! First of all, every one would ask why the king remained twelve years in the forest? Secondly, why should the king's daughter remain unmarried all that while? This would be regarded as absurd.

Even if she could have got so far without a quarrel, still there would have been a great hue and cry about the marriage itself. First, it never happened. Secondly, how could there be a marriage between a princess of the Warrior Caste and a boy of the priestly Brahman Caste? Her readers would have imagined at once that the writer was preaching against our social customs in an underhand way. And they would write letters to the papers.

So I pray with all my heart that my grandmother may be born a grandmother again, and not through some cursed fate take birth as her luckless grandson.

So with a throb of joy and delight, I asked Grannie: "What then?"

Grannie went on: "Then the princess took her little husband away in great distress, and built a large palace with seven wings, and began to cherish her husband with great care."

I jumped up and down in my bed and clutched at the bolster more tightly than ever and said: "What then?"

Grannie continued: "The little boy went to school and learned many lessons from his teachers, and as he grew up his class-fellows began to ask him: 'Who is that beautiful lady who lives with you in the palace with the seven wings?'"

The Brahman's son was eager to know who she was. He could only remember how one day he had been gathering sticks, and a great disturbance arose. But all that was so long ago that he had no clear recollection.

Four or five years passed in this way. His companions always asked him: "Who is that beautiful lady in the palace with the seven wings?" And the Brahman's son would come back from school and sadly tell the princess: "My school companions always ask me who is that beautiful lady in the palace with the seven wings, and I can give them no reply. Tell me, oh, tell me, who you are!"

---

[2]Such childhood marriages used to be quite common in India, although they are illegal today. The idea was to guarantee that the girl was married while still a virgin. The couple were not expected to consummate the relationship (and often not even to live together) until she reached puberty. A case like this in which the boy marries an older woman would be quite rare, but perhaps appealing to a romantic young boy.

The princess said: "Let it pass to-day. I will tell you some other day." And every day the Brahman's son would ask: "Who are you?" and the princess would reply: "Let it pass to-day. I will tell you some other day." In this manner four or five more years passed away.

At last the Brahman's son became very impatient, and said: "If you do not tell me to-day who you are, O beautiful lady, I will leave this palace with the seven wings." Then the princess said: "I will certainly tell you to-morrow."

Next day the Brahman's son, as soon as he came home from school, said: "Now, tell me who you are." The princess said: "To-night I will tell you after supper, when you are in bed."

The Brahman's son said: "Very well;" and he began to count the hours in expectation of the night. And the princess, on her side, spread white flowers over the golden bed, and lighted a gold lamp with fragrant oil, and adorned her hair, and dressed herself in a beautiful robe of blue, and began to count the hours in expectation of the night.

That evening when her husband, the Brahman's son, had finished his meal, too excited almost to eat, and had gone to the golden bed in the bedchamber strewn with flowers, he said to himself: "To-night I shall surely know who this beautiful lady is in the palace with the seven wings."

The princess took for her the food that was left over by her husband, and slowly entered the bedchamber. She had to answer that night the question, who was the beautiful lady who lived in the palace with the seven wings. And as she went up to the bed to tell him she found a serpent had crept out of the flowers and had bitten the Brahman's son. Her boy-husband was lying on the bed of flowers, with face pale in death.

My heart suddenly ceased to throb, and I asked with choking voice: "What then?"

Grannie said: "Then . . ."

But what is the use of going on any further with the story? It would only lead on to what was more and more impossible. The boy of seven did not know that, if there were some "What then?" after death, no grandmother of a grandmother could tell us all about it.

But the child's faith never admits defeat, and it would snatch at the mantle of death itself to turn him back. It would be outrageous for him to think that such a story of one teacherless evening could so suddenly come to a stop. Therefore the grandmother had to call back her story from the ever-shut chamber of the great End, but she does it so simply: it is merely by floating the dead body on a banana stem on the river, and having some incantations read by a magician. But in that rainy night and in the dim light of a lamp death loses all its horror in the mind of the boy, and seems nothing more than a deep slumber of a single night. When the story ends, the tired eyelids are weighed down with sleep. Thus it is that we send the little body of the child floating on the back of sleep over the still water of time, and then in the morning read a few verses of incantation to restore him to the world of life and light.

Translated by Rabindranath Tagore and C. F. Andrews

Mokshodayani Mukhopadhyay: The Bengali Babu (1882)

*The writer comes from a distinguished family of scholars and nationalist politicians working for Indian independence. The journal she published in 1870—*Banga Mahila (Woman of Bengal)*—was one of the first attempts at publishing by a an Indian woman. The journal stood for women's rights, particularly the right to higher education. The poem from which this excerpt is taken is from her first collection:* Bana Prasun (A Bunch of Wild Flowers), *published in 1882. This poem created a controversy as it was a reply to the misogynist poem of a well-known contemporary poet, Hemachandra Bandhopadhyay, called "Bengalir Meye" ("Bengali Woman").*

What is the attitude of the writer toward the babu? Which of his qualities does she particularly satirize? Why is it ironic that he prides himself on not drinking? Why would an advocate of Indian independence take this sort of attitude toward the babu?

Who's that rushing through his breakfast and bath?
The Bengali babu![1] He's terribly pressed:
The sahib[2] will scold him, should he be late
So he's got to get ready, and bustles about.
There he comes, decked in trousers and jacket!
On his head a pith helmet, tied round with a scarf,

Just like a basket! He can't bear to wait
For anything. Loses his temper and shouts.
Furious, he'll slap or snap at his boy
If the child should happen to call out, "Father!"
Everything's a rush, but he takes his own time
Over his hookah,[3] and puffs it at ease.
Should his heart soften, as he dreams in the smoke,
A half-chewed betel leaf[4] will console the child.
The carriage costs five annas, but it hurts him to walk.
Alas, there goes our Bengali babu!

Alas, there goes our Bengali babu!
He slaves away from ten till four,
Carrying his servitude like a peddler's wares.
A lawyer or magistrate, or perhaps a schoolmaster,
A subjudge, clerk, or overseer:
The bigger the job, the greater his pride;
The babu thinks he's walking on air.
Red in the face from the day's hard labor,
He downs pegs of whiskey to relax when he's home.
He's transported with pride at the thought of his rank—

---

[1]A babu is a clerk, usually a subsidiary one in an English colonial office.
[2]The colonial boss.
[3]Water-pipe for smoking tobacco.
[4]A mild stimulant.

But faced with a sahib, he trembles in fear!
Then he's obsequious, he mouths English phrases,
His own tongue disgusts him, he heaps it with curses.
The babu's learned English, he swells with conceit
And goes off in haste to deliver a speech.
He flounders while speaking, and stumbles and stutters,
But he's speaking in *English:* you must come and hear.

Alas, there goes our Bengali babu!
The lackey's livery is shed when he's home.
Bare-chested in slippers, he's a sight to be seen;
Clad in plain cloth, pleated by his servant,
He relaxes in slippers, or in native sandals.[5]
He enjoys his tobacco, lolls about on cushions;
Hookah at his mouth, he thinks he's in heaven.
The sitting room's resplendent, and echoes with laughter,
The spittoon's in front of them, but they spit on the mat.

Alas, there goes our Bengali babu!
Cane in hand, wearing shoes, smoking a cheroot;[6]
Some, sahib-fashion, are hatted and coated.
Not a thought of religion, they lie about and sing,
Crying out on occasion "Bring the tobacco and pan!"[7]

The oil lamp burns brightly, they can't wait to impress.
Their valor's displayed to any fool who passes.
With his cronies the babu plays cards or chess.
Alas, there he sits, the Bengali babu!

He longs to be fair, scrubs vigorously with soap;
Rubs with a towel till his skin peels off;
Parts his hair in front in the style of Prince Albert,[8]
Scents himself liberally, and reeks like a civet. . . .

He has fashionable tastes. He loves watching plays;
His mouth stuffed with betel, he smiles with a twist.
He roars like a bull, "Excellent! Encore!"
And by the grace of the shopkeeper, he gets a lungful of smoke.
Head over heels in debt, but he won't leave his pleasures,
Alas, there goes our Bengali babu!
Here's one who doesn't drink, swells with pride at the thought—
The country's deliverance lies in his hand!

---

[5]Not really sandals, but a kind of slipper, worn and popularized by Iswarchandra Vidyasagar.
[6]Cigar.
[7]Betel leaf and areca nut, chewed for relaxation.
[8]Husband of Queen Victoria.

He writes himself down as a Brahmo[9] and turns religious,
Tradesmen and peddlers are amazed at his sermons—
One becomes Brahmo to emancipate women,
Drags out of seclusion the ladies of his clan;
Another, a drunkard, is liberated by drink,
And launches a struggle to deliver the country.
The babu speaks a patter of Bengali and English
But he berates the English with all his heart.
These sports are but nocturnal; wiping his mouth, in the morning
The babu is respectful and sober[10] again.

Translated by Supriya Chaudhury

[9]Follower of the "Brahmo Samaj," a Bengali nationalist movement founded by Rammohan Roy.

[10] The Bengali word is *bhadra,* a term implying a variety of characteristics such as decent, genteel, respectable.

Mohandas K. Gandhi: *Indian Home Rule* (1909)

The popular image of Gandhi in the West involves a saintly manner and "passive resistance." In fact he was a skillful lawyer whose techniques of nonviolent protest were anything but passive and who could be fearlessly outspoken in defense of his beloved India. In this imaginary dialogue, Gandhi is replying to the question of an interviewer (here labeled "READER") as to how he would address "extremists" seeking independence from Britain. Gandhi's replies are labeled "EDITOR."

What does Gandhi say the proper role of the British in India should be?

EDITOR:

I would say to the extremists: "I know that you want Home Rule[1] for India; it is not to be had for your asking. Everyone will have to take it for himself. What others get for me is not Home Rule but foreign rule; therefore, it would not be proper for you to say that you have obtained Home Rule if you have merely expelled the English. I have already described the true nature of Home Rule. This you would never obtain by force of arms. Brute-force is not natural to Indian soil. You will have, therefore, to rely wholly on soul-force. You must not consider that violence is necessary at any stage for reaching our goal." I would say to the moderates: "Mere petitioning is derogatory; we thereby confess inferiority. To say that British rule is indispensable, is almost a denial of the Godhead. We cannot say that anybody or anything is indispensable except God. Moreover, common sense should tell us that to state that, for the time being, the presence of the English in India is a necessity, is to make them conceited.

"If the English vacated India, bag and baggage, it must not be supposed that she would be widowed. It is possible that those who are forced to observe peace under their pressure would fight after their withdrawal. There can be no advantage in suppressing an eruption; it must have its vent. If, therefore, before we can remain at peace, we must fight amongst ourselves, it is better that we do so.[2] There is no occasion for a third party to protect the weak. It is this so-called protection which has unnerved us. Such protection can only make the weak weaker. Unless we realize this, we cannot have Home Rule. I would paraphrase the thought of an English divine [3] and say that anarchy under Home Rule were better than orderly foreign rule. Only, the meaning that the learned divine attached to Home Rule is different from Indian Home Rule according to my conception. We have to learn, and to teach others, that we do not want the tyranny of either English rule or Indian rule."

If this idea were carried out, both the extremists and the moderates could join hands. There is no occasion to fear or distrust one another.

READER:

What then, would you say to the English?

---

[1]Independence, self-government.

[2]Gandhi thus foresees the possibility of something like the divisive violence that occurred at Independence, even though it was to break his heart and take his life.

[3]Clergyman.

EDITOR:

To them I would respectfully say: "I admit you are my rulers. It is not necessary to debate the question whether you hold India by the sword or by my consent. I have no objection to your remaining in my country, but although you are the rulers; you will have to remain as servants of the people. It is not we who have to do as you wish, but it is you who have to do as we wish. You may keep the riches that you have drained away from this land, but you may not drain riches henceforth. Your function will be, if you so wish, to police India; you must abandon the idea of deriving any commercial benefit from us. We hold the civilization that you support to be the reverse of civilization. We consider our civilization to be far superior to yours. If you realize this truth, it will be to your advantage and, if you do not, according to your own proverb,[4] you should only live in our country in the same manner as we do. You must not do anything that is contrary to our religions. It is your duty as rulers that for the sake of the Hindus you should eschew beef, and for the sake of Mahomedans[5] you should avoid bacon and ham. We have hitherto said nothing because we have been cowed down, but you need not consider that you have not hurt our feelings by your conduct. We are not expressing our sentiments either through base selfishness or fear, but because it is our duty now to speak out boldly. We consider your schools and courts to be useless. We want our own ancient schools and courts to be restored. The common language of India is not English but Hindi. You should, therefore, learn it. We can hold communication with you only in our national language.

"We cannot tolerate the idea of your spending money on railways and the military. We see no occasion for either. You may fear Russia; we do not. When she comes we shall look after her. If you are with us, we may then receive her jointly. We do not need any European cloth. We shall manage with articles produced and manufactured at home. You may not keep one eye on Manchester[6] and the other on India. We can work together only if our interests are identical.

---

[4]"When in Rome, do as the Romans do."

[5]An old English term for "Muslim." Note that Gandhi is already trying to be sensitive to both religions. This was the issue that in the end defeated him.

[6]The center of the English cotton-weaving trade. One of Gandhi's most important campaigns was to persuade Indians to wear only traditional Indian homespun garments, boycotting English imports.

P. Lankesh: Bread (1970)

Lankesh has had a varied career. He has taught at the University of Bangalore, Karnataka, and has produced and directed films. He has also been a journalist and editor and publishes his own newspaper in Kannada. His published works include twenty volumes of poetry, fiction, drama and an edited anthology of Kannada poetry. His translations into Kannada include works by Sophocles and Baudelaire.

What kind of person is the woman in this story? Explain the reactions of the other people to her complaint.

Summer. Wherever it was shady, there were people. Wherever it was damp, there were houseflies. When she got down at Singarapete[1] railway station, she hadn't noticed lots of things: coolies[2] scurrying here and there; a station full of dirty-limbed, ragged people, babies clutched in their armpits. Colorful pieces of paper, meaningless to her, were stuck all over the walls. Behind the station, on one side, smoke was rising from earth to sky. On the way into town, there were several processions. She'd tried to read the banners and posters of many of the processions, but couldn't. She'd tried to discuss some things with her daughter who'd just had a baby but the daughter seemed a bit scared. Afraid that her mother was trying to probe into her husband's affairs, she had dodged the questions. The son-in-law gave her no chance to speak when he came home from the office. She gave her daughter the foodstuffs and everything she had brought for her, nursed her after the delivery for a week. She was now on her way back to the railway station with her tiny trunk and traveling bag. Her daughter had given her fruit and flat bread for the journey.

It was about four miles from her daughter's house to the station. She did think of taking a horse-cart instead of trying to walk the distance in the hot sun. But she had walked all the way, unwilling to fork out two rupees for a cart.

"Walked four miles. They say this dump is a station. There's not even standing room," she grumbled to the person next to her, standing near a pillar on the crowded platform. But that person just stood there, unmoved.

At her foot was a gob of someone's snot covered with a swarm of flies—when they came close to her own feet, she felt queasy. She looked around, but decided to stay put as there seemed to be no place of refuge from the invasion of flies. She got very curious about the silent motionless person who stood there under a full head of hair; long hair falling from the crown of the head; from shoulder to ankle a dirty green cloth. She coughed, to attract attention. The person turned around slowly, mechanically. It was a man, not a woman. A face spent in fever, big pits under his eyes, countless lines on his face—a face full of anger and pain. She felt uneasy. She quietly dragged her trunk and bag a little away from the pillar. But he too moved a little and looked her in the eyes. She tried to look away, but couldn't. If she started out from there, he might follow her. There were people milling all around—people going about their own business indifferent to her problem. She wanted to stop some of them and tell them about this man. But she couldn't find the courage. Well, she said to herself, and stood there stubbornly. There were many others like her, waiting near other pillars with baskets, bags, cooking vessels. Dirty people, they sit anywhere at all,

[1]Small town in the state of Karnataka in south India.

[2]Porters who carry luggage.

spit any place; the more she looked, the dizzier she seemed to get. Then a gong struck, announcing an arriving train. She thought of asking someone when approximately the train might arrive, but her tongue stuck in her mouth. A railway clerk was writing something on a blackboard near the gate. After he left, she could see what it was: "TRAIN DELAYED BY ONE HOUR."

The man was looking elsewhere. She felt a little better.

She wished she could join her children at once, and hear their voices. She was also famished. She was unaccustomed to eating in public, with everybody looking on. Still the belly accepts only one answer. Quietly she opened the bag and drew out the bread. She undid the packet and put it on her lap, thinking of saving at least two pieces of bread for her little baby. As she put aside one and started folding up the paper packet, the man with the long hair gazed at her, his eyes popping. Then she knew that his eyes were not fevered or unhappy, just hungry. She thought she could give him one of the pieces of bread. But she didn't want to get too familiar with him. She had suspicions, fears. So she tried wrapping up the bread in some haste, when he directly pounced on her, grabbed all of it and started cramming it into his mouth. She was startled out of her skin by what happened so fast. "Ho! Ho! Thief! Thief!" she screamed.

People slowly gathered around her. One of them, a thin tall cruel-eyed man, stared at her and asked, "What happened?"

She was trembling. "This man stole my—my—"

"Stole your what?"

"My bread. That's what he's eating."

The long-haired hungry man had already bitten off and finished half of it. He didn't seem to be aware of the world around him. His dhoti[3] didn't quite cover his thighs, his shirt was open at the chest. Long matted hair, unkempt beard. The world seemed dumbstruck at his single-mindedness. Some men grumbled something; some left the scene; others were neutral. The tall thin man with the cruel eyes asked again: "Why scream so loud for such a small thing? You know why he stole it, don't you?"

Some people laughed at his dry-voiced question.

Her helplessness grew. She shivered uncontrollably. Trying to force a sound out of her throat, she said: "Can't you see it, he grabbed it from my hand?"

"He was hungry, that's why." The answer was very direct. He got hungry, so he took it: a proper answer. But the roused, disturbed mind fumbled for something that had to be said, and made her say:

"If he'd asked me, I'd have given it to him myself. He needn't have grabbed . . ." But her words dissolved in the hubbub around her. Some laughed, some sneered. Down her neck, close to her chest, hot breaths and teasing voices that made her break out in a sweat. A weak-limbed wide-eyed creature raised his voice and said: "We know all about people like you. This has gone on too long. Don't try and fool us now. Tell us, take an oath on your baby's head and tell us: would you really have given it if he'd asked for it, would you really?"

"Anyone can take any oath," sneered another man.

She got into a rage at these country dogs barking at a woman instead of coming to her help; it didn't matter even if she died now. She cried out bravely:

"Who are you to get me to take oaths? I would have given it if I wished; if not, I wouldn't have. Aren't you ashamed to scold a poor woman when this cur grabs food from her hand and devours it? Don't any of you have wives, children?" She spat. "Dogs!"

[3]Traditional garment covering men's lower bodies.

"So we're dogs, are we?"

"What else? Get out of my way. Don't touch me."

"Why do dogs need wives and children?" "Give that whore one in the face!" "Look, look at this woman's cheek!"

"If you touch my hand, I'll pick up my sandals. Will you move aside, or else . . ." As she said this, her voice grew louder. It became a scream. Trampled underfoot, her bag and trunk seemed to have disappeared. Numberless people from all over the station crowded there. "Thu!" she spat out viciously. The gathered crowd laughed, clapped hands; a thousand eyes stared at her. This was her first such experience. She had a feeling she was standing stark naked, she was scared she'd do something vile in the pressure of circumstance. Then began the people's murmur, panic. Someone said, "Police!" At a distance, a policeman was coming towards her, parting the crowd on both sides. She felt the breath of new life. Her fear turned into a fit of weeping. She wept helplessly in a loud voice. The policeman came in a hurry, asking something. His face and body were sweating. He had an ugly devouring look. As soon as he came near enough, he seized her bag, went straight to the beggar, grabbed the bread in his hand, and hit him on the head with his stick.

The crowd had stood motionless so far. But when the stick struck the bread-thief, there was a wave of anger. The anger was itching to become action. The policeman struck the beggar again. Blood began to flow. He stood there stunned by the blow. The policeman, too, was probably scared. He started pushing people with his stick, saying, "Go now, get away from here." She was staring at the thief; there was blood running down him. The crowd held the policeman by his stick and asked, "Why did you hit him?" It looked as if any minute the policeman would be torn to pieces by the crowd, when she said, "Please, don't hit anyone, please." She went closer to the "thief" who was bleeding badly. She couldn't touch him though she wanted to. Shivering, she looked around for her trunk and bag.

The policeman stood by, scared himself. "Look here, madam. It's you that's responsible for this mess. You'd better leave." Trying to please the crowd, he added, "We lose our heads because of people like you." But she couldn't have left then. She wanted to take out fruit from her handbag and distribute it to the "thief" and to the whole crowd. She took the fruit out of the bag, and took out the face cream, the powder, the baby socks and dolls that were in the bag along with the fruit, and held them out, her hands in a gesture of giving—but no one took anything. She tried to say, "Excuse me." But the words didn't come. From her faint hands, the fruit and the socks fell to the ground.

Then a distant whistle and a fearful military cry was heard. The crowd tried to disperse. But it wasn't easy to get through a dense milling crowd. Everyone scrambled, everyone got into everyone else's way. The policeman, who had begun to adopt a somewhat neutral position in the meantime, plucked up new spirit and started beating the crowd with his stick. She said, "No, no, please." Nobody heard her say it.

The reserve force was soon on the crowd. The policeman said to her, "Look here, these people are always getting into trouble, come away. They'll all run now," and pulled her by the hand. A police hand curved around her shoulders and caressed a breast. She tried to escape it. "Why are they beating up the people? Please. No. Don't beat them. No, I won't come. You leave me alone and go your way." But he didn't let her go, his khaki chest pressed against her sweating breasts. The policeman said, "Have you gone off your head? Come, woman, or we'll be hurt. Come away."

The reserve force kept up a fierce pressure. The people moved back far away and watched, with cruel, revengeful eyes. But the bread thief stood bleeding near the same old pillar and still stared at her. The policeman dragged her brutally across and gave her over to the reserve force. They stood guard around her as if she were some princess. She wished she could run from there and join the crowd. She wished she could scream out what she felt.

But the police surrounded her, behind her a van. Left, right, left, right. As if they'd conquered a country, they marched with her. "Where to?" she asked. "O come with us. We'll send you home," said one of them. Tears welled up in her eyes. She turned around. Between the bars of the station, the walls and the sacks, she could see the beggar. His eyes, full of anger, fever, and hunger still seemed to look only at her. As she looked on, he seemed to walk straight in her direction. She wiped her eyes and looked again. There was no one there. The filthy body odor of policemen. When she closed her eyes, he was there again—a green shirt, a dhoti that didn't quite cover his thighs, hunger in his eyes, and drenched with blood.

Translated by A. K. Ramanujan

Faiz Ahmed Faiz (1914–1978): Selected Poems

One of the foremost poets in the Indian sub-continent, Faiz Ahmed Faiz was born in Sialkot in Pakistan. He studied philosophy and English literature, but poetry and politics preoccupied him more than anything else. For writing poetry that always antagonizes the ruling élite and challenges colonial and feudal values, like such rebellious writers as Ngugi of Kenya and Darwish of Palestine, Faiz had to go to jail repeatedly during both colonial and postcolonial times in Pakistan. Inspired by the Marxist ideology, Faiz's poetry exhibits a strong sense of commitment to lower-class people, yet it always maintains a unique beauty nourished by the long, rich tradition of Urdu literature. His love poems are as appealing as his political poems, and he is considered primarily responsible for shaping poetic diction in contemporary Urdu poetry.

Which poems deal with love, and which ones with politics? What evidence is there that Faiz is a courageous poet? What is his attitude towards loneliness and death?

Loneliness

Loneliness like a good, old friend
visits my house to pour wine in the evening.
And we sit together, waiting for the moon,
and for your face to sparkle in every shadow.

Last Night

Last night your lost memory visited my heart
as spring visits the wilderness quietly,
as the breeze echoes the silence of her footfalls
in the desert,
as peace slowly, softly descends on one's sickness.

Tonight

Do not strike the chord of sorrow tonight!
Days burning with pain turn to ashes.
Who knows what happens tomorrow?
Last night is lost; tomorrow's frontier wiped out:
Who knows if there will be another dawn?
Life is nothing, it's only tonight!
Tonight we can be what the gods are!

Do not strike the chord of sorrow, tonight!
Do not repeat stories of sufferings now,
Do not complain, let your fate play its role,
Do not think of tomorrows, give a damn—
Shed no tears for seasons gone by,
All sighs and cries wind up their tales,
Oh, do not strike the same chord again!

Speak

Speak, your lips are free.
Speak, it is your own tongue.
Speak, it is your own body.
Speak, your life is still yours.

See how in the blacksmith's shop
The flame burns wild, the iron glows red;
The locks open their jaws,
And every chain begins to break.

Speak, this brief hour is long enough
Before the death of body and tongue:
Speak,'cause the truth is not dead yet,
Speak, speak, whatever you must speak.

Stanza

If they snatch my ink and pen,
I should not complain,
For I have dipped my fingers
In the blood of my heart.
I should not complain
Even if they seal my tongue,
For every ring of my chain
Is a tongue ready to speak.

My Interview

The wall has grown all black, up to the circling roof.
Roads are empty, travellers all gone. Once again
My night begins to converse with its loneliness;
My visitor I feel has come once again.
Henna stains one palm, blood wets another;
One eye poisons, the other cures.

None leaves or enters my heart's lodging;
Loneliness leaves the flower of pain unwatered,
Who is there to fill the cup of its wound with color?

My visitor I feel has come once again,
Of her own will, my old friend—her name
Is Death: a friend in need, yet an enemy—
The murderess and the sweetheart!

Translated by Azfar Hussain

Akhtaruzzaman Elias (1943-1997): *Dream Book* (1996)

Elias was a major Bengali fiction writer particularly noted for his subtle sense of humor, realistic use of dialogue and dialect, and for his Marxist commitment to the lower class in both towns and villages in Bangladesh. His last major novel, called Khoabnama *(*Dream Book*), is set in rural Bangladesh during a long historical period spanning several centuries. Some of the major characters in this novel are landless farmers, who still constitute a large segment of the population in Bangladesh. The novel weaves together numerous stories and episodes of struggles, frustrations, hopes, and dreams of these people. What follows is an episode in which the landless farmer Tameez wants to work on the land owned by a large farmer (Abdul Aziz) in an arrangement known as "sharecropping," which has a long tradition in many countries, and used to be common in the Southern United States. The landed farmer provides the land itself and the landless farmer not only cultivates it and produces crops but also provides seeds and other necessary means of cultivation. When crops are finally produced, the landed farmer receives two thirds of the crop and the landless farmer gets only one. Besides showing how exploitative this system is, the passage also portrays part of a well-known historical struggle of landless farmers against sharecropping.*

Contrast the way Tameez is living with the way his ancestors lived as explained in the last paragraph.

Tameez pays a price for his decision. He leaves Khiyar[1] in order to become a sharecropper in his own village. He stomachs all kinds of criticisms. He does not have a cow. He does not have a plow or a yoke or a harrow; nor does he have a single *cowrie*[2] to buy even a handful of seed. So how can anyone possibly trust his ability to sharecrop? With hands together, however, Tameez desperately prays for a piece of land. He tries to persuade the landowner, Sharafat Mondol, to lease him at least a bit of land. He also tells Mondol that he will be reimbursed for the expenses of cultivation after the harvest.

Tameez's proposal sounds attractive. It is not that such sharecropping arrangements have not worked in the past. But Sharafat Mondol's eldest son, Abdul Aziz, is a clever and cautious man. He lives in Joypur where he works as a clerk at an office of land registration. There is perhaps no one in the entire village of Lathidanga who can match his knowledge of matters relating to land. So Abdul Aziz pays in advance only half the prices of cows and other means of production like ploughs, yokes, harrows, and seeds. He whispers to himself, 'you have nothing yet you want to sharecrop, eh? Well, then, you should simply follow whatever terms and conditions I dictate now."

But Abdul Kader comments, "These folks have been here for a long time. Even Tameez's father once worked on our land. . . ."

But landless farmers have meanwhile gone out of bounds. Their agitation[3] has already begun in town and it seems that the wave of protest may soon reach this eastern part of the

[1]The name of a village in northern Bangladesh.
[2]"Cowrie" means "penny."
[3]This is a historical reference to the uprising of landless peasants against large farmers in Bengal in the nineteenth century during British colonial rule (1757-1947). The protesting farmers demanded larger shares of the crops.

village across the Korotoya River. Farmers in Khiyar are now insisting on two shares out of three, wanting to give only one to the landowner. Of course you can always demand whatever you want—you don't have to pay taxes for speaking out. But the farmers argue that one important fact remains unchanged: the landlord cannot command the land to walk into his courtyard and deliver the crop. Or does he suppose that land is a heron that it can fly in a flash from that monstrous *Arjun*[4] in Kamarpara to the tree overlooking the mansion of the Mondols? What the hell does he know about the value of land? Does he know that plowing even a tiny piece of land costs at least a pound of human blood, oozing from the body like salt?

Abdul Aziz of course watches the uprising in Khiyar—a nagging pain in the ass, of course—while he also wonders if it will soon make the peasants' blood boil in his own locality. Yet he feels no compulsion to please anyone in particular. All he wants is simply the full enforcement of the sharecropping rules in his locality. "Follow the rules or get the hell out of my land"—that's the only policy Abdul Aziz seems to care for.

How can Tameez soothe these anxieties of Abdul Aziz? Abdul Aziz is simply Abdul Aziz: one who effortlessly writes his name in English "M. A. Aziz" at one solid stretch[5], one who attends all kinds of meetings and forums, who retails—whenever he gets a chance to do this—all the horrid stories of oppressions Hindus have inflicted on Muslims, and who therefore urges all Muslims to unite under the banner of the Muslim League[6] so as to put an end to those oppressions, But now even Abdul Aziz cannot help scratching his head. Whatever may happen, the fact still remains: Abdul Aziz holds a position in an office of land registration in Joypur where his both hands stay equally alive and active. But as he leaves Joypur to spend a few days in his village, his left hand turns uncomfortably passive,[7] although it daily wipes the shit from his ass after his inevitable response to the inescapable call of nature. Abdul Aziz, however, compensates for the momentary inactivity of his left hand by the unleashed activity of his tongue and teeth.

Tameez himself watched farmers make a great commotion to the West.[8] But does he like all this fuss himself? No, he doesn't. He still believes the landowner should dictate the terms of sharecropping arrangement simply because he *is* the owner of land. Yet these landless farmers, armed with weapons, have tried to claim the larger share of the crop. To halt this move, however, some landowners have hired a group of workers to harvest the fields. Although Tameez comes from the eastern part of the country, he has easily gotten

---

[4]The name of a tree.

[5]The language of the majority of people in Bangladesh today is Bengali. During the British colonial rule (1757-1947), people who could read, write, or use English—the language of the colonizer—were held in great esteem and benefited from certain social and economic privileges which others without knowledge of English simply could not share.

[6]The leading sectarian political party led by middle-and upper-class Muslim activists. The other sectarian political party led by middle-and upper-class Hindu activists is known as Congress. During the British colonial rule in India (1757-1947), when Bangladesh was part of India, these two parties, which came into being in the twentieth century, were not only involved in anti-colonial struggles against the British rulers but were also responsible for much of the tension between Hindus and Muslims on the Indian subcontinent.

[7]The activity of the left hand has a specific local meaning in Bangladesh: while the right hand does the assigned job, the left hand takes the money as a bribe. The fact that Tameez is a corrupt and dishonest man is indicated by the activity of his left hand.

[8]The western part of the country.

one of these jobs. The landowners have, it seems, also informed and bribed the police. And how many places can be policed at once?

That day Tameez had begun harvesting in a cheerful mood because he had been offered a wage-rate better than usual. He was working enthusiastically, thinking that the sooner he finished harvesting the paddy, the better. But as soon as the sun had reached the middle of the sky, he heard the angry demonstrating farmers swooping in. But God-the-Great saved him: he broke into a run before they could catch him by the scruff of his neck. Even the thin wives and daughters of the angry farmers joined in with brooms, large knives, potatoes, and sticks. Had not he run through the field or had not he quickly leapt over the harvest lying scattered in the field, he would have surely received at least a mighty blow from a broom or even a whacking blow of a cooking potato or two. Who knew? Perhaps he did receive one or two. If a woman beats a man, it is unlikely that he will spread word of it. By the time Tameez reachedf the landowner's courtyard, he felt their fuss was absolutely pointless and disgusting. Land is after all *Lakshmi*[9] and crops are her offspring. If the crops are caught in a tug of war, the very body of the land gets hurt![10] Crops are the soul of the soul of the landowner. Tameez was anguished by the mob's sheer insensitivity to the sufferings of the land. eTrue, his father and grandfather and great grandfather had all lived on fishing; they were not traditional land-farmers. Yet Tameez empathized with the pain of the land. A long time ago, long before Tameez was born, the legendary largest type of fish—the *Baghar* fish, as it was called—used to add to the spectacle of the famous *Poradaha*[11] fair, simply because none but Tameez's great grandfather—Baghar-the-boatman—could catch it. This is why Tameez's father later adopted the name of his own grandfather, the name of the famous fish-catcher, to keep the glory of his family alive. This ancestral glory, however, ended with Tameez's father, who had been known more as Baghar's grandson than as anything else. And Tameez today is known as simply as Tameez.

Translated by Azfar Hussain

---

[9]*Lakshmi* is the Hindu goddess of prosperity.

[10]Land is often personified in Bengali literature.

[11]The name of a semi-urban area in the northern part of Bangladesh.

Kishwar Naheed: We Sinful Women

Kishwar Naheed is an outspoken Pakistani feminist and has broached many controversial issues concerning women. She was an editor of the prestigious monthly Maah-i Nahu *for several years. A prolific writer, her poetry deals with a wide variety of subjects: love, hysterectomy, sexism, censorship, American intervention in Pakistan and other socio-political issues. Some of her published work includes the volumes of poetry:* Lips that Speak, Unnamed Journey, Poems, Alleyways: the Sun, Doorways, Amidst Reproaches, Complete Poems, *and* The Colour Pink within a Black Border *and the prose works* Woman 'twixt Dreams and Dust, Come Back Africa, *and* Women in the Mirror of Psychology.

What connections are made in this poem between women, their bodies, and sin?

It is we sinful women
who are not awed by the grandeur of those who wear gowns

who don't sell our lives
who don't bow our heads
who don't fold our hands together.

It is we sinful women
while those who sell the harvests of our bodies
become exalted
become distinguished
become the just princes of the material world.

It is we sinful women
who come out raising the banner of truth
up against barricades of lies on the highways
who find stories of persecution piled on each threshold
who find the tongues which could speak have been severed.

It is we sinful women.
Now, even if the night gives chase
these eyes shall not be put out.
For the wall which has been razed
don't insist now on raising it again.
It is we sinful women
who are not awed by the grandeur of those who wear gowns

who don't sell our bodies
who don't bow our heads
who don't fold our hands together.

Translated by Rukhsana Ahmad

China 1900–Present

Lu Xun: The Wise Man, the Fool, and the Slave (1925)

Lu Xun (1881-1936) is probably the most important Chinese author of the 20th century. Left-wing, like most authors of his time, his early death prevented him from suffering the roller-coaster treatment of left-wing intellectuals by the Communist government after 1949. Lu Xun was born into a gentry family in Shao-hsing (Che-kiang province). His father's chronic disease and subsequent death brought financial difficulties to the family. Moreover, since it had been Lu Xun that had to regularly go to the pawnshop in order to buy more expensive and ineffectual Chinese medicine for his ailing father, it gave Lu Xun the determination to study western medicine. Having studied in Japan for several years, he went to a show of lantern slides on the Russo-Japanese War (1904–5). A slide depicting the execution of a Chinese claimed to be a Russian spy made such a profound impression on Lu Xun that he decided to quit studying medicine and become, instead, a writer. It was not the execution itself but the throngs of able-bodied, sturdy Chinese witnessing it in complete apathy that shocked him. His fellow country-men, Lu Xun concluded, needed to be awakened, their spirit needed to be changed and the best way to reach them was through literature. In his subsequent writings, his essays, short stories, and novels, he used irony and at times scathing sarcasm to rouse the Chinese people into taking an active part in their own fate and future.

What is the moral of this story? How would you apply this story to the situation in contemporary China? Do you think it could also be read as a parable within the context of American society today?

A slave did nothing but look for people to whom to pour out his woes. This was all he would and all he could do. One day he met a wise man. "Sir!" he cried sadly, tears streaming from his eyes. "You know, the life I lead is less than human. I may not have a single meal all day, and if I do it is only husks of sorghum which not even a pig or dog would eat. Not to mention that there is only one small bowl of it. . . ."

"That's really pitiful," the wise man commiserated.

"Isn't it?" His spirits rose. "Then I work all day and all night. At dawn I carry water, at dusk I cook the dinner; in the morning I run errands, in the evening I grind wheat; when it's fine I wash the clothes, when it's wet I hold the umbrella; in winter I mind the boiler, in summer I wave the fan. At midnight I boil mushrooms, and wait on our master at his gambling parties; but never a tip do I get, only sometimes the strap. . . ."

"Dear me . . ." The wise man sighed, and the rims of his eyes looked a little red as if he were going to shed tears.

"I can't go on like this, sir. I must find some way out. But what can I do?"

"I am sure things will improve. . . ."

"Do you think so? I certainly hope so. But now that I've told you my troubles and you've been so sympathetic and encouraging, I already feel much better. It shows there is still some justice in the world."

A few days later, though, he felt aggrieved again and found someone else to whom to pour out his woes.

"Sir!" he exclaimed, shedding tears. "You know, where I live is even worse than a pigsty. My master doesn't treat me like a human being; he treats his dog ten thousand times better. . . ."

"Confound him!" The other swore so loudly that he startled the slave. The other man was a fool.

"All I have to live in, sir, is a tumble-down one-roomed hut, damp, cold, and swarming with bedbugs. They bite me like anything when I lie down to sleep. The place stinks and hasn't a single window. . . ."

"Can't you ask your master to have a window made?"

"How can I do that?"

"Well, show me what it's like."

The fool followed the slave to his hut, and began to pound the mud wall.

"What are you doing, sir?" The slave was horrified.

"I am opening a window for you."

"This won't do! The master will curse me."

"Let him!" The fool continued to pound away.

"Help! A bandit is breaking down the house! Come quickly or he will knock down the wall!" Shouting and sobbing, the slave rolled frantically on the ground. A whole troop of slaves came out and drove away the fool. Roused by the outcry, the last one to come slowly out was the master.

"A bandit tried to break down our house. I gave the alarm, and together we drove him away!" The slave spoke respectfully and triumphantly.

"Good for you!" The master praised him.

Many callers came that day to express concern, among them the wise man.

"Sir, because I made myself useful, the master praised me. When you said the other day that things would improve, you were really showing foresight." He spoke very hopefully and happily.

"That's right". . . . replied the wise man, and seemed happy for his sake.

Translated by Gladys Yang

K'ang Yu-wei: Utopian Marriage (1885)

K'ang Yu-wei (1858-1927), a native of Canton, was the leading figure in the Chinese reform movement of 1898. Having won the confidence of the emperor, K'ang's propositions of radical changes in the Chinese education system, its legal system, and the organization of its military forces along with the abolition of age-old customs such as foot-binding were implemented by imperial edicts in the summer of 1898. The strong opposition of conservatives, however, led to a coup d'état against the Kuang-hsu emperor and the execution of reformers who had not fled the country in time. K'ang had fled to Japan and spent the next 15 years outside China. Even after the Revolution of 1911 had made China a republic, he continued to actively support the return of the Manchu dynasty and the founding of a constitutional monarchy which he considered the type of government best suited for China. K'ang wrote his first draft of the Ta-t'ung shu (How to Achieve the Great Harmony) *in 1884-1885. It was completed in 1902, but only parts of it had been published until in 1935, after K'ang's death, the first complete edition appeared.*

In this voluminous book, K'ang is giving a detailed description of his ideal society, a society without the boundaries that in K'ang's opinion are responsible for most of the suffering in the world. The world will be unified under a one-world government. The same language should be spoken by everyone. Racial boundaries will be abolished through centuries of interracial marriages or the extinction of "unfit" races. State ownership will have erased the boundaries between rich and poor. The sexes will be completely equal in their rights. While child-bearing will remain a highly esteemed prerogative of the female sex, children will be raised and educated in public institutions to allow women to work. Having grown up in public institutions, members of the Ta-t'ung society will be unlikely to have particular concern for their own families and will give equal consideration to all other human beings, thus there will be no more family boundaries. Only laziness, the idolization of an individual, competition, and abortion will be prohibited in the Ta-t'ung society. K'ang shows himself a keen observer of contemporary western systems and societies (e.g., in arguing for the abolition of races he uses the United States as an example: even in a free and democratic society people do not mix as long as there are racial distinctions). Yet his book also shows him indebted to Chinese traditional thought. His depiction of the nine sources of suffering has a Buddhist ring. His conviction that this existing world could be improved to an extent that suffering might be overcome completely shows him very much imbued with the optimism of the Confucian tradition.

Explain whether you think K'ang's regulations for marriage would really achieve his goal: to end all suffering due to unhappy marriages.

When human morality has reached the perfection it will attain in One World, there will be few distinctions which would give rise to barriers between human beings. While monarchical states, both past and present, have differentiated nobles from plebeians by the relative elegance of their dress, yet in America the sort of clothing worn by the people's leaders and by the common people themselves is identical. We have not yet heard that this practice is disadvantageous to good government, while its benefit is to show the equality of all the people. If this is all right for rulers and subjects, how much more so for men and women!

Regulations should be made for clothing, the clothing of men and women to be uniformly the same. In the Era of Complete Peace and Equality, all persons will be independent and free clothing that is unusual will not be harmful to the public weal, and in everything people may do as they will. Men and women may dress in any way, even in the old style if they wish. However, in public meetings, when formal dress is worn, men and women will all adopt the same style, and may not wear different colors, in order to revert to complete unity. There being no distinctions of form or color, there will of course be no difference in their manner of behavior. This being so, women will not be regarded as different from men when, as teachers, superiors, officials, or rulers, they hold office and perform their duties.

All marriages of men and women will be by the personal choice of the parties. Their affections and will in this matter being mutual, they will then form an alliance. This alliance will be called an "intimate relations contract." We will not have the old terms of husband and wife. For, since men and women will be entirely equal and independent, their love contracts will be like treaties of peace between two states: there will be no distinctions of either party being unimportant or important, one superior or inferior. Should there be the slightest distinction of superior and inferior, then the relationship of the contracting parties would be that of half lord and half vassal, and we could not call it an alliance. The marriage alliance should only be like the joining together of two friends, nothing more.

Alliances of men and women should have a time-limit, and may not be life contracts. For all whom we call humans necessarily have natures which are unlike. Metal is hard, water is soft; *yin* and *yang* promote differing conditions; charity (*jen*) and avarice are each to be found among human beings; sweetness and bitterness differ in goodness to the taste; wisdom and stupidity are differing degrees; progressive and reactionary are differing characteristics. Thus, those who are in love never have exactly identical principles in their natures (or never have exactly identical ideas or ideals), and it is easy for them to come to consider each other as perverse and peculiar. Therefore, no matter who they are, people can merely vow to be united, but find it very difficult to hold to their union for long. If they are compelled to it, there will inevitably be quarreling between them. They may see each other but not speak; or they may live apart to the end of their lives; or they may hate each other and get divorced; or they may secretly scheme to poison each other. Innumerable are those in the world, past and present, who, because of being compelled to be united to the end of their days, have eaten bitterness, or lost their lives. If they desire to end their relationship, then this would damage their reputation and be thought immoral, unfeeling, and unpleasant. If in consequence they do not desire to end it, then they sit, the wife regarding this wild husband, the husband regarding this cruel wife as perverse and unreasonable. It is difficult for them to be content for a single breath, being forced to put up with this situation all their lives. Therefore, even for those with the natural endowments of worthies and sages, there is absolutely no principle through which they can for a long period be mutually happy while mutually united.

Furthermore, human affections are such that upon seeing someone different, one thinks of changing. Familiarity breeds boredom. Only novelty is desired; only beauty is loved. Supposing an alliance was made formerly, whereby one obtained a beautiful person as one's spouse; but then one sees someone whose ability and learning are still higher, whose appearance is still more beautiful, whose temperament is still more congenial, whose wealth is still richer: then love will assuredly be born, and one will assuredly think of changing one's relationships. And after that, there will again be new persons one will see who will excite the desire for novelty and change. The years and months are not the same; those we love are still more unlike. Hence we necessarily follow our feelings, abandon the old, and scheme for the new. . . .

Again, the old practice of the Age of Disorder was based upon the fact that the idea of husband-and-wife was solely for the purpose of transmitting posterity. This being the private duty of the individual man, it was therefore unavoidable that unions should be constrained to exist for life. The husband and wife being permanently fastened together, then the father and sons were always related to each other. But now, when the Age attains to Complete Equality, men and women will be equal, and each will have their own independence. People having been nurtured by the government may not be private individuals of one surname, but will be "Heaven's people" of the world. The matter of men and women will concern only the satisfaction of the human feelings, and not the regulation of the transmission of the line from father to son.

And how can we take the constrained union for life, and thereby create suffering and difficulties for human natures? Thus, to compel union is also immoral. . . .

Therefore we cannot but fix a time-limit to the contracts, to enable the parties easily to honor them. Then, if they have new loves, it will not be hard to wait for a little while. The term of the contract must not be too short, and so human propagation will not become too promiscuous. Thus we can bring about that many desires will yet not poison the body. When two persons love each other forever, they may of course remain united all their lives. Should they form new relationships, they will be permitted to change their arrangements; their former love being renewed, they may also renew their former alliance. In everything there will be freedom; thus we will accord with human nature and harmonize with natural principles.

Translated by Laurence G. Thompson

Quotations from Chairman Mao Tse-Tung

For a short period in the late sixties the "Little Red Book" containing the thoughts of Chinese Communist Party Chairman Mao Zedong (or as his name was spelled in English at the time "Mao Tse-Tung") was one of the most intensively-studied books in the world. Assembled by party editors from old speeches and writings of Mao, it was intended as a guide for those involved in the Cultural Revolution of 1966–1969. Mao argued that the Chinese Revolution had become rigid and betrayed its basic principles. To reinvigorate it, he invited young people to join the Red Guards and attack "bourgeois" elements in society. Everyone in China was forced to gather in study groups to spend hours discussing every line of the Quotations *and applying them to their lives. The book was also studied by Maoists abroad, including in the U.S. The results were disastrous. Millions died, many others were imprisoned for "incorrect" thoughts such as liking Western music or advocating Confucianism, many of China's brightest and most creative people were forced to abandon their jobs to labor on collective farms, and a whole generation lost its chance at education as it charged around the countryside attacking the previous generation. The translation used here is that issued by the party itself through Foreign Languages Press in Beijing in the second edition of 1966.*

"To Be Attacked by the Enemy Is Not a Bad Thing but a Good Thing" (May 26, 1939)

How does Mao turn criticism into an advantage?

I hold that it is bad as far as we are concerned if a person, a political party, an army or a school is not attacked by the enemy, for in that case it would definitely mean that we have sunk to the level of the enemy. It is good if we are attacked by the enemy, since it proves that we have drawn a clear line of demarcation between the enemy and ourselves. It is still better if the enemy attacks us wildly and paints us as utterly black and without a single virtue; it demonstrates that we have not only drawn a clear line of demarcation between the enemy and ourselves but achieved a great deal in our work.

Speech at the Chinese Communist Party's National Conference on Propaganda Work (March 12, 1957)

This passage was used to justify the intensive "reeducation" sessions which tried to bring all Chinese people into line. The final qualifying phrases were usually ignored.

In our country bourgeois and petty-bourgeois ideology, anti-Marxist ideology, will continue to exist for a long time. Basically, the socialist system has been established in our country. We have won the basic victory in transforming the ownership of the means of production, but we have not yet won complete victory on the political and ideological fronts. In the ideological field, the question of who will win in the struggle between the proletariat and the bourgeoisie has not been really settled yet. We still have to wage a protracted struggle against bourgeois and petty-bourgeois ideology. It is wrong not to understand this and to give up ideological struggle. All erroneous ideas, all poisonous weeds, all ghosts and monsters, must be subjected to criticism; in no circumstance should they be allowed to spread unchecked. However, the criticism should be fully reasoned, analytical and convincing, and not rough, bureaucratic, metaphysical or dogmatic.

"On the People's Democratic Dictatorship" (June 30, 1949)

The ultimate goal of Marxists was not unlike that of anarchists: the complete abolition of state power and the establishment of direct democracy among the people. However both Marx and Lenin had argued that a period of transition called "socialism" was necessary, in which the state would organize the conditions necessary for its own abolition. But the only Communist states which abolished themselves, like the Soviet Union, did so in order to transform themselves into conventional states.

What reasons does Mao give for not abolishing state power right away? (This speech was given immediately after the triumph of the Communists.)

"Don't you want to abolish state power?" Yes, we do, but not right now; we cannot do it yet. Why? Because imperialism still exists, because domestic reaction still exists, because classes still exist in our country. Our present task is to strengthen the people's state apparatus—mainly the people's army, the people's police and the people's courts—in order to consolidate national defense and protect the people's interests.

"Problems of War and Strategy" (November 6, 1938)

In its original context this saying meant that the Communists would never be allowed to come to power in China without a successful violent revolution. In the context of the Cultural Revolution it meant that the Chinese People's Army had to play a leading role in sustaining, purifying, and spreading Communism. And abroad it was often used to justify revolutionary terrorism.

Every Communist must grasp the truth, "Political power grows out of the barrel of a gun."

Speech at the Moscow Meeting of Communist and Workers' Parties (November 18, 1957)

Mao was widely ridiculed abroad for stating that the U.S. and its nuclear arsenal were "paper tigers." Many supposed that Mao would have willingly plunged the world into a nuclear war out of sheer ignorance. But it seems more probable that, lacking such arms himself, he used his most powerful weapon: the bluff. The bomb was not a very effective tool of diplomacy because the threat it posed was only as credible as the willingness of any nation to plunge the world into a holocaust, very probably destroying itself in the process. Mao had every reason to let the world think he was not afraid of the bomb no matter what his private thoughts might have been.

I have said that all the reputedly powerful reactionaries are merely paper tigers. The reason is that they are divorced from the people. Look! Was not Hitler a paper tiger? Was Hitler not overthrown? I also said that the tsar of Russia, the emperor of China and Japanese imperialism were all paper tigers. As we know, they were all overthrown. U.S. imperialism has not yet been overthrown and it has the atom bomb. I believe it also will be overthrown. It, too, is a paper tiger.

"Some Questions Concerning Methods of Leadership" (June 1, 1943)

This is the core of the ideology that made the Cultural Revolution so appealing to many young idealists; but in the end learning from the people turned out to mean learning only from Chairman Mao and his allies.

In all the practical work of our Party, all correct leadership is necessarily "from the masses, to the masses." This means: take the ideas of the masses (scattered and unsystematic ideas) and concentrate them (through study turn them into concentrated and systematic ideas), then go to the masses and propagate and explain these ideas until the masses embrace them as their own, hold fast to them and translate them into action, and test the correctness of these ideas in such action. Then once again concentrate ideas from the masses and once again go to the masses so that the ideas are persevered in and carried through. And so on, over and over again in an endless spiral, with the ideas becoming more correct, more vital and richer each time. Such is the Marxist theory of knowledge.

Introductory note to "Women Have Gone to the Labor Front" (1955)

Women had been oppressed in China as much as anywhere on earth, and Mao often spoke of the important role they would play in building Communism. Many concrete advances were made for women; however, except for his wife Jian Qing, who was very influential during the Cultural Revolution, women were generally relegated to subordinate positions in the party leadership.

In order to build a great socialist society, it is of the utmost importance to arouse the broad masses of women to join in productive activity. Men and women must receive equal pay for equal work in production. Genuine equality between the sexes can only be realized in the process of the socialist transformation of society as a whole.

On the Correct Handling of Contradictions Among the People (February 27, 1957)

Of all the quotations in the "Little Red Book" none is more inspiring or chilling than this. It comes from a brief period of reform in the fifties known as the "Hundred Flowers Campaign" during which Mao encouraged complete freedom of thought, including criticism of the Party. The result was much more vigorous debate than Mao had expected and the period ended with an abrupt crackdown against those who had raised their voices in opposition. It could stand as a critique of the failures of the Cultural Revolution itself, which tried to settle ideological questions by force under the guise of debate.

Letting a hundred flowers blossom and a hundred schools of thought contend is the policy for promoting the progress of the arts and the sciences and a flourishing socialist culture in our land. Different forms and styles in art should develop freely and contend freely. We think that it is harmful to the growth of art and science if administrative measures are used to impose one particular style of art or school of thought and to ban another. Questions of right and wrong in the arts and sciences should be settled through free discussion in artistic and scientific circles and through practical work in these fields. They should not be settled in summary fashion.

Lo Ch'ing: Protest Posters (January 1979)

Lo Ch'ing, born on Taiwan of parents who fled the 1947 Communist revolution in China, is a distinuished painter as well as poet. In the following poem he salutes the efforts of mainland protesters advocating more political freedom during the period of post-Mao economic reform dominated by Deng Xiaoping. The principal technique of protest during this period was the mounting of handwritten posters, an idea borrowed from Mao's own Red Guards.

What metaphor from nature does Lo Ch'ing use to praise the power of the posters?

For Wei Ching-sheng[1] *and his companions*

They issue the rules continuously:
Nail the white clouds onto the wide blue sky
Paint the frozen rivers onto the parched earth

But stealthily we
Stick the posters onto
The vacant, hopeless eyes
Solidifying our strength in each
Hand with its pulsating veins

If they are white clouds, then let them flow and flap
Flapping as posters of incomparable purity flap
Caught in the hungry, eye-straining gaze of the world

Each word of protest
Becoming a drop of sweet summer rain
Melting a million frozen rivers and streams
Overflowing into hands interlaced with veins like subway maps
Seeping through the paper dikes that their rules have glued together

Translated Joseph Roe Allen

---

[1]Wei Ching-sheng was one of the leaders of the poster movement, and was imprisoned for a long term as a result, along with several others. In the 1989 pro-democracy protests, he was considered one of the main inspirations for the activists. Although now released from prison, he is still under governmental surveillance.

Japan 1900–Present

Hirokichi Numajiri: Poverty in a Rural Village

Japan's urbanized prosperity is so familiar that it is difficult to realize that only a few generations ago most Japanese lived in extreme poverty, farming under the harshest of conditions. The following narrative of life in the village of Tsukji-machi a century ago consists of the recollections of a peasant born in 1888 whose grandfather had been a blacksmith.

What were the main difficulties faced by the local farmers? What recourse did the peasants have when landlords set conditions that were too harsh? Why was infanticide practiced so widely? The killing of unwanted children has been extremely common in many cultures. One estimate put the infanticide rate in Medieval Europe at around 50%.

My grandfather was an agricultural blacksmith. He rented a shop on the main street in Omura where he made and mended hoes, rakes, and other farm tools. All farmers in those days plowed by hand and, after many years of use, these implements got worn down. A farm tool could be mended only by grafting a new piece of metal onto the worn part of its blade. Grandfather must have been pretty good at his trade because people from as far away as Oda used to bring him their old sickles and hoes, wrapped up in carrying cloths.

The furnace for firing the iron was fueled by charcoal; Grandfather always insisted that only pinewood charcoal was good enough. The bellows was operated with your right foot and right hand: a length of string was tied to your big toe and this you pulled in alternation with another piece of string held in your hand. The other hand was then free to hold down and turn the piece of iron you were working on. At the same time, another blacksmith would hammer away at the red-hot iron, flattening and beating it out.

Eventually, when my grandfather was so old he could mend no more than a couple of hoes a day, he decided it was time to retire. He was an excellent blacksmith, though, and his work was sorely missed.

I was about seven when the war in China started in 1896. Four or five men from the village went off to serve in the army, and I remember everyone went down to the banks of the River Sakura to see them off. Back then, however, there was no bridge across and the men had to use the ferry. Getting horses across was more of a problem: the ferry was too small, so they were made to splash down into the river and wade to the other bank.

There were almost no carts on the roads in those days: it was only after the war with Russia in 1904 that handcarts and horse-drawn vehicles first appeared on the main roads leading into Tsuchiura. It was about that time, too, that Suijin Bridge was built across the Sakura.

There were about thirty families living in our village then; of these maybe ten owned their own horse. At the back of the house belonging to the village headman was a piece of ground we called the "repair yard," and at a certain time each year the villagers brought their horses here and a vet, paid for by all the villagers, would come along and clip the horses' hooves. Alongside the "repair yard" was a building where the old people of the village used to meet; they'd pray there and then chat together over a cup of green tea.

In Oshita, one of the staging posts along the highway, there used to be a tea house. The place today is just waste ground where buses are parked, but back then we had a small one-story building with three whores working in it. It was a long trip into Tsuchiura then, made even more difficult because there weren't any bridges across the river, so all the young men from the surrounding countryside used to come to this house for a bit of fun. But it's become much easier to travel into town now, and the tea house, along with much of everything else, has disappeared.

My father died suddenly, mainly from overwork, when I was seven, and from then on, young as I was, I had to go out into the fields and help my mother. Since we were tenants and didn't have any land of our own, there was no alternative. The annual rent for land that yielded about twenty-four sacks of rice per acre was twelve sacks, so it was damned hard work for tenant farmers to make a living. Still, there were so many people who wanted to rent a field or two that the landlord could tell you, "If you think the rent's too high, you can always leave;" you had no choice—you put up with the conditions and got on with working the land as hard as you could.

If the weather throughout the summer had been bad, some of the tenants would be forced to go along and beg him, with tears in their eyes, to reduce the rice rent a bit. And like as not the reply would be: "If you can't afford to pay, you'll just have to get off the land." In bad years you had no choice but to give the landlord most of your harvest, though this was really meant to feed your own family.

Some of the landlords were so plain cruel and heartless that their tenants were driven to murdering them. The villagers in those days used to make a type of firework called a "lightning," which was let off as part of the celebrations during festivals. The firework was made by putting gunpowder into a wooden tube, and fixing a bamboo hoop firmly around the end to stop it splitting. One landlord, apparently, was killed by a "lightning" that someone threw into the room where he was sleeping. Another was beaten to death up in the mountains. These things all happened a long time ago, of course.

Once you'd paid in the rice rent, even in a good year you were lucky if you had enough left over to keep your family going for as much as six months. Rice for the rest of the year had to be bought with extra income from doing casual work, in the gravel pits or with a roadmending gang.

Many houses in our village didn't have their own bath. People without baths would wash at home in a tub of cold water most days, and then once every week or so they'd go along and use a neighbor's. Yes, I suppose that out of the thirty or so houses in the village, only five or six had their own baths. I don't know about other villages, but in our area the problem was that, even if you could put up the money for a proper wooden tub, there just wasn't enough fuel available to heat the water. If we'd had some woodland of our own, we could have cut down some trees and used the timber for fuel; around here, though, trespassing in the landlord's woods in the mountains was forbidden, and even collecting fallen leaves wasn't permitted. We certainly couldn't afford to buy firewood, not even for cooking, and instead we had to burn straw, usually bundles of rice straw. But we could never get hold of enough of it, so we used to go and cut dead reeds on the riverbank and use those too. And since there would never have been enough fuel to heat a bath as well, most families were left without one.

When it rained, the farmers in those days used to wear straw raincoats and bamboo hats. During the hottest months of the year we wore *himino,* short coats made of thin straw, used for keeping the sun off. The *himino* let the air circulate around your body and kept you surprisingly cool. They were worn by peasants in this area until as late as the 1950s.

Because everyone was so hard up around here, "thinning out" the newborn was quite widely practiced. The number of children killed just depended, I'm told, on how strict the local policeman was. An officious and bloody-minded cop might well notice that a woman, whom he'd previously seen several months pregnant, no longer was, but there weren't any new babies around. If he'd started poking around for reasons, it would have caused all sorts of trouble for the villagers. So with this sort of man in the neighborhood there was nothing for it but to let an unwanted baby live. On the other hand, if a slack new policeman was appointed to the area, the "thinning out" rate would rapidly increase. The situation was so bad that the number of kids in each grade of the primary school varied a good deal, depending on who'd been the local constable at the time they were born.

You know, I remember when I was at primary school we used to use a wick dipped in kerosene for light. Some families used proper oil lamps, but more common were simple wicks because they needed a lot less oil. My family sometimes couldn't even afford the kerosene for a wick; so to provide the light to do my homework by, I often had to go out into the fields and collect fireflies, which I put in a paper bag. In those days, near the paddy fields, there were an awful lot of fireflies, so many in fact you could feel them brushing against your face as you walked along. If you put them into a bag they gave off a palish glow. I'd hold the bag near my exercise book, and it would give off just about enough light for me to practice writing my Chinese characters.

Translated by Garry O. Evans

Yosano Akiko (1878-1942): Tangled Hair (1935)

Yosano, also known as "Ho Sho," helped to revolutionize modern Japanese poetry early in the 20th Century. She also translated into modern Japanese the masterpiece of her nation's most famous woman author: Murasaki Shikibu's Tale of Genji and founded a school for girls. *She applied a modern style to traditional Japanese poetic forms. In this brief poem she uses a traditional image: tangled hair as a symbol of disordered thoughts, but treats it in a surrealistically modern fashion.*

Hair all tangled this morning—
Shall I smooth it
With spring rain
Dripping from the jet-black
Wings of swallows?

Translated by Sanford Goldstein and Seishi Shinoda

Yasunari Kawabata: The Grasshopper and the Bell Cricket (1924)

Yasunari Kawabata was one of Japan's great modern novelists, but as a young man he also excelled in writing very short stories which he called "palm-of-the-hand-stories," as if they were small, delicate objects which could be held in the palm of one's hand. Like haiku, these tales suggest much on the basis of a very slight incident. There is a long tradition in Japan of children keeping insects as pets in delicate cages. The bell cricket is particularly prized for its cry, considered a symbol of autumn, and often referred to in classic haiku.

How does the boy in the story show he likes the girl especially without saying so to her? What development shows the children as creative? How are Kiyoko and Fujio united without their being aware of it? What do the final paragraphs tell us about Kawabata's attitudes toward adult love?

Walking along the tile-roofed wall of the university, I turned aside and approached the upper school. Behind the white board fence of the school playground, from a dusky clump of bushes under the black cherry trees, an insect's voice could be heard. Walking more slowly and listening to that voice, and feeling reluctant to part with it, I turned right so as not to leave the playground behind. When I turned to the left, the fence gave way to an embankment planted with orange trees. At the corner, I exclaimed with surprise. My eyes gleaming at what they saw up ahead, I hurried forward with short steps.

At the base of the embankment was a bobbing cluster of beautiful varicolored lanterns, such as one might see at a festival in a remote country village. Without going any farther, I knew that it was a group of children on an insect chase among the bushes of the embankment. There were about twenty lanterns. Not only were there crimson, pink, indigo, green, purple, and yellow lanterns, but one lantern glowed with five colors at once. There were even some little red store-bought lanterns. But most of the lanterns were beautiful square ones that the children had made themselves with love and care. The bobbing lanterns, the coming together of children on this lonely slope—surely it was a scene from a fairy tale?

One of the neighborhood children had heard an insect sing on this slope one night. Buying a red lantern, he had come back the next night to find the insect. The night after that, there was another child. This new child could not buy a lantern. Cutting out the back and front of a small carton and papering it, he placed a candle on the bottom and fastened a string to the top. The number of children grew to five, and then to seven. They learned how to color the paper that they stretched over the windows of the cutout cartons, and to draw pictures on it. Then these wise child-artists, cutting out round, three-cornered, and lozenge leaf shapes in the cartons, coloring each little window a different color, with circles and diamonds, red and green, made a single and whole decorative pattern. The child with the red lantern discarded it as a tasteless object that could be bought at a store. The child who had made his own lantern threw it away because the design was too simple. The pattern of light that one had had in hand the night before was unsatisfying the morning after. Each day, with cardboard, paper, brush, scissors, penknife, and glue, the children made new lanterns out of their hearts and minds. Look at my lantern! Be the most unusually beautiful! And each night, they had gone out on their insect hunts. These were the twenty children and their beautiful lanterns that I now saw before me.

Wide-eyed, I loitered near them. Not only did the square lanterns have old-fashioned patterns and flower shapes, but the names of the children who had made them were cut in squared letters of the syllabary. Different from the painted-over red lanterns, others (made of thick cutout cardboard) had their designs drawn onto the paper windows, so that the candle's light seemed to emanate from the form and color of the design itself. The lanterns brought out the shadows of the bushes like dark light. The children crouched eagerly on the slope wherever they heard an insect's voice.

"Does anyone want a grasshopper?" A boy, who had been peering into a bush about thirty feet away from the other children, suddenly straightened up and shouted.

"Yes! Give it to me!" Six or seven children came running up. Crowding behind the boy who had found the grasshopper, they peered into the bush. Brushing away their outstretched hands and spreading out his arms, the boy stood as if guarding the bush where the insect was. Waving the lantern in his right hand, he called again to the other children.

"Does anyone want a grasshopper? A grasshopper!"

"I do! I do!" Four or five more children came running up. It seemed you could not catch a more precious insect than a grasshopper. The boy called out a third time.

"Doesn't anyone want a grasshopper?"

Two or three more children came over.

"Yes. I want it."

It was a girl, who just now had come up behind the boy who'd discovered the insect. Lightly turning his body, the boy gracefully bent forward. Shifting the lantern to his left hand, he reached his right hand into the bush.

"It's a grasshopper."

"Yes. I'd like to have it."

The boy quickly stood up. As if to say "Here!" he thrust out his fist that held the insect at the girl. She, slipping her left wrist under the string of her lantern, enclosed the boy's fist with both hands. The boy quietly opened his fist. The insect was transferred to between the girl's thumb and index finger.

"Oh! It's not a grasshopper. It's a bell cricket." The girl's eyes shone as she looked at the small brown insect.

"It's a bell cricket! It's a bell cricket!" The children echoed in an envious chorus.

"It's a bell cricket. It's a bell cricket."

Glancing with her bright intelligent eyes at the boy who had given her the cricket, the girl opened the little insect cage hanging at her side and released the cricket in it.

"It's a bell cricket."

"Oh, it's a bell cricket," the boy who'd captured it muttered. Holding up the insect cage close to his eyes, he looked inside it. By the light of his beautiful many-colored lantern, also held up at eye level, he glanced at the girl's face.

Oh, I thought. I felt slightly jealous of the boy, and sheepish. How silly of me not to have understood his actions until now! Then I caught my breath in surprise. Look! It was something on the girl's breast that neither the boy who had given her the cricket, nor she who had accepted it, nor the children who were looking at them noticed.

In the faint greenish light that fell on the girl's breast, wasn't the name "Fujio" clearly discernible? The boy's lantern, which he held up alongside the girl's insect cage, inscribed his name, cut out in the green papered aperture, onto her white cotton kimono. The girl's lantern, which dangled loosely from her wrist, did not project its pattern so clearly, but still one could make out, in a trembling patch of red on the boy's waist, the name "Kiyoko." This chance interplay of red and green—if it was chance or play—neither Fujio nor Kiyoko knew about.

Even if they remembered forever that Fujio had given her the cricket and that Kiyoko had accepted it, not even in dreams would Fujio ever know that his name had been written in green on Kiyoko's breast or that Kiyoko's name had been inscribed in red on his waist, nor would Kiyoko ever know that Fujio's name had been inscribed in green on her breast or that her own name had been written in red on Fujio's waist.

Fujio! Even when you have become a young man, laugh with pleasure at a girl's delight when, told that it's a grasshopper, she is given a bell cricket; laugh with affection at a girl's chagrin when, told that it's a bell cricket, she is given a grasshopper.

Even if you have the wit to look by yourself in a bush away from the other children, there are not many bell crickets in the world. Probably you will find a girl like a grasshopper whom you think is a bell cricket.

And finally, to your clouded, wounded heart, even a true bell cricket will seem like a grasshopper. Should that day come, when it seems to you that the world is only full of grasshoppers, I will think it a pity that you have no way to remember tonight's play of light, when your name was written in green by your beautiful lantern on a girl's breast.

Translated by Lane Dunlop & J. Martin Holman

Masuji Ibuse: *Black Rain* (1966)

Ibuse's novel is a narrative of the consequences of the nuclear bombing of Hiroshima on August 6, 1945, based on the journals of and interviews with survivors. It combines vivid realistic detail with an effectively understated picture of the emotional impact of the bombing on its victims. In the following passage the narrator walks with his wife and niece through the ruins of the city, unaware that they have already absorbed doses of radiation which will gradually sicken them. Food was already in very short supply before the bombing, and they were lucky to have relatives in the countryside who had sent them a little parched rice. Ibuse does not place the blame for the bombing entirely on the U.S. The book contains criticisms of the militarism of the Japanese government, as in the speech by a soldier burning corpses: "If only we'd been born in a country, *not a damn-fool* state."

Which image from the following passages do you find the most moving? Why?

Walking made my toes hurt so that I nearly danced with the pain. The others were complaining of the pain too. I myself must have walked some ten or eleven miles already. My wife had walked five or six, and Yasuko about five. We ate parched rice as we walked. We would thrust a hand into the cloth bag my wife was carrying, take out a handful and, putting it in our mouths, chew on it as we walked. It gradually turned to sugar, and tasted sweet in the mouth; it was better than either the water or the cucumber. The most effective way seemed to be to chew as one walked, although I could understand why travelers in olden times took parched rice with them as rations for the journey. Finally, one gulped it down, then took another handful out of the cloth bag and put it in one's mouth. Parched rice may be very unappetizing-looking, but I gave thanks in my heart to my wife's folk for sending it.

The main highway was dotted with refugees. Just as I had overheard the people in the bamboo grove saying, the houses by the roadside all had their doors and shutters fastened. Where there was a roofed gateway, its doors were shut fast. Outside one of the gates with shut doors lay a bundle of straw scorched by fire. I wondered if passing refugees had set fire to it.

However far we went, still the houses along the road had their doors shut. Here the breeze was cool, unlike the hot breath of the town, and ripples were running over the rice plants in the paddy fields. The fathers from the Catholic church[1] on the north side of Yamamoto Station went running past us at top speed, carrying a stretcher. With them was one father, a man past middle age, whom I had often seen on the Kabe-bound train on my way to work. He came panting along far behind the others carrying the stretcher, and as he passed me he glanced into my face and nodded briefly in recognition. "Good luck to you," I called after him.

At last, we reached Yamamoto Station. From here on, the trains were running. A train was standing in the station, every coach full, but we managed to squeeze our way into the vestibule of one of them. Wedged tight, I tried to make more room by nudging at a bundle directly in front of me. Wrapped in a cloth, it rested on the shoulders of a woman of about thirty. Somehow, it felt different from a bundle of belongings, so I tried touching it furtively with my hand. I contacted what felt like a human ear: a child seemed to be in the

---

[1]There was a considerable number of Catholics in Hiroshima.

bundle. To carry a child in such a fashion was outrageous. It was almost certain to suffocate in such a crush.

"Excuse me Ma'am," I said softly. "Is it your child in here?"

"Yes," she said in a scarcely audible voice. "He's dead."

"I'm sorry," I said, taken aback. "I didn't know. . . . I really must apologize, to be pushing and . . ."

"Not at all," she said gently. "None of us can help it in such a crowd." She hitched the bundle up, bent her head, and was seized with a fit of weeping.

"It was when the bomb burst," she said through her sobs. "The sling of his hammock broke, and he was dashed against the wall and killed. Then the house started to burn, so I wrapped him in a quilt cover and brought him away on my back. I'm taking him to my old home in Imori, so I can bury him in the cemetery there."

She stopped weeping, and ceased talking at the same time. I could not bring myself to address her any further.

A kite[2] was wheeling in the air above the wires. The cicadas were chirping, and a dabchick was bustling about the pond with waterlilies by the side of the highway. A perfectly commonplace scene that somehow seemed quite extraordinary. . . .

The conductor announced the train's imminent departure, and a fiercer clamor arose from those who had not succeeded in getting on. The train lurched forward and stopped, lurched and stopped again.

"What the hell're you up to? Are you starting or aren't you?" bellowed a voice, to be followed by another voice that launched into a speech somewhere inside the coach: "Ladies and gentlemen, you can see for yourselves how sadly decadent the National Railways have become. Concerned only with carrying black market goods, they have nothing but contempt for the ordinary passenger. . . ." But this time the train glided smoothly into motion, and the rest of the speech was lost forever in the clatter of its wheels. . . .

Nearing Kamiya-cho, I came upon a number of men who looked like soldiers. With gauze masks over their mouths and noses, they were tending to three or four fires which they had built in separate places. As I drew nearer, I saw that they had made the fires in holes about six feet square dug in the ground, and were fetching corpses and throwing them in the flames. For fuel, they were using old railway ties, and the crackling of the ties as they burned gave the pyres an added touch of horror beneath the blazing sun. I looked, and from the trunks of the bodies could see pale blue, slender flames rising, to be caught up at once in the fierce red flames leaping higher all about them.

Body after body the soldiers brought, on door panels and sheets of corrugated iron, to fling them unceremoniously, face up, into the flames before trudging off silently on their next mission. They had bent up the corners of the corrugated iron sheets for ease in carrying. They must have been working under orders from a superior officer; whatever emotions they felt, their expressions gave no clue. The only sign of feeling seemed to be in their military boots, which were slow-moving and leaden. When there were so many bodies in a pit that the flames died down, they would dump the bodies they brought on the ground by the edge. Sometimes, the jolt would bring a mass of maggots and liquid corruption gushing from the corpse's mouth. When a body was dumped

[2]Vulture.

too close to the fire, the heat would bring the maggots wriggling out in panic all over it. And occasionally the shock of hitting the ground would do something to the joints of a corpse, so that it reminded me of Pinocchio, in the children's tale, with all the pins removed from his wooden limbs. If even Pinocchio, poor plaything of wood and metal pins, was supposed to have felt pain in his own wooden way when he barked his shin against something, what of these the dead, who had once been human beings?

"These stiffs are getting out of hand," muttered the soldier at the front end of a piece of corrugated iron.

"If only we'd been born in a *country,* not a damn-fool *state,"* said his companion wistfully.

That exchange was the only human sound I heard there. The body on the improvised stretcher lay in a tight huddle, a Pinocchio with every single pin removed . . .

All unconsciously, I had started murmuring tathe "Sermon on Mortality"[3] to myself. Hiroshima was no more. . . . Yet who could have foreseen that its end would be of such horror as this?

Translated by John Bester

[3]A Buddhist ritual text. The narrator will later find himself drafted to read the funeral service endlessly over the dead.

Europe 1900–Present

Sigmund Freud: *The Interpretation of Dreams* (1900)

Despite the widely-recognized failure of Freudian psychotherapy to heal disturbed people effectively and the rejection of many of his major theories Freud remains one of the most influential figures of the 20th century. Freud's basic insight that our minds preserve memories and emotions which are not always consciously available to us has transformed the way humanity views itself ever since. Freud said that there had been three great humiliations in human history: Galileo's discovery that we were not the center of the universe, Darwin's discovery that we were not the crown of creation, and his own discovery that we are not in control of our own minds. The tendency of modern people to trace their problems to childhood traumas or other repressed emotions begins with Freud. One of Freud's more important discoveries is that emotions buried in the unconscious surface in disguised form during dreaming, and that the remembered fragments of dreams can help uncover the buried feelings. Whether or not the mechanism is exactly as Freud describes it, many people have derived insights into themselves from studying their dreams, and most modern people consider dreams emotionally significant, unlike our ancestors who often saw them either as divine portents or as the bizarre side-effects of indigestion. Freud claims that dreams are wish-fulfillments, and will ultimately argue that those wishes are the result of repressed or frustrated sexual desires. The anxiety surrounding these desires turns some dreams into nightmares.

Explain what Freud means by "dreams of convenience."

Dreams are not comparable to the spontaneous sounds made by a musical instrument struck rather by some external force than by the hand of a performer; they are not meaningless, not absurd, they do not imply that one portion of our stockpile of ideas sleeps while another begins to awaken. They are a completely valid psychological phenomenon, specifically the fulfillment of wishes; they can be classified in the continuity of comprehensible waking mental states; they are constructed through highly complicated intellectual activity.

But as soon as we delight in this discovery, a flood of questions assails us. If, according to dream analysis, the dream represents a fulfilled wish, what creates the astonishing and strange form in which this wish-fulfillment is expressed? What transformation have the dream thoughts undergone to shape the manifest dream which we remember when awake? Through what means has this transformation taken place? What is the source of the material which has been reworked into the dream? Where do the many peculiarities which we notice in dream thoughts come from, for instance that they may be mutually contradictory? Can a dream tell us something new about our inner psychological processes? Can its content correct the opinions that we have held during our waking hours?

I suggest that we set these questions aside for the moment and follow one particular path further. We have learned that a dream represents a fulfilled wish. Our next concern will be to discover whether this is a universal characteristic of dreams. . . We must leave open the possibility that the meaning may not be the same in every dream. Our first dream was a wish-fulfillment; but perhaps another will prove to be a fulfilled fear; a third might contain a reflex; a fourth may simply reproduce a memory. Are there other wish-dreams? Or perhaps nothing but wish-dreams exist.

It is easy to demonstrate that dreams often have the character of blatant wish-fulfillments; so much so that one wonders why the language of dreams was not understood long ago. For instance, there is a dream that I can experience at will, experimentally, as it were. When I eat sardines, olives, or other strongly salted foods in the evening, I am awakened in the night by thirst. But the awaking is always preceded by a dream with the same content: I gulp the water down; and it tastes delicious to me as only a cool drink can when one is dying of thirst; and then I wake up and really have to drink. The cause of this simple dream is the thirst which I feel when I awaken. This feeling causes the desire to drink, and the dream shows me this desire fulfilled. It thereby serves a function which I can easily guess. I am a good sleeper, unaccustomed to being awakened by any need. If I can slake my thirst by dreaming that I am drinking, I don't need to wake up in order to be satisfied. Thus this is a convenience dream. The dream is substituted for action, as so often in life.

Recently this same dream occurred in a somewhat modified form. I had become thirsty even before sleeping and drained the glass of water which was standing on the nightstand next to my bed. A few hours later during the night I had a new attack of thirst which was more inconvenient. In order to get some water I would have had to get up and take the glass standing on my wife's nightstand. I dreamed therefore that my wife gave me a drink out of a vessel. This vessel was an Etruscan funerary urn which I had brought back from a trip to Italy and had since given away. However, the water in it tasted so salty (plainly because of the ashes) that I had to wake up. It is easy to see how neatly this dream arranged matters; since it its only aim was wish-fulfillment, it could be completely egotistical. A love of convenience is not really compatible with consideration for others. The introduction of the funerary urn is probably another wish-fulfillment; I was sorry that I didn't own the vessel any more—just as the water glass beside my wife was inaccessible. The urn also fit the growing salty taste which I knew would force me to wake up.

I very commonly had such dreams of convenience in my youth. Always used to working deep into the night, it was always difficult for me to wake up early. I used to dream then that I was out of bed and standing in front of the washstand. Eventually I had to recognize that I was not up, but meanwhile I had slept some more. The same lazy dream in a particularly witty form was told to me by one of my colleagues who evidently shared my sleepyheadedness. The landlady he rented rooms near the hospitals from had strong instructions to wake him up at the right time every morning; but she had a difficult time carrying out these orders. One morning he was sleeping especially sweetly. The woman called into the room, "Mr. Pepi, get up. You have to go to the hospital." At that point the sleeper dreamed that he was lying in a bed in a room in the hospital, on which was a placard which read "Pepi H., medical student, age 22." Dreaming, he said to himself, "Since I am already in the hospital, I don't have to go there," so he turned over and slept on. Thus he openly confessed the cause of his dream.

It is just as easy to discover wish-fulfillment in some other dreams that I have collected from normal people. A friend who knows my dream theory and had shared it with his wife said to me one day, "I must tell you that my wife dreamed yesterday that she had her period. You know what that means." Certainly I knew; since the young woman had dreamed that she had her period, it meant that her period had not come. I could well believe that she would liked to have enjoyed her freedom a little longer before beginning the burdens of motherhood. It was a clever way of announcing the onset of her pregnancy. Another friend writes me that his wife recently dreamed that she noticed drops of milk on her blouse front. This is always a sign of pregnancy, but not a first pregnancy; the young mother wanted to have more milk for the second child than she had had for the first. . . .

These examples will perhaps be enough to show that dreams which can only be understood as wish-fulfillments, and which clearly reveal their content, occur often and under manifold circumstances. These mostly short and simple dreams stand out pleasantly in contrast with the confused and overly complex dream compositions which have mostly absorbed the attention of writers. . . .

We recognize that we might have gotten at the understanding of the concealed meaning of dreams by the shortest path if we had simply followed common ways of speaking. Proverbs indeed sometimes speak dismissively of dreams; people think they are being properly scientific when they say, "Dreams are froth." But in common usage dreams are predominantly the fulfillers of dreams. We cry out, delighted, "I would never have imagined such a thing even in my wildest dreams" when we find that reality has surpassed our expectations. . . .

There still remain anxiety dream[1] as a special subdivision of dreams with a painful content whose interpretation as wish-fulfillment dreams will be most unwillingly accepted by the unenlightened. However, I can deal briefly with anxiety dreams here; they do not represent another aspect of the problems posed by dreams; rather it is a matter of understanding above all neurotic anxiety. The anxiety that we feel in dreams is only apparently explained by the dream's content. When we try to discover the meaning of a dream's content, we note that the anxiety felt in a dream is no better explained by its content than the anxiety felt in a phobia[2] is explained by the mental image which induces the phobia. For instance, is it quite true that one may fall out of a window, and therefore one may reasonably exert a certain amount of caution around a window; but this does not explain why in its phobic form the fear is so powerful and the sufferer pursued by the fear far beyond its cause. The same explanation is valid for Phobias as for anxiety dreams. The anxiety is in both cases only loosely linked to the association, and actually derives from another source.

Since dream anxiety is intimately related to neurotic anxiety I must explain the first by reference to the second. In a short publication on anxiety neurosis . . . I argued that neurotic anxiety derives from sexual life, and is the expression of unsatisfied desire which has been diverted from its goal. This formula has since then been proven valid. It enables us now to say that the sexual content of anxiety dreams is the result of transformation of sexual desire.

Translated by Paul Brians

---

[1]Nightmares.
[2]Irrational fear.

V. I. Lenin: *What Is to Be Done?* (1902)

When Lenin tried to organize a Marxist revolutionary party in Russia, he faced a dilemma. The ultimate goal of Marxist Communism was absolute freedom; but the only realistic vehicle for attaining that goal was a disciplined party. He was irritated by the dissent and controversy which raged in revolutionary circles. In this famous treatise he outlined his ideas on freedom in powerful words that to later generations read like a denunciation of freedom as it is normally understood. Implemented by Lenin himself after the 1917 revolution and exacerbated by Stalin, they transformed Marx's dream of a "dictatorship of the proletariat" (absolute rule by the people, depriving the old ruling class of its power) into its opposite, a dictatorship over *the proletariat. In later decades, the rationale for repression outlined here was advanced again and again by dictatorial Communist governments as they argued that the small "vanguard" of the proletariat was capable of leading the masses for their own good, even in opposition to their express will.*

Why does he argue no criticism can be made of socialist ideology?

"Freedom"—it's a great word, but under the flag of "freedom of industry" the most rapacious of wars were conducted. Under the banner of "freedom of labor" workers have been robbed. The very same internal hypocrisy is contained in the contemporary phrase "freedom to criticize." People who are truly convinced that they have advanced the frontier of science would not demand freedom for new ideas to coexist next to old, but to replace them. . . .

We are walking in a small, tight group along a steep and difficult path, firmly joining hands. We are surrounded by enemies, and must continue almost always under their fire. We have freely and consciously decided to unite to fight the enemy and not stumble into the neighboring marsh, where dwell those who from the beginning have reproached us for separating into a special group and choosing the path of struggle, and not the path of compromise. And now some of us are beginning to cry: "Let's go into the marsh!" And when we start to shame them, they object: "What a backward people you are! And aren't you ashamed to deny us the freedom to call you to a better way? Oh yes, gentlemen, you are free not only to call us, but to go anywhere you like, even if it's into the marsh. We even consider the marsh to be the right place for you, and are ready to assist you as best we can to move you there. But just let go of our hands—don't clutch at us and soil the great word "freedom," because we too are "free" to go where we like—free to fight with the marsh and with those who turn to the marsh. . . .

We said that Social-Democratic consciousness could not exist among the workers. But it could be brought to them from without. The history of all countries testifies that workers left exclusively to their own strength can cultivate only a trade union consciousness—that is the belief in the need to unite into a union, struggle against the bosses, press the government to pass needed labor legislation, etc. The doctrine of Socialism grew out of philosophic, historical, and economic theories which were worked out by the educated representatives of the propertied class, the intelligentsia. The founders of modern scientific socialism, Marx and Engels, belonged themselves to the bourgeois intelligentsia. Just as in Russia, the theoretical doctrine of Social-Democracy arose quite independently from spontaneous growth of a worker's movement, but arose rather as a natural and inevitable result of the development of ideas among the revolutionary socialist intelligentsia. . . .

The lack of preparedness of the majority of revolutionaries, a completely natural phenomenon, could not provoke any particular dangers. Once the tasks were correctly organized, once there was the energy for the repeated attempts to execute these tasks, the temporary failures were only half of the problem. Revolutionary experience and organizational skill come with time only if there is a desire to cultivate the necessary qualities, and if there is a consciousness of one's shortcomings which in revolutionary activity is more than half-way towards their correction.

But what was only half of the problem became full-blown when this consciousness began to fade (although it was very alive in the previously mentioned groups), when there appeared people—and even Social-Democratic organs—that were ready to make shortcomings virtuous and even tried to theoretically substantiate their cringing and bowing before spontaneity. . . .

Since there can be no talk of an independent ideology developed by the working masses in the process of their movement, the only choice is: bourgeois or socialist ideology. There is no middle way (for mankind has not developed any "third" ideology), and generally speaking, in a society torn by class opposition there could never be a non-class or an above-class ideology. Therefore any belittlement of socialist ideology, any dismissal of it signifies the strengthening of bourgeois ideology. There is discussion of spontaneity. But spontaneous development of the workers movement leads to its subordination to the bourgeois ideology. . . .

I could continue my exemplary analysis of the statutes, but I think that what's been said is enough. A small, tight, solid nucleus of the most dependable, experienced and hardened workers having trustworthy representatives in the main regions and connected by all the rules of secrecy with the organization of revolutionaries can quite capably, with the widest support of the masses and without any formal organization, fulfill all functions of a professional organization, in a manner desirable to a Social-Democratic movement. Only in this way can we secure the consolidation and development of a Social-Democratic trade-union movement, despite all the gendarmes.

It may be rejected that an organization that is so loose and not well formed, that its membership is in no way enrolled or registered can even be called an organization. It can be. It's not the name I'm after. But this "memberless organization" will do everything required and guarantee from the very outset the solid connection of our future trade unions to Socialism. Who but an incorrigible utopian would want a broad organization of workers with elections, reports, and universal suffrage under absolutism?

The moral from this is simple: if we begin with a solid foundation of strong organization of revolutionaries, we can guarantee the stability of the movement as a whole and realize the goals of Social-Democracy and of trade unions. If we, however, begin with a wide workers' organization, supposedly the most accessible to the masses (but in fact is the most accessible to the gendarmes, and makes revolutionaries most accessible to the police) we shall not achieve one goal nor the other. . . ."

Translated by Jane Scales

Aleksander Solzhenitsin: *The Gulag Archipelago* (1973)

At the 1956 Communist Party Congress of the U.S.S.R., Premier Nikita Khruschev delivered a speech which was not reported in the press, "revealing" Stalin's crimes to hundreds of party members who had loyally supported him during more than two decades of terror and repression. The imprisonment and murder of millions was called the product of a deviation from true Marxism-Leninism, built on the "cult of personality." One of the victims of this repression was Aleksander Solzhenitsin, who was shuttled from prison camp to prison camp (in what he called the "Gulag [an acronym for 'The Chief Administration of Corrective Labor Camps'] Archipelago") for eight years for the crime of having made derogatory remarks about Stalin in correspondence with a friend. At first Solzhenitsin's writings about the horrors he and those he met had experienced were supported by Khruschev, but he was soon seen as dangerous even to the reformed Party. He was exiled in 1969 for having continued to publish his novels and articles abroad, and the next year received the Nobel Prize for literature. The Gulag Archipelago *especially enraged the Soviet leadership, for it sought to demonstrate, through hundreds of stories meticulously researched and detailed while the author was in prison and after, that torture and repression had not begun with Stalin, nor ended with him. He became an outspoken critic of the entire Soviet era. His brilliant, bitter sarcasm made him popular among anti-Communists abroad. After a lengthy residence in the United States, he returned to live in post-Communist Russia in 1994.*

What means were used to persuade people to confess to crimes which they had not committed?

If the intellectuals in the plays of Chekhov[1] who spent all their time guessing what would happen in twenty, thirty, or forty years had been told that in forty years interrogation by torture would be practiced in Russia; that prisoners would have their skulls squeezed within iron rings; that a human being would be lowered into an acid bath; that they would be trussed up naked to be bitten by ants and bedbugs; that a ramrod heated over a primus stove would be thrust up their anal canal (the "secret brand"); that a man's genitals would be slowly crushed beneath the toe of a jackboot; and that, in the luckiest possible circumstances, prisoners would be tortured by being kept from sleeping for a week, by thirst, and by being beaten to a bloody pulp, not one of Chekhov's plays would have gotten to its end because all the heroes would have gone off to insane asylums.

Yes, not only Chekhov's heroes, but what normal Russian at the beginning of the century, including any member of the Russian Social Democratic Workers' Party, could have believed, would have tolerated, such a slander against the bright future? What had been acceptable under Tsar Aleksei Mikhailovich in the seventeenth century, what had already been regarded as barbarism under Peter the Great, what might have been used against ten or twenty people in all during the time of Biron in the mid-eighteenth century, what had already become totally impossible under Catherine the Great, was all being practiced during the flowering of the glorious twentieth century—in a society based on socialist principles, and at a time when airplanes were flying and the radio and talking films had already appeared—not by one scoundrel alone in one secret place only, but by tens of thousands of

[1]The ineffectual nobles depicted in the plays of Anton Chekhov (1860–1904), particularly in *The Cherry Orchard,* were often interpreted as expressing the exhaustion of the pre-Revolutionary regime.

specially trained human beasts standing over millions of defenseless victims.

Was it only that explosion of atavism which is now evasively called "the cult of personality" that was so horrible? Or was it even more horrible that during those same years, in 1937 itself, we celebrated Pushkin's centennial? And that we shamelessly continued to stage those self-same Chekhov plays, even though the answers to them had already come in? Is it not still more dreadful that we are now being told, thirty years later, "Don't talk about it!"? If we start to recall the sufferings of millions, we are told it will distort the historical perspective! If we doggedly seek out the essence of our morality, we are told it will darken our material progress! Let's think rather about the blast furnaces, the rolling mills that were built, the canals that were dug . . . no, better not talk about the canals. . . .[2] Then maybe about the gold of the Kolyma? No, maybe we ought not to talk about that either. . . .[3] Well, we can talk about anything, so long as we do it adroitly, so long as we glorify it. . . .

It is really hard to see why we condemn the Inquisition. Wasn't it true that beside the autos-da-fe,[4] magnificent services were offered the Almighty? It is hard to see why we are so down on serfdom. After all, no one forbade the peasants to work every day. And they could sing carols at Christmas too. And for Trinity Day the girls wove wreaths. . . .

The principle of our interrogation consists further in depriving the accused of even a knowledge of the law. . . .

Of the hundreds of prisoners I knew who had gone through interrogation and trial, and more than once too, who had served sentences in camp and in exile, none had ever seen the Code or held it in his hand!

It was only when both codes were thirty-five years old and on the point of being replaced by new ones that I saw them, two little paperback brothers, the UK or Criminal Code, and the UPK or Code of Criminal Procedure, on a newsstand in the Moscow subway (because they were outdated, it had been decided to release them for general circulation).

I read them today touched with emotion. For example, the UPK—the Code of Criminal Procedure:

"Article 136: The interrogator does not have the right to extract testimony or a confession from an accused by means of compulsion and threats." (It was as though they had foreseen it!)

Those familiar with our atmosphere of suspicion will understand why it was impossible to ask for the Code in a people's court or in the District Executive Committee. Your interest in the Code would be an extraordinary phenomenon: you must either be preparing to commit a crime or be trying to cover your tracks.

"Article 111: The interrogator is obliged to establish clearly all the relevant facts, both those tending toward acquittal and any which might lessen the accused's measure of guilt."

But it was I who helped establish Soviet power in October! It was I who shot Kolchak! I took part in the dispossession of the kulaks! I saved the state ten million rubles in lowered

---

[2]These were some of the most murderous slave-labor projects.

[3]Solzhenitsin is alluding to well-known projects carried out at the cost of immense suffering.

[4]The ceremonies during which the Spanish Inquisition burned those they had convicted of heresy or witchcraft.

production costs! I was wounded twice in the war! I have three orders and decorations.[5]

"You're not being tried for that!" History . . . the bared teeth of the interrogator: "Whatever good you may have done has nothing to do with the case."

"Article 139: The accused has the right to set forth his testimony in his own hand, and to demand the right to make corrections in the deposition written by the interrogator."

Oh, if we had only known that in time! But what I should say is: If that were only the way it really was! We were always vainly imploring the interrogator not to write "my repulsive, slanderous fabrications" instead of "my mistaken statements," or not to write "our underground weapons arsenal" instead of "my rusty Finnish knife."

If only the defendants had first been taught some prison science! If only interrogation had been run through first in rehearsal, and only afterward for real. . . .

The loneliness of the accused! That was one more factor in the success of unjust interrogation! The entire apparatus threw its full weight on one lonely and inhibited will. From the moment of his arrest and throughout the entire *shock* period of the interrogation the prisoner was, ideally, to be kept entirely alone. In his cell, in the corridor, on the stairs, in the offices, he was not supposed to encounter others like himself, in order to avoid the risk of his gleaning a bit of sympathy, advice, support from someone's smile or glance. The *Organs* did everything to blot out for him his future and distort his present: to lead him to believe that his friends and family had all been arrested and that material proof of his guilt had been found. . . .

In 1938 Ivanov-Razumnik found *one hundred forty* prisoners in a standard Butyrki cell intended for twenty-five—with toilets so overburdened that prisoners were taken to the toilet only once a day, sometimes at night; and the same thing was true of their outdoor walk as well. It was Ivanov-Razumnik who in the Lubyanka reception "kennel" calculated that for weeks at a time there were *three* persons for each square yard of floor space (just as an experiment, try to fit three people into that space!) In this "kennel" there was neither ventilation nor a window, and the prisoners' body heat and breathing raised the temperature to 40 or 45 degrees Centigrade—104 to 113 degrees Fahrenheit—and everyone sat there in undershorts with their winter clothing piled beneath them. Their naked bodies were pressed against one another, and they got eczema from one another's sweat. They sat like that for *weeks at a time,* and were given neither fresh air nor water—except for gruel and tea in the morning.

And if at the same time the latrine bucket replaced all other types of toilet (or if, on the other hand, there was no latrine bucket for use between trips to an outside toilet, as was the case in several Siberian prisons); and if four people ate from one bowl, sitting on each other's knees; and if someone was hauled out for interrogation, and then someone else was pushed in beaten up, sleepless, and broken; and if the appearance of such broken men was more persuasive than any threats on the part of the interrogators; and if, by then, death and any camp whatever seemed easier to a prisoner who had been left unsummoned for months than his tormented current situation—perhaps this really did replace the theoretically ideal isolation in solitary. And you could not always decide in such a porridge of people with whom to be forthright; and you could not always find someone from whom to seek advice. And you would believe in the tortures and beatings not when the interrogator threatened you with them but when you saw their results on other prisoners.

---

[5]This paragraph imagines the defenses of those who had supported and carried out repressive and even genocidal acts but who found themselves in their turn accused of treason.

You could learn from those who had suffered that they could give you a salt-water douche in the throat and then leave you in a box for a day tormented by thirst (Karpunich). Or that they might scrape the skin off a man's back with a grater till it bled and then oil it with turpentine. (Brigade Commander Rudolf Pintsov underwent both treatments. In addition, they pushed needles under his nails, and poured water into him to the bursting point—demanding that he confess to having *wanted* to turn his brigade of tanks against the government during the November parade.)[6] And from Aleksandrov, the former head of the Arts Section of the All-Union Society for Cultural Relations with Foreign Countries, who has a broken spinal column which tilts to one side, and who cannot control his tear ducts and thus cannot stop crying, one can learn how *Abakumov* himself could beat—in 1948.

Yes, yes, Minister of State Security Abakumov himself did not by any means spurn such menial labor. (A Suvorov at the head of his troops!) He was not averse to taking a rubber truncheon in his hands every once in a while. And his deputy Ryumin was even more willing. He did this at Sukhanovka in the "Generals'" interrogation office. The office had imitation-walnut paneling on the walls, silk portieres at the windows and doors, and a great Persian carpet on the floor. In order not to spoil all this beauty, a dirty runner bespattered with blood was rolled out on top of the carpet when a prisoner was being beaten. When Ryumin was doing the beating, he was assisted not by some ordinary guard but by a colonel. "And so," said Ryumin politely, stroking his rubber truncheon, which was four centimeters—an inch and a half—thick, "you have survived trial by sleeplessness with honor." (Alexander D. had cleverly managed to last a month "without sleep" by sleeping while he was standing up.) "So now we will try the club. Prisoners can't take more than two or three sessions of this. Let down your trousers and lie down on the runner." The colonel sat down on the prisoner's back. A.D. was going to *count* the blows. He didn't yet know about a blow from a rubber truncheon on the sciatic nerve when the buttocks have disappeared as a consequence of prolonged starvation. The effect is not felt in the place where the blow is delivered—it explodes inside the head. After the first blow the victim was mad with pain and broke his nails on the carpet. Ryumin beat away, trying to hit accurately. The colonel pressed down on A.D.'s torso—this was just the right sort of work for three big shoulder-board stars, assisting the all-powerful Ryumin! (After the beating the prisoner could not walk and, of course, was not carried. They just dragged him along the floor. What was left of his buttocks was soon so swollen that he could not button his trousers, and yet there were practically no scars. He was hit by a violent case of diarrhea, and, sitting there on the latrine bucket in solitary, A.D. guffawed. He went through a second and a third session, and his skin cracked, and Ryumin went wild, and started to beat him on the stomach, breaking through the intestinal wall and creating an enormous hernia through which A.D.'s intestines protruded. The prisoner was taken off to the Butyrki hospital with a case of peritonitis, and for the time being their attempts to compel him to commit a foul deed were suspended.)

That is how they can torture you too! After that it could seem a simple fatherly caress when the Kishinev interrogator Danilov beat Father Viktor Shipovalnikov across the back of the head with a poker and pulled him by his long hair. (It is very convenient to drag a

---

[6]In actual fact, he did *lead* his brigade at the parade, but for some reason he did not *turn* it against the government. But this was not taken into account. However, after these most varied tortures, he was sentenced to ten years by the OSO. To that degree, the gendarmes themselves had no faith in their achievements. [Note by Solzhenitsin.]

priest around in that fashion; ordinary laymen can be dragged by the beard from one corner of the office to the other. And Richard Ohola—a Finnish Red Guard, and a participant in the capture of British agent Sidney Reilly, and commander of a company during the suppression of the Kronstadt revolt—was lifted up with pliers first by one end of his great mustaches and then by the other, and held for ten minutes with his feet off the floor.)

But the most awful thing they can do with you is this: undress you from the waist down, place you on your back on the floor, pull your legs apart, seat assistants on them (from the glorious corps of sergeants!) who also hold down your arms; and then the interrogator (and women interrogators have not shrunk from this) stands between your legs and with the toe of his boot (or of her shoe) gradually, steadily, and with ever greater pressure crushes against the floor those organs which once made you a man. He looks into your eyes and repeats and repeats his questions or the betrayal he is urging on you. If he does not press down too quickly or just a shade too powerfully, you still have fifteen seconds left in which to scream that you will confess to everything, that you are ready to see arrested all twenty of those people he's been demanding of you, or that you will slander in the newspapers everything you hold holy. . . .

And may you be judged by God, but not by people. . . .

"There is no way out! You have to confess to everything!" whisper the stoolies who have been planted in the cell.

"It's a simple question: hang onto your health!" say people with common sense.

"You can't get new teeth," those who have already lost them nod at you.

"They are going to convict you in any case, whether you confess or whether you don't," conclude those who have got to the bottom of things.

"Those who don't sign get shot!" prophesies someone else in the corner. "Out of vengeance! So as not to risk any leaks about how they conduct interrogations."

"And if you die in the interrogator's office, they'll tell your relatives you've been sentenced to camp without the right of correspondence. And then just let them look for you."

If you are an orthodox Communist, then another orthodox Communist will sidle up to you, peering about with hostile suspicion, and he'll begin to whisper in your ear so that the uninitiated cannot overhear:

"It's our duty to support Soviet interrogation. It's a combat situation. We ourselves are to blame. We were too softhearted; and now look at all the rot that has multiplied in the country. There is a vicious secret war going on. Even here we are surrounded by enemies. Just listen to what they are saying! The Party is not obliged to account for what it does to every single one of us—to explain the whys and wherefores. If they ask us to, that means we should sign."

And another orthodox Communist sidles up:

"I signed denunciations against thirty-five people, against all my acquaintances. And I advise you too: Drag along as many names as you can in your wake, as many as you can. That way it will become obvious that the whole thing is an absurdity and they'll let everyone out!"

But that is precisely what the *Organs* need. The conscientiousness of the orthodox Communist and the purpose of the NKVD[7] naturally coincide. Indeed, the NKVD needs just that arched fan of names, that fat multiplication of them. That is the mark of quality of their work, and these are also new patches of woods in which to set out snares. "Your

---

[7]Acronym for "People's Secretariat of Internal Affairs," the secret police.

accomplices, accomplices! Others who share your views!" That is what they keep pressing to shake out of everyone. They say that R. Ralov named Cardinal Richelieu[8] as one of his accomplices and that the Cardinal was in fact so listed in his depositions—and no one was astonished by this until Ralov was questioned about it at his rehabilitation proceedings in 1956.

Translated by Thomas P. Whitney

[8]Notorious chief minister of Louis XIII of France, unlikely to have plotted against the Soviet government since he had died in 1642.

The Balfour Declaration (1917)

The British Foreign Secretary, Arthur James Balfour, wrote to Jewish leader Lord Rothschild, to assure him that his government supported the ideal of providing a homeland for the Jews. The British hoped thereby to win more Jewish support for the Allies in the First World War. The "Balfour Declaration" became the basis for international support for the founding of the modern state of Israel. The letter was published a week later in The Times *of London as reproduced here.*

What condition does the declaration place on England's support for the establishment of a Jewish state in Palestine?

Foreign Office
November 2nd, 1917

Dear Lord Rothschild:

I have much pleasure in conveying to you, on behalf of His Majesty's
Government, the following declaration of sympathy with Jewish Zionist aspirations which has been submitted to, and approved by, the Cabinet:

His Majesty's Government view with favor the establishment in Palestine of a national home for the Jewish people, and will use their best endeavors to facilitate the achievement of this object, it being clearly understood that nothing shall be done which may prejudice the civil and religious rights of existing non-Jewish communities in Palestine, or the rights and political status enjoyed by Jews in any other country.

I should be grateful if you would bring this declaration to the knowledge of the Zionist Federation.

Yours,
Arthur James Balfour

John McCrae: In Flanders Fields (1915)

Canadian poet John McCrae was a medical officer in both the Boer War and World War I. A year into the latter war he published in Punch *magazine, on December 8, 1915, the sole work by which he would be remembered. This sonnet commemorates the deaths of thousands of young men who died in Flanders during the grueling battles there. It created a great sensation, and was used widely as a recruiting tool, inspiring other young men to join the Army. Legend has it that he was inspired by seeing the blood-red poppies blooming in the fields where many friends had died. In 1918 McCrae died at the age of 40, in the way most men died during that war, not from a bullet or bomb, but from disease: pneumonia, in his case.*

Compare the mood in the first two stanzas with that in the third. Can you explain why people during the war interpreted it primarily as a pro-war poem although it was often read later as an anti-war poem? Who is the speaker in this poem? What does the speaker want his listeners to do?

In Flanders fields the poppies blow[1]
Between the crosses, row on row
   That mark our place; and in the sky
   The larks, still bravely singing, fly
Scarce heard amid the guns below.

We are the Dead. Short days ago
We lived, felt dawn, saw sunset glow,
   Loved and were loved, and now we lie
         In Flanders fields.

Take up our quarrel with the foe:
To you from failing hands we throw
   The torch; be yours to hold it high.
   If ye break faith with us who die
We shall not sleep, though poppies grow
         In Flanders fields.

---

[1]Bloom.

e. e. cummings: my sweet old etcetera (1926)

Many of the soldiers who went through the nightmare of World War I were deeply disillusioned by the experience. The alienation of these men from the society that had sent them off to combat is bitterly reflected in this poem by e. e. cummings, who developed an idiosyncratic style which involved avoiding capital letters (even in the spelling of his own name) and playing with the way that the sense flows from one line to the next. The tendency of civilians to gloss over the horrors of war is reflected in the word "etcetera," which shifts its meaning continuously throughout this poem.

If the soldier doesn't care about the war, what does he care about?

my sweet old etcetera
aunt lucy during the recent

war could and what
is more did tell you just
what everybody was fighting

for,
my sister

isabel created hundreds
(and
hundreds) of socks not to
mention shirts fleaproof earwarmers

etcetera wristers etcetera, my
mother hoped that

i would die etcetera
bravely of course my father used
to become hoarse talking about how it was
a privilege and if only he
could meanwhile my

self etcetera lay quietly
in the deep mud et

cetera
(dreaming,
et
   cetera, of
Your smile
eyes knees and of your Etcetera)

William Butler Yeats: The Second Coming (1921)

Yeats was attracted to the occult and fashioned an elaborate mythology to explain human experience. "The Second Coming," written after the catastrophe of World War I and with communism and fascism rising, is a compelling glimpse of an inhuman world about to be born. The Christian era was about to give way to an ominous period represented by the rough, pitiless beast in the poem.

Why is Bethlehem chosen to be the birthplace of the beast?

Turning and turning in the widening gyre[1]
The falcon cannot hear the falconer;
Things fall apart; the center cannot hold;
Mere anarchy is loosed upon the world,
The blood-dimmed tide is loosed, and everywhere
The ceremony of innocence is drowned;
The best lack all conviction, while the worst
Are full of passionate intensity.

Surely some revelation is at hand;
Surely the Second Coming[2] is at hand;
The Second Coming! Hardly are those words out
When a vast image out of *Spiritus Mundi*[3]
Troubles my sight: somewhere in sands of the desert
A shape with lion body and the head of a man,
A gaze blank and pitiless as the sun,
Is moving its slow thighs, while all about it
Reel shadows of the indignant desert birds.
The darkness drops again; but now I know
That twenty centuries[4] of stony sleep
Were vexed to nightmare by a rocking cradle,
And what rough beast, its hour come round at last
Slouches towards Bethlehem to be born?

---

[1]Spiral, making the figure of a cone.
[2]"Second Coming" refers to the promised return of Christ on Doomsday, the end of the world; but in Revelation 13 Doomsday is also marked by the appearance of a monstrous beast.
[3]Spirit of the world.
[4]2,000 years; the creature has been held back since the birth of Christ.

Adolf Hitler: "Nation and Race" from *Mein Kampf* (1923)

It has often been said that if the world had taken Hitler's Mein Kampf *("My Struggle") seriously when it was first published, much of the suffering caused by World War II might have been prevented. But who could have imagined that this obscure figure writing in prison would rise to absolute power in Germany and actually attempt to carry out his vicious policies? The following passage is a sample of the antisemitic ravings that fueled the "Final Solution," the Nazis' attempt to exterminate the Jews. Unfortunately similar vicious rhetoric still circulates in many countries today, including the U.S. Like many racists, he begins by appealing to the fear of rape by members of the hated "race."*

What does Hitler say was the goal of the Russian Revolution?

For hours the black-haired Jew boy, diabolic joy in his face, waits in ambush for the unsuspecting girl whom he defiles with his blood and thus robs her from her people. With the aid of all means he tries to ruin the racial foundations of the people to be enslaved. Exactly as he himself systematically demoralizes women and girls, he is not scared from pulling down the barriers of blood and race for others on a large scale. It was and is the Jews who bring the negro to the Rhine, always with the same concealed thought and the clear goal of destroying, by the bastardization which would necessarily set in, the white race which they hate, to throw it down from its cultural and political height and in turn to rise personally to the position of master.

For a racially pure people, conscious of its blood, can never be enslaved by the Jew. It will forever only be the master of bastards in this world.

Thus he systematically tries to lower the racial level by a permanent poisoning of the individual.

In the political sphere, however, he begins to replace the idea of democracy by that of the dictatorship of the proletariat.[1]

In the organized mass of Marxism he has found the weapon which makes him now dispense with democracy and which allows him, instead, to enslave and to "rule" the people dictatorially with the brutal fist.

He now works methodically towards the revolution in a twofold direction: economically and politically.

Thanks to his international influence, he ensnares with a net of enemies those peoples which put up a too violent resistance against the enemy from within, he drives them into war, and finally, if necessary, he plants the flag of revolution on the battlefield.

In the field of economics he undermines the State until the social organizations which have become unprofitable are taken from the State and submitted to his financial control.

Politically he denies to the State all means of self-preservation, he destroys the bases of any national self-dependence and defense, he destroys the confidence in the leaders, he derides history and the past, and he pulls down into the gutter everything which is truly great.

In the domain of culture he infects art, literature, theater, smites natural feeling, overthrows all conceptions of beauty and sublimity, of nobility and quality, and in turn he pulls the people down into the confines of his own swinish nature.

---

[1]The Marxist-Leninist term for a communist form of government.

Religion is ridiculed, customs and morality are presented as outlived, until the last supports of a nationality in the fight for human existence in this world have fallen.

Now begins the great, final revolution. The Jew, by gaining the political power, casts off the few cloaks which he still wears. The democratic national Jew becomes the blood Jew and the people's tyrant. In the course of a few years he tries to eradicate the national supporters of intelligence, and, while he thus deprives the people of their natural spiritual leaders, he makes them ripe for the slave's destiny of permanent subjugation.

The most terrible example of this kind is offered by Russia where he killed or starved about thirty million people with a truly diabolic ferocity, under inhuman tortures, in order to secure to a crowd of Jewish scribblers and stock exchange robbers[2] the rulership over a great people.

But the end is not only the end of the freedom of the peoples oppressed by the Jew, but also the end of these peoples' parasites themselves. With the death of the victim this peoples' vampire will also die sooner or later.

Translated by John Chamberlain, et al.

[2]A persistent delusion of antisemites is the belief that Jews are somehow simultaneously super-capitalists and communists.

Elie Wiesel: *Night* (1960)

The late Terrence de Pres, in a foreword to a book on Eli Wiesel, wrote, "Every age produces the event which defines it, and in our time the Holocaust is ours. It demands that one face the kind of limitless horror our technological and bureaucratic civilization makes possible." As most students know the Holocaust refers to the Nazi plan to exterminate all the Jews of Europe. This monstrous event, which took the lives of six million Jews and four million other persons considered undesirable by the Hitler regime, has subsequently raised disturbing questions about human nature and, among some religious thinkers, theological questions about the justice of the Christian and Jewish God. Eli Wiesel was deported from his Hungarian village at age fifteen; he and his family were sealed in box cars and transported to Auschwitz, the largest of the Nazi death camps. There he saw his mother and youngest sister for the last time. He writes, "'Men to the left! Women to the right!' Eight words spoken quietly, indifferently, without emotion. Eight short, simple words. Yet that was the moment when I parted from my mother." His mother and sister were gassed and fed into the crematoria ovens. Wiesel and his father sustained one another during a long period of deprivation and cruelty, but the father died before the death camps were liberated by the Allies in 1945. The selection that follows is taken from the fifth chapter of his memoir Night *and presents the dehumanizing process of Auschwitz and the human and spiritual consequences on the prisoners. In light of his thoughts of God while in the death camp, it is worth noting that the boy was deeply involved with Judaism before he was deported. After the War Wiesel tried to return to the living. He studied at the Sorbonne in Paris, became a writer of more than twenty books, worked vigorously for many humanitarian causes and in 1986 was awarded the Nobel Peace Prize. But as he said in a recent interview, he has never fully recovered from the experience of evil of the Holocaust.*

What is the significance of the prisoners' forgetting to say kaddish *at the end of this selection?*

The summer was coming to an end. The Jewish year was nearly over.

On the eve of Rosh Hashanah,[1] the last day of that accursed year, the whole camp was electric with the tension which was in all our hearts. In spite of everything, this day was different from any other. The last day of the year. The word "last" rang very strangely. What if it were indeed the last day?

They gave us our evening meal, a very thick soup, but no one touched it. We wanted to wait until after prayers. At the place of assembly, surrounded by the electrified barbed wire, thousands of silent Jews gathered, their faces stricken.

Night was falling. Other prisoners continued to crowd in, from every block, able suddenly to conquer time and space and submit both to their will.

"What are You, my God," I thought angrily, "compared to this afflicted crowd, proclaiming to You their faith, their anger, their revolt? What does Your greatness mean, Lord of the Universe, in the face of all this weakness, this decomposition, and this decay? Why do You still trouble their sick minds, their crippled bodies?"

Ten thousand men had come to attend the solemn service, heads of the blocks, Kapos,[2] functionaries of death.

"Bless the Eternal. . . ."

---

[1]The Jewish New Year.

[2]Prisoners who worked for the camp guards, supervising other prisoners.

The voice of the officiant had just made itself heard. I thought at first it was the wind.

"Blessed be the Name of the Eternal!"

Thousands of voices repeated the benediction; thousands of men prostrated themselves like trees before a tempest.

"Blessed be the Name of the Eternal!"

Why, but why should I bless Him? In every fiber I rebelled. Because He had had thousands of children burned in His pits? Because He kept six crematories working night and day, on Sundays and feast days? Because in His great might He had created Auschwitz, Birkenau, Buna, and so many factories of death? How could I say to Him: "Blessed art Thou, Eternal, Master of the Universe, Who chose us from among the races to be tortured day and night, to see our fathers, our mothers, our brothers, end in the crematory? Praised be Thy Holy Name, Thou Who hast chosen us to be butchered on Thine altar?"

I heard the voice of the officiant rising up, powerful yet at the same time broken, amid the tears, the sobs, the sighs of the whole congregation:

"All the earth and the Universe are God's!"

He kept stopping every moment, as though he did not have the strength to find the meaning beneath the words. The melody choked in his throat.

And I, mystic that I had been, I thought:

"Yes, man is very strong, greater than God. When You were deceived by Adam and Eve, You drove them out of Paradise. When Noah's generation displeased You, You brought down the Flood. When Sodom no longer found favor in Your eyes, You made the sky rain down fire and sulfur. But these men here, whom You have betrayed, whom You have allowed to be tortured, butchered, gassed, burned, what do they do? They pray before You! They praise Your name!"

"All creation bears witness to the Greatness of God!"

Once, New Year's Day had dominated my life. I knew that my sins grieved the Eternal; I implored his forgiveness. Once, I had believed profoundly that upon one solitary deed of mine, one solitary prayer, depended the salvation of the world.

This day I had ceased to plead. I was no longer capable of lamentation. On the contrary, I felt very strong. I was the accuser, God the accused. My eyes were open and I was alone—terribly alone in a world without God and without man. Without love or mercy. I had ceased to be anything but ashes, yet I felt myself to be stronger than the Almighty, to whom my life had been tied for so long. I stood amid that praying congregation, observing it like a stranger.

The service ended with the Kaddish.[3] Everyone recited the Kaddish over his parents, over his children, over his brothers, and over himself.

We stayed for a long time at the assembly place. No one dared to drag himself away from this mirage. Then it was time to go to bed and slowly the prisoners made their way over to their blocks. I heard people wishing one another a Happy New Year!

I ran off to look for my father. And at the same time I was afraid of having to wish him a Happy New Year when I no longer believed in it.

He was standing near the wall, bowed down, his shoulders sagging as though beneath a heavy burden. I went up to him, took his hand and kissed it. A tear fell upon it. Whose was that tear? Mine? His? I said nothing. Nor did he. We had never understood one another so

[3]Prayer for the dead.

clearly.

The sound of the bell jolted us back to reality. We must go to bed. We came back from far away. I raised my eyes to look at my father's face leaning over mine, to try to discover a smile or something resembling one upon the aged, dried-up countenance. Nothing. Not the shadow of an expression. Beaten.

Yom Kippur.[4] The Day of Atonement.

Should we fast? The question was hotly debated. To fast would mean a surer, swifter death. We fasted here the whole year round. The whole year was Yom Kippur. But others said that we should fast simply because it was dangerous to do so. We should show God that even here, in this enclosed hell, we were capable of singing His praises.

I did not fast, mainly to please my father, who had forbidden me to do so. But further, there was no longer any reason why I should fast. I no longer accepted God's silence. As I swallowed my bowl of soup, I saw in the gesture an act of rebellion and protest against Him.

And I nibbled my crust of bread.

In the depths of my heart, I felt a great void.

The SS[5] gave us a fine New Year's gift.

We had just come back from work. As soon as we had passed through the door of the camp, we sensed something different in the air. Roll call did not take so long as usual. The evening soup was given out with great speed and swallowed down at once in anguish.

I was no longer in the same block as my father. I had been transferred to another unit, the building one, where, twelve hours a day, I had to drag heavy blocks of stone about. The head of my new block was a German Jew, small of stature, with piercing eyes. He told us that evening that no one would be allowed to go out after the evening soup. And soon a terrible word was circulating—selection.

We knew what that meant. An SS man would examine us. Whenever he found a weak one, a *musulman* as we called them, he would write his number down: good for the crematory.

After soup, we gathered together between the beds. The veterans said:

"You're lucky to have been brought here so late. This camp is paradise today, compared with what it was like two years ago. Buna was a real hell then. There was no water, no blankets, less soup and bread. At night we slept almost naked, and it was below thirty degrees. The corpses were collected in hundreds every day. The work was hard. Today, this is a little paradise. The Kapos had orders to kill a certain number of prisoners every day. And every week—selection. A merciless selection. . . . Yes, you're lucky."

"Stop it! Be quiet!" I begged. "You can tell your stories tomorrow or on some other day."

They burst out laughing. They were not veterans for nothing.

"Are you scared? So were we scared. And there was plenty to be scared of in those days."

The old men stayed in their corner, dumb, motionless, hunted. Some were praying.

An hour's delay. In an hour, we should know the verdict —death or a reprieve.

And my father? Suddenly I remembered him. How would he pass the selection? He had aged so much. . . .

---

[4]Day for atoning for one's sins.

[5]Elite corps of Nazi security, often associated with running concentration camps.

The head of our block had never been outside concentration camps since 1933. He had already been through all the slaughterhouses, all the factories of death. At about nine o'clock, he took up his position in our midst:

"Achtung !"[6]

There was instant silence.

"Listen carefully to what I am going to say." (For the first time, I heard his voice quiver.) "In a few moments the selection will begin. You must get completely undressed. Then one by one you go before the SS doctors. I hope you will all succeed in getting through. But you must help your own chances. Before you go into the next room, move about in some way so that you give yourselves a little color. Don't walk slowly, run! Run as if the devil were after you! Don't look at the SS. Run, straight in front of you!"

He broke off for a moment, then added:

"And, the essential thing, don't be afraid!"

Here was a piece of advice we should have liked very much to be able to follow.

I got undressed, leaving my clothes on the bed. There was no danger of anyone stealing them this evening.

Tibi and Yossi, who had changed their unit at the same time as I had, came up to me and said:

"Let's keep together. We shall be stronger."

Yossi was murmuring something between his teeth. He must have been praying. I had never realized that Yossi was a believer. I had even always thought the reverse. Tibi was silent, very pale. All the prisoners in the block stood naked between the beds. This must be how one stands at the last judgment.

"They're coming!"

There were three SS officers standing round the notorious Dr. Mengele, who had received us at Birkenau. The head of the block, with an attempt at a smile, asked us:

"Ready?"

Yes, we were ready. So were the SS doctors. Dr. Mengele was holding a list in his hand: our numbers. He made a sign to the head of the block: "We can begin!" As if this were a game!

The first to go by were the "officials" of the block: *Stubenaelteste,* Kapos, foremen, all in perfect physical condition of course! Then came the ordinary prisoners' turn. Dr. Mengele took stock of them from head to foot. Every now and then, he wrote a number down. One single thought filled my mind: not to let my number be taken; not to show my left arm.

There were only Tibi and Yossi in front of me. They passed. I had time to notice that Mengele had not written their numbers down. Someone pushed me. It was my turn. I ran without looking back. My head was spinning: you're too thin, you're weak, you're too thin, you're good for the furnace. . . . The race seemed interminable. I thought I had been running for years. . . . You're too thin, you're too weak. . . . At last I had arrived exhausted. When I regained my breath, I questioned Yossi and Tibi:

"Was I written down ?"

"No," said Yossi. He added, smiling: "In any case, he couldn't have written you down, you were running too fast. . . ."

I began to laugh. I was glad. I would have liked to kiss him. At that moment, what did the others matter! I hadn't been written down.

Those whose numbers had been noted stood apart, abandoned by the whole world.

---

[6]Attention!

Some were weeping in silence.

The SS officers went away. The head of the block appeared, his face reflecting the general weariness.

"Everything went off all right. Don't worry. Nothing is going to happen to anyone. To anyone."

Again he tried to smile. A poor, emaciated, dried-up Jew questioned him avidly in a trembling voice:

"But . . . but, *Blockaelteste,*[7] they did write me down !"

The head of the block let his anger break out. What! Did someone refuse to believe him!

"What's the matter now? Am I telling lies then? I tell you once and for all, nothing's going to happen to you! To anyone! You're wallowing in your own despair, you fool!"

The bell rang, a signal that the selection had been completed throughout the camp.

With all my might I began to run to Block 36. I met my father on the way. He came up to me:

"Well? So you passed?"

"Yes. And you?"

"Me too."

How we breathed again, now! My father had brought me a present—half a ration of bread obtained in exchange for a piece of rubber, found at the warehouse, which would do to sole a shoe.

The bell. Already we must separate, go to bed. Everything was regulated by the bell. It gave me orders, and I automatically obeyed them. I hated it. Whenever I dreamed of a better world, I could only imagine a universe with no bells.

Several days had elapsed. We no longer thought about the selection. We went to work as usual, loading heavy stones into railway wagons. Rations had become more meager: this was the only change.

We had risen before dawn, as on every day. We had received the black coffee, the ration of bread. We were about to set out for the yard as usual. The head of the block arrived, running.

"Silence for a moment. I have a list of numbers here. I'm going to read them to you. Those whose numbers I call won't be going to work this morning; they'll stay behind in the camp."

And, in a soft voice, he read out about ten numbers. We had understood. These were numbers chosen at the selection. Dr. Mengele had not forgotten.

The head of the block went toward his room. Ten prisoners surrounded him, hanging onto his clothes:

"Save us ! You promised . . . ! We want to go to the yard. We're strong enough to work. We're good workers. We can . . . we will . . ."

He tried to calm them, to reassure them about their fate, to explain to them that the fact that they were staying behind in the camp did not mean much, had no tragic significance.

"After all, I stay here myself every day," he added.

It was a somewhat feeble argument. He realized it, and without another word went and shut himself up in his room.

The bell had just rung.

---

[7]Senior block kapo.

"Form up !"

It scarcely mattered now that the work was hard. The essential thing was to be as far away as possible from the block, from the crucible of death, from the center of hell.

I saw my father running toward me. I became frightened all of a sudden.

"What's the matter?"

Out of breath, he could hardly open his mouth.

"Me, too . . . me, too . . . ! They told me to stay behind in the camp."

They had written down his number without his being aware of it.

"What will happen ?" I asked in anguish.

But it was he who tried to reassure me.

"It isn't certain yet. There's still a chance of escape. They're going to do another selection today . . . a decisive selection."

I was silent.

He felt that his time was short. He spoke quickly. He would have liked to say so many things. His speech grew confused; his voice choked. He knew that I would have to go in a few moments. He would have to stay behind alone, so very alone.

"Look, take this knife," he said to me. "I don't need it any longer. It might be useful to you. And take this spoon as well. Don't sell them. Quickly! Go on. Take what I'm giving you!"

The inheritance.

"Don't talk like that, father." (I felt that I would break into sobs.) "I don't want you to say that. Keep the spoon and knife. You need them as much as I do. We shall see each other again this evening, after work."

He looked at me with his tired eyes, veiled with despair. He went on:

"I'm asking this of you . . . Take them. Do as I ask, my son. We have no time . . . Do as your father asks."

Our Kapo yelled that we should start.

The unit set out toward the camp gate. Left, right! I bit my lips. My father had stayed by the block, leaning against the wall. Then he began to run, to catch up with us. Perhaps he had forgotten something he wanted to say to me. . . . But we were marching too quickly. . . . Left, right!

We were already at the gate. They counted us, to the din of military music. We were outside.

The whole day, I wandered about as if sleepwalking. Now and then Tibi and Yossi would throw me a brotherly word. The Kapo, too, tried to reassure me. He had given me easier work today. I felt sick at heart. How well they were treating me! Like an orphan! I thought: even now, my father is still helping me.

I did not know myself what I wanted—for the day to pass quickly or not. I was afraid of finding myself alone that night. How good it would be to die here!

At last we began the return journey. How I longed for orders to run!

The military march. The gate. The camp.

I ran to Block 36.

Were there still miracles on this earth? He was alive. He had escaped the second selection. He had been able to prove that he was still useful. . . . I gave him back his knife and spoon.

Akiba Drumer left us, a victim of the selection. Lately, he had wandered among us, his eyes glazed, telling everyone of his weakness: "I can't go on . . . It's all over. . . ." It was impossible to raise his morale. He didn't listen to what we told him. He could only repeat that all was over for him, that he could no longer keep up the struggle, that he had no strength left, nor faith. Suddenly his eyes would become blank, nothing but two open wounds, two pits of terror.

He was not the only one to lose his faith during those selection days. I knew a rabbi from a little town in Poland, a bent old man, whose lips were always trembling. He used to pray all the time, in the block, in the yard, in the ranks. He would recite whole pages of the Talmud [8] from memory, argue with himself, ask himself questions and answer himself. And one day he said to me: "It's the end. God is no longer with us."

And, as though he had repented of having spoken such words, so clipped, so cold, he added in his faint voice:

"I know. One has no right to say things like that. I know. Man is too small, too humble and inconsiderable to seek to understand the mysterious ways of God. But what can I do? I'm not a sage, one of the elect, nor a saint. I'm just an ordinary creature of flesh and blood. I've got eyes, too, and I can see what they're doing here. Where is the divine Mercy? Where is God? How can I believe, how could anyone believe, in this merciful God?"

Poor Akiba Drumer, if he could have gone on believing in God, if he could have seen a proof of God in this Calvary, [9] he would not have been taken by the selection. But as soon as he felt the first cracks forming in his faith, he had lost his reason for struggling and had begun to die.

When the selection came, he was condemned in advance, offering his own neck to the executioner. All he asked of us was:

"In three days I shall no longer be here. . . . Say the Kaddish for me."

We promised him. In three days' time, when we saw the smoke rising from the chimney, we would think of him. Ten of us would gather together and hold a special service. All his friends would say the Kaddish.

Then he went off toward the hospital, his step steadier, not looking back. An ambulance was waiting to take him to Birkenau.

These were terrible days. We received more blows than food; we were crushed with work. And three days after he had gone we forgot to say the Kaddish.

Translated by Stella Rodway

---

[8] The vast commentary on the Torah, or Jewish law.

[9] The hill in Jerusalem where the ancient Romans executed prisoners, including Jesus.

Simone de Beauvoir: *The Second Sex* (1949–1950)

No feminist thinker has had more widespread influence than Simone de Beauvoir. An important modern novelist and scholar, she explored in her classic work The Second Sex *many of the issues that are still being hotly debated today, though she was writing during a period when feminism was at a low point in its influence. In this passage she examines certain limiting images and stereotypes that had been traditionally associated with women. Thirty years ago she would have been known primarily as the companion of philosopher Jean-Paul Sartre. Today she is more famous than he. She begins by describing some of the many ways in which men have seen "woman" in nature.*

What attitudes toward the "female" aspects of nature that de Beauvoir describes in the first paragraph is common among them? Why do you think she objects to these attitudes? What is she complaining about in the second paragraph? Can you think of examples of what de Beuavoir means when she says that men urge women to break the moral code which they otherwise argue for? Do you think she is correct in saying that women have to be more ingenious than men in dealing with the requirements of morality upon them? Explain your answer. Do you think women act less naturally around men than around women? If they do, what do you think are the causes of this different behavior?

Man finds again in woman bright stars and dreamy moon, the light of the sun, the shade of grottoes; and, conversely, the wild flowers of thickets, the proud garden rose are women. Nymphs, dryads, sirens, undines, fairies haunt the fields and woods, the lakes, oceans, moorland. Nothing lies deeper in the hearts of men than this animism.[1] For the sailor, the sea is a woman, dangerous, treacherous, hard to conquer, but cherished the more for his effort to subdue her. The proud mountain, rebellious, virginal, and wicked, is a woman for the alpinist[2] who wills, at the peril of his life, to violate her. It is sometimes asserted that these comparisons reveal sexual sublimation; but rather they express an affinity between woman and the elements that is as basic as sexuality itself. Man expects something other than the assuagement of instinctive cravings from the possession of a woman; she is the privileged object through which he subdues Nature. But other objects can play this part. Sometimes man seeks to find again upon the body of young boys the sandy shore, the velvet night, the scent of honeysuckle. But sexual penetration is not the only manner of accomplishing carnal possession of the earth. In his novel *To a God Unknown,* Steinbeck presents a man who has chosen a mossy rock as a mediator between himself and nature; in *Chatte,* Colette describes a young husband who has centered his love on his favorite cat, because, through this wild and gentle animal, he has a grasp on the sensual universe which the too human body of his wife fails to give him. The Other can be incarnated in the sea, the mountain, as perfectly as in woman; they oppose to man the same passive and unforeseen resistance that enables him to fulfill himself; they are an unwillingness to overcome, a

[1]Belief that spirits dwell within natural objects.
[2]Mountain-climber in the Alps.

prey to take possession of. If sea and mountain are women, then woman is also sea and mountain for her lover.[3]

But it is not casually given to any woman whatever to serve in this way as intermediary between man and the world; man is not satisfied merely to find in his partner sex organs complementary to his own. She must incarnate the marvelous flowering of life and at the same time conceal its obscure mysteries. Before all things, then, she will be called upon for youth and health, for as man presses a living creature in his embrace, he can find enchantment in her only if he forgets that death ever dwells in life. And he asks for still more: that his loved one be beautiful. The ideal of feminine beauty is variable, but certain demands remain constant; for one thing, since woman is destined to be possessed, her body must present the inert and passive qualities of an object. Virile[4] beauty lies in the fitness of the body for action, in strength, agility, flexibility; it is the manifestation of transcendence animating a flesh that must never sink back upon itself. The feminine ideal is symmetrical[5] only in such societies as Sparta, Fascist Italy, and Nazi Germany, which destine woman for the State and not for the individual, which regard her exclusively as mother and make no place for eroticism.[6]

But when woman is given over to man as his property, he demands that she represent the flesh purely for its own sake.[7] Her body is not perceived as the radiation of a subjective personality, but as a thing sunk deeply in its own immanence; it is not for such a body to have reference to the rest of the world, it must not be the promise of things other than itself; it must end the desire it arouses. . . .

Woman knows that the masculine code is not hers, that man takes for granted she will not observe it since he urges her to abortion, adultery, wrongdoing, betrayals, and lies, which he condemns officially. She therefore calls upon other women to help define a set of "local rules," so to speak, a moral code specially for the female sex. It is not merely through malevolence that women comment on and criticize the behavior of their friends interminably; in order to pass judgment on others and to regulate their own conduct, women need much more moral ingenuity than do men.

What gives values to such relations among women is the truthfulness they imply. Confronting man, woman is always playacting; she lies when she makes believe that she accepts her status as the inessential other, she lies when she presents to him an imaginary person-

---

[3]A significant phrase of Samivel is cited by Bachelard (*La Terre et les rêvereies de la volonte*): 'These mountains lying around me in a circle I have ceased little by little to regard as enemies to fight, as females to trample upon, or as trophies to conquer so as to provide for myself and for others true witness of my own worth.' The ambivalence woman-mountain is established through the common idea of 'enemy to fight,' "trophy,' and 'witness' of power (note by de Beauvoir).

[4]Male.

[5]The same as the male ideal (women were urged to be athletically fit in Sparta, just like the men).

[6]That is, the Spartans, Fascists, and Nazis all valued women only as mothers.

[7]Be careful not to read this sentence literally; de Beauvoir is not arguing that women are actually owned by men; only that in traditional societies they are commonly treated like property. In the second half of the sentence, she is saying that men in such cultures value women less as potential mothers for their children than as sexual partners for themselves. In a sense, they *become* sex.

age through mimicry, costumery, studied phrases. These histrionics[8] require a constant tension; when with her husband, or with her lover, every woman is more or less conscious of the thought: 'I am not being myself'; the male world is harsh, sharp-edged, its voices are too resounding, the lights too crude, the contacts rough. With other women, a woman is behind the scenes; she is polishing her equipment, but not in battle; she is getting her costume together, preparing her make-up, laying out her tactics; she is lingering in dressing-gown and slippers in the wings before making her entrance on the stage; she likes this warm, easy, relaxed atmosphere. In *Le Képi* Colette shows us two friends peacefully sewing and discussing little details of the work, exchanging small confidences, practicing new make-ups. And in contrast with this quiet scene is one in which preparations are being made for one of the friends to meet a young man. The atmosphere is more serious; there are to be no tears: the make-up! An unbought dress is regretted; fine silk stockings must be borrowed; to wear or not to wear a flower must be decided; there are so many questions! In such circumstances women help one another, discuss their social problems, each creating for the others a kind of protecting nest; and what they do and say is genuine.

Translated by H. M. Parshley

[8]Acting

Latin America & The Caribbean 1900–Present

Pablo Neruda: Anguish of Death

Chilean poet Pablo Neruda received the Nobel Prize for literature in 1971. In the "Anguish of Death" he writes of the Spanish conquest of the Inca, referring to the requerimiento, *the practice whereby the Spaniards would extend a Bible to American peoples with the demand that they convert to Christianity. Understanding neither Spanish nor what a European-style book was, the leader often dropped the text on the ground, providing the signal for the Spaniards to attack. Nevertheless, this bogus ceremony fulfilled Queen Isabella's requirement that Native Americans be offered Christianity: only if they refused, were they to be conquered by force. The outcome was usually that described in Neruda's poem.*

Why does Neruda write of a "visitor from another planet?" Why does he call the Bible "a piece of a basket, a fruit?"

In Cajamarca, the anguish of death began.

The youthful Atahualpa, sky-blue stamen,
illustrious tree, listened to the wind
carry the faint murmur of steel.
There was a confused
light, an earth-tremor from the coast,
an unbelievable galloping—
rearing and power—
from iron and iron, among the weeds.
The governors were arriving.
The Inca[1] came out to the music
surrounded by his nobles.

The visitors
from another planet, sweaty and bearded,
go to do reverence.
The chaplain,
Valverde, treacherous heart, rotten jackal,
brings forward a strange object, a piece
of a basket, a fruit,
perhaps from the same planet from which the horses come.

---

[1]"Inca" is the title of the ruler of the Incas.

Atahualpa takes it. He does not know
what it is made of; it doesn't shine, it makes no noise,
and he lets it fall, smiling.

"Death;
vengeance, kill, I will absolve you,"
the jackal of the murderous cross cries out.
Thunder draws near the robbers.
Our blood is shed in its cradle.

The young princes gather like a chorus
around the Inca, in the hour of the anguish of death.

Ten thousand Peruvians fell
under crosses and swords, the blood
moistened the robes of Atahualpa.
Pizarro, the cruel hog from western Spain,
had the slender arms of the Inca
tied up. Night has now come down
over Peru like a live coal that is black.

Translated by James Wright

Jorge Luis Borges: The Library of Babel[1] (1941)

You may have heard it said that if a hundred monkeys were placed in a room with a hundred typewriters and allowed to hit the keyboards at random for an infinite amount of time they would eventually produce by pure chance all possible texts. Hidden somewhere among heaps of linguistic rubbish would be brilliant literary works and other invaluable writings; but as Argentinian fabulist Borges points out, how would we ever find them? Whereas in the Renaissance a diligent scholar could hope to read all the European books in existence, we are awash in a sea of information but in many ways considerably less well informed than our ancestors. The story also reflects the consciousness of modern people that the universe is a vast, mostly empty wasteland. The sense of radical aloneness and absurdity which this consciousness produces suffuses the tale. Yet the human spirit does triumph in the limited domain of literature, through the brilliance of his expression and the sparkle of his wit.

What kinds of books have people especially searched for in the Library?

By this art you may contemplate the variation of the 23 letters . . .
—*The Anatomy of Melancholy,* Part 2, Sect. II, Mem. IV.

The universe (which others call the Library) is composed of an indefinite, perhaps an infinite, number of hexagonal galleries,[2] with enormous ventilation shafts in the middle, encircled by very low railings. From any hexagon the upper or lower stories are visible, interminably. The distribution of the galleries is invariable. Twenty shelves—five long shelves per side—cover all sides except two; their height, which is that of each floor, scarcely exceeds that of an average librarian. One of the free sides gives upon a narrow entrance way, which leads to another gallery, identical to the first and to all the others. To the left and to the right of the entrance way are two miniature rooms. One allows standing room for sleeping; the other, the satisfaction of fecal necessities. Through this section passes the spiral staircase, which plunges down into the abyss and rises up to the heights. In the entrance way hangs a mirror, which faithfully duplicates appearances. People are in the habit of inferring from this mirror that the Library is not infinite (if it really were, why this illusory duplication?); I prefer to dream that the polished surfaces feign and promise infinity. . . .

Light comes from some spherical fruits called by the name of lamps. There are two, running transversally, in each hexagon. The light they emit is insufficient, incessant.

Like all men of the Library, I have traveled in my youth. I have journeyed in search of a book, perhaps of the catalogue of catalogues; now that my eyes can scarcely decipher what I write, I am preparing to die a few leagues from the hexagon in which I was born. Once dead, there will not lack pious hands to hurl me over the banister; my sepulcher shall be the unfathomable air: my body will sink lengthily and will corrupt and dissolve in the wind engendered by the fall, which is infinite. I affirm that the Library is interminable.

[1]According to Genesis 11: 5–9 God multiplied the languages of those who were trying to build a tower to Heaven in Babel so that their inability to communicate with each other would defeat them. A Library of Babel would be therefore a library which hides rather than disseminates knowledge.
[2]The shape of these galleries suggests an enormous beehive.

The idealists argue that the hexagonal halls are a necessary form of absolute space or, at least, of our intuition of space. They contend that a triangular or pentagonal hall is inconceivable. (The mystics claim that to them ecstasy reveals a round chamber containing a great book with a continuous back circling the walls of the room; but their testimony is suspect; their words, obscure. That cyclical book is God.) Let it suffice me, for the time being, to repeat the classic dictum: *The Library is a sphere whose consummate center is any hexagon, and whose circumference is inaccessible.*[3]

Five shelves correspond to each one of the walls of each hexagon; each shelf contains thirty-two books of a uniform format; each book is made up of four hundred and ten pages; each page, of forty lines; each line, of some eighty black letters. There are also letters on the spine of each book; these letters do not indicate or prefigure what the pages will say. I know that such a lack of relevance, at one time, seemed mysterious. Before summarizing the solution (whose disclosure, despite its tragic implications, is perhaps the capital fact of this history), I want to recall certain axioms.

The first: The Library exists *ab aeterno.*[4] No reasonable mind can doubt this truth, whose immediate corollary is the future eternity of the world. Man, the imperfect librarian, may be the work of chance or of malevolent demiurges; the universe, with its elegant endowment of shelves, of enigmatic volumes, of indefatigable ladders for the voyager, and of privies for the seated librarian, can only be the work of a god. In order to perceive the distance which exists between the divine and the human, it is enough to compare the rude tremulous symbols which my fallible hand scribbles on the end pages of a book with the organic letters inside: exact, delicate, intensely black, inimitably symmetric.

The second: *The number of orthographic symbols is twenty-five.*[5] This bit of evidence permitted the formulation, three hundred years ago, of a general theory of the Library and the satisfactory resolution of the problem which no conjecture had yet made clear: the formless and chaotic nature of almost all books. One of these books, which my father saw in a hexagon of the circuit number fifteen ninety-four, was composed of the letters MCV perversely repeated from the first line to the last. Another, very much consulted in this zone, is a mere labyrinth of letters, but on the next-to-the-last page, one may read *O Time your pyramids.* As is well known: for one reasonable line or one straightforward note there are leagues of insensate cacophony, of verbal farragoes and incoherencies. (I know of a wild region whose librarians repudiate the vain superstitious custom of seeking any sense in books and compare it to looking for meaning in dreams or in the chaotic lines of one's hands. . . . They admit that the inventors of writing imitated the twenty-five natural symbols, but they maintain that this application is accidental and that books in themselves mean nothing. This opinion—we shall see—is not altogether false.)

For a long time it was believed that these impenetrable books belonged to past or remote languages. It is true that the most ancient men, the first librarians, made use of a language quite different from the one we speak today; it is true that some miles to the right the

---

[3]A parody of St. Thomas Aquinas' definition of God as a circle whose center is everywhere and whose circumference is nowhere.

[4]Eternally, has always existed.

[5]The original manuscript of the present note does not contain digits or capital letters. The punctuation is limited to the comma and the period. These two signs, plus the space sign and the twenty-two letters of the alphabet, make up the twenty-five sufficient symbols enumerated by the unknown author. [*Author's note*]

language is dialectical and that ninety stories up it is incomprehensible. All this, I repeat, is true; but four hundred and ten pages of unvarying MCVs do not correspond to any language, however dialectical or rudimentary it might be. Some librarians insinuated that each letter could influence the next, and that the value of MCV on the third line of page 71 was not the same as that of the same series in another position on another page; but this vague thesis did not prosper. Still other men thought in terms of cryptographs; this conjecture has come to be universally accepted, though not in the sense in which it was formulated by its inventors.

Five hundred years ago, the chief of an upper hexagon[6] came upon a book as confusing as all the rest but which contained nearly two pages of homogenous lines. He showed his find to an ambulant decipherer, who told him the lines were written in Portuguese. Others told him they were in Yiddish. In less than a century the nature of the language was finally established: it was a Samoyed-Lithuanian dialect of Guaraní, with classical Arabic inflections. The contents were also deciphered: notions of combinational analysis, illustrated by examples of variations with unlimited repetition. These examples made it possible for a librarian of genius to discover the fundamental law of the Library. This thinker observed that all the books, however diverse, are made up of uniform elements: the period, the comma, the space, the twenty-two letters of the alphabet. He also adduced a circumstance confirmed by all travelers: *There are not, in the whole vast Library, two identical books.* From all these incontrovertible premises he deduced that the Library is total and that its shelves contain all the possible combinations of the twenty-odd orthographic symbols (whose number, though vast, is not infinite); that is, everything which can be expressed, in all languages. Everything is there: the minute history of the future, the autobiographies of the archangels, the faithful catalogue of the Library, thousands and thousands of false catalogues, a demonstration of the fallacy of these catalogues, a demonstration of the fallacy of the true catalogue, the Gnostic gospel of Basilides, the commentary on this gospel, the commentary on the commentary of this gospel, the veridical[7] account of your death, a version of each book in all languages, the interpolations of every book in all books.

When it was proclaimed that the Library comprised all books, the first impression was one of extravagant joy. All men felt themselves lords of a secret, intact treasure. There was no personal or universal problem whose eloquent solution did not exist—in some hexagon. The universe was justified, the universe suddenly expanded to the limitless dimensions of hope. At that time there was much talk of the Vindications: books of apology and prophecy, which vindicated for all time the actions of every man in the world and established a store of prodigious arcana [8] for the future. Thousands of covetous persons abandoned their dear natal hexagons and crowded up the stairs, urged on by the vain aim of finding their Vindication. These pilgrims disputed in the narrow corridors, hurled dark maledictions, strangled each other on the divine stairways, flung the deceitful books to the bottom of the tunnels, and died as they were thrown into space by men from remote regions. Some went mad. . . .

---

[6]Formerly, for each three hexagons there was one man. Suicide and pulmonary diseases have destroyed this proportion. My memory recalls scenes of unspeakable melancholy: there have been many nights when I have ventured down corridors and polished staircases without encountering a single librarian. *[Author's note]*

[7]True.

[8]Secret knowledge.

The Vindications do exist. I have myself seen two of these books, which were concerned with future people, people who were perhaps not imaginary. But the searchers did not remember that the calculable possibility of a man's finding his own book, or some perfidious variation of his own book, is close to zero.

The clarification of the basic mysteries of humanity—the origin of the Library and of time—was also expected. It is credible that those grave mysteries can be explained in words: if the language of the philosophers does not suffice, the multiform Library will have produced the unexpected language required and the necessary vocabularies and grammars for this language.

It is now four centuries since men have been wearying the hexagons. . . .

There are official searchers, *inquisitors.* I have observed them carrying out their functions: they are always exhausted. They speak of a staircase without steps where they were almost killed. They speak of galleries and stairs with the local librarian. From time to time they will pick up the nearest book and leaf through its pages, in search of infamous words. Obviously, no one expects to discover anything.

The uncommon hope was followed, naturally enough, by deep depression. The certainty that some shelf in some hexagon contained precious books and that these books were inaccessible seemed almost intolerable. A blasphemous sect suggested that all searches be given up and that men everywhere shuffle letters and symbols until they succeeded in composing, by means of an improbable stroke of luck, the canonical books. The authorities found themselves obliged to issue severe orders. The sect disappeared, but in my childhood I still saw old men who would hide out in the privies for long periods of time, and, with metal disks in a forbidden dicebox, feebly mimic the divine disorder.

Other men, inversely, thought that the primary task was to eliminate useless works. They would invade the hexagons, exhibiting credentials which were not always false, skim through a volume with annoyance, and then condemn entire bookshelves to destruction: their ascetic, hygienic fury is responsible for the senseless loss of millions of books. Their name is execrated; but those who mourn the "treasures" destroyed by this frenzy, overlook two notorious facts. One: the Library is so enormous that any reduction undertaken by humans is infinitesimal. Two: each book is unique, irreplaceable, but (inasmuch as the Library is total) there are always several hundreds of thousands of imperfect facsimiles—of works which differ only by one letter or one comma. Contrary to public opinion, I dare suppose that the consequences of the depredations committed by the Purifiers have been exaggerated by the horror which these fanatics provoked. They were spurred by the delirium of storming the books in the Crimson Hexagon: books of a smaller than ordinary format, omnipotent, illustrated, magical.

We know, too, of another superstition of that time: the Man of the Book. In some shelf of some hexagon, men reasoned, there must exist a book which is the cipher [9] and perfect compendium of *all the rest:* some librarian has perused it, and it is analogous to a god. Vestiges of the worship of that remote functionary still persist in the language of this zone. Many pilgrimages have sought Him out. For a century they trod the most diverse routes in vain. How to locate the secret hexagon which harbored it? Someone proposed a regressive approach: in order to locate book A, first consult book B which will indicate the location of A; in order to locate book B, first consult book C, and so on ad infinitum. . . .

[9]Code.

I have squandered and consumed my years in adventures of this type. To me, it does not seem unlikely that on some shelf of the universe there lies a total book.[10] I pray the unknown gods that some man—even if only one man, and though it have been thousands of years ago!—may have examined and read it. If honor and wisdom and happiness are not for me, let them be for others. May heaven exist, though my place be in hell. Let me be outraged and annihilated, but may Thy enormous Library be justified, for one instant, in one being.

The impious assert that absurdities are the norm in the Library and that anything reasonable (even humble and pure coherence) is an almost miraculous exception. They speak (I know) of "the febrile Library, whose hazardous volumes run the constant risk of being changed into others and in which everything is affirmed, denied, and confused as by a divinity in delirium." These words, which not only denounce disorder but exemplify it as well, manifestly demonstrate the bad taste of the speakers and their desperate ignorance. Actually, the Library includes all verbal structures, all the variations allowed by the twenty-five orthographic symbols, but it does not permit of one absolute absurdity. It is pointless to observe that the best book in the numerous hexagons under my administration is entitled *Combed Clap of Thunder;* or that another is called *The Plaster Cramp;* and still another *Axaxaxas Mlö.* Such propositions as are contained in these titles, at first sight incoherent, doubtless yield a cryptographic or allegorical justification. Since they are verbal, these justifications already figure, *ex hypothesi,* in the Library. I can not combine certain letters, as *dhcmrlchtdj,* which the divine Library has not already foreseen in combination, and which in one of its secret languages does not encompass some terrible meaning. No one can articulate a syllable which is not full of tenderness and fear, and which is not, in one of those languages, the powerful name of some god. To speak is to fall into tautologies. This useless and wordy epistle itself already exists in one of the thirty volumes of the five shelves in one of the uncountable hexagons—and so does its refutation. (An *n* number of possible languages makes use of the same vocabulary; in some of them, the symbol *library* admits of the correct definition *ubiquitous and everlasting system of hexagonal galleries,* but *library* is *bread* or *pyramid* or anything else, and the seven words which define it possess another value. You who read me, are you sure you understand my language?)

Methodical writing distracts me from the present condition of men. But the certainty that everything has been already written nullifies or makes phantoms of us all. I know of districts where the youth prostrate themselves before books and barbarously kiss the pages, though they do not know how to make out a single letter. Epidemics, heretical disagreements, the pilgrimages which inevitably degenerate into banditry, have decimated the population. I believe I have mentioned the suicides, more frequent each year. Perhaps I am deceived by old age and fear, but I suspect that the human species—the unique human species—is on the road to extinction, while the Library will last on forever: illuminated, solitary, infinite, perfectly immovable, filled with precious volumes, useless, incorruptible, secret.

Infinite I have just written. I have not interpolated this adjective merely from rhetorical habit. It is not illogical, I say, to think that the world is infinite. Those who judge it to be

---

[10]I repeat: it is enough that a book be possible for it to exist. Only the impossible is excluded. For example: no book is also a stairway, though doubtless there are books that discuss and deny and demonstrate this possibility and others whose structure corresponds to that of a stairway. [*Author's note*]

limited, postulate that in remote places the corridors and stairs and hexagons could inconceivably cease—a manifest absurdity. Those who imagined it to be limitless forget that the possible number of books is limited. I dare insinuate the following solution to this ancient problem: *The Library is limitless and periodic.* If an eternal voyager were to traverse it in any direction, he would find, after many centuries, that the same volumes are repeated in the same disorder (which, repeated, would constitute an order: Order itself). My solitude rejoices in this elegant hope.[11]

Translated by Anthony Kerrigan

[11]Letizia Alvarez de Toledo has observed that the vast Library is useless. Strictly speaking, *one single volume* should suffice: a single volume of ordinary format, printed in nine or ten type body, and consisting of an infinite number of infinitely thin pages. (At the beginning of the seventeenth century, Cavalieri said that any solid body is the superposition of an infinite number of planes.) This silky vade mecum would scarcely be handy: each apparent leaf of the book would divide into other analogous leaves. The inconceivable central leaf would have no reverse. [*Author's note*]

Gabriela Mistral: I Am Not Alone (1922)

Gabriela Mistral, a Nobel laureate, is one of Chile's most distinguished writers. After an early love affair, tragically ended by the untimely death of her lover, she lived a life of self-described desolation, yearning for, but never experiencing motherhood. She turned her personal tragedy into beautiful poetry which offers intellectual and spiritual love, compassion, and courageous nurturance to others, especially children or others in need of protection.

What contrast is the poet drawing between the "deserted" world and her own state? Why is she "not alone?"

The night, it is deserted
from the mountains to the sea.
But I, the one who rocks you,
I am not alone!

The sky, it is deserted
for the moon falls to the sea.
But I, the one who holds you,
I am not alone !

The world, it is deserted.
All flesh is sad you see.
But I, the one who hugs you,
I am not alone!

Translated by Mary Gallwey

Gabriela Mistral: Tiny Feet (1922)

How does the poet make the child's tiny feet express its suffering?

A child's tiny feet,
Blue, blue with cold,
How can they see and not protect you?
Oh, my God!

Tiny wounded feet,
Bruised all over by pebbles,
Abused by snow and soil!

Man, being blind, ignores
that where you step, you leave
A blossom of bright light,
that where you have placed
your bleeding little soles
a redolent tuberose grows.

Since, however, you walk
through the streets so straight,
you are courageous, without fault.

Child's tiny feet,
Two suffering little gems,
How can the people pass, unseeing.

Translated by Mary Gallwey

Juana de Ibarbourou: The Hour (1918)

Juana de Ibarbourou, a Uruguayan poet, celebrates human life as a manifestation of nature. Many of her poems express the idea that death, though inevitable, is not final, but that the individual will transmigrate into another form, often returning as some kind of luxuriant floral growth. Her insistent demand, immediate and sensual, frankly expressed in the poem below, displays her desire to live life to the fullest before the death of the body. This theme, common in Western poetry from the Classical period forward, is known in Latin as Carpe diem, *"Seize the day."*

What is the poet's attitude toward her lover? What arguments is she using to persuade him to make love with her?

Take me now, while it is early
and I bear dahlia buds[1] in my hand

Take me now while still
my hair is dark.

Now, while I have fragrant flesh
and limpid eyes and rosy skin.

Now, while my nimble foot
wears the living sandal of spring.

Now, while on my lip is laughter
like a quickly shaken bell.

Afterwards . . . Oh! I know
that I will have none of these later.

And your desire then will be useless
like an offering placed on a tomb.

Take me now while it's still early
and my hands full of tuberoses.[2]

Today, no later. Before night falls
and the flower's fresh center wilts.

Today, not tomorrow. Oh, beloved, can't you see
that the vine will become a cypress tree?[3]

Translated by Mary Gallwey

---

[1]A symbol of youth.
[2]A lily-like flower.
[3]A symbol of death.

Rubén Darío (1867-1916): To Roosevelt (1905)

Theodore Roosevelt was the individual who most represented the US incursions into Latin America that outraged even nonpolitical poets such as Rubén Darío (Nicaragua, 1867-1916). Latin Americans had admired the energy, wealth, and democracy of the United States, but now they feared the bullying of their northern neighbor. President Roosevelt supported a 1903 revolution in Panama that resulted in the annexation by the U.S. of territory for the Panama Canal, and in 1904 proclaimed a corollary to the Monroe Doctrine which justified the use of the U.S. military to "police" Latin America.

What positive qualities does Darío boast Latin America has? What are the main characteristics he associates with Roosevelt and the United States?

It is with the voice of the Bible, or the verse of Walt Whitman,
that I should come to you, Hunter,
primitive and modern, simple and complicated,
with something of Washington and more of Nimrod.[1]

You are the United States,
you are the future invader
of the naive America that has Indian blood,
that still prays to Jesus Christ and still speaks Spanish.

You are the proud and strong exemplar of your race;
you are cultured, you are skillful; you oppose Tolstoy[2]
And breaking horses, or murdering tigers,
you are an Alexander-Nebuchadnezzar.[3]
(You are a professor of Energy
as today's madmen say.)

You think that life is fire,
that progress is eruption,
that wherever you shoot
you hit the future.

No.

The United States is potent and great.
When you shake there is a deep tremor
that passes through the enormous vertebrae of the Andes.

---

[1]Nimrod is said to be a "mighty hunter" in Genesis 10:8-9. Roosevelt was renowned for his hunting prowess.
[2]Roosevelt was much in the news in 1905 because of his role in mediating an end to the Russo-Japanese War. Tolstoy, one of Russia's greatest writers, was an ardent pacifist and advocate of the poor.
[3]A combination of two ancient empire-builders: Alexander the Great of Macedon and the Babylonian conqueror of Jerusalem.

If you clamor, it is heard like the roaring of a lion.
Hugo[4] already said it to Grant: The stars are yours.
(The Argentine sun, ascending, barely shines,
and the Chilean star rises . . .) You are rich.
You join the cult of Hercules to the cult of Mammon,[5]
and illuminating the road of easy conquest,
Liberty raises its torch in New York.

But our America, that has had poets
since the ancient times of Netzahualcoyotl,[6]
that has walked in the footprints of great Bacchus
who learned Pan's alphabet at once;[7]
that consulted the stars, that knew Atlantis[8]
whose resounding name comes to us from Plato,
that since the remote times of its life
has lived on light, on fire, on perfume, on love,
America of the great Montezuma, of the Inca,
the fragrant America of Christopher Columbus,
Catholic America, Spanish America,
the America in which noble Cuahtemoc said:
"I'm not in a bed of roses";[9] that America
that trembles in hurricanes and lives on love,
it lives, you men of Saxon eyes and barbarous soul.
And it dreams. And it loves, and it vibrates, and it is the daughter of the Sun.
Be careful. Viva Spanish America!
There are a thousand cubs loosed from the Spanish lion.
Roosevelt, one would have to be, through God himself,
the fearful Rifleman and strong Hunter,
to manage to grab us in your iron claws.

And, although you count on everything, you lack one thing: God!

Translated by Bonnie Frederick

[4]Victor Hugo, French poet and radical activist, was living in exile when he hailed Ulysses S. Grant's United States as heir to the democratic tradition which had been betrayed in France.

[5]Hercules represents power; Mammon, wealth.

[6]A famous Aztec warrior-poet.

[7]Pan was in Greek mythology inventor of the alphabet. Darío is stressing that the Aztecs and other Native American peoples had writing long before the coming of the Europeans.

[8]There is a Latin American tradition that claims that the vanished civilization of Atlantis, described in Plato's *Timaeus* and *Critias* was actually located in the Western Hemisphere.

[9]These are the words said to have been utterered stoically by the successor to Montezuma when he was being tortured by the Spanish after the defeat of the Aztecs to encourage one of his fellow Aztecs not to betray his people.

Gabriel García Márquez: The Handsomest Drowned Man in the World: A Tale for Children (1968)

Novelist and short story writer García Márquez was raised by grandparents who immersed him in the folklore and legends of his native Colombia. After a global career as a journalist, he settled in Mexico, where he continues to pursue a distinguished career as a writer. His literary technique has been called "magical realism," because it often treats extraordinary and even supernatural events as if they were perfectly ordinary: an approach to narrative García Márquez claims he learned from his grandmother. The following selection reveals his keen sense of place and character, as well as the folkways of death.

What does the story have to say about the ways in which people deal with death?

The first children who saw the dark and slinky bulge approaching through the sea let themselves think it was an enemy ship. Then they saw it had no flags or masts and they thought it was a whale. But when it washed up on the beach, they removed the clumps of seaweed, the jellyfish tentacles, and the remains of fish and flotsam, and only then did they see that it was a drowned man.

They had been playing with him all afternoon, burying him in the sand and digging him up again, when someone chanced to see them and spread the alarm in the village. The men who carried him to the nearest house noticed that he weighed more than any dead man they had ever known, almost as much as a horse, and they said to each other that maybe he'd been floating too long and the water had got into his bones. When they laid him on the floor they said he'd been taller than all other men because there was barely enough room for him in the house, but they thought that maybe the ability to keep on growing after death was part of the nature of certain drowned men. He had the smell of the sea about him and only his shape gave one to suppose that it was the corpse of a human being, because the skin was covered with a crust of mud and scales.

They did not even have to clean off his face to know that the dead man was a stranger. The village was made up of only twenty-odd wooden houses that had stone courtyards with no flowers and which were spread about on the end of a desert-like cape. There was so little land that mothers always went about with the fear that the wind would carry off their children and the few dead that the years had caused among them had to be thrown off the cliffs. But the sea was calm and bountiful and all the men fit into seven boats. So when they found the drowned man they simply had to look at one another to see that they were all there.

That night they did not go out to work at sea. While the men went to find out if anyone was missing in neighboring villages, the women stayed behind to care for the drowned man. They took the mud off with grass swabs, they removed the underwater stones entangled in his hair, and they scraped the crust off with tools used for scaling fish. As they were doing that they noticed that the vegetation on him came from faraway oceans and deep water and that his clothes were in tatters, as if he had sailed through labyrinths of coral. They noticed too that he bore his death with pride, for he did not have the lonely look of other drowned men who came out of the sea or that haggard, needy look of men who drowned in rivers. But only when they finished cleaning him off did they become aware of the kind of man he was and it left them breathless. Not only was he the tallest, strongest, most virile, and best built man they had ever seen, but even though they were looking at him there was no room for him in their imagination.

They could not find a bed in the village large enough to lay him on nor was there a table solid enough to use for his wake. The tallest men's holiday pants would not fit him, nor the fattest ones' Sunday shirts, nor the shoes of the one with the biggest feet. Fascinated by his huge size and his beauty, the women then decided to make him some pants from a large piece of sail and a shirt from some bridal brabant linen[1] so that he could continue through his death with dignity. As they sewed, sitting in a circle and gazing at the corpse between stitches, it seemed to them that the wind had never been so steady nor the sea so restless as on that night and they supposed that the change had something to do with the dead man. They thought that if that magnificent man had lived in the village, his house would have had the widest doors, the highest ceiling, and the strongest floor, his bedstead would have been made from a midship frame held together by iron bolts, and his wife would have been the happiest woman. They thought that he would have had so much authority that he could have drawn fish out of the sea simply by calling their names and that he would have put so much work into his land that springs would have burst forth from among the rocks so that he would have been able to plant flowers on the cliffs. They secretly compared him to their own men, thinking that for all their lives theirs were incapable of doing what he could do in one night, and they ended up dismissing them deep in their hearts as the weakest, meanest, and most useless creatures on earth. They were wandering through that maze of fantasy when the oldest woman, who as the oldest had looked upon the drowned man with more compassion than passion, sighed:

"He has the face of someone called Esteban."

It was true. Most of them had only to take another look at him to see that he could not have any other name. The more stubborn among them, who were the youngest, still lived for a few hours with the illusion that when they put his clothes on and he lay among the flowers in patent leather shoes his name might be Lautaro. But it was a vain illusion. There had not been enough canvas, the poorly cut and worse sewn pants were too tight, and the hidden strength of his heart popped the buttons on his shirt. After midnight the whistling of the wind died down and the sea fell into its Wednesday drowsiness. The silence put an end to any last doubts: he was Esteban. The women who had dressed him, who had combed his hair, had cut his nails and shaved him were unable to hold back a shudder of pity when they had to resign themselves to his being dragged along the ground. It was then that they understood how unhappy he must have been with that huge body since it bothered him even after death. They could see him in life, condemned to going through doors sideways, cracking his head on crossbeams, remaining on his feet during visits, not knowing what to do with his soft, pink, sea lion hands while the lady of the house looked for her most resistant chair and begged him, frightened to death, sit here, Esteban, please, and he, leaning against the wall, smiling, don't bother, ma'am, I'm fine where I am, his heels raw and his back roasted from having done the same thing so many times whenever he paid a visit, don't bother, ma'am, I'm fine where I am, just to avoid the embarrassment of breaking up the chair, and never knowing perhaps that the ones who said don't go, Esteban, at least wait till the coffee's ready, were the ones who later on would whisper the big boob finally left, how nice, the handsome fool has gone. That was what the women were thinking beside the body a little before dawn. Later, when they covered his face with a handkerchief so that the light would not bother him, he looked so forever dead, so defenseless, so much like their men that the first furrows of tears opened in their hearts. It was one of the

[1]Especially fine linen, imported from the city of Brabant, now in Belgium.

younger ones who began the weeping. The others coming to, went from sighs to wails, and the more they sobbed the more they felt like weeping, because the drowned man was becoming all the more Esteban for them, and so they wept so much, for he was the most destitute, most peaceful, and most obliging man on earth, poor Esteban. So when the men returned with the news that the drowned man was not from the neighboring villages either, the women felt an opening of jubilation in the midst of their tears.

"Praise the Lord," they sighed, "he's ours!"

The men thought the fuss was only womanish frivolity. Fatigued because of the difficult nighttime inquiries, all they wanted was to get rid of the bother of the newcomer once and for all before the sun grew strong on that arid, windless day. They improvised a litter with the remains of foremasts and gaffs, tying it together with rigging so that it would bear the weight of the body until they reached the cliffs. They wanted to tie the anchor from a cargo ship to him so that he would sink easily into the deepest waves, where fish are blind and divers die of nostalgia, and bad currents would not bring him back to shore, as had happened with other bodies. But the more they hurried, the more the women thought of ways to waste time. They walked about like startled hens, pecking with the sea charms on their breasts, some interfering on one side to put a scapular[2] of the good wind on the drowned man, some on the other side to put a wrist compass on him, and after a great deal of *get away from there, woman, stay out of the way, look, you almost made me fall on top of the dead man,* the men began to feel mistrust in their livers and started grumbling about why so many main-altar decorations for a stranger, because no matter how many nails and holy-water jars he had on him, the sharks would chew him all the same, but the women kept piling on their junk relics, running back and forth, stumbling, while they released in sighs what they did not in tears, so that the men finally exploded with *since when has there ever been such a fuss over a drifting corpse, a drowned nobody, a piece of cold Wednesday meat.* One of the women, mortified by so much lack of care, then removed the handkerchief from the dead man's face and the men were left breathless too.

He was Esteban. It was not necessary to repeat it for them to recognize him. If they had been told Sir Walter Raleigh, even they might have been impressed with his gringo accent, the macaw on his shoulder, his cannibal killing blunderbuss, but there could be only one Esteban in the world and there he was, stretched out like a sperm whale, shoeless, wearing the pants of an undersized child, and with those stony nails that had to be cut with a knife. They only had to take the handkerchief off his face to see that he was ashamed, that it was not his fault that he was so big or so heavy or so handsome, and if he had known that this was going to happen, he would have looked for a more discreet place to drown in, seriously, I even would have tied the anchor off a galleon around my neck and staggered off a cliff like someone who doesn't like things in order not to be upsetting people now with this Wednesday dead body, as you people say, in order not to be bothering anyone with this filthy piece of cold meat that doesn't have anything to do with me. There was so much truth in his manner that even the most mistrustful men, the ones who felt the bitterness of endless nights at sea fearing that their women would tire of dreaming about them and begin to dream of drowned men, even they and others who were harder still shuddered in the marrow of their bones at Esteban's sincerity.

That was how they came to hold the most splendid funeral they could conceive of for an abandoned drowned man. Some women who had gone to get flowers in the neighboring villages returned with other women who could not believe what they had been told, and

---

[2]A sleeveless garment worn over one's clothes as a sign of religious devotion.

those women went back for more flowers when they saw the dead man, and they brought more and more until there were so many flowers and so many people that it was hard to walk about. At the final moment it pained them to return him to the waters as an orphan and they chose a father and mother from among the best people, and aunts and uncles and cousins, so that through him all the inhabitants of the village became kinsmen. Some sailors who heard the weeping from a distance went off course and people heard of one who had himself tied to the mainmast, remembering ancient fables about sirens. While they fought for the privilege of carrying him on their shoulders along the steep escarpment by the cliffs, men and women became aware for the first time of the desolation of their streets, the dryness of their courtyards, the narrowness of their dreams as they faced the splendor and beauty of their drowned man. They let him go without an anchor so that he could come back if he wished and whenever he wished, and they all held their breath for the fraction of centuries the body took to fall into the abyss. They did not need to look at one another to realize that they were no longer all present, that they would never be. But they also knew that everything would be different from then on, that their houses would have wider doors, higher ceilings, and stronger floors so that Esteban's memory could go everywhere without bumping into beams and so that no one in the future would dare whisper the big boob finally died, too bad, the handsome fool has finally died, because they were going to paint their house fronts gay colors to make Esteban's memory eternal and they were going to break their backs digging for springs among the stones and planting flowers on the cliffs so that in future years at dawn the passengers on great liners would awaken, suffocated by the smell of gardens on the high seas, and the captain would have to come down from the bridge in his dress uniform, with his astrolabe, his pole star, and his row of war medals and, pointing to the promontory of roses on the horizon, he would say in fourteen languages, look there, where the wind is so peaceful now that it's gone to sleep beneath the beds, over there, where the sun's so bright that the sunflowers don't know which way to turn, yes, over there, that's Esteban's village.

Translated by Gregory Rabassa

Gustavo Gutiérrez: *A Theology of Liberation: History, Politics and Salvation* (1973)

Some Latin American priests responded to the liberal papacy of Pope John XXIII by rejecting the Church's traditional alliance with the rich and powerful in most countries for a more socially concerned way of thought called "liberation theology." Blending Marxism with liberal Catholicism, they engaged in struggles to win better living conditions for the poor. They attained widespread support among those they sought to help and vigorous opposition from the powerful, including the hierarchy of the Church. When Catholicism turned more conservative, their writings were severely censured and their programs halted. Yet they continue to inspire many, both inside and outside the Catholic Church, who wish to combine social activism with religious faith. The Peruvian founding father of liberation theology here attacks the traditional interpretation of the gospel which sees asceticism as spiritually improving. The poverty of spirit of which the gospel speaks has for Gutiérrez nothing to do with material impoverishment.

According to Gutiérrez, what was the purpose of the communism practiced by the early Christians?

Material poverty is a scandalous condition. Spiritual poverty is an attitude of openness to God and spiritual childhood. Having clarified these two meanings of the term poverty we have cleared the path and can now move forward towards a better understanding of the Christian witness of poverty. We turn now to a third meaning of the term: poverty as a commitment of solidarity and protest.

We have laid aside the first two meanings. The first is subtly deceptive; the second partial and insufficient. In the first place, if material poverty is something to be rejected, as the Bible vigorously insists, then a witness of poverty cannot make of it a Christian ideal. This would be to aspire to a condition which is recognized as degrading to man. It would be, moreover, to move against the current of history. It would be to oppose any idea of the domination of nature by man and the consequent and progressive creation of better conditions of life. And finally, but not least seriously, it would be to justify, even if involuntarily, the injustice and exploitation which is the cause of poverty.

On the other hand, our analysis of the Biblical texts concerning spiritual poverty has helped us to see that it is not directly or in the first instance an interior detachment from the goods of this world, a spiritual attitude which becomes authentic by incarnating itself in material poverty. Spiritual poverty is something more complete and profound. It is above all total availability to the Lord. Its relationship to the use or ownership of economic goods is inescapable, but secondary and partial. Spiritual childhood—an ability to receive, not a passive acceptance—defines the total posture of human existence before God, men, and things.

How are we therefore to understand the evangelical meaning of the witness of a real, material, concrete poverty? *Lumen gentium*[1] invites us to look for the deepest meaning of Christian poverty in Christ: "Just as Christ carried out the work of redemption in poverty and under oppression, so the Church is called to follow the same path in communicating to men the fruits of salvation. Christ Jesus, though He was by nature God . . . emptied himself, taking the nature of a slave (Philippians 2:6), and being rich, he became poor (2

[1] *A Light to the Nations,* by a team of liberal theological professors in Argentina in 1966.

Corinthians 8:9) for our sakes. . . .

The taking on of the servile and sinful condition of man, as foretold in Second Isaiah, is presented by Paul as an act of voluntary impoverishment: "For you know how generous our Lord Jesus Christ has been: He was rich, yet for your sake he became poor, so that through his poverty you might become rich" (2 Corinthians 8:9). This is the humiliation of Christ, his kenosis (Philippians 2:6-11). But he does not take on man's sinful condition and its consequences to idealize it. It is rather because of love for and solidarity with men who suffer in it. It is to redeem them from their sin and to enrich them with his poverty. It is to struggle against human selfishness and everything that divides men and enables there to be rich and poor, possessors and dispossessed, oppressors and oppressed.

Poverty is an act of love and liberation. It has a redemptive value. If the ultimate cause of man's exploitation and alienation is selfishness, the deepest reason for voluntary poverty is love of neighbor. Christian poverty has meaning only as a commitment of solidarity with the poor, with those who suffer misery and injustice. The commitment is to witness to the evil which has resulted from sin and is a breach of communion. It is not a question of idealizing poverty, but rather of taking it on as it is—an evil—to protest against it and to struggle to abolish it. As Ricoeur[2] says, you cannot really be with the poor unless you are struggling against poverty. Because of this solidarity—which must manifest itself in specific action, a style of life, a break with one's social class—one can also help the poor and exploited to become aware of their exploitation and seek liberation from it. Christian poverty, an expression of love, is solidarity with the poor and is a protest against poverty. This is the concrete, contemporary meaning of the witness of poverty. It is a poverty lived not for its own sake, but rather as an authentic imitation of Christ; it is a poverty which means taking on the sinful condition of man to liberate him from sin and all its consequences.

Luke[3] presents the community of goods in the early Church as an ideal. "All whose faith had drawn them together held everything in common" (Acts 2:44); "not a man of them claimed any of his possessions as his own, but everything was held in common" (Acts 4:33). They did this with a profound unity, one "in heart and soul" (ibid.). But as J. Dupont correctly points out, this was not a question of erecting poverty as an ideal, but rather of seeing to it that there were no poor: "They had never a needy person among them, because all who had property in land or houses sold it, brought the proceeds of the sale, and laid the money at the feet of the apostles; it was then distributed to any who stood in need" (Acts 4:34-35). The meaning of the community of goods is clear: to eliminate poverty because of love of the poor person. Dupont rightly concludes, "If goods are held in common, it is not therefore in order to become poor for love of an ideal of poverty; rather it is so that there will be no poor. The ideal pursued is, once again, charity, a true love for the poor."

We must pay special attention to the words we use. The term poor might seem not only vague and churchy, but also somewhat sentimental and aseptic. The "poor" person today is the oppressed one, the one marginated from society, the member of the proletariat struggling for his most basic rights; he is the exploited and plundered social class, the country struggling for its liberation. In today's world the solidarity and protest of which we are

---

[2]French philosopher Paul Ricoeur, who advocates social activism

[3]Author of the book of Acts, which traces events in the history of the early Christian church.

speaking have an evident and inevitable "political" character insofar as they imply liberation. To be with the oppressed is to be against the oppressor. In our times and on our continent to be in solidarity with the "poor," understood in this way, means to run personal risks—even to put one's life in danger. Many Christians—and non-Christians—who are committed to the Latin American revolutionary process are running these risks. And so there are emerging new ways of living poverty which are different from the classic "renunciation of the goods of this world."

Only by rejecting poverty and by making itself poor in order to protest against it can the Church preach something that is uniquely its own: "spiritual poverty," that is, the openness of man and history to the future promised by God. Only in this way will the Church be able to fulfill authentically—and with any possibility of being listened to—its prophetic function of denouncing every injustice to man. And only in this way will it be able to preach the word which liberates, the word of genuine brotherhood.

Only authentic solidarity with the poor and a real protest against the poverty of our time can provide the concrete, vital context necessary for a theological discussion of poverty. The absence of a sufficient commitment to the poor, the marginated, and the exploited is perhaps the fundamental reason why we have no solid contemporary reflection on the witness of poverty.

For the Latin American Church especially, this witness is an inescapable and much-needed sign of the authenticity of its mission.

Translated by Sister Caridad Inda and John Eagleson

Louise Bennett: Colonization in Reverse

Louise Bennett is a popular Jamaican poet now living in Canada who artfully uses the island dialect to comment on contemporary Caribbean life. Jamaica was a former British colony, and she points out that one of the unexpected consequences of the empire-building of the past is the continued influx of former colonists into the former colonial nations. Just as the legacy of slavery lives on, so does that of colonialism. As the comments about the lazy woman named Jane reflect, Bennett's verse is not militant: she sees human frailty on all sides; but she surely means to call attention to the fact that the British cannot logically ignore the needs of those it once claimed to protect.

The narrator seems proud of this form of "colonization;" how do her words actually constitute a critique of classic colonialism?

Wat a joyful news, Miss Mattie,
I feel like me heart gwine burs'
Jamaica people colonizin
Englan in reverse.

By de hundred, by de t'ousan
From country and from town,
By de ship-load, by de plane-load
Jamaica is Englan boun.

Dem a-pour out o' Jamaica,
Everybody future plan
Is fe[1] get a big-time job
An settle in de mother lan.

What a islan! What a people!
Man an woman, old an young
Jusa pack dem bag an baggage
An tun history upside dung![2]

Some people don't like travel,
But fe show dem loyalty
Dem all a-open up cheap-fare-
To-Englan agency.

An week by week dem shippin off
Dem countryman like fire,
Fe immigrate an populate
De seat o' de Empire.

---

[1]To.
[2]Turn history upside down.

Oonoo[3] see how life is funny,
Oonoo see de tunabout,
Jamaica live fe box bread
Outa English people mout'.

For wen dem catch a Englan,
An start play dem different role,
Some will settle down to work
An some will settle fe de dole.

Jane say de dole is not too bad
Because dey payin' she
Two pounds a week fe seek a job
Dat suit her dignity.

Me say Jane will never find work
At the rate how she dah-look,
For all day she stay pon Aunt Fan couch
An read love-story book.

Wat a devilment a Englan!
Dem face war an brave de worse,
But I'm wonderin' how dem gwine stan'
Colonizin' in reverse.

---

[3]Oh now.

Derek Walcott: Hurucan

A graduate of the University of West Indies in Kingston, Jamaica, Derek Walcott grew up a "divided child," black with a white grandparent, Methodist in a Catholic country (the island of St. Lucia). Both dramatist and poet, his work reflects the varied roots of Caribbean culture. In this work he uses the Spanish word for "hurricane" to allude to the region's Spanish past, but it is the vanished Native Americans of the islands that he is really celebrating. The poem begins with a flash of lightning and a torrential downpour which lead to the windstorm itself, the only god who has survived the massacre of the ancient culture, now returned to assert his power. Even as observors grasp for alien metaphors to describe him, he is the god of the place. Walcott won the Nobel Prize for literature in 1992.

What historical event has made the god angry? What at the end of the poem symbolizes Hurucan's power over modern civilization?

I.

Once branching light startles the hair of the coconuts,
and on the villas' asphalt roofs, rain
resonates like pebbles in a pan,
and only the skirts of surf
waltz round the abandoned bandstand,
and we hear the telephone cables
hallooing like fingers tapped over an Indian's mouth,
once the zinc roofs begin wrenching their nails
like freight uncrated with a crowbar,
we remember you[1] as the possible
deity of the whistling marsh-canes,
we doubt that you were ever slain
by the steel Castilian[2] lances
of a thousand horizons,
deity of the yellow-skinned ones
who thatched your temple with plantains.[3]

When the power station's blackout
grows frightening as amnesia,
and the luxury resorts
revert to the spear-tips of candles,
and the swimming pools in their marsh-light
multiply with hysterical lilies
like the beaks of fledglings uttering your name,
when lightning fizzles out

[1]"Hurucan," personified as the god of hurricanes.
[2]Spanish, referring to the Spanish invaders whose arrival led to the almost complete extermination of the original inhabitants of the islands.
[3]A relative of the banana.

in the wireless,[4] we can see and hear
the streaming black locks of clouds,
flesh the gamboge[5] of lightning,
and the epicanthic, almond-shaped eye[6]
of the whirling cyclops,[7]
runner through the cloud-smoke,
our ocean's marathon strider,
the only survivor
of their massacred deities

whose temples change
like the clouds over Yucatán
in the copper twilight over Ecuador,
runner who can grip the mares' tails
of galloping cirrus,[8]
vaulting the dead conquistadors of the helmeted palms.[9]
You'd never reply
to the name of the northern messenger[10]
whose zigzagging trident
pitchforks the oaks like straw,
nor to the thunderous tambours
of Shango;[11] you rage
till we get your name right,
till the surf and bent palms dance
to your tune, even if, at your entrance,
clouds plod the horizon like caparisoned[12] camels,
and the wind begins to unwhirl
like a burnoose;[13] you abhor
all other parallels
but our own,
Hurucan.

---

[4]Radio.

[5]A bright yellow dye.

[6]The epicanthic fold of the upper eyelid is what gives "almond-shaped" Asian eyes their distinctive appearance; Native Americans possess it as well, their distant ancestors being related to the ancient peoples of Siberia. The storm has an eye, but it is an Indian eye.

[7]One-eyed monster of classical mythology.

[8]"Mares' tails" is a popular name for high, wispy cirrus clouds.

[9]The coconut palm trees are fancifully compared to the old Spanish conquistadors; the coconut shells are their battle helmets.

[10]Thor is the Norse god of lightning, associated with oak trees. Here he represents European culture.

[11]Shango or Xango is a West African God of storms whose cult is still observed in some parts of the Caribbean.

[12] Cloth-draped.

[13]The long robe worn by Arab nomads.

You scream like a man whose wife is dead,
like a god who has lost his race,
you yank the electric wires with wet hands.

Then we think of a different name
than the cute ones christened by radar,[14]
in the sludge that sways
next day by the greased pierheads
where a rowboat still rocks in fear,
and Florida now flares to your flashbulb
and the map of Texas rattles,[15]
and we lie awake in the dark
by the dripping stelae of candles,[16]
our heads gigantified on the walls,[17]
and think you, still running
with tendons feathered with lightning,
water-worrier, whom the chained trees
strain to follow,
havoc, reminder, ancestor,
and, when morning enters, pale
as an insurance broker,[18]
god.

II.

The sea almond's dress
is drenched in the morning,
the leaves drip on their clotheslines[19]
like wax drops from candles,
the pent waves circle their fences
like witless sheep.
A freighter is parked
on the coastal road to the airport,
and the birds won't be back
for some time. The chairs
around the bandstand are heaped up
like the morning after your dance,

---

[14]The Weather Service assigns personal names in alphabetical order to all tropical storms, and tracks them on radar.

[15]Caribbean storms often move onto the U.S. mainland.

[16]Since the broken electric lines have cut off the electricity, the only light comes from candles. Stelae are pillars.

[17]The candles cast huge shadows.

[18]The insurance brokers are pale because they are aghast at how much they will have to pay to repair the damage.

[19]Seaweed is hanging from clotheslines. This passage describes the disarray and wreckage left behind by the storm.

and the worms we have buried underground
spark and stutter again.[20] Roofs
are scattered all over the hillsides
like cards dropped during a shoot-out,
and the sea starts the pompous thunder
of a military funeral
as spray shoots up round the kiosk
where the Police Band played.

We return the pieces of fear
to their proper place,
the shelf at the back of the mind—
the artifacts, the Carib[21] arrowheads,
the pin-pierced amulets,
and that force whose weather vanes
are the slow-spinning frigates.
Your name fades again in the grounded
flights; there in dark hangars
the mineral patience of cattle—
a cold sweat slides down the silver
hides of the empty planes.

---

[20]When the ground becomes too saturated with water, worms emerge on the surface to keep from drowning; these are compared to underground electrical wires.
[21]The Caribs are one of the original native peoples of the Caribbean, now remembered only through their artifacts.

North America 1900–Present

T. S. Eliot: The Preludes (1917)

T. S. Eliot was born in St. Louis and educated at Harvard University, but most of his adult life was passed in London. In the vanguard of the artistic movement known as Modernism, Eliot was a unique innovator in poetry and The Waste Land *(1922) stands as one of the most original and influential poems of the twentieth century. As a young man he suffered a religious crisis and a nervous breakdown before regaining his emotional equilibrium and Christian faith. His early poetry, including "Preludes," deals with spiritually exhausted people who exist in the impersonal, tawdry modern city. "Preludes" impressionistically captures the impoverished spiritual lives of those living in a lonely, sordid, decadent culture.*

Eliot was an important literary critic who once observed, "The only way of expressing emotion in the form of art is by finding an "objective correlative;" in other words, a set of objects, a situation, a chain of events, which shall be the formula of that particular emotion. . . ." Can one find an "objective correlative" in "Preludes" that results in a specific emotion?

I

The winter evening settles down
With smell of steaks in passageways.
Six o'clock.
The burnt-out ends of smoky days.
And now a gusty shower wraps
The grimy scraps
Of withered leaves about your feet
And newspapers from vacant lots;
The showers beat
On broken blinds and chimneypots,
And at the corner of the street
A lonely cab-horse steams and stamps.
And then the lighting of the lamps.

II

The morning comes to consciousness
Of faint stale smells of beer
From the sawdust-trampled street
With all its muddy feet that press
To early coffee-stands.

With the other masquerades
That time resumes,
One thinks of all the hands
That are raising dingy shades
In a thousand furnished rooms.

III

You tossed a blanket from the bed
You lay upon your back, and waited;
You dozed, and watched the night revealing
The thousand sordid images
Of which your soul was constituted;
They flickered against the ceiling.
And when all the world came back
And the light crept up between the shutters
And you heard the sparrows in the gutters,
You had such a vision of the street
As the street hardly understands;
Sitting along the bed's edge, where
You curled the papers from your hair,
Or clasped the yellow soles of feet
In the palms of both soiled hands.

IV

His soul stretched tight across the skies
That fade behind a city block,
Or trampled by insistent feet
At four and five and six o'clock;
And short square fingers stuffing pipes,
And evening newspapers, and eyes
Assured of certain certainties,
The conscience of a blackened street
Impatient to assume the world.

I am moved by fancies that are curled
Around these images, and cling:
The notion of some infinitely gentle
Infinitely suffering thing.

Wipe your hand across your mouth, and laugh;
The worlds revolve like ancient women
Gathering fuel in vacant lots.

Robert Frost: The Road Not Taken (1915)

This poem is usually interpreted as an assertion of individualism, but critic Lawrence Thompson has argued that it is a slightly mocking satire on a perennially hesitant walking partner of Frost's who always wondered what would have happened if he had chosen their path differently.

What evidence can you find in the poem to support each of these views?

Two roads diverged in a yellow wood,
And sorry I could not travel both
And be one traveler, long I stood
And looked down one as far as I could
To where it bent in the undergrowth;

Then took the other, as just as fair,
And having perhaps the better claim,
Because it was grassy and wanted wear;
Though as for that the passing there
Had worn them really about the same.

And both that morning equally lay
In leaves no step had trodden black.
Oh, I kept the first for another day!
Yet knowing how way leads on to way,
I doubted if I should ever come back.

I shall be telling this with a sigh
Somewhere ages and ages hence:
Two roads diverged in a wood, and I—
I took the one less traveled by,
And that has made all the difference.

H. D. (Hilda Doolittle): Sea Poppies (1916)

In the late 19th and early 20th centuries Japanese arts made a considerable impact on the West. The traditional Japanese esthetic of understatement, subtlety and refinement had great appeal for a generation that was rebelling against romantic excess. Japanese prints influenced impressionist painters, Japanese music influenced impressionist composers, and the compact art of the Japanese haiku transformed the thinking of many western poets. Particularly strongly influenced were the Imagists, a group of English and American poets who strove for a highly compressed yet natural kind of poetry. One of the more prominent Imagists was the American Hilda Doolittle, who in her collection Sea Garden *published a series of poems about flowers beside the ocean. The result is both longer and more elaborate than a* waka *or* haiku, *but strives for the same concentrated attention to simple but beautiful elements of nature.*

Compare this poem with Basho's haiku. What does it have in common with them? What is different about it?

Amber husk
fluted with gold,
fruit on the sand
marked with a rich grain,

treasure
spilled near the shrub-pines
to bleach on the boulders:

your stalk has caught root
among wet pebbles
and drift flung by the sea
and grated shells
and split conch-shells.

Beautiful, wide-spread,
fire upon leaf,
what meadow yields
so fragrant a leaf
as your bright leaf?

Claude McKay: If We Must Die (1919)

In 1919 there was a wave of race riots consisting mainly of white assaults on black neighborhoods in a dozen American cities. Jamaican-born writer Claude McKay responded by writing this sonnet, urging his comrades to fight back. It had a powerful impact, then and later.

For what reason does McKay say even a doomed resistance is worth while?

If we must die, let it not be like hogs
Hunted and penned in an inglorious spot,
While round us bark the mad and hungry dogs,
Making their mock at our accursed lot.
If we must die, O let us nobly die,
So that our precious blood may not be shed
In vain; then even the monsters we defy
Shall be constrained to honor us though dead!
O kinsmen we must meet the common foe!
Though far outnumbered let us show us brave,
And for their thousand blows deal one deathblow!
What though before us lies the open grave?
Like men we'll face the murderous, cowardly pack,
Pressed to the wall, dying, but fighting back!

Malcolm X: Declaration of Independence, December 4, 1963

Not long after he made his first trip to Mecca and other parts of the Middle East, Malcolm X began to drift away from Elijah Muhammad, founder of the Nation of Islam (informally called the "Black Muslims"). The tension erupted into an open break when Malcolm reacted to the Kennedy assassination in a way that brought widespread condemnation of the Nation. Malcolm proceeded to announce the founding of a rival organization in this speech. The experience of seeing in Mecca Muslims of all races worshipping side by side had challenged his belief in racial separation, but it had not made him less militant or outspoken against racism in America. He was constantly being contrasted in the press with Martin Luther King, Jr., who advocated Gandhian nonviolent resistance to combat racism. In a little more than a year he was dead, shot down by assassins from the Nation of Islam.

Why does Malcolm X reject moving back to Africa as the complete answer to the problems of African-Americans?

Because 1964 threatens to be a very explosive year on the racial front, and because I myself intend to be very active in every phase of the American Negro struggle for *human rights,* I have called this press conference this morning in order to clarify my own position in the struggle—especially in regard to politics and nonviolence.

I am and always will be a Muslim. My religion is Islam. I still believe that Mr. Muhammad's analysis of the problem is the most realistic, and that his solution is the best one. This means that I too believe the best solution is complete separation, with our people going back home, to our own African homeland.

But separation back to Africa is still a long-range program, and while it is yet to materialize, 22 million of our people who are still here in America need better food, clothing, housing, education and jobs *right now.* Mr. Muhammad's program does point us back homeward, but it also contains within it what we could and should be doing to help solve many of our own problems while we are still here.

Internal differences within the Nation of Islam forced me out of it. I did not leave of my own free will. But now that it has happened, I intend to make the most of it. Now that I have more independence of action, I intend to use a more flexible approach toward working with others to get a solution to this problem.

I do not pretend to be a divine man, but I do believe in divine guidance, divine power, and in the fulfillment of divine prophecy. I am not educated, nor am I an expert in any particular field—but I am sincere, and my sincerity is my credentials.

I'm not out to fight other Negro leaders or organizations. We must find a common approach, a common solution, to a common problem. As of this minute, I've forgotten everything bad that the other leaders have said about me, and I pray they can also forget the many bad things I've said about them.

The problem facing our people here in America is bigger than all other personal or organizational differences. Therefore, as leaders, we must stop worrying about the threat that we seem to think we pose to each other's personal prestige, and concentrate our united efforts toward solving the unending hurt that is being done daily to our people here in America.

I am going to organize and head a new mosque in New York City, known as the Muslim Mosque, Inc. This gives us a religious base, and the spiritual force necessary to rid our people of the vices that destroy the moral fiber of our community.

Our political philosophy will be black nationalism. Our economic and social philosophy will be black nationalism. Our cultural emphasis will be black nationalism. . . .

The political philosophy of black nationalism means: we must control the politics and the politicians of our community. They must no longer take orders from outside forces. We will organize, and sweep out of office all Negro politicians who are puppets for the outside forces.

Our accent will be upon youth: we need new ideas, new methods, new approaches. We will call upon young students of political science throughout the nation to help us. We will encourage these young students to launch their own independent study, and then give us their analysis and their suggestions. We are completely disenchanted with the old, adult, established politicians. We want to see some new faces—more militant faces.

Concerning the 1964 elections: we will keep our plans on this a secret until a later date—but we don't intend for our people to be the victims of a political sellout again in 1964.

The Muslim Mosque, Inc., will remain wide open for ideas and financial aid from all quarters. Whites can help us, but they can't join us. There can be no black-white unity until there is first some black unity. There can be no workers' solidarity until there is first some racial solidarity. We cannot think of uniting with others, until after we have first united among ourselves. We cannot think of being acceptable to others until we have first proven acceptable to ourselves. One can't unite bananas with scattered leaves.

Concerning nonviolence: it is criminal to teach a man not to defend himself when he is the constant victim of brutal attacks. It is legal and lawful to own a shotgun or a rifle. We believe in obeying the law.

In areas where our people are the constant victims of brutality, and the government seems unable or unwilling to protect them, we should form rifle clubs that can be used to defend our lives and our property in times of emergency, such as happened last year in Birmingham; Plaquemine, Louisiana; Cambridge, Maryland; and Danville, Virginia. When our people are being bitten by dogs, they are within their rights to kill those dogs.

We should be peaceful, law-abiding—but the time has come for the American Negro to fight back in self-defense whenever and wherever he is being unjustly and unlawfully attacked.

If the government thinks I am wrong for saying this, then let the government start doing its job.

Gary Snyder: Buddhism and the Coming Revolution (1969)

During "the sixties" (c. 1967–1973) many American and European young people challenged the values of their elders in a wide variety of movements, the most famous of which was the campaign against the Vietnam War. But for those involved in the self-defined "counterculture" of the period, the goal was not the mere ending of the war in Southeast Asia, but the revolutionary transformation of society. One of the most eloquent voices of the period belonged to Gary Snyder, who as a member of the "Beat Generation" had already begun to explore Buddhism. He was approaching middle age when the youth rebellion of the sixties broke out, but he spoke for many young people who defined their search for new values by seeking guidance from non-Western cultures, Native American and Asian in particular.

How does Snyder link Buddhism with the idea of cultural revolution?

Buddhism holds that the universe and all creatures in it are intrinsically in a state of complete wisdom, love and compassion; acting in natural response and mutual interdependence. The personal realization of this from-the-beginning state cannot be had for and by one-"self" because it is not fully realized unless one has given the self up, and away.

In the Buddhist view, that which obstructs the effortless manifestation of this is Ignorance, which projects into fear and needless craving. Historically, Buddhist philosophers have failed to analyze out the degree to which ignorance and suffering are caused or encouraged by social factors, considering fear-and-desire to be given facts of the human condition. Consequently the major concern of Buddhist philosophy is epistemology and "psychology" with no attention paid to historical or sociological problems. Although Mahayana Buddhism has a grand vision of universal salvation, the *actual* achievement of Buddhism has been the development of practical systems of meditation toward the end of liberating a few dedicated individuals from psychological hangups and cultural conditionings. Institutional Buddhism has been conspicuously ready to accept or ignore the inequalities and tyrannies of whatever political system it found itself under. This can be death to Buddhism, because it is death to any meaningful function of compassion. Wisdom without compassion feels no pain.

No one today can afford to be innocent, or indulge himself in ignorance of the nature of contemporary governments, politics and social orders. The national polities of the modern world maintain their existence by deliberately fostered craving and fear: monstrous protection rackets. The "free world" has become economically dependent on a fantastic system of stimulation of greed which cannot be fulfilled, sexual desire which cannot be satiated and hatred which has no outlet except against oneself, the persons one is supposed to love, or the revolutionary aspirations of pitiful, poverty-stricken marginal societies like Cuba or Vietnam. The conditions of the Cold War have turned all modern societies—Communist included—into vicious distorters of man's true potential. They create populations of "preta"—hungry ghosts, with giant appetites and throats no bigger than needles. The soil, the forests and all animal life are being consumed by these cancerous collectivities; the air and water of the planet is being fouled by them.

There is nothing in human nature or the requirements of human social organization which intrinsically requires that a culture be contradictory, repressive and productive of violent and frustrated personalities. Recent findings in anthropology and psychology make this more and more evident. One can prove it for himself by taking a good look at his own nature through meditation. Once a person has this much faith and insight, he must be led to a deep concern with the need for radical social change through a variety of hopefully non-violent means.

The joyous and voluntary poverty of Buddhism becomes a positive force. The traditional harmlessness and refusal to take life in any form has nation-shaking implications. The practice of meditation, for which one needs only "the ground beneath one's feet" wipes out mountains of junk being pumped into the mind by the mass media and supermarket universities. The belief in a serene and generous fulfillment of natural loving desires destroys ideologies which blind, maim and repress—and points the way to a kind of community which would amaze "moralists" and transform armies of men who are fighters because they cannot be lovers.

Avatamsaka (Kegon) Buddhist philosophy sees the world as a vast interrelated network in which all objects and creatures are necessary and illuminated. From one standpoint, governments, wars, or all that we consider "evil" are uncompromisingly contained in this totalistic realm. The hawk, the swoop and the hare are one. From the "human" standpoint we cannot live in those terms unless all beings see with the same enlightened eye. The Bodhisattva[1] lives by the sufferer's standard, and he must be effective in aiding those who suffer.

The mercy of the West has been social revolution; the mercy of the East has been individual insight into the basic self/void. We need both. They are both contained in the traditional three aspects of the Dharma path: wisdom (prajna), meditation (dhyana), and morality (sila). Wisdom is intuitive knowledge of the mind of love and clarity that lies beneath one's ego-driven anxieties and aggressions. Meditation is going into the mind to see this for yourself—over and over again, until it becomes the mind you live in. Morality is bringing it back out in the way you live, through personal example and responsible action, ultimately toward the true community (sangha) of "all beings." This last aspect means, for me, supporting any cultural and economic revolution that moves clearly toward a free, international, classless world. It means using such means as civil disobedience, outspoken criticism, protest, pacifism, voluntary poverty and even gentle violence if it comes to a matter of restraining some impetuous redneck. It means affirming the widest possible spectrum of non-harmful individual behavior—defending the right of individuals to smoke hemp, eat peyote, be polygynous,[2] polyandrous[3] or homosexual. Worlds of behavior and custom long banned by the Judaeo-Capitalist-Christian-Marxist West. It means respecting intelligence and learning, but not as greed or means to personal power. Working on one's own responsibility, but willing to work with a group. "Forming the new society within the shell of the old"—the I.W.W.[4] slogan of fifty years ago.

The traditional cultures are in any case doomed, and rather than cling to their good aspects hopelessly it should be remembered that whatever is or ever was in any other culture can be reconstructed from the unconscious, through meditation. In fact, it is my own view that the coming revolution will close the circle and link us in many ways with the most creative aspects of our archaic past. If we are lucky we may eventually arrive at a totally integrated world culture with matrilineal descent, free-form marriage, natural-credit communist economy, less industry, far less population and lots more national parks.

---

[1]Incarnation of the Buddha; in some forms of Buddhism every believer is a bodhisattva.
[2]Having more than one wife.
[3]Having more than one husband.
[4]Industrial Workers of the World, a radical, highly innovative grass-roots labor organization which had its period of greatest influence just before World War I.

Rachel Carson: *Silent Spring* (1962)

Deforestation, toxic waste, endangered species, air and water pollution . . . not to mention overpopulation, the "greenhouse effect," and depletion of the ozone layer—it is impossible to live in today's world without being aware of at least some of these environmental hazards. Yet little more than three decades ago, Environmentalism did not exist in the common vocabulary. No one talked about these issues because people did not think about them. Indeed, they did not even know about them. Then Rachel Carson, a zoologist with the U.S. Fish and Wildlife service who had done postgraduate work at Johns Hopkins University, published Silent Spring. *It was the clarion call of perhaps the first eco-warrior. A spring with no birdsong? Unimaginable! and yet—as Carson so clearly pointed out—entirely possible. Worse, the poisons that killed insects and birds were toxic to humans as well. Public response was immediate and powerful. In a very real sense, mass environmentalism began with Rachel Carson's* Silent Spring.

What are the two roads of which Carson writes?

There was once a town in the heart of America where all life seemed to live in harmony with its surroundings. The town lay in the midst of a checkerboard of prosperous farms, with fields of grain and hillsides of orchards where, in spring, white clouds of bloom drifted above the green fields. In autumn, oak and maple and birch set up a blaze of color that flamed and flickered across a backdrop of pines. Then foxes barked in the hills and deer silently crossed the fields, half hidden in the mists of the fall mornings.

Along the roads, laurel, viburnum and alder, great ferns and wildflowers delighted the traveler's eye through much of the year. Even in winter the roadsides were places of beauty, where countless birds came to feed on the berries and on the seed heads of the dried weeds rising above the snow. The countryside was, in fact, famous for the abundance and variety of its bird life, and when the flood of migrants was pouring through in spring and fall, people traveled from great distances to observe them. Others came to fish the streams, which flowed clear and cold out of the hills and contained shady pools where trout lay. So it had been from the days many years ago when the first settlers raised their houses, sank their wells, and built their barns.

Then a strange blight crept over the area and everything began to change. Some evil spell had settled on the community, mysterious maladies swept the flocks of chickens; the cattle and sheep sickened and died. Everywhere was a shadow of death. The farmers spoke of much illness among their families. In the town the doctors had become more and more puzzled by new kinds of sickness appearing among their patients. There had been several sudden and unexplained deaths, not only among adults but even among children, who would be stricken suddenly while at play and die within a few hours.

There was a strange stillness. The birds, for example—where had they gone? Many people spoke of them, puzzled and disturbed. The feeding stations in the backyards were deserted. The few birds seen anywhere were moribund; they trembled violently and could not fly. It was a spring without voices. On the mornings that had once throbbed with the dawn chorus of robins, catbirds, doves, jays, wrens, and scores of other bird voices there was now no sound; only silence lay over the fields and woods and marsh.

On the farms the hens brooded, but no chicks hatched. The farmers complained that they were unable to raise any pigs—the litters were small and the young survived only a few days. The apple trees were coming into bloom but no bees droned among the blossoms, so there was no pollination and there would be no fruit.

The roadsides, once so attractive, were now lined with browned and withered vegetation as though swept by fire. These, too, were silent, deserted by all living things. Even the streams were now lifeless. Anglers no longer visited them, for all the fish had died.

In the gutters under the eaves and between the shingles of the roofs, a white granular powder still showed a few patches; some weeks before it had fallen like snow upon the roofs and the lawns, the fields and streams.

No witchcraft, no enemy action had silenced the rebirth of new life in this stricken world. The people had done it themselves.

This town does not actually exist, but it might easily have a thousand counterparts in America or elsewhere in the world. I know of no community that has experienced all the misfortunes I describe. Yet every one of these disasters has actually happened somewhere, and many real communities have already suffered a substantial number of them. A grim specter has crept upon us almost unnoticed, and this imagined tragedy may easily become a stark reality we all shall know.

What has already silenced the voices of spring in countless towns in America? This book is an attempt to explain. . . .

We stand now where two roads diverge. But unlike the roads in Robert Frost's familiar poem, they are not equally fair. The road we have long been traveling is deceptively easy, a smooth superhighway on which we progress with great speed, but at its end lies disaster. The other fork of the road—the one "less traveled by"—offers our last, our only chance to reach a destination that assures the preservation of our earth.

The choice, after all, is ours to make. If, having endured much, we have at last asserted our "right to know," and if, knowing, we have concluded that we are being asked to take senseless and frightening risks, then we should no longer accept the counsel of those who tell us that we must fill our world with poisonous chemicals; we should look about and see what other course is open to us.

A truly extraordinary variety of alternatives to the chemical control of insects is available. Some are already in use and have achieved brilliant success. Others are in the stage of laboratory testing. Still others are little more than ideas in the minds of imaginative scientists, waiting for the opportunity to put them to the test. All have this in common: they are *biological* solutions, based on understanding of the living organisms they seek to control and of the whole fabric of life to which these organisms belong. Specialists representing various areas of the vast field of biology are contributing—entomologists, pathologists, geneticists, physiologists, biochemists, ecologists—all pouring their knowledge and their creative inspirations into the formation of a new science of biotic controls.

Through all these new, imaginative, and creative approaches to the problem of sharing our earth with other creatures there runs a constant theme, the awareness that we are dealing with life—with living populations and all their pressures and counterpressures, their surges and recessions. Only by taking account of such life forces and by cautiously seeking to guide them into channels favorable to ourselves can we hope to achieve a reasonable accommodation between the insect hordes and ourselves.

The current vogue for poisons has failed utterly to take into account these most fundamental considerations. As crude a weapon as the cave man's club, the chemical barrage has been hurled against the fabric of life—a fabric on the one hand delicate and destructible, on the other miraculously tough and resilient, and capable of striking back in unexpected ways. These extraordinary capacities of life have been ignored by the practitioners of chemical control who have brought to their task no "high-minded orientation," no humility before the vast forces with which they tamper.

The "control of nature" is a phrase conceived in arrogance born of the Neanderthal age of biology and philosophy, when it was supposed that nature exists for the convenience of man. The concepts and practices of applied entomology for the most part date from that Stone Age of science. It is our alarming misfortune that so primitive a science has armed itself with the most modern and terrible weapons, and that in turning them against the insects it has also turned them against the earth.

Stanley Kauffman: The Necessary Film (1971)

A novelist, essayist, drama critic, and college teacher, Stanley Kauffmann is best known as the longtime critic of films for The New Republic. *His comments on film have been collected in several books over the last four decades. Kauffmann demonstrates a keen understanding of the technical demands of film, and his observations on acting performances, owing a good deal to his familiarity with the theater, are particularly persuasive. The essay below, written a quarter-century ago, reminds us of the peculiar psychological value of all art, what Kauffmann calls our recognition of a double life, and how film, more than other arts, highlights this hidden life.*

Considering that there have been many changes in movies since this essay was written, which of Kauffmann's observations do you think still hold true?

When the first moving picture flashed onto a screen, the double life of all human beings became intensified. That double life consists, on the one hand, of actions and words and surfaces, and, on the other, of secrets and self-knowledges, self-ignorances, self-ignorings. That double life has been part of man's existence ever since art and religion were invented to make sure that he became aware of it. In the past century, religion has receded further and further as revealer of that double life, and art has taken over more and more of the function; and when the film art came along, it made that revelation of doubleness inescapable, more attractive. On the screen are facts; which at the same time are symbols; and they thus invoke doubleness at every moment, in every kind of picture. They stir up the concealments in our lives, both those concealments we like and those we don't like, they shake our histories and our hopes into our consciousness. Not completely, by any means. (Who could stand it?) Not more grandly or deeply than do other arts. But more quickly and surely.

Think of this process as applying to every frame of film and it is clear that when we sit before a screen, we run risks unprecedented in human history. A poem may or may not touch us, a play or novel may never get near us. But films are inescapable. (In fact, with poor films, we often have the sensation of fighting our way out of them.) When two screen lovers kiss, in any film, that kiss has a minimum inescapability which is stronger than in other arts—both as an action before us and as a metaphor of the kissingness in our lives. Each of us is pinned privately to that kiss in some degree of pleasure or pain or enlightenment. In period films or modern dramas, in musicals or political epics, in Westerns or farces, our beings are in some measure summoned up before our private vision.

And I suggest that the fundamental way, conscious or not, in which we determine the quality of a film is by the degree to which the reexperiencing of ourselves coincides with our pride, our shames, our hopes, our honor. Finally, distinctions among films arise from the way they please or displease us with ourselves: not whether they please or displease but how.

This is true, I believe, in every art today; it is not a cinema monopoly. But in film it is becoming more true more swiftly and decisively because the film has a much smaller heritage of received esthetics to reassess; because the film is bound more closely to the future than other arts seem to be; and because the film confronts us so immediately, so seductively, and so shockingly with at least some truth about what we have been doing with ourselves.

To the degree that film exposes a viewer to this truth of himself, in his experience of the world or of fantasy, in his options of actions or of privacy, to the degree that he can thus accept a film as worthy of himself or better than himself, to that degree a film is necessary to him; and it is that necessity, I suggest, that ultimately sets its value.

Throughout history, two factors have formed men's taste in any art—knowledge of that art and knowledge of life—and obviously this is still true, but the function of taste seems to be altering. As formalist esthetic canons seem less and less tenable, standards in art and life become more and more congruent, and the function of taste seems increasingly to be the selection and appraisal of the works that are most valuable—most necessary—to the individual's existence. So our means for evaluating films become more and more involved with our means for evaluating experience: not identical with our standards in life but certainly related—and, one hopes, somewhat braver.

Of course the whole process means that men feed on themselves, on their own lives variously rearranged by art, as a source of values. But despite other prevalent beliefs in the past, we are coming to see that men have always been the source of their own values. In the century in which this liberation, this responsibility, has become increasingly apparent, the intellect of man has simultaneously provided a new art form, the film, that can make the most of it.

Tim O'Brien: The Man I Killed (1990)

Tim O'Brien has become the most famous novelist to have written out of his experience of being a soldier in the Vietnam War. He says that he became a soldier because he was afraid to follow his convictions into exile in Canada, and he has devoted much of his career to describing the experiences of that war with passion and precision to bring home the reality of war. In The Things They Carried, *the book from which this selection comes, he admits that this story is partly a composite and not strict autobiography; but it reflects vividly the experiences he and others like him underwent. In this story O'Brien imagines the typical "Viet Cong" as being a person much like himself. Bringing the dead to life through the imagination is a critical feat for him, because war is made possible only through dehumanizing the enemy. A quarter century after the American soldier could not bring himself to talk, he finds his voice in O'Brien's story.*

What qualities make the dead soldier particularly sympathetic?

His jaw was in his throat, his upper lip and teeth were gone, his one eye was shut, his other eye was a star-shaped hole, his eyebrows were thin and arched like a woman's, his nose was undamaged, there was a slight tear at the lobe of one ear, his clean black hair was swept upward into a cowlick at the rear of the skull, his forehead was lightly freckled, his fingernails were clean, the skin at his left cheek was peeled back in three ragged strips, his right cheek was smooth and hairless, there was a butterfly on his chin, his neck was open to the spinal cord and the blood there was thick and shiny and it was this wound that had killed him. He lay face-up in the center of the trail, a slim, dead, almost dainty young man. He had bony legs, a narrow waist, long shapely fingers. His chest was sunken and poorly muscled—a scholar, maybe. His wrists were the wrists of a child. He wore a black shirt, black pajama pants, a gray ammunition belt, a gold ring on the third finger of his right hand. His rubber sandals had been blown off. One lay beside him, the other a few meters up the trail. He had been born, maybe, in 1946 in the village of My Khe near the central coastline of Quang Ngai Province, where his parents farmed, and where his family had lived for several centuries, and where, during the time of the French, his father and two uncles and many neighbors had joined in the struggle for independence. He was not a Communist. He was a citizen and a soldier. In the village of My Khe, as in all of Quang Ngai, patriotic resistance had the force of tradition, which was partly the force of legend, and from his earliest boyhood the man I killed had listened to stories about the heroic Trung sisters and Tran Hung Dao's famous rout of the Mongols and Le Loi's final victory against the Chinese at Tot Dong. He had been taught that to defend the land was a man's highest duty and highest privilege. He accepted this. It was never open to question. Secretly, though, it also frightened him. He was not a fighter. His health was poor, his body small and frail. He liked books. He wanted someday to be a teacher of mathematics. At night, lying on his mat, he could not picture himself doing the brave things his father had done, or his uncles, or the heroes of the stories. He hoped in his heart that he would never be tested. He hoped the Americans would go away. Soon, he hoped. He kept hoping and hoping, always, even when he was asleep.

"Oh, man, you fuckin' trashed the fucker," Azar said. "You scrambled his sorry self, look at that, you did, you laid him out like Shredded fuckin' Wheat."

"Go away," Kiowa said.

"I'm just saying the truth. Like oatmeal."

"Go," Kiowa said.

"Okay, then, I take it back," Azar said. He started to move away, then stopped and said, "Rice Krispies, you know? On the dead test, this particular individual gets A-plus."

Smiling at this, he shrugged and walked up the trail toward the village behind the trees.

Kiowa kneeled down.

"Just forget that crud," he said. He opened up his canteen and held it out for a while and then sighed and pulled it away. "No sweat, man. What else could you do?"

Later, Kiowa said, "I'm serious. Nothing *anybody* could do. Come on, Tim, stop staring."

The trail junction was shaded by a row of trees and tall brush. The slim young man lay with his legs in the shade. His jaw was in his throat. His one eye was shut and the other was a star-shaped hole.

Kiowa glanced at the body.

"All right, let me ask a question," he said. "You want to trade places with him? Turn it all upside down—you *want* that? I mean, be honest."

The star-shaped hole was red and yellow. The yellow part seemed to be getting wider, spreading out at the center of the star. The upper lip and gum and teeth were gone. The man's head was cocked at a wrong angle, as if loose at the neck, and the neck was wet with blood.

"Think it over," Kiowa said.

Then later he said, "Tim, it's a *war.* The guy wasn't Heidi—he had a weapon, right? It's a tough thing, for sure, but you got to cut out that staring."

Then he said, "Maybe you better lie down a minute."

Then after a long empty time he said, "Take it slow. Just go wherever the spirit takes you."

The butterfly was making its way along the young man's forehead, which was spotted with small dark freckles. The nose was undamaged. The skin on the right cheek was smooth and fine-grained and hairless. Frail-looking, delicately boned, the young man had never wanted to be a soldier and in his heart had feared that he would perform badly in battle. Even as a boy growing up in the village of My Khe, he had often worried about this. He imagined covering his head and lying in a deep hole and closing his eyes and not moving until the war was over. He had no stomach for violence. He loved mathematics. His eyebrows were thin and arched like a woman's, and at school the boys sometimes teased him about how pretty he was, the arched eyebrows and long shapely fingers, and on the playground they would mimic a woman's walk and make fun of his smooth skin and his love for mathematics. He could not make himself fight them. He often wanted to, but he was afraid, and this increased his shame. If he could not fight little boys, he thought, how could he ever become a soldier and fight the Americans with their airplanes and helicopters and bombs? It did not seem possible. In the presence of his father and uncles, he pretended to look forward to doing his patriotic duty, which was also a privilege, but at night he prayed with his mother that the war might end soon. Beyond anything else, he was afraid of disgracing himself, and therefore his family and village. But all he could do, he thought, was wait and pray and try not to grow up too fast.

"Listen to me," Kiowa said. "You feel terrible, I know that."

Then he said, "Okay, maybe I *don't* know."

Along the trail there were small blue flowers shaped like bells. The young man's head was wrenched sideways, not quite facing the flowers, and even in the shade a single blade of sunlight sparkled against the buckle of his ammunition belt. The left cheek was peeled back in three ragged strips. The wounds at his neck had not yet clotted, which made him seem animate even in death, the blood still spreading out across his shirt.

Kiowa shook his head.

There was some silence before he said, "Stop *staring.*"

The young man's fingernails were clean. There was a slight tear at the lobe of one ear, a sprinkling of blood on the forearm. He wore a gold ring on the third finger of his right hand. His chest was sunken and poorly muscled—a scholar, maybe. For years, despite his family's poverty, the man I killed had been determined to continue his education in mathematics. The means for this were arranged, perhaps, through the village liberation cadres, and in 1964 the young man began attending classes at the university in Saigon, where he avoided politics and paid attention to the problems of calculus. He devoted himself to his studies. He spent his nights alone, wrote romantic poems in his journal, took pleasure in the grace and beauty of differential equations. The war, he knew, would finally take him, but for the time being he would not let himself think about it. He had stopped praying; instead, now, he waited. And as he waited, in his final year at the university, he fell in love with a classmate, a girl of seventeen, who one day told him that his wrists were like the wrists of a child, so small and delicate, and who admired his narrow waist and the cowlick that rose up like a bird's tail at the back of his head. She liked his quiet manner; she laughed at his freckles and bony legs. One evening, perhaps, they exchanged gold rings.

Now one eye was a star.

"You okay?" Kiowa said.

The body lay almost entirely in shade. There were gnats at the mouth, little flecks of pollen drifting above the nose. The butterfly was gone. The bleeding had stopped except for the neck wounds.

Kiowa picked up the rubber sandals, clapping off the dirt, then bent down to search the body. He found a pouch of rice, a comb, a fingernail clipper, a few soiled piasters, a snapshot of a young woman standing in front of a parked motorcycle. Kiowa placed these items in his rucksack along with the gray ammunition belt and rubber sandals.

Then he squatted down.

"I'll tell you the straight truth," he said. "The guy was dead the second he stepped on the trail. Understand me?

"We all had him zeroed. A good kill—weapon, ammunition, everything." Tiny beads of sweat glistened at Kiowa's forehead. His eyes moved from the sky to the dead man's body to the knuckles of his own hands. "So listen, you have to pull your shit together. Can't just sit here all day."

Later he said, "Understand?"

Then he said, "Five minutes, Tim. Five more minutes and we're moving out."

The one eye did a funny twinkling trick, red to yellow. His head was wrenched sideways, as if loose at the neck, and the dead young man seemed to be staring at some distant object beyond the bell-shaped flowers along the trail. The blood at the neck had gone to a deep purplish black. Clean fingernails, clean hair—he had been a soldier for only a single day. After his years at the university, the man I killed returned with his new wife to the village of My Khe, where he enlisted as a common rifleman with the 48th Vietcong Battalion. He knew he would die quickly. He knew he would see a flash of light. He knew he would fall dead and wake up in the stories of his village and people.

Kiowa covered the body with a poncho.

"Hey, Tim, you're looking better," he said. "No doubt about it. All you needed was time—some mental R&R."[1]

Then he said, "Man, I'm sorry."

Then later he said, "Why not talk about it?"

Then he said, "Come on, man, talk."

He was a slim, dead, almost dainty young man of about twenty. He lay with one leg bent beneath him, his jaw in his throat, his face neither expressive nor inexpressive. One eye was shut. The other was a star-shaped hole.

"Talk to me," Kiowa said.

---

[1] Rest and recreation.

Sherman Alexie: The Trial of Thomas-Builds-the-Fire (1993)

Sherman Alexie is a poet and fiction writer and a member of the Spokane/Coeur d'Alene Indian tribe. Alexie writes in a style that mixes history and fiction, fact and fantasy, past and present. Much of Alexie's work explores how the long history of white attempts to destroy or dominate Indian culture continues to shape the lives of Indians living today, and portrays how Indians continue to resist through humor, anger, love and story-telling. His work points out that while many whites purport to love and respect Indians long dead (as in movies like "Dances With Wolves"), few show any interest in, knowlege of, or connection with the millions of Indians living today who struggle against many of the same injustices inflicted on their ancestors.

In what various ways does this story connect the past and the present?

> Someone must have been telling lies about Joseph K., for without having done anything wrong he was arrested one fine morning.
> —Franz Kafka

Thomas Builds-the-Fire waited alone in the Spokane tribal holding cell while BIA[1] officials discussed his future, the immediate present, and of course, his past.

"Builds-the-Fire has a history of this kind of behavior," a man in a BIA suit said to the others. "A storytelling fetish accompanied by an extreme need to tell the truth. Dangerous."

Thomas was in the holding cell because he had once held the reservation postmaster hostage for eight hours with the idea of a gun and had also threatened to make significant changes in the tribal vision. But that crisis was resolved years ago as Thomas surrendered voluntarily and agreed to remain silent. In fact, Thomas had not spoken in nearly twenty years. All his stories remained internal; he would not even send letters or Christmas cards.

But recently Thomas had begun to make small noises, form syllables that contained more emotion and meaning than entire sentences constructed by the BIA. A noise that sounded something like rain had given Esther courage enough to leave her husband, tribal chairman David WalksAlong, who had been tribal police chief at the time of Thomas Builds-the-Fire's original crime. WalksAlong walked along with BIA policy so willingly that he took to calling his wife a savage in polyester pants. She packed her bags the day after she listened to Thomas speak; Thomas was arrested the day after Esther left.

Now Thomas sat quietly in his cell, counting cockroaches and silverfish. He couldn't sleep, he didn't feel like eating. Often he closed his eyes and stories came to him quickly, but he would not speak. He nodded and laughed if the story was funny; cried a little when the stories were sad; pounded his fists against his mattress when the stories angered him.

"Well, the traveling judge is coming in tomorrow," one guy in a BIA suit said to the others. "What charges should we bring him up on?"

"Inciting a riot? Kidnapping? Extortion? Maybe murder?" another guy in a BIA suit asked, and the others laughed.

"Well," they all agreed. "It has to be a felony charge. We don't need his kind around here anymore."

[1]Bureau of Indian Affairs, the U.S. government agency that oversees life on Indian reservations. Some Indians work for and with the BIA, many others fight against it as a force of control and repression of Indian culture.

Later that night, Thomas lay awake and counted stars through the bars in his window. He was guilty, he knew that. All that was variable on any reservation was how the convicted would be punished.

The following report is adapted from the original court transcript.

"Mr. Builds-the-Fire," the judge said to Thomas. "Before we begin this trial, the court must be certain that you understand the charges against you."

Thomas, who wore his best ribbon shirt[2] and decided to represent himself, stood and spoke a complete sentence for the first time in two decades.

"Your Honor," he said. "I don't believe that the exact nature of any charges against me have been revealed, let alone detailed."

There was a hush in the crowd, followed by exclamations of joy, sadness, etc. Eve Ford, the former reservation postmaster held hostage by Thomas years earlier, sat quietly in the back row and thought to herself, *He hasn't done anything wrong.*

"Well, Mr. Builds-the-Fire," the judge said. "I can only infer by your sudden willingness to communicate that you do in fact understand the purpose of this trial."

"That's not true."

"Are you accusing this court of dishonesty, Mr. Builds-the-Fire?"

Thomas sat down, to regain his silence for a few moments.

"Well, Mr. Builds-the-Fire, we're going to dispense with opening remarks and proceed to testimony. Are you ready to call your first witness?"

"Yes, I am, Your Honor. I call myself as first and only witness to all the crimes I'm accused of and, additionally, to bring attention to all the mitigating circumstances."

"Whatever," the judge said. "Raise your right hand and promise me you'll tell the whole truth and nothing but the truth."

"Honesty is all I have left," Thomas said.

Thomas Builds-the-Fire sat in the witness stand, closed his eyes, and spoke this story aloud:

"It all started on September 8, 1858. I was a young pony, strong and quick in every movement. I remember this. Still, there was so much to fear on that day when Colonel George Wright took me and 799 of my brothers captive. Imagine, 800 beautiful ponies stolen at once. It was the worst kind of war crime. But Colonel Wright thought we were too many to transport, that we were all dangerous. In fact, I still carry his letter of that day which justified the coming slaughter:

'Dear Sir:

'As I reported in my communication of yesterday the capture of 800 horses on the 8th instant, I have now to add that this large band of horses composed the entire wealth of the Spokane chief Til-co-ax. This man has ever been hostile; for the last two years he has been constantly sending his young men into the Walla Walla valley, and stealing horses and cattle from the settlers and from the government. He boldly acknowledged these facts when he met Colonel Steptoe, in May last. Retributive justice has now overtaken him; the blow has been severe but well merited. I found myself embarrassed with these 800 horses. I could not hazard the experiment of moving with such a number of animals (many of them very wild) along with my large train; should a stampede take place, we might not

---

[2]A colorful ceremonial shirt.

only lose our captured animals, but many of our own. Under those circumstances, I determined to kill them all, save a few in service in the quartermaster's department and to replace broken-down animals. I deeply regretted killing these poor creatures, but a dire necessity drove me to it. This work of slaughter has been going on since 10 o'clock of yesterday, and will not be completed before this evening, and I shall march for the Coeur d'Alene Mission tomorrow.

Very respectfully, your obedient servant,

G. WRIGHT, Colonel 9th Infantry, Commanding.'[3]

"Somehow I was lucky enough to be spared while hundreds of my brothers and sisters fell together. It was a nightmare to witness. They were rounded into a corral and then lassoed, one by one; and dragged out to be shot in the head. This lasted for hours, and all that dark night mothers cried for their dead children. The next day, the survivors were rounded into a single mass and slaughtered by continuous rifle fire."

Thomas opened his eyes and found that most of the Indians in the courtroom wept and wanted to admit defeat. He then closed his eyes and continued the story:

"But I was not going to submit without a struggle. I would continue the war. At first I was passive, let one man saddle me and ride for a while. He laughed at the illusion of my weakness. But I suddenly rose up and bucked him off and broke his arm. Another man tried to ride me, but I threw him and so many others, until I was lathered with sweat and blood from their spurs and rifle butts. It was glorious. Finally they gave up, quit, and led me to the back of the train. They could not break me. Some may have wanted to kill me for my arrogance, but others respected my anger, my refusal to admit defeat. I lived that day, even escaped Colonel Wright, and galloped into other histories."

Thomas opened his eyes and saw that the Indians in the courtroom sat up straight, combed their braids gracefully, smiled with Indian abandon.

"Mr. Builds-the-Fire," the judge asked. "Is that the extent of your testimony?"

"Your Honor, if I may continue, there is much more I need to say. There are so many more stories to tell."

The judge looked at Thomas Builds-the-Fire for an instant, decided to let him continue. Thomas closed his eyes, and a new story was raised from the ash of older stories:

"My name was Qualchan and I had been fighting for our people, for our land. It was horrendous, hiding in the dirt at the very mouth of the Spokane River where my fellow warrior, Moses, found me after he escaped from Colonel Wright's camp. Qualchan, he said to me. You must stay away from Wright's camp. He means to hang you. But Wright had taken my father hostage and threatened to hang him if I did not come in. Wright promised he would treat me fairly. I believed him and went to the colonel's camp and was immediately placed in chains. It was then I saw the hangman's noose and made the fight to escape. My wife also fought beside me with a knife and wounded many soldiers before she was subdued. After I was beaten down, they dragged me to the noose and I was hanged with six other Indians, including Epseal, who had never raised a hand in anger to any white or Indian."

Thomas opened his eyes and swallowed air hard. He could barely breathe and the courtroom grew distant and vague.

---

[3]This letter is a verbatim copy of the actual historical document. Colonel Wright led the U.S. military force in the 1850s that suppressed attempts by the Spokane, Coeur d'Alene, and Palouse Indians to resist the invasion of white miners and settlers into their lands.

"Mr. Builds-the-Fire," the judge asked and brought Thomas back to attention. "What point are you trying to make with this story?"

"Well," Thomas said. "The City of Spokane is now building a golf course named after me, Qualchan, located in that valley where I was hanged."

The courtroom burst into motion and emotion. The judge hammered his gavel against his bench. The bailiff had to restrain Eve Ford, who had made a sudden leap of faith across the room toward Thomas.

"Thomas," she yelled. "We're all listening."

The bailiff had his hands full as Eve slugged him twice and then pushed him to the ground. Eve stomped on the bailiff's big belly until two tribal policemen tackled her, handcuffed her, and led her away.

"Thomas," she yelled. "We hear you."

The judge was red-faced with anger; he almost looked Indian. He pounded his gavel until it broke.

"Order in the court," he shouted. "Order in the fucking court."

The tribal policemen grew in number. Many were Indians that the others had never seen before. The policemen swelled in size and forced the others out of the courtroom. After the court was cleared and order restored, the judge pulled his replacement gavel from beneath his robe and continued the trial.

"Now," the judge said. "We can go about the administration of justice."

"Is that real justice or the idea of justice?" Thomas asked him, and the judge flew back into anger.

"Defense testimony is over," he said. "Mr. Builds-the Fire, you will now be cross examined."

Thomas watched the prosecuting attorney approach the witness stand.

"Mr. Builds-the-Fire," he said. "Where were you on May 16, 1858?"

"I was in the vicinity of Rosalia, Washington, along with 799 other warriors, ready to battle with Colonel Steptoe and his soldiers."

"And could you explain exactly what happened there that day?"

Thomas closed his eyes and told this story:

"My name was Wild Coyote and I was just sixteen years old and was frightened because this was to be my first battle. But we were confident because Steptoe's soldiers were so small and weak. They tried to negotiate a peace, but our war chiefs would not settle for anything short of blood. You must understand these were days of violence and continual lies from the white man. Steptoe said he wanted peace between whites and Indians, but he had cannons and had lied before, so we refused to believe him this time. Instead, we attacked at dawn and killed many of their soldiers and lost only a few warriors. The soldiers made a stand on a hilltop and we surrounded them, amazed at their tears and cries. But you must understand they were also very brave. The soldiers fought well, but there were too many Indians for them on that day. Night fell and we retreated a little as we always do during dark. Somehow the surviving soldiers escaped during the night, and many of us were happy for them. They had fought so well that they deserved to live another day."

Thomas opened his eyes and found the prosecuting attorney's long nose just inches from his own.

"Mr. Builds-the-Fire, how many soldiers did you kill that day?"

Thomas closed his eyes and told another story:

"I killed one soldier right out with an arrow to the chest. He fell off his horse and didn't move again. I shot another soldier and he fell off his horse, too, and I ran over to him to take his scalp but he pulled his revolver and shot me through the shoulder. I still have the scar. It hurt so much that I left the soldier and went away to die. I really thought I was going to die, and I suppose the soldier probably died later. So I went and lay down in this tall grass and watched the sky. It was beautiful and I was ready to die. It had been a good fight. I lay there for part of the day and most of the night until one of my friends picked me up and said the soldiers had escaped. My friend tied himself to me and we rode away with the others. That is what happened."

Thomas opened his eyes and faced the prosecuting attorney.

"Mr. Builds-the-Fire, you do admit, willingly, that you murdered two soldiers in cold blood and with premeditation?"

"Yes, I killed those soldiers, but they were good men. I did it with sad heart and hand. There was no way I could ever smile or laugh again. I'm not sorry we had to fight, but I am sorry those men had to die."

"Mr. Builds-the-Fire, please answer the question. Did you or did you not murder those two soldiers in cold blood and with premeditation?"

"I did."

Article from the Spokesman-Review, *October 7, 19—.*

Builds-the-Fire to Smolder in Prison

WELLPINIT, WASHINGTON—Thomas Builds-the-Fire, the self proclaimed visionary of the Spokane Tribe, was sentenced today to two concurrent life terms in the Walla Walla State Penitentiary. His many supporters battled with police for over eight hours following the verdict.

U.S. District Judge James Wright asked; "Do you have anything you want to say now, Mr. Builds-the-Fire?" Builds-the-Fire simply shook his head no and was led away by prison officials.

Wright told Builds-the-Fire that the new federal sentencing guidelines "require the imposition of a life sentence for racially motivated murder." There is no possibility for parole, said U.S. Prosecuting Attorney, Adolph D. Jim, an enrolled member of the Yakima Indian Nation.

"The only appeal I have is for justice," Builds-the-Fire reportedly said as he was transported away from this story and into the next.

Thomas Builds-the-Fire sat quietly as the bus traveled down the highway toward Walla Walla State Penitentiary. There were six other prisoners: four African men, one Chicano, and a white man from the smallest town in the state.

"I know who you are," the Chicano said to Thomas. "You're that Indian guy did all the talking."

"Yeah," one of the African men said. "You're that story-teller. Tell us some stories, chief, give us the scoop."

Thomas looked at these five men who shared his skin color, at the white man who shared this bus which was going to deliver them into a new kind of reservation, barrio, ghetto, logging-town tin shack. He then looked out the window, through the steel grates on the windows, at the freedom just outside the glass. He saw wheat fields, bodies of water, and bodies of dark-skinned workers pulling fruit from trees and sweat from thin air.

Thomas closed his eyes and told this story.

Acknowledgements for *Reading About the World Vol. II*, edited by Paul Brians, et al.

eo Africanus: "Description of Timbuktu," trans. © *1996 Paul Brians.*

oems 10, 74, 196, 46 from The Devotional Poems of Mirabai, trans. A.J. Alston (1980). Reprinted by permisson of Motilala Banarsidaas Publishers.

'abir: Selected Songs, trans. © *1999 Azfar Hussain.*

'ang-His: The Sacred Edicts, P'u Sung-ling: "Painting on the Wall" trans. © *1994 Lydia Gerber.*

'Monkey" by Wu Cheng-En, translated by Arthur Waley, pp. 11-19. Copyright © *1943 by John Day Co. Used by permission of Grove/Atlantic, Inc.*

poems from Matsuo Basho, pp. 44, 48, 53, 57. Reprinted with the permission of Macmillan Library Reference USA, a division of Ahsuog, Inc. from IATSUO BASHO, by Makoto Ueda. Copyright © *1970 by Twayne Publishers, Inc.*

The Love Suicides at Sonezaki, Scene Three" from Major Plays of Chikamatsu, translated by Donald Keene, pp. 51-56. Copyright © *1961 Columbia 'niversity Press. Reprinted with permission from the publisher.*

The Lady and Her Five Suitors," François Rabelais: "Letter from Gargantua to his son Pantagruel," René Descartes: Discourse on Method, Michel de Iontaigne: On Cannibals, trans. © *1994 Paul Brians.*

'ulius Excluded from Heaven: A Dialogue" by Desierius Erasmus from Collected Works of Erasmus: Literary and Educational Writings, 5/e, A.H.T. evy editor, translated by Michael J. Heath. Copyright © *1986 by University of Toronto Press. Reprinted by permission.*

The First Day: On Sunspots" from Dialogue on the Great World Systems by Galileo Galilei, trans. Thomas Salusbury & Giorgio de Santillana '953), pp. 62-69. Reprinted by permisison of The University of Chicago Press.

onnets 18 & 24 by Louise Labé from Louise Labé's Complete Works, pp. 114, 120, trans. Edith Farrell (1986).

xcerpts from The Discovery and Conquest of Mexico, pp. 318-321, 422-442, by Bernal Diaz del Castillo, trans. Maudslay (1956). Published by arrar, Straus & Giroux.

etter to Princess Doña Juana by Doña Isabel de Guevara and Letter to his nephew by Andres García, pp. 14-17 and 144-146 from Letters and People 'the Spanish Indies, Sixteenth Century, James Lockhart & Enrique Otte, eds. (1976). Reprinted by permission of Cambridge University Press.

A Response to Jealousy" by Sor Juana Ines de la Cruz, trans. © *1994 Susan Swan. Reprinted by permission.*

uan del Valle y Caviedes: "The Privileges of the Poor," trans. © *1994 Mary Gallwey.*

o. 118-199 from "Radhika Santwanam" by Muddupalani, translated by B.V.L. Narayanarow. Reprinted by permission of The Feminist Press at the 'ity University of New York, from Susie Tharu and K. Lalita, Women Writing in India: 600 B.C. to the Present, vol. 1, edited by Susie Tharu and K. alita. Copyright 1991 by Susie Tharu and K. Lalita.

'ung Hsiu-Ch'uan: "A Visit to Heaven" Li Ju-chen: "The Land of the Great," trans. © *1994 Lydia Gerber.*

'in tse-hsu's letter to Queen Victoria" from China's Response to the West, by Ssu-Yu Teng and John K. Fairbank. Copyright © *1954, 1979, 1981 by e President and Fellows of Harvard College. Reprinted by permission of Harvard University Press.*

Musui's Story" from Musui's Story: The Autobiography of a Tokugawa Samurai, pp. 151-155 by Katsu Kokichi, translated by Teruko Craig. 'opyright © *1988 The Arizona Board of Regents. Reprinted by permission of the University of Arizona Press.*

The 'Pill' of the Three Religions" by Fukuzumi Masae from Sources of Japanese Tradition, pp. 583-586, translated by William de Bary and Donald eene. Copyright © *1958 Columbia University Press. Reprinted with permission from the publisher.*

'hinese vs. Western Learning" from The Autobiography of Fukuzawa Yukichi, trans. Eiichi Kiyooka (1947), pp. 218-221, 228-231. Reprinted by ermission of The Hokuseido Press.

'oltaire: A Treatise on Toleration, trans. © *1994 Richard Hooker.*

xcerpts from The Social Contract, pp. 3-22 by Jean-Jacques Rousseau, trans. G.D.H. Cole.

'rologue in Heaven" by Johann Wolfgang Goethe in Faust: The Original German and New Translation and Introduction, pp. 83, 85, 87, 89, 91. 'ranslation copyright © *1961 by Walter Kaufmann. Used by permission of Doubleday, a division of Random House, Inc.*

mile Zola: Germinal, trans. © *1994 Paul Brians.*

The Death of God" from The Gay Science, pp. 95-96, by Friedrich Nietzsche, translated by Walter Kaufmann. Copyright © *1974 by Random House, ıc. Reprinted by permission of Random House, Inc.*

"Letter to Elena" by Maria Eugenia Echenique from La Ondina del Plata (14 November 1875): 486-88, translated by Bonnie Frederick (1999).

"He and She" by Silvia Fernandez, trans. Bonnie Frederick. Reprinted by permission.

Silvia Fernández: "He and She," trans. © 1994 The Palouse Translation Project, reprinted by permission of Bonnie Frederick.

"A Canary's Ideas" by Joaquim Maria Machado de Assis from The Devil's Church and Other Stories, trans. Jack Schmitt and Lorie Ishimatsu, pp. 12- 129, © 1977. By permission of the University of Texas Press.

Excerpts from Civil Disobedience by Henry David Thoreau Miscellanies by Henry David Thoreau, pp. 131-132, 149-150.

"Because I could not stop for death" and "After Great Pain a Formal Feeling Comes" by Emily Dickinson reprinted by permission of the publishers and the Trustees of Amherst College from The Poems of Emily Dickinson, Thomas H. Johnson, ed., Cambridge, Mass.: The Belknap Press of Harvard University Press, Copyright © 1951, 1955, 1979, 1983 by the President and Fellows of Harvard College.

"Wild Nights—Wild Nights!" by Emily Dickinson in Selected Poems of Emily Dickinson, James Reeves, ed., Heinemann, 1959, pp. 18-19.

Excerpt from Chapter 4 of Things Fall Apart, by Chinua Achebe (1959), pp. 20-24. Reprinted by permission of Heinemann Educational Publishers, a division of Reed Educational & Professional Publishing Ltd.

"The Return" by Ngugi wa Thiong'o in Secret Lies (1975), pp. 49-54. Reprinted by permission of Heinemann Educational Publishers, a division of Reed Educational & Professional Publishing Ltd.

"Poet's Lament on the Death of his Wife" by Raage Ugaas from Somali Poetry: An Introduction (© 1964), translated by B.W. Andrezejewski & I.M. Lewis, pp. 64-66. Reprinted with permission of Oxford University Press.

"Long, long, have you held" by Leopold Sedar Senghor from The Collected Poetry, p. 121, edited by Melvin Dixon (Charlottesville: Virginia, 1991). Reprinted with permission of the University Press of Virginia

"Black Skin, White Masks" by Frantz Fanon, pp. 230-232, translated by Charles Lam Markmann. Copyright © 1967 by Grove Press, Inc. Used by permission of Grove/Atlantic, Inc.

"We are at War!" in Africa Contemporary Record: Annual Survey and Documents, 1968-1969. pp. 721-722.

Nelson Mandela Inaugural Address, May 10, 1994. Reprinted by permission of the African National Congress.

"Half a Day" from The Time and the Place and Other Stories by Naguib Mahfouz. Copyright © 1991 by the American University in Cairo Press. Used by permission of Doubleday, a division of Random House, Inc.

"Identity Card" by Mahmoud Darwish in Selected Poems (1973), trans. Ian Wedde & Fawwaz Tuqan, pp. 24-25. Reprinted by permission of Carcanet Press, Ltd.

"America, the Great Satan" by the Ayatollah Khomeni in Islam and Revolution (1981), pp. 304-306, trans. Hamid Algar. Reprinted by permission o Mizan Press.

"A Little Arab Girl's First Day at School" by Assia Djebar from Fantasia: An Algerian Cavalcade, trans. Dorothy S. Blair. Reprinted by permission o Quartet Books Ltd.

"We Sinful Women" by Kishwar Naheed, pp. 31, 33, from We Sinful Women: Contemporary Urdu Feminist Poetry, edited by Rukhsana Ahmad, fi published in Great Britain by The Women's Press Ltd, 1991, 34 Great Sutton Street, London EC1V 0LQ, is used by permission of The Women's Pre Ltd.

"The Veil," from DEATH OF AN EX-MINISTER (1987) by Narwal El Saadawi, pp. 31-35, translated by Shirley Eber, originally published by Methuen. Reprinted by permission of Random House, UK, Ltd.

Pages 219-21, Mokshodayani Mukhopadhyay from "Bagalir Babu" ("The Bengali Babu"). Translated by Supriya Chaudhury. 219-221. Reprinted b permission of The Feminist Press at the City University of New York, from Susie Tharu and K. Lalita, Women Writing in India: 600 B.C. to the Present, vol. 1, edited by Susie Tharu and K. Lalita. Copyright 1991 by Susie Tharu and K. Lalita.

"Bread" by P. Lankesh in New Writing in India (1974), trans. A.K. Ramanujan. Reprinted by permission.

Faiz Ahmed Faiz: Selected Poems, Akhtaruzzaman Elias: "Dream Book," trans. © 1994 Azfar Hussain.

"The Wise Man, the Fool, and the Slave" from Silent China: Selected Writings of Lu Xun (1973), edited and translated by Gladys Yang, pp. 128-1 1973. Reprinted by permission of Oxford University Press.

"How to Achieve the Great Harmony" by K'ang Yu-wei in Ta T'ung Shu: The One-World Philosophy of K'ang Yu-wei (1958), pp. 162-165, trans Laurence Thompson. Reprinted by premission of Routledge.

"Protest Posters" by Lo Ch'ing in Forbidden Games and Video Poems: The Poetry of Yan Mu and Lo Ch'ing (1995), trans. Joseph Allen, p. 315. Reprinted by permission of University of Washington Press.

"Poverty in Rural Japan" in Memories of Silk and Straw: A Self Portrait of Small-Town Japan, pp. 25-28, by Dr. Junichi Saga. Tranlated by Gary O. vans. Published by Kodansha International Ltd. English translation copyright © 1987 Kodansha International. Reprinted by permisison. All rights eserved.

'Tangled Hair" by Yosano Akiko, from Tangled Hair (1987), trans. Sanford Goldstein & Seishi Shinoda. Reprinted by permission of Charles E. Tuttle o., Inc. of Boston, Massachusetts and Tokyo, Japan.

'The Grasshopper and the Bell Cricket" by Yasunari Kawabata from Palm-of-the-Hand Stories, pp. 12-15, translated by Lane Dunlop & J. Martin Iolman. Translation copyright © 1988 by Lane Dunlop and J. Martin Holman. Reprinted by permission of North Point Press, a division of Farrar, traus & Giroux, Inc.

xcerpts from Black Rain, by Masuji Ibuse, pp. 113-114, 161-162, translated by John Bester. Published by Kodansha International Ltd. English anslation copyright © 1969 Kodansha International. Reprinted by permission. All rights reserved.

igmund Freud: The Interpretation of Dreams, trans. © 1994 Paul Brians.

/. I. Lenin: What Is to Be Done? trans. © 1994 Jane Scales.

xcerpts from The Gulag Archipelago 1918-1956: An Experiment in Literary Investigation I-II by Alexandr I. Solzhenitsyn, pp. 93-94, 121-129. opyright © 1973 by Aleksandr I. Solzhenitsyn. English language translation © 1973, 1974 by Harper & Row Publishers, Inc. Reprinted by ermission of HarperCollins Publishers, Inc.

'my sweet old etcetera" by e.e. cummings, copyright 1926, 1945, © 1991 by the Trustees for the e.e. cummings Trust. Copyright © 1985 by George ames Firmage, from COMPLETE POEMS: 1904-1962 by e.e. cummings, edited by George J. Firmage. Reprinted by permission of Liveright ublishing Corporation.

'The Second Coming" by William Butler Yeats. Reprinted by permission of Simon & Schuster from The Poems of W.B. Yeats, A New Edition, pp. 184-85, edited by Richard J. Finneran. Copyright 1924 by Macmillan Publishing Company, renewed 1952 by Bertha Georgie Yeats.

'Nation and Race" from Mein Kampf, Adolf Hitler, pp. 448-451, translated by Ralph Manheim. Copyright © 1943, renewed 1971 by Houghton Aifflin Company. Reprinted by permission of Houghton Mifflin Company. All rights reserved.

'Night" by Eli Wiesel from Night, Dawn, Day, pp. 73-83, trans. Stella Rodway. Copyright © 1960 by MacGibbon & Kee. Copyright renewed © 988 by The Collins Publishing Group. Reprinted by permission of Hill and Wang, a division of Farrar, Straus & Giroux, Inc.

xcerpt from The Second Sex by Simone de Beauvoir, trans. H.M. Parshley, pp. 165-166, 571. Copyright 1952 and renewed 1980 by Alfred A. Knopf, nc. Reprinted by permission of the publisher.

'Anguish of Death" reprinted from NERUDA AND VALLEJO: SELECTED POEMS, pp. 77, 79, edited by Robert Bly, Beacon Press, Boston, 1971, 993. Copyright © 1993 Robert Bly. Reprinted with his permission.

'The Library of Babel" from Ficciones, by Jorge Luis Borges, pp. 79-88, translated by Anthony Kerrigan. Copyright © 1962 by Grove Press, Inc. Used y permission of Grove/Atlantic, Inc.

abriela Mistral: "Tiny Feet," Juana de Ibarbourou: "The Hour," trans. © 1994 Mary Gallwey.

ubén Darío: "To Roosevelt," trans. © 1994 Bonnie Frederick.

'The Handsomest Drowned Man in the World: A Tale for Children," pp. 98-108 from Leaf Storm and Other Stories by Gabriel Garcia Marquez. opyright © 1971 by Gabriel Garcia Marquez. Reprinted by permission of HarperCollins Publishers, Inc.

xcerpt from A Theology of Liberation: History, Politics and Salvation by Gustavo Gutierrez, pp. 299-302, trans. Sister Caridad Inda and John agleson. Maryknoll, N.Y.: Orbis Books, 1988. Reprinted by permission.

'Colonization in Reverse" by Louise Bennett from Jamaica Labrish (1966). Reprinted by permission of the author, Louis Bennett. All rights reserved.

'Hurucan" from Collected Poems 1948-1984, pp. 423-426 by Derek Walcott. Copyright © 1986 by Derek Walcott. Reprinted by permission of arrar, Straus & Giroux, Inc.

'Preludes" by T.S. Eliot in The Complete Poems and Plays 1909-1950, pp. 12-13. Reprinted by permission of Faber and Faber Ltd, publishers.

'Sea Poppies" by H.D. from COLLECTED POEMS, 1912-1944 (1952). Copyright © 1982 by The Estate of Hilda Doolittle. Reprinted by ermission of New Directions Publishing Corp.

'A Declaration of Independence" by Malcolm X in Malcolm X Speaks, pp. 20-22, George Breitman, ed. Copyright © 1965, 1989 by Betty Shabazz nd Pathfinder Press. Reprinted by permission.

'Buddhism and the Coming Revolution" by Gary Snyder from Earth House Hold: Technical Notes and Queries to Fellow Dharma Revolutionaries, pp. 0-93. Copyright © 1969 by Gary Snyder. Reprinted by permission of New Directions Publishing Corp.

'Silent Spring" by Rachel Carson, pp. 1-3, 277-279. Copyright © 1962 by Rachel L. Carson, renewed 1990 by Roger Christie. Reprinted by permission f Houghton Mifflin Co. All rights reserved.